WAR, RELIGION AND SERVICE

POLITICS AND CULTURE IN NORTH-WESTERN EUROPE 1650–1720

Series Editors

Dr Tony Claydon, University of Wales, Bangor, UK
Dr Hugh Dunthorne, University of Wales Swansea, UK
Dr Charles-Edouard Levillain, Université de Lille 2, France
Dr Esther Mijers, University of Reading, UK
Dr David Onnekink, Universiteit Utrecht/Universiteit Leiden, The Netherlands

Focusing on the years between the end of the Thirty Years' War and the end of the War of Spanish Succession, this new monograph series seeks to broaden scholarly knowledge of this crucial period that witnessed the solidification of Europe into centralised nation states and created a recognisably modern political map. Bridging the gap between the early modern period of the Reformation and the eighteenth century of colonial expansion and industrial revolution these years provide a fascinating era of study in which nationalism, political dogma, economic advantage, scientific development, cultural interests and strategic concerns began to overtake religion as the driving force of European relations and national foreign policies.

The period under investigation, *c.*1650–1720, corresponds to the decline of Spanish power and the rise of French hegemony that was only to be finally broken following the defeat of Napoleon in 1815. This shifting political powerbase presented opportunities and dangers for many countries, resulting in numerous alliances between formerly hostile nations attempting to consolidate or increase their international influence, or restrain that of a rival. Three of the most influential nations at this time, France, Great Britain and The Netherlands, were all at some stage during this period either at war or in alliance with one another.

Despite this being a formative period in the formation of the European landscape, there has been remarkably little joined-up research that studies events from an international, rather than national perspective. By providing a forum that encourages scholars to engage with the subject of politics, diplomacy, war and international relations on a broad European basis, it is hoped that a greater understanding of this pivotal era will be forthcoming.

War, Religion and Service

Huguenot Soldiering, 1685–1713

Edited by

MATTHEW GLOZIER
The University of Sydney, Australia

DAVID ONNEKINK
Universiteit Utrecht/ Universiteit Leiden, The Netherlands

ASHGATE

Published by
Ashgate Publishing Limited
Gower House
Croft Road
Aldershot
Hampshire GU11 3HR
England

Ashgate Publishing Company
Suite 420
101 Cherry Street
Burlington, VT 05401–4405
USA

Ashgate website: http://www.ashgate.com

British Library Cataloguing in Publication Data
War, religion and service : Huguenot soldiering, 1685–1713. – (Politics and culture in north-west Europe, 1650–1720)
    1. Huguenots – Europe – History – 17th century 2. Huguenots – Europe – History – 18th century 3. French – Europe – History – 17th century 4. French – Europe – History – 18th century 5. War – Religious aspects – Christianity 6. Europe – History, Military – 1648–1789 7. Europe – History – 1648 – 1715
    I. Glozier, Matthew II. Onnekink, David
    940.2'52

Library of Congress Cataloging-in-Publication Data
War, religion and service : Huguenot soldiering, 1685–1713 / edited by Matthew Glozier and David Onnekink.
    p. cm. – (Politics and culture in North-West Europe 1650–1720)
    Includes bibliographical references and index.
    ISBN-13: 978-0-7546-5444-5 (alk. paper)
    1. Europe – History, Military – 1648–1789. 2. Huguenots – Europe – History – 17th century. 3. Mercenary troops – Europe – History – 17th century. 4. Huguenots – Europe – History – 18th century. 5. Mercenary troops – Europe – History – 18th century. I. Glozier, Matthew. II. Onnekink, David.

    D273.5.W37 2007
    355.3'54088284509032–dc22

2006033560

ISBN 978-0-7546-5444-5

Printed and bound in Great Britain by MPG Books Ltd, Bodmin, Cornwall.

Contents

List of Illustrations

Notes on Contributors

Professor Matthias Asche is Professor of Early Modern History at the University of Tübingen. His habilitation thesis (Tübingen) was a study of the resettlement of Brandenburg after the Thirty Years' War. His current areas of study include Early Modern European history generally, history of university, education and sciences, as well as comparative land and denominational history. Professor Asche is also deeply interested in European migration history.

Dr Paola Bianchi is Lecturer in Modern History at the University of Aosta, and formerly a post-doctoral Fellow at the University of Padua. Her PhD thesis on the military reforms of Vittorio Amedeo II (1684–1730) has been published as *Onore e mestiere. Le riforme militari nel Piemonte del Settecento* (Honour and Career: Military Reforms in Eighteenth-Century Piedmont) (2002). Her current interest is in educational experiences of the grand tour and cosmopolitanism in Turin. She is President of the Laboratory of Historical Studies on the states of Piedmont and Savoy.

Sir Peter de la Billière, KCB, KBE, DSO, MC and bar, joined the army as a private in the King's Shropshire Light Infantry and was later commissioned. His first tours of duty included Japan and Korea. After Egypt he joined the SAS, taking over as Commanding Officer of 22nd SAS in January 1972, at the age of 37. Later, he led the counter-terrorist team that took shape, under Operation Pagoda, following the Munich Olympics massacre. He managed problems in Northern Ireland, the Iranian Embassy Siege and the Falklands War. With the Iraqi invasion of Kuwait, he was appointed Commander, British Forces Middle East. After the First Gulf War, he became Special Advisor to the Minister of Defence on Middle East matters. He retired from active service in June 1992.

Professor John Childs is Professor of Military History and Director of the Centre for Military History at the University of Leeds. He is also chairman of the Battlefields Panel of English Heritage, a trustee of the Royal Armouries and an occasional adviser to the Ministry of Defence. He has published numerous books on the history of warfare in the early modern period, most recently *La Guerre au XVIIe siècle* (2004) and *The Williamite Wars in Ireland* (2007).

Dr Andreas Flick is President of the Huguenot Society of Germany (Deutsche Hugenotten Gesellschaft) and a pastor of the Evangelical Reformed Church in Celle. He has written and published extensively on the Huguenots in northern Germany.

Dr Matthew Glozier is an Honorary Associate of the Centre for Medieval Studies at the University of Sydney. His books include *The Huguenot Soldiers of William of Orange and the Glorious Revolution of 1688* (2002) and *Scottish Soldiers in France in the Age of the Sun King* (2004). His most recent publication is a study of Frederick Herman von Schomberg, entitled *Marshal Schomberg, 1615–1690: 'the ablest soldier of his age'* (2005).

Dr Detlef Harms gained his PhD at the University of Potsdam. He has written widely on the army of Brandenburg-Prussia, and specifically on its foreign officer corps. His published work includes *Vom Lehns- und Ritterheer zum Söldnerheer. Zur Entwicklung des Militärwesens im deutschen Feudalreich vom Beginn des 14. bis zum Beginn des 16. Jahrhunderts* (1990), and 'Das städtische Militärwesen im Spätmittelalter', *Militärgeschichte*, 5 (1990).

Dr Harman Murtagh is an authority on Ireland's military history on which he has published widely. He was for many years editor of *Irish Sword* and is Vice-President of the Irish Commission for Military History. He has a strong research interest in the Jacobite/Williamite war in Ireland 1689–91, having published 'The Irish Jacobite Army, 1689–91', *Irish Sword*, 70 (1990) and 'The War in Ireland, 1689–91', in W. A. Maguire (ed.), *Kings in Conflict* (1990).

Dr David Onnekink is a postdoctoral fellow and Lecturer at the universities of Utrecht and Leiden. He is interested in British and Dutch politics in the late seventeenth century and is currently working on a project on ideology and Dutch foreign policy, 1672–1713. His publications include *The Anglo-Dutch Favourite: The Career of Hans Willem Bentinck, 1st Earl of Portland (1649–1709)* (2007). He has co-edited (with Dr Raymond Fagel) *Oorlog en Samenleving in de Nieuwe Tijd* (2005) and (with Dr Esther Mijers) *Redefining William III: The Impact of the King-Stadholder in International Context* (2007).

Philip Rambaut, DSC, is author of the only existing biography of Feversham: *Louis de Durfort-Duras, second Earl of Feversham* (1988). His work also appears in the *Proceedings of the Huguenot Society of Great Britain and Ireland*, 25 (1989–93) and in P. Rambaut and R. Vigne, *Britain's Huguenot War Leaders* (2003).

Dianne W. Ressinger has produced the definitive English-language version of the memoirs of the Revd Jaques Fontaine (Huguenot Society, new series 2, 1997) and recently published the first ever English edition of the memoirs of Isaac Dumont de Bostaquet (Huguenot Society, new series 4, 2005).

Dr Helmut Schnitter taught at the University of Potsdam, Germany, and has published widely on the Huguenots in the army of Brandenburg-Prussia. His most important works include *Unter dem rotten Adler. Réfugiés im brandeburgischen Heer Ende des 17. Anfang des 18. Jahrhundert* (1996) and 'Die Réfugiés in der brandenburgischen Armee', in G. Bregulla (ed.), *Hugenotten in Berlin* (1988).

Dr D. J. B. Trim is Lecturer in History at Newbold College and Co-Director of its Centre for the Study of Religious and Cultural Diversity. He is a Fellow of the Royal Historical Society, a Visiting Fellow in the Department of History, University of Reading, and Associate Editor of *The Journal of the Society for Army Historical Research*.

Randolph Vigne recently retired from his position as long-time General Editor of the publications of the Huguenot Society of Great Britain and Ireland. He has authored many important studies of various aspects of the Huguenots in Great Britain, Ireland, South Africa and elsewhere, and numerous articles by him appear in the Society's *Proceedings* and other journals. He has also edited a number of book-length studies, including *Guillaume Chenu de Chalezac: The 'French Boy'* (1993) and (with Charles Littleton) *From Strangers to Citizens* (2001).

Foreword

General Sir Peter de la Billière, KCB, KBE, DSO, MC and bar (rtd.)

The British Army is no stranger to recruits from foreign countries and it has been my privilege to serve with men from many nations from as far afield as Fiji, Hong Kong and New Zealand to mention a few. They made fine soldiers with many of them winning gallantry awards. Contemporary times are no stranger to wars of religion, and Northern Ireland and the international Islamic conflicts are the most recent scenes of such action. Today's events reflect the role played by religion in war in the Middle Ages and the early modern period in Europe.

For 250 years the French Protestants suffered persecution while the rulers of France with few exceptions, but notably Henry IV who proclaimed the Edict of Nantes, created a single Catholic state. Freedom of worship came on the eve of the Revolution of 1789 and was enshrined in the Declaration of the Rights of Man. It is not surprising that many thousands of Protestants gallantly refused to abjure and at great risk emigrated to other states throughout Europe and the world. That so many of them were accomplished artisans in their trade, including that of soldiering, became France's loss and Europe's gain. To this day many people of distinction in professions and trades are descended from Huguenot ancestors; as with my family they take great pride in their lineage and would no doubt wish that their predecessors had had the opportunity to maintain more positive connections with their former motherland.

Courage became an inherent quality of the migrant Huguenots and in no profession was this more apparent than amongst those who enlisted into the armies of European nations. Huguenot generals and senior commanders abound in sixteenth- and seventeenth-century armies, in particular the English army benefited from their presence. The extraordinary example of Friedrich Hermann von Schomberg, who ultimately commanded thousands of Huguenot officers in the Irish campaigns, stands out. Though a Marshal of France he chose to leave his adopted motherland rather than obey Louis XIV's request to abjure his faith and then became the Field Marshal of the Brandenburg army. He concluded his career as second-in-command to William III and was appointed Knight of the Garter and Master of the Ordnance.

Huguenot soldiers were a force to be reckoned with throughout Europe and this volume is the first attempt to bring together in a scholarly study essays treating the Huguenots as soldiers in Europe. Their story is often fascinating and sometimes poignant as they aided International Protestantism against Catholic foes across Europe, while remaining 'under the cross' in their homeland of France. This book contains chapters analysing their efforts internationally prior to the 1685 revocation of the Edict of Nantes which sealed their fate in France. Their role as mercenaries and freedom fighters for International Protestantism is explored together with the complex political motivation that underscored their involvement abroad in the pre-

Revocation era. Chapters examine the Huguenot rationale for joining foreign armies and the dynamics of the 'Protestant International' of which they were a prominent part. Their role in European armies after the Revocation is covered by a number of expert studies of Huguenot refugees in the armies of Britain, the Netherlands, Russia, Brandenburg-Prussia, Brunswick-Lüneburg-Celle and Savoy-Piedmont. Chapters also treat the Huguenot legacy, focusing on the ageing generation of refugees and their descendants' contributions to the countries of their adoption. This book contains studies of the Huguenots as a group in various countries and examines the lives and action of some individual French refugee commanders who led armies consisting of their compatriots. By combining biographical studies of eminent figures with broader consideration of group experience this book presents a wide-ranging and thought provoking collection of material. It is the first study of its kind to treat consistently the military contribution made by Huguenots to armies outside France at the high point of their importance as a historical group.

I take pride in my association with this important literary salutation to Europe's Huguenot ancestors. They were brave entrepreneurial people: they have made a significant contribution to the prosperity and security of Europe and they stand acknowledged as upholders of democratic and religious freedom.

The authors are to be congratulated for their valuable contribution to history: their book will occupy a prominent position in my library and that of others who have an interest in this period and these people.

Acknowledgements

Thanks must go to Mrs Vivien Costello, of the Huguenot Society of Great Britain and Ireland, for her tireless support of this volume, and for translating much of the German material into English. The editors would also like to thank Mr Randolph Vigne for his encouragement and assistance throughout the production of this book. The editors also wish to thank Professor John Miller for his advice and guidance, which greatly benefitted the volume in terms of its scope and direction.

The index and cumulative bibliography were constructed by Matthew Glozier.

List of Abbreviations

AECP	Archives étrangères, *correspondance politique*, Quai d'Orsay (Paris)
AEMD	Archives étrangères, *mémoires et documents*, Quai d'Orsay
AG	Archives de la guerre, Château de Vincennes (Paris)
Bib. Inst.	Bibliothèque de l'Institute (Paris)
Bib. Maz.	Bibliothèque Mazarine (Paris)
BL, Add. MS	British Library (London), Additional Manuscripts
BN	Bibliothèque Nationale (Paris)
BN, f. Fr.	Bibliothèque Nationale de France, *fonds Française*
BN, MS Fr.	Bibliothèque Nationale de France, *manuscrits Française*
Bod. Lib.	Bodleian Library (Oxford)
BSG	Bibliothèque Saint-Genèviève (Paris)
CARAN	Centre Accueil de la Recherche des Archives Nationales (Paris)
CSPDom.	*Calendar of State Papers Domestic*
CTB	*Calendar of Treasury Books*
DNB	Dictionary of National Biography
GAL	Gemeentearchief van Leiden (Netherlands)
HMC	Royal Commission on Historical Manuscripts (UK), Reports
HNA	Het Nationaal Archief (The Hague) (formerly Algemeen Rijksarchief)
TNA	The National Archives (Kew) (formerly PRO)
NAS	National Archives of Scotland (Edinburgh)
NLS	National Library of Scotland (Edinburgh)
SG	States General of the United Provinces of the Netherlands
SHAT	Service Historique de l'armée de terre, Château de Vincennes (Paris)
SPV	State Papers Venetian
WO	War Office

Note on spelling

All names of persons have been spelt in the original language of their native country, with the exception of William III, who is much better known by the anglicised form of his name, and Louis of Nassau, as he was referred to by French Huguenots.

Glossary

Adjutant. An officer who assists the colonel in regimental administrative duties, and is specially selected for the purpose.

Blind. A piece of wood set across the top of a trench to support hurdles and bavines filled with earth in order to cover in the trench and protect it from gun fire.

Brevet. Not a regimental rank, but a temporary army one. It applies to field service and a brevet major, for example, continues to serve as a captain in his regiment, the higher rank only being assumed in field manoeuvres.

Cadet. A volunteer, serving in the hope of obtaining a commission. Some entire regiments consisted of cadets, or well-born youths training for commissions. The majority of cadets attached to Huguenot regiments succeeded as few appear in this rank on later pension lists. Their status and pay approximate those of sergeants.

Captain-lieutenant. The senior lieutenant ranking next for promotion, who commanded the colonel's company.

Chevaux-de-frises. Stakes of wood tied together with iron and driven into the ground as an obstacle to cavalry.

Counter-mine. A tunnel of the defenders to discover the mines of attackers.

Counterscarp. The slope of the moat nearest the open country.

En seconde. A term applied to officers appointed to a regiment in the absence of the officer holding the 'standing' or permanent commission. For example, following the disaster at Almanza, where a number of officers were taken prisoner, *en seconde* officers took their place pending release.

Hornworks. Rectangular outworks providing enfilading fire down the length of the curtain wall and flanking all approaches by the attackers.

Maréchal de camp. A rank in the French army equivalent to major-general.

Ravelin. A small, triangular work with only two faces and no angles, built in the moat before the curtain wall where the moat made a salient angle.

Redout. A small square fort with no angles which was always detached from the main fortifications.

Reformé/reformado. An officer placed on half-pay, additional to the strength of a regiment, forming a kind of reserve.

Scarp. The slope of the ditch nearest the town.

Troop. Applied to the cavalry, whereas 'company' is used in the infantry. Regiments were divided into troops or companies, each commanded by a captain.

Introduction

Matthew Glozier and David Onnekink
*The University of Sydney, Australia/Universiteit Utrecht/Universiteit Leiden,
The Netherlands*

This volume examines the reception and employment of Huguenot soldiers in the armies of the Dutch Republic, Britain, Brandenburg-Prussia, Russia and Savoy between the revocation of the Edict of Nantes in 1685 and the 1713 Treaty of Utrecht. Huguenots had served abroad since the French Wars of Religion. Due to the forced exodus after 1685, however, large numbers would take service in the armies of foreign princes, who eagerly sought their expertise and experience in their efforts to develop professional standing armies. Two decades of almost continuous warfare in the 1690s and 1700s assured employment for the Huguenot soldiers. They mostly served in the Protestant armies of the coalition against Louis XIV. War, religion and service thus form the main theme of this volume of essays, which elaborates the high-point of the story of the Huguenot soldiers between 1685 and 1713.

It is a story typified by the experiences of the de La Billière family.[1] This family from the heartland of Protestantism in France's south, possessed a martial tradition dating back to the thirteenth century. Like many members of the *petite noblesse* they adopted Calvin's dictates and became firm Protestants.[2] A the time of the 1685 Revocation, Charles de La Cour, seigneur de La Billière, was forced to choose between obeying his king and following the dictates of his heart. He chose obedience, thus securing the family possessions and ensuring the survival of the family in France. Of his four sons, two took flight for the sake of liberty of conscience, and joined their great-uncle, Pierre de La Cour de La Gardiolle. Gardiolle died a refugee in London, while his nephews, Paul and Pierre, fought under William III in Ireland and the Netherlands. The first of them to be naturalised was Pierre, in 1701. Ironically, at the time of the Peace of Ryswick in 1698, Pierre and Paul were on leave in Brussels where they met their brothers, François and Charles, who had remained in France and fought for King Louis. This was the only time post-Revocation that they would see one another, but their relationship was maintained through letters, in which there appears no trace of animosity through fighting on opposite sides in the great conflict.[3] Family members continued to face one another in wars throughout the eighteenth century until the last on the line in France, Louis Marie de la Cour de

---

1   For the history of this family, see Sir B. B. Burke, *A Genealogical and Heraldic History of the Colonial Gentry*, ed. A. P. Burke (2 vols, London, 1891–5), vol. 2, pp. 418–20; F. P. de Labillière, *History of a Cevenol Family: A Paper read before the Huguenot Society of London, January 11, 1888* (London, 1888).

2   See the will of Fulcrand de La Cour, Seigneur de La Billière, 30 March 1637, in which he declared himself to be a Protestant: Burke, *Colonial Gentry*, p. 418.

3   Burke, *Colonial Gentry*, p. 420.

La Gardiolle, fell foul of Admiral Nelson at the battle of the Nile. In Britain the only remaining male line of the de La Billière family served the professions in church, army and law.

The unique history of Huguenot soldiering has attracted much interest from historians, and it is useful to say something of its early historiography. Here Samuel Smiles can be mentioned, one of the first to broadcast the significant role played by Huguenots in the events of 1688. Smiles bemoaned the lack of knowledge in the English-speaking world of the number and nature of French Protestant military service. However, he himself referred to earlier complaints by the French themselves that so many of their countrymen had been, seemingly, forgotten by the British. It is worth quoting at some length the plea of the French historian Jules Michelet for the inclusion of Huguenots in the story of William III's army:

> The army of William was strong precisely in that Calvinistic element which James [II] repudiated in England – I mean in our Huguenot soldiers, the brothers of the Puritans. I am astonished that Macaulay has thought fit to leave this circumstance in the background. I cannot believe that great England, with all her glories and her inheritance of Liberty, is unwilling nobly to avow the part which we Frenchmen had in her deliverance. In the Homeric enumeration which the historian gives of the followers of William, he [Macaulay] reckons up English, Germans, Dutch, Swedes, Swiss, with the picturesque detail of their arms, uniforms, and all, down even to the two hundred negroes with their black faces set off by embroidered turbans and white feathers who followed the body of English gentry led by the Earl of Macclesfield. But he did not see our Frenchmen. Apparently the proscribed Huguenot soldiers who followed William did not do honour to the Prince by their clothes! Doubtless many of them wore the dress in which they had fled France – and it had become dusty, worn, and tattered.[4]

Robin Gwynn has sought to defend Macaulay, claiming his appreciation of the Huguenots was greater than that of most nineteenth-century Britons.[5] The problem for Michelet was not that Macaulay had said nothing of them, but that he said too little in his otherwise thorough (if stridently Whiggish) narrative of the 'Glorious Revolution' of 1688. Yet, while Smiles was responsible for presenting the British public with the achievements of the Huguenots in all walks-of-life, continental historians had already done much to establish the facts of refugee service in the armies of Europe. In particular, the research of Pierre Charles Weiss and Eugene and Emily Haag has stood the test of time.[6] It is important to note that these early and thorough historians placed on record information (primarily in biographical form) of

---

4   J. Michelet, *Louis XIV et la Revocation de l'Edit de Nantes* (Histoire de France, vol. 13, Paris, 1860), pp. 418–19. Cited in S. Smiles, *The Huguenots: Their Settlements, Churches, and Industries in England and Ireland* (London, fourth edition 1870), pp. 184–5.

5   R. D. Gwynn, 'Patterns in the Study of Huguenot Refugees in Britain: past, present and future', in I. Scouloudi (ed.), *Huguenots in Britain and their French Background, 1550–1800* (London, 1987), pp. 217–18.

6   C. Weiss, *Histoire des réfugiés protestants de France depuis la révocation de l'Édit de Nantes jusqu'à nos jours* (2 vols, Paris, 1853); E. and E. Haag, *La France Protestante, ou Vies des Protestants Français qui se sont fait un nom dans l'histoire depuis les premiers temps de la Réformation jusqu'à la reconnaissance du principe de la liberté des cultes par*

Huguenot soldiers which has not been significantly tested or stretched till the present day. However, even these authors drew upon older published works that pre-dated the emergence of History as an academic discipline.

The Haags based their pioneering, multi-volume work on original manuscript material in France, the majority of it still extant. Weiss based much of his incisive comments on a combination of printed primary sources, supplemented by secondary works. His comments on the Huguenots in Germany (and Brandenburg-Prussia especially) are a good case in point, being based on primary sources, such as Ancillon. He also relied upon the magisterial eighteenth-century works of Erman and Reclam, and on Beckman.[7] Pierre Jurieu and Frederick the Great also feature among the sources used by Weiss for the Huguenots in Germany.[8] In this way Weiss presented to the French reading public much information on the role and contribution of the Huguenots in countries as diverse as Germany, Sweden, Denmark-Norway and Russia (though there was little published material for him to digest here).

The same approach, though arguably more purely antiquarian in its scope, was adopted by Emmanuel Orentin Douen in France and D. C. A. Agnew in England, who both worked through the lists of abjurations, imprisonments, fines and pensions maintained by the *archives nationals* among other sources.[9] Limited in approach to the Huguenots of Paris, Douen nevertheless demonstrated the value of manuscript sources for the study of the Huguenots. Agnew's interest was far more general, though he confined himself to Huguenots in the British Isles. This is evidence of the depth of interest created by earlier authors such as Weiss and Haag in France and Smiles in England. These two nations were brought together in the form of Baron F. de Schickler, whose work on the English refuge of the Huguenots complimented his ongoing research in France.[10]

Among other effects, these published works prompted the establishment of societies aimed at the study of the Huguenots generally. The Huguenot Society of London and that of South Carolina (both established in 1885) became natural homes for the investigation of the refugees and their descendants in national context. However, the loser in all this was the very internationalism inherent to the Huguenots diaspora from 1685, the very period of focus for this study of refugee soldiers.

---

l'Assemblée Nationale; ouvrage précédé d'une notice historique sur le Protestantisme en France, et suivi de pièces justificatives (9 vols, Paris, 1846–59).

7   C. Ancillon, *Histoire de l'établissement des Français réfugiés en Brandebourg* (Berlin, 1690); J. P. Erman and P. C. F. Reclam, *Mémoires pour servir à l'histoire des Réfugiés François dans les États du Roi* (9 vols, Berlin, 1782–99); J. Beckmann, *Historische Beschreibung der Chur und Mark Brandenburg* (2 vols, Berlin, 1751–3).

8   Frederick the Great, *Histoire de mon temps. Instruction militaire du Roi de Prusse pour ses Généraux. Instruction secrète ... contenant les ordres secrèts ... Traduite de l'original allemand par le Prince de Ligne* (Berlin, 1788); P. Jurieu, *Lettres pastorales* (Rotterdam, 1688).

9   E. O. Douen, *La révocation de l'Edit de Nantes a Paris, d'après des documents inedits* (3 vols, Paris, 1894); D. C. A. Agnew, *Protestant Exiles from France in the Reign of Louis XIV* (Edinburgh, 1866; 3 vols, London, second edition 1871).

10   Baron F. de Schickler, *Les Eglises du Refuge en Angleterre* (3 vols, Paris, 1892).

Early statements about the Huguenots as soldiers after 1685 were, however, accepted as fact. While much of the biographical detail of their lives has remained sound, little has been done to test the wider implication of their services to the armies of Europe. As a result of this interaction between long-accepted truths and recent scholarship, Robin Gwynn has charted the fortunes of Huguenot research in the English-speaking world, concluding that only recently has there emerged new interest among academic historians in the Huguenots.[11] Much new research has focused on reconstructing the French Protestant 'world', while other works have treated them within various contexts; as one group of immigrants among many, or as soldiers within broader expatriate communities of foreign servicemen.[12]

This volume focuses on the significance and nature of Huguenot soldiering between 1685 and 1713, but tries to widen the scope by charting their European experience by studying their role in England, Ireland, the United Provinces, Brandenburg, Savoy and Russia.[13] The chapters in this book are grouped by national perspectives but deal with similar themes that cut right through this division; the themes of religion, service and war. An introductory chapter by David Trim provides a panoramic overview and analysis of the origins of Huguenot soldiering. He shows how the origins of the military skills of Huguenots must be traced back to the sixteenth century Wars of Religion. The Huguenots' experience in the wars initiated a military tradition which would endure until the late seventeenth century.

The theme of refuge and religion deals with the direct results of the cataclysmic decision of Louis XIV to revoke the Edict of Nantes in 1685. Thousands of refugees who were determined to keep their religion fled France and were dispersed over Europe – mostly travelling to England, Brandenburg and the United Provinces. Dianne Ressinger, for instance, describes the fortunes of one of them, Isaac Dumont de Bostaquet, who fled to The Hague and, although no professional soldier, was committed and obliged to take up arms in the service of William III. Two biographical chapters highlight the difficulties of some of the greatest officers of Huguenot origin. Randolph Vigne analyses the career of Henri de Massue de Ruvigny, Earl of Galway, who fled France in 1685 and became one of the highest officers in King William's army, as well as a patron of Huguenot refugees in Ireland. Louis de Durfort-Duras, Earl of Feversham, had left France before 1685 and served in the armies of Charles II and James II, as Philip Rambaut describes. Detlef Harms as well shows how

---

11   R. D. Gwynn, 'Patterns in the Study of Huguenot Refugees in Britain: past, present and future', in I. Scouloudi (ed.), *Huguenots in Britain and their French Background*, pp. 217–36 (second revised edition, Brighton and Portland, 2000).

12   R. A. Mentzer and A. Spicer (eds), *Society and Culture in the Huguenot World, 1559 to 1685* (Cambridge, 2002); R. Vigne and C. Littleton (eds), *From Strangers to Citizens: The Integration of Immigrant Communities in Britain, Ireland and Colonial America, 1550–1750* (Brighton and Portland, 2001); M. R. Glozier, *The Huguenot Soldiers of William of Orange and the Glorious Revolution of 1688: The Lions of Judah* (Brighton and Portland, 2002).

13   The most thorough overview of the Huguenot regiments in Britain between 1688 and 1713 is V. Costello, 'Researching Huguenot officers in the British army, 1688–1713', *The Genealogists' Magazine: Journal of the Society of Genealogists*, 28/8 (December 2005): 335–54.

the 'unfortunate banished people from France' found refuge in Brandenburg after 1685.

The second and main theme of this volume, service, is undoubtedly the actual contribution of Huguenot soldiers to foreign armies. It was perhaps the army of Louis XIV that first distinguished itself through its superior quality. Through the expulsion of the Huguenots, military expertise was unwittingly exported and utilised by foreign princes, in the process of building up professional standing armies. As Philip Rambaut shows, Huguenot soldiers were already attracted to England under Charles II and James II, partly through the efforts of the Earl of Feversham, but as John Childs argues, the mass of Huguenot soldiers entered Britain after the revocation of the Edict of Nantes. In the United Provinces as well Huguenot soldiers contributed to the augmentation of the army at the eve of the Nine Years' War and were, moreover, instrumental in the success of the Glorious Revolution in 1688–9, as Matthew Glozier and David Onnekink point out. Huguenot soldiers were actively being sought in Brandenburg, as Matthias Asche, Detlef Harms and Helmut Schnitter show, through the 1685 Edict of Potsdam. But they were also recruited from France before 1685, making them less poor refugees and rather professional armies that played a vital role in the development of the Brandenburg army. Andreas Flick and Paola Bianchi study the contribution of Huguenots to the building-up of the standing army of the Dukes of Brunswick-Lüneburg and Savoy-Piedmont. After the Nine Years' War many Huguenots were demobilised but were eagerly sought by Peter the Great to enrol in the Russian army, as Matthew Glozier describes. That Huguenot soldiers could also cause friction in the armies in which they served is shown by David Onnekink, who analyses the reception and perception of Huguenots in the English army.

The last theme, war, returns in most of the articles. The Huguenots, forced to leave their native country after 1685, became soldiers in the armies of the Grand Alliance that turned against the Sun King. The only article that deals primarily with actual warfare though is by Harman Murtagh, who discusses the Irish campaigns. In England, the United Provinces and Brandenburg, Huguenots often fought in separate regiments that distinguished themselves on the battlefield, but these were mostly disbanded at the end of the Nine Years' War, after which Huguenots continued to fight in the War of the Spanish Succession but not in distinct regiments. Although the story of the Huguenot soldiers did not end in 1713, the Peace of Utrecht marks a crucial watershed after which French Protestants continued to serve abroad but not in distinct regiments or in grand wars.

The themes war, religion and service form the essence of historiography on Huguenot soldiers and have done so for a long time, but in this volume several additional themes emerge which may provide a direction for future research. Traditional (Huguenot) military historiography has largely focused on regiments and warfare. With the rise of the New Military History or 'War and Society' schools in the 1980s, emphasising the 'socialization of military history',[14] attention has increasingly been paid to the integration of soldiers in the foreign armies, their professional contribution and their social context. Migrating French Huguenot

---

14 See C. Jones, 'New Military History for Old? War and Society in Early Modern Europe', *European Studies Review*, 12 (1982): 97–108.

soldiers distinguished themselves by their service record in foreign armies and were instrumental in the spread of knowledge about military affairs and so the development of professional armies outside France. They also established themselves as part of French communities abroad that developed new sets of loyalty and identity and formed part of international family networks. Three further themes therefore emerge from the articles in this volume: the contribution of professionalism and experience, the transfer of loyalties and the shifting identities.

Huguenot soldiers contributed to the professionalisation of European armies in several ways. Firstly, they brought with them experience from many years in the best army in Europe. As Trim shows, the Huguenots had a long established tradition of military service. On the whole Huguenot soldiers had a good reputation. William III held his Huguenot regiments in high regard. A similar picture arises, for instance, from the articles of Glozier, Flick, Asche and Bianchi, showing how Huguenot regiments contributed to the professionalisation of the armies of Russia, Celle, Brandenburg and Savoy. Still their skills should not be overestimated, since many soldiers, such as Isaac Dumont de Bostaquet for instance, as Ressinger points out, had had almost no military experience before taking service in the Dutch army.

Another way in which Huguenots contributed to the professionalisation of European armies was more indirectly. They brought with them knowledge of military literature as Schnitter points out, and as he and Glozier show, were at the forefront of the establishment of military academies. Schnitter also points out that their knowledge helped the Brandenburgers to reorganise the regiments in a way that contributed to their effectiveness. According to Harms as well 'The adoption of the French regimental structure and appropriate army tactics' were beneficial to the Brandenburg army. Trim argues that the clientele structures of the following of the Huguenot nobility also helped in creating well organised regiments. Most authors also point to the fact that Huguenots had the reputation of being well-disciplined, an important factor in the development of professional armies.

A second theme that emerges from the articles is that of loyalty, or rather of conflicting or transferring allegiances. A soldier serves his king, but many Huguenots were obliged to break their oath, flee for the sake of their religion and serve another prince. As Trim argues, during the religious wars many Huguenot soldiers served God before the king, and were consequently regarded as deserters by Catholics. Many mercenaries and soldiers of fortune served whoever would pay them, but in the age of emerging standing armies after the Thirty Years' War this would increasingly become problematic. Ressinger contends that 'Dumont's loyalty was always with the King', and argues out that William III had Huguenot officers take a new oath of loyalty to the States-General in order to break their ties with the French king.

The case of Huguenot soldiers in France may have been exceptional, as many Catholic princes, such as the Duke of Savoy, as Bianchi shows, had no qualms about establishing Protestant regiments of seasoned Huguenot soldiers. As John Childs shows, even James II, who tended to promote Catholic officers, was prepared to appoint Feversham as chief commander, as he had been a loyal friend. Feversham was even entrusted to suppress the Protestant Monmouth rebellion in 1685. But even so, many Huguenots like Bostaquet must have felt the pressure of such conflicting loyalties. Rambaut asks whether Feversham's loyalty to James II in turn was 'misplaced'; Miremont, for instance, indeed refused to fight for James II against William, but the Duke of Schomberg looked down on Marlborough when he deserted James II. Each officer had to make up his mind which choice to make. Where Huguenots served in the armies of Protestant princes, however, their loyalty and commitment was rather seen to increase. William III had every reason to trust his Huguenot officers, as Murtagh points out, even more than his English commanders. Onnekink, however, shows how some English pamphleteers suspected Huguenot soldiers of treasonable behaviour.

A last theme that comes out of this volume is that of identity. Ressinger illustrates the loyalty among Huguenot officers in the Dutch Republic; such mutual bonds guaranteed the continuous existence of Huguenot soldiering after 1685, and their organisation in Huguenot regiments in their identification as such. As Trim shows, their identity was in many ways entangled with their zeal for their religion, which indeed was 'the very essence' of their existence. Huguenots were able to maintain their identity and reputation abroad through the organisation of specifically Huguenot regiments. Bianchi, for instance, points out how important it was for Huguenots and Waldensians to maintain their identity by serving in distinct regiments in the Savoyard army. However, as Childs points out, they were not unique in serving abroad, as most European armies were polyglot and multicultural. Still, in this age of professionalisation, some degree of 'nationalisation' of the standing army reduced the reliance of princes on mercenary auxiliary regiments. In England in particular, as Childs shows, the separate Huguenot regiments were unusual and disappeared altogether after the end of the Nine Years' War.

Huguenot soldiers were often part of larger French exile communities who remained distinct in the societies in which they were embedded. Ressinger and Flick, for instance, provide insights into the customs and fortunes of these communities in the United Provinces and Celle, and the ways in which the soldiers formed a part of those communities. Belonging to these larger exiled French communities undoubtedly strengthened the ability of the mercenary soldiers to regard themselves as Huguenots, and they continued to do so until after 1713 all hope of return to France was lost. Still, their self-perceived identity must have eroded over time, especially after a second migration. Glozier, for instance, describes how Huguenots who had fled to Brandenburg after 1685 ended up in Russia after the Nine Years' War, by which time they could be regarded as 'Germanised Huguenots' building up a new life in Russia.

There remains the question of how important the 'construction' of identities was. As Childs points out, Huguenot soldiers were 'paraded as religious refugees' by William III to strengthen his own image as a Protestant prince. It was precisely William's identification of his Huguenot soldiers with his Protestant cause that would be criticised. Pamphleteers and MPs in England, as Onnekink shows, often regarded William's Huguenot regiments as mercenary armies, mistrusted their loyalties and forced many of them to remain outsiders by opposing acts of naturalisation. Even if they had lived for a prolonged time in their new countries and were naturalised, they were, as Rambaut points out about Feversham, 'considered very much a foreigner and not always to be trusted'. Indeed, the perception of these foreign soldiers was often negative.

In conclusion, it can be argued, as Harms writes, that 'the Huguenots distinguished themselves by demonstrating an ethos of loyalty to the state, religious piety and, usually, an assiduous attitude to duty and discipline'. It is the aim of this volume to offer a new overview, focused in time but diverging in geographical perspective, of the nature, contribution and actions of the Huguenot soldiers, but also to pose new questions and open up new avenues for research.

Chapter 1

Huguenot Soldiering *c.*1560–1685
The Origins of a Tradition[1]

D. J. B. Trim

Newbold College, UK

When the Edict of Fontainebleau (1685) ended France's experiment in religious toleration, the French Calvinist military experience was already a century-and-a-quarter old; thus, the Huguenot soldiers who served across Europe from 1685 to 1713 were followers in a long tradition. The characteristics and qualities of Huguenot soldiering after 1685 did not emerge out of a vacuum and, therefore, this essay focuses on the history of Huguenot soldiers in foreign service in the preceding 125 years. The factors that made Huguenot soldiering distinctive, long-lasting, and successful are best understood in the context of its origins and development.

The military history of French Calvinists has not received the attention it deserves from modern scholarship. Studies of early-modern French armies have focused overwhelmingly on Royal and Catholic armies, reflecting, partly, the fact that government records naturally survived better than those of the rebellious Huguenots and perhaps, in part, that the royal armies, as the antecedents of the great armies of Louis XIV and Napoleon, naturally attract the attention of military historians.[2] Even histories of Calvinists and Calvinism in sixteenth- and seventeenth-century France do insufficient justice to the Huguenot penchant for military service.[3] The exception

1   I gratefully acknowledge funding from the British Academy, the French Protestant Church of London and the University of London Central Research Fund, that made possible research in Paris.

2   Key works on the French army in the sixteenth and seventeenth centuries are F. Lot, *Recherches sur les effectifs des armées françaises des Guerres d'Italie aux Guerres de Religion 1494–1562* (Paris, 1962); D. Potter, *War and Government in the French Provinces: Picardy 1470–1560* (Cambridge, 1993); J. B. Wood, *The King's Army: Warfare, Soldiers, and Society during the Wars of Religion in France, 1562–1576* (Cambridge, 1996); D. Parrott, *Richelieu's Army: War, Government and Society in France, 1624–1642* (Cambridge, 2001); J. A. Lynn, *Giant of the Grand Siècle: The French Army, 1610–1715* (Cambridge, 1997); and G. Rowlands, *The Dynastic State and the Army under Louis XIV: Royal Service and Private Interest, 1661–1701* (Cambridge, 2002).

3   Studies of sixteenth-century Huguenot soldiering are few and short: for example J. de Pablo, 'Contribution à l'étude de l'histoire des institutions militaires huguenotes, ii. L'armée huguenote entre 1562 et 1573', *Archiv für Reformationsgeschichte*, 48 (1957): 192–216; R. S. Love, '"All the King's Horsemen": The Equestrian Army of Henri IV, 1585–1598', *Sixteenth Century Journal*, 22 (1991): 511–33; D. J. B. Trim, 'Edict of Nantes: Product of military success or failure?', in K. Cameron, M. Greengrass and P. Roberts (eds), *The Adventure of*

is the body of scholarship on French immigrants to Britain and Ireland: while mainly exploring religious, cultural and commercial dimensions of the Huguenots it has produced a number of works that additionally consider the military role of French Protestant immigrants in Britain, Ireland and the Atlantic world.[4] However, these studies have tended to focus on the period after the mass emigrations of the 1680s. This tends to create an impression that the history of Huguenot soldiering is the history of Huguenot *émigrés* in the British army in the Nine Years' War (1688–97) and the War of the Spanish Succession (1702–13). Yet the contribution of Huguenot soldiers to the wars against Louis XIV was not restricted to the British army.

This is one reason why this essay focuses on Huguenot service with foreign, rather than French, armies in the 125 years before 1685, providing the context for the foreign service that came after. But in fact, the French Calvinist military experience was generally a foreign one, throughout the sixteenth and seventeenth centuries. Many Huguenots served with foreign armies even during the Wars of Religion (1562–1629).[5] In particular, they developed a very close relationship with the rebellious provinces of the Netherlands and their leader, Willem I, Prince of Orange, which continued after his death in 1584. Throughout the seventeenth century, a large French (and overwhelmingly Protestant) contingent was an important part of the army of the United Provinces of the Netherlands, playing a key role in Dutch campaigns; but Huguenots also served as individuals or in small groups in armies across Europe. In a very real sense, then, Huguenot soldiering had *always* been about mercenary soldiering; after 1685 there was probably a quantitative change in Huguenot soldiering (in that the numbers of Huguenot soldiers in foreign service increased), but not a qualitative one.

The long-term history of Huguenot soldiering is important because it can help to answer some of the obvious questions about the French Calvinist military

---

Religious Pluralism in Early Modern France (Oxford, Bern, New York, 2000), pp. 85–99; and essays in *L'Amiral de Coligny et son temps* (Paris, 1974); and *Colloques l'Avènement d'Henri IV*, ed. J. and D. Biarritz, vol. 1 'Quatrième centenaire de la bataille de Coutras (Coutras, 16–18 octobre 1987)' (Pau, 1988–92 [1988]). Studies of the Huguenot naval effort are not cited here.

4   See R. Gwynn, *Huguenot Heritage: The History and Contribution of the Huguenots in Britain* (London, 1985; reprinted Brighton, Portland, 2001), esp. ch. 9; R. Gwynn, 'The Huguenots in Britain, the "Protestant International" and the Defeat of Louis XIV', in R. Vigne and C. Littleton (eds), *From Strangers to Citizens: The Integration of Immigrant Communities in Britain, Ireland and Colonial America, 1550–1750* (London, Brighton, 2001), p. 413 et seq.; the articles collected and republished in R. Vigne and P. Rambaut, *Britain's Huguenot War Leaders* (London, 2002); and M. R. Glozier, *The Huguenot Soldiers of William of Orange and the Glorious Revolution of 1688: The Lions of Judah* (Brighton, Portland, 2002). The *apparatus criticus* of, in particular, Gwynn and Glozier direct the reader to the wealth of (often short) articles in sometimes obscure periodicals which, nevertheless, do illuminate the Huguenot role in the wars of the 1680s and 1690s.

5   I adopt here the periodisation of M. P. Holt, *The French Wars of Religion 1562–1629* (Cambridge, 1995) rather than the more traditional one of 1562–98, although the hostilities of the 1600s were not on the whole as widespread nor as long as the civil wars of the sixteenth century: see Trim, 'Edict of Nantes', pp. 86–7, 98.

experience, especially in its golden age at the end of the seventeenth century. How were Huguenots mobilised by foreign armies? In what countries did they prefer to serve and why? This may, in turn, give an insight into why so many served. What was the social composition of Huguenot units? And what explains their combat effectiveness? The Huguenots were a significant group in the European mercenary market for so long partly because of their fighting qualities, but also, in part, because they were relatively easy to mobilise. This reflected, firstly, the great influence of the nobility on the Calvinist movement and, secondly, the fact that the Huguenots – partly due to the military threat they faced in France throughout the sixteenth century and partly, perhaps, to the nature of Calvinism – were a heavily militarised group within French society. The Huguenots abroad always included veterans of the French royal and other armies, around whom other recruits could be formed into capable fighting units. Equally, the clientage ties of nobles and the Presbyterian structure of church organisation both lent themselves to military mobilisation – this was especially true in France during the wars of religion, but was also true for French Calvinists in foreign armies. Finally, the Huguenots' confessional zeal made them exceptionally fine combat troops. They generally served only Protestant powers and showed great commitment and zeal in opposing the expansionist design of the Habsburgs and, later, the 'Sun King' of France.

I

Huguenot soldiering originated around the year 1560. Individual Huguenots served (some with distinction) in the French royal armies during the Italian (or Habsburg-Valois) Wars in the 1540s–1550s, but there was no such thing as 'Huguenot soldiering' as a group experience until after the emergence of the Huguenots as a clear, distinct and powerful group amongst the French nobility. This occurred after the death of Henri II in July 1559. It is notable that, whereas Calvinists were at most some 10–12 per cent of the total population of France, they may have comprised almost a third of the provincial nobility, including a goodly number of greater nobles and princes of the blood. They were not distributed evenly across the country – whereas only one in a hundred of the *noblesse* of northern Mayenne was a Calvinist, it was one in four of the nobles of the Beauce, more than one in three of those of Quercy, and 40 per cent of the nobility of Saintonge and the *election* of Bayeux.[6]

The Huguenot nobles 'came out' in the three years after Henri II's death as protectors of their common co-religionists against local persecutors and Catholic mobs, while in 1560 the Calvinist Louis I de Bourbon, Prince de Condé, led an aristocratic conspiracy to seize, by force if necessary, control of the regency of the

---

6   D. Potter, 'The French Protestant Nobility in 1562: The "Associacion de Monseigneur le Prince de Condé"', *French History*, 15 (2001): 310; J.-M. Constant, 'The Protestant Nobility in France during the Wars of Religion: A Leaven of Innovation in a Traditional World', in P. Benedict *et al.* (eds), *Reformation, Revolt and Civil War in France and the Netherlands, 1555–1585* (Amsterdam, 1999), pp. 70–71; and cf. P. Benedict, 'The Dynamics of Protestant Militancy: France, 1555–1563', ibid., p. 37.

boy-King Charles IX.[7] Calvinism's ability to attract nobles and its organised nature made its adherents a political force that could not be swept away through repression. Furthermore, not only did the Reformed faith attract nobles, but probably a majority of them were drawn from the *noblesse d'epée* (the nobility of the sword) – almost 90 per cent of Calvinist nobles in the Beauce, for example.[8]

This preponderance ensured that French Calvinism was militant and militarised, and guaranteed the existence of Huguenot soldiering as a distinct subject. This became evident during the first episode in the history of Huguenot soldiering, which came in 1562 with the outbreak of the first of eight wars of religion that were to occupy most of the succeeding 36 years.

In the first war (1562–3) the Huguenots were able to muster troops sufficient for both a main army in the Loire valley, under the Prince de Condé and Gaspard II de Coligny, Seigneur de Châtillon and Admiral of France, and a secondary force, operating in Normandy. Added to these were some regional defence forces. The infantry units were composed mostly of volunteers raised through the various local reformed churches. Condé envisaged, when appealing to the reformed consistories of France in April 1562, that each should 'use such means as you have promptly to furnish soldiers'; the Calvinist system of consistories and local and regional synods lent itself to military organisation by companies and regiments. The regional synod of Guyenne, for example, 'resolved to have each church form an *enseigne* [infantry company] ... and to group these into regiments by colloquys'.[9]

In addition, however, the Huguenot forces drew heavily on the affinities of the nobles – especially for their cavalry. An *estat* from 1562, of the 'princes, lords, knights, gentlemen and captains with the Prince de Condé who have resolved to live and die together to maintain the gospel in France', indicates that Condé had some 4,000 nobles with him, mostly in mounted units.[10] Similarly, in the second civil war (1567–8), the Huguenot army was distinguished by its high proportion of nobles.[11] Several of the Protestant leaders were captains of their own companies of *gens d'armes* – the elite, aristocratic heavy cavalry that was the hard core of

---

7   Benedict, 'Dynamics of Protestant Militancy', pp. 42–3; N. M. Sutherland, 'Calvinism and the Conspiracy of Amboise', *History*, 47 (1962): 111–38.

8   Constant, 'The Protestant Nobility in France during the Wars of Religion', p. 72.

9   'Mémoires du Prince de Condé', in J.-F. Michaud and J.-J.-F. Poujoulat (eds), *Nouvelle collection des mémoires pour servir à l'histoire de France, depuis le XIIIe siècle jusqu'à la fin du XVIIIe*, series 1 (32 vols, Paris, 1836–44), vol. 6 (1839), p. 629, Condé to the *églises réformées de France*, 7 April 1562; Benedict, 'Dynamics of Protestant Militancy', pp. 42–4 (at 43); A. Thierry, 'L'Homme de guerre dans l'œuvre d'Agrippa d'Aubigné', in G.-A. Pérouse, A. Thierry and A. Tournon (eds), *L'Homme de guerre au XVIe siècle* (Saint-Etienne: Université de Saint-Etienne, 1992), p. 145.

10   Potter, 'The French Protestant Nobility in 1562': 313–28, printing TNA, SP 70/41, fols 50–56, *Estat de partie des princes, seigneurs, chevalliers de l'ordre, gentishommes, capitaynes de l'associacion de Monseigneur le prince de Condé qui ont resolu de vivre et mourir ensemble pour maintainir l'evangille en France*, 7 September 1562 (collated with Bibliothèque Nationale [hereafter BN] BL, Lans. MS 5, fol. 181).

11   For example Bib. Maz., MS 2,620, fol. 17 and MS 2,619, fol. 35, *Sommation... du Roy a ceux de la nouvelle relligion qui esoyent en armes a ste Denis*, December 1567, and

France's standing army. The rank-and-file of these *compagnies d'ordonnance* (or *gendarmerie*) were mostly a Captain's friends, extended family and clients.[12] As a result, such men tended to stick together; thus, the Huguenots were able to draw off a few entire units of the royal army.[13] Even when they were not so tightly bound together, they sometimes took the bulk of a unit, as for example in 1568, when Henri-Robert, Duc de Bouillon, joined the Huguenot army: he evidently was followed by 70 per cent of his *compagnie de gendarmerie* of 100 lances, as a new company of 30 was put in its place on the royal establishment.[14] In addition, great Protestant nobles were able to draw on their affinities to create new units, of both cavalry and infantry.[15] Furthermore, many reformed-leaning aristocratic rank-and-file of the *gendarmerie* made individual decisions to serve the Calvinist cause, leaving their companies to join the Protestant forces, again as individuals.[16] The Catholics would have called this desertion but, for the men in question, they were simply obeying God, rather than man (as Acts 5:29 enjoins). Such veterans, together with individual volunteers, whether from churches or noble affinities, had to be formed into new units – a not inconsiderable task, but one which, in practice, occurred swiftly. This probably suggests that most, or at least the core, of each unit were men who knew each other already, as members of the same local church or of the same noble client affinity.

---

undertaking of Charles IX with Huguenot nobility (the latter undated but almost certainly from March 1568: see Wood, *The King's Army*, p. 21).

12   See K. B. Neuschel, *Word of Honour: Interpreting Noble Culture in Sixteenth-Century France* (Ithaca NY, London, 1989); R. R. Harding, *Anatomy of a Power Elite: The Provincial Governors of Early Modern France* (New Haven CT, 1978), pp. 20–1; S. P. Kettering, 'Patronage and Kinship in Early Modern France', *French Historical Studies*, 16 (1989): 409–10, 418; Wood, *The King's Army*, p. 139; and, for example, BN, MS Fr. 25,801, no. 185, the *roolle de la montre* (muster roll) of the *gendarmerie* company of Charles de La Rochefoucauld, 9 June 1567.

13   Certainly in the first civil war: see Potter, 'The French Protestant Nobility in 1562': 308–9, 309 n.12, citing *CSPFor.*, vol. 5 (1562), p. 279, no. 571; see also BN, MS Fr. 3,185, fols 73–4 (summary of *gendarmerie* musters, April–June 1563), which shows that, within weeks of the end of the first civil war, Huguenot nobles (including Condé, Coligny and La Rochefoucauld) had their *compaignies de gendarmerie* again, so that probably the latter had served under their captains' command throughout the first war. The Huguenot captains retained their companies to the beginning of the second civil war and they were again placed on the royal establishment after both the second and third wars.

14   BN, MS Fr. 3,193, fol. 198, *Estat du paiement des Compagnies du gendarmerie*, January 1568. The Duc de Bouillon's status as a Huguenot is discussed below.

15   Potter, 'The French Protestant Nobility in 1562': 309–10, 313–23 *passim*; and see also, for example, TNA, SP70/47, fol. 197v, *estat* of garrison of Dieppe, December 1562: in two companies of arquebusiers commanded by the Comte de Montgomery, 52 out of 460 men (11 per cent) were *gentilshommes*.

16   For example, Jehan de Saint-Jehan at the start of the third civil war left the company of Philip de La Roche, Sieur de Fontanilles and went to England: see BN, *Nouvelles acquisitions françaises* 8,628, fol. 37, the muster roll of 15 September 1569.

II

How the first Huguenot soldiers were mobilised in the first and second civil wars in France during the 1560s is important because it set a pattern for Huguenot soldiering in Europe for the rest of the sixteenth and seventeenth centuries. Of course, French Protestant soldiering was initially against the French crown and this indicates why Huguenot soldiering was mostly mercenary soldiering – there was consistently a strong incentive for Huguenots to go abroad. Mercenary service was a good way to make a living, but it was especially *à propos* for members of the nobility, whose *raison d'être* was making war. For much of the last four decades of the sixteenth century (and again at times in the first three decades of the seventeenth century), the Huguenots fought against the Valois and Bourbon monarchs for the right to practise their religion. Even during this period of focus on their native land, however, their military endeavours were still connected to wider international and Protestant war efforts. Firstly, in France the Huguenots frequently fought alongside foreign Protestant forces – German, English, Welsh, Scottish and Swiss. Secondly, throughout this period, French Protestants served not just in France, but in other theatres of war.

In the first war of religion, in 1562–3 the Huguenots were aided by English troops sent by Elizabeth I; in the first, second, third, fifth and eighth civil wars they hired large numbers of German mercenaries.[17] The most important chapter in the history of mutual co-operation and military interchange with foreign Protestants began in 1569. Willem I, Prince of Orange, leader of the revolt of the Netherlands, had been badly defeated by the Spanish in 1568, the year the third war of religion had started; the following spring, Willem took the remnants of his army into France and joined the main Protestant field army under Condé and Coligny. Willem's brother, Louis (or Lodewijk) van Nassau, took command of the French privateering fleet based at La Rochelle.[18] He remained in command until the end of the war in August 1570 – indeed, it was he who gave the ultimate order to the fleet to disarm.[19] During the brief period of peace between the third and fourth wars of religion, there was a renewed Turkish threat in the Mediterranean. A force of Huguenots served the Venetians against the infidels in 1571 and French Protestants may have been among the French troops that fought for the Spanish in the crusade of Lepanto.[20]

In May 1572, Willem and Louis of Nassau launched a renewed revolt in the Netherlands. Louis was responsible for leading an uprising in the south. He took Valenciennes and Mons with an army made up of Huguenots, Dutch exiles, English volunteers and some German mercenaries, with two Huguenots, de Poyet and the

---

17   A. Corvisier, 'Les Guerres de Religion, 1559–1598', in P. Contamine (ed.), *Histoire militaire de France* (4 vols, Paris, 1992–4), vol. 1 'Des origines à 1715', p. 320.

18   Lodewijk van Nassau was such a transnational operator that he was not just a Dutch figure. To the Huguenot soldiers (from whose perspective this story is told) he was always 'Louis'.

19   BN, MS Fr. 18,587, fol. 539, *acte* of Louis de Nassau, 15 May 1572.

20   F. Braudel, *The Mediterranean and the Mediterranean World in the Age of Philip II*, trans. S. Reynolds (London, 1973), p. 1105.

celebrated François de La Noüe, as his deputies.[21] It was an integral part of the plan that they would be reinforced by a Huguenot contingent under Jean de Hangest, Seigneur de Genlis, as a prelude to what Coligny, briefly chief adviser of King Charles IX, planned would be a French declaration of war on Spain and the despatch of a royal army into the southern Netherlands. When de Genlis was defeated the King lost his nerve, resulting in the Saint-Bartholomew's massacre; then Willem van Oranje, leading a German mercenary army to aid his brother, was driven back into Germany; and thus the garrison of Mons was cut off and – eventually – forced to accept terms. But the mostly Huguenot garrison, despite their isolation, facing elite Spanish troops, made a splendid defence: 'The brave Defence of Count Lodowick, assisted by Mounsieur de La Noüe ... and many of the French Nobility, made the Siege of Mons very long and difficult. The Spaniards fired above 20,000 Canon-shot against it.'[22] This southern extension of the second Dutch revolt of 1572 demonstrates well how Huguenots, Dutch and English co-operated towards a common end. And although the grand design failed, it was French troops, both in the planning and execution, which formed the major element of Louis of Nassau's army. Huguenot troops also rallied to Flushing, after it rebelled and formed part of the forces serving the States of Zealand.[23]

The following year, in the spring of 1573, the Comte de Montgomery mustered an Anglo-French expedition in Plymouth to intervene in the fourth civil war (precipitated by the Saint-Bartholomew's massacre). When peace in France was concluded in the summer of 1573, Montgomery sent his Huguenot and English troops to the Netherlands to aid the sorely pressed Willem I. They arrived in July 1573 and went straight into action around the hard-pressed city of Haarlem, but the city fell later that month. A few Huguenot volunteers were already serving with Willem, including de Poyet, who in August Willem appointed his *maître de camp general* (commander of a separate field army). In August, less than a month after Haarlem fell, de Poyet and his army stormed St Geertruidenberg with a force of 'English, Scottish, French and Flemish companies', as one of his British soldiers later recalled. It was the first city captured by the rebels for a year and a major boost

21   De Poyet has thus far defied further identification: see A. E. C. Simoni, 'Walter Morgan Wolff: An Elizabethan Soldier and His Maps', *Quaerendo*, 26 (1996): 66–8. One Henri Poyet was a trooper in Schomberg's Horse in Ireland in the 1690s, but the question of the two men's relationship must remain open: HMC, *House of Lords*, vol. 3, p. 406.

22   L. Aubery du Maurier, *The Lives of all the Princes of Orange, from William the Great, Founder of the Common-wealth of the United Provinces* (1682), trans. T. Brown (London, 1693), p. 32; see also R. Williams, *A Briefe Discourse of Warre* (1590), p. 21; and *The Actions of the Lowe Countries* (1618), pp. 83–94, 98 [page nos are in *The Works of Sir Roger Williams*, ed. J. X. Evans (Oxford, 1972)]; BN, MS Fr. 18,587, fols 541–3, *Discours de la deffaicte des troupes du Sʳ de Genlis*; and D. J. B. Trim, 'Fighting "Jacob's Wars": The Employment of English and Welsh Mercenaries in the European Wars of Religion: France and the Netherlands, 1562–1610', PhD thesis (University of London, 2002), p. 112.

23   For example, in Baron J. Kervyn de Lettenhove (ed.), *Relations politiques des Pays-Bas et de l'Angleterre, sous le règne de Philippe II* (11 vols, Brussels, 1882–1900), vol. 6, pp. 454, 458, 457, nos 2435, 2438, 2437, anon. reports to Sir William Cecil, 12 and 16 July 1572, and convention between magistrates of Flushing and Colonel Gilbert, 15 July 1572.

to their morale. Willem's multinational force operated in 1573–4 against the Spanish besiegers of Leiden; the successful defence of the city was a decisive moment in the history of the Dutch Revolt.[24] De Poyet, meanwhile, retained command of a separate army in the field until he returned to France in May 1574.[25] Huguenot companies were still in service with the rebels when the mutiny of the Spanish army in 1576 led to all the provinces of the Netherlands joining Holland and Zealand in revolt against Spain. The companies employed by the States of Holland had their own *maître de Camp des compagnies françoises*, one Antoine de La Garde, who had first served in Holland in 1572.[26]

Huguenot participation in the campaigns in the Netherlands during 1572–6 was the start of a close association with the Dutch rebels-cum-republic that lasted till the War of the Spanish Succession. French and Dutch Calvinists regarded the wars in France and the Netherlands, waged against the often-allied Catholic French and Spanish monarchies, as essentially the same conflict against idolatrous, anti-Christian religion. The Spanish had sent troops from the Netherlands to aid the Crown in the first war of religion, so it was also in the French Protestants' best interests to aid their fellow Calvinists in the Netherlands. Furthermore, the Netherlandish and Huguenot nobility were extensively intermarried. The Counts of Egmont, Lalaing, Hornes and Rennenburg and the Prince of Epinoy were all part of the extended Montmorency family, one of the greatest noble clans in France, and their cousins included such Huguenot leaders as the Seigneur de Genlis and Admiral de Coligny, and possibly the Prince de Porcien. Willem van Oranje married as his fourth wife Louise de Coligny, the Admiral's daughter, having earlier wed (and buried) as his third wife, Charlotte de Bourbon, a cousin of Louis de Condé and Henri de Bourbon, King of Navarre.[27] For ideological, strategic and familial reasons the Huguenots identified the Dutch Revolt as a cause worth fighting for, and the Netherlands drew many Huguenot soldiers.

The newly United Provinces of the Netherlands still had need of an army to fight Spain. Huguenots provided a ready source of recruits, especially since there was a

---

24   D. J. B. Trim, 'Immigrants, the Indigenous Community and International Calvinism', in N. Goose and L. Luu (eds), *Immigrants in Tudor and Early Stuart England* (Brighton, Portland, 2005), p. 212; GAL, *Archief der Secretarie* 1033, fols 12r, 43v, 'Rekening' of payments made to units of Willem of Orange's army, 1572–5; *Koninklijk Huisarchief* (hereafter KH), The Hague, A 11/XIV I/12, fols 341r, 2r–v, Willem to de Poyet and Commission to same, 3 July and 1 August 1573; Williams, 'Actions of the Lowe Countries', in *Works*, ed. Evans, pp. 135–6, 138 n. 240; Lettenhove, *Relations Politiques*, vol. 10, p. 812, no. 2625, Thomas Morgan to Lord Burghley, 13 September 1573; GAL, *Archief der Secretarie* 1334, n. fol, receipts of payments to Captains Duran and d'Aultrain, Leiden, 1574.

25   KH, A 11/XIV I/12, fol. 396, Willem to officers of de Poyet's army, 15 May 1574.

26   HNA, *Collectie Ortell* 35, Muster rolls of companies of Captain Duran and M. de La Garde, November 1575; F. J. G. ten Raa and F. de Bas (eds), *Het Staatsche Leger 1568–1795* (vols 1–4, Breda, 1911–18), vol. 1, p. 28.

27   G. Parker, *The Dutch Revolt* (London, 1977; 1990 edition), pp. 271, 273, genealogical tables 1, 3; Potter, 'The French Protestant Nobility in 1562': 313 n. 3: the title of Prince de Porcien was used by Antoine de Croy, who was, presumably, related to the great Netherlands' noble family of Croy.

relatively prolonged period of uneasy peace in France after the sixth war of religion concluded in 1577. With peace at home, some French soldiers found employment in Muscovy, though their confessional allegiance is uncertain.[28] But the majority of Huguenots who served abroad did so in Dutch pay. Three new companies of Huguenot infantry joined the Dutch army in the autumn of 1577 and a steady stream followed thereafter. From 1579 two French infantry regiments were in Dutch pay.

François de La Noüe rivals Coligny and Montgomery for the status of greatest Huguenot soldier of the sixteenth century. La Noüe had been one of the chief Captains under Louis of Nassau at Mons in 1572, and was now Colonel of the first of these Huguenot regiments, of 12 companies. Antoine de La Garde commanded the second, of 10 companies. The total Huguenot establishment in Dutch pay was 2,500 men in the two infantry regiments, plus 400 Horse, of which half were *edelen* (noblemen).[29]

In August 1578, de La Noüe was appointed *maréchal-de-camp* by the States General and made Commander-in-Chief of the States' forces in Flanders later that year; de la Garde was, like de La Noüe, appointed to the States' Council of War. La Noüe held command of the Dutch army of Flanders until his capture by the Spanish in the aftermath of a defeat in May 1580. He was regarded highly by his employers who, in addition to appointing him to senior army command, consulted him on wider strategic and political issues. He was regarded by the Spanish as sufficient a threat that, after they captured him in May 1580, they notoriously refused to ransom him unless he agreed to have his eyes put out. De la Garde, meanwhile, commanded the defence of Breda in 1581, and for his efforts was made Governor of the important fortress of Bergen-op-Zoom, a post he held until his death in 1583.[30]

In 1581–2 there was a great influx of French Catholics, when the Duc d'Anjou, the French king's younger brother, briefly allied with the States General. He eventually fell out with them over religious, political and financial issues, but, throughout Anjou's time in the Low Countries and on into 1585, some Huguenot companies remained in Dutch pay. Among them was a company of 100 lancers under de La Noüe's son, Odet, Seigneur de Téligny, who remained in the Netherlands until 1585, holding from July 1584 the rank of General of the Cavalry.[31] In the early 1580s, Huguenots contributed to the efforts made by Dom Antonio, pretender to the Portuguese throne, to oust Philip II of Spain – the chance to weaken the Habsburg King was an attraction to the Calvinist soldiers and sailors who took part. Much of this effort was naval, but in 1582–3 Huguenots served in the amphibious expedition

28   G. P. Herd, 'General Patrick Gordon of Auchleuchries – A Scot in Seventeenth-Century Russian Service', PhD thesis (University of Aberdeen, 1993), p. 135.

29   GAL, *Stadsarchief* 3021, Prince of Orange to SG, 4 January 1580; Ten Raa and de Bas (eds), *Het Staatsche Leger*, vol. 1, pp. 56–57, 61, 160.

30   P. Kervyn de Volkaersbeke (ed.), *Correspondance de François de La Noue, surnommé Bras-de-Fer, accompagnée de notes historiques et précédée de la vie de ce grand capitaine* (8 vols, Gand, Paris, 1854), vol. 7, pp. 56–210 *passim*; AEMD, France, 242, fols 32r–37r, De La Noüe to SG, 27 December 1577; Ten Raa and de Bas (eds), *Het Staatsche Leger*, vol. 1, pp. 51, 244–5.

31   Ibid., pp. 63–4, 108, 173, 183.

led by Philippe Strozzi (who, ironically, in the third civil war had commanded royal troops against the Huguenots) that attempted to seize the Azores for Antonio.[32]

III

In 1584 the Wars of Religion had resumed, and from 1585 to 1598 the Huguenots' attention was fixed on France, where Henri de Navarre battled to become Henri IV of France and to settle the civil wars. Few Huguenots served in foreign armies in these years; some with German forces, but only when they intervened in France. In 1587, Guillaume-Robert de La Marck, Duc de Bouillon and sovereign Prince of Sedan, was joint commander of a large army, paid for largely by Elizabeth I of England, that entered France to aid Henri de Navarre and the Protestant cause. Ultimately defeated by Catholic forces under the Duc de Guise, the army consisted mostly of mercenaries. First among them were Germans, led by Baron von Dohna, both cavalry (the *reiters*, whose fame lent their name to the entire force in contemporary French usage) and infantry (*landsknechts*). There were also Swiss infantry, led by Bouillon; but some Huguenots served with them.[33] Bouillon's own status – German or Huguenot – is debatable. Sedan was a principality of the Holy Roman Empire (and Bouillon was disputed between France and the Empire), so he could be regarded as German. In practice, however, while the rulers of the several small sovereign principalities on the borders of (or actually within) France were regarded by contemporaries as 'foreign princes in France' (*princes estrangers en France*), they were well-integrated into French aristocratic kinship networks. They owned large estates within France, commanded French armies and acted as *gouverneurs* of French provinces, and were integral members of the French court and political scene. Bouillon was himself a Calvinist (like his father before him); he was a cousin of Navarre and brother-in-law of one of the Huguenot military leaders, Henri de La Tour (who inherited the duchy on Guillaume-Robert's death in 1588). Bouillon could thus be classified as a Huguenot himself, rather than a German.[34] In any event, the presence of French Calvinists serving alongside his mercenaries does not invalidate the point that Huguenot soldiering from the mid-1580s was for 15 years occupied with France itself.

---

32   See B. Dietz, 'Privateering in North-West European Waters, 1568 to 1572', PhD thesis (University of London, 1959), pp. 424, 426, 428; J.-F. Dubost, *La France italienne* (Paris, 1997), p. 203. Dom Antonio was based at La Rochelle for a time: for example BN, *Collection Dupuy* 500, fol. 15, Antonio to Pope Sixtus V, 2 August 1585.

33   BN, MS Fr. 704, fols 69–70, 86 and 72, *Estat de larmee des reistres* and *articles et capitulation* of the army of the Prince de Conty, Duc de Bouillon and Baron d'Hone (Dohna) (both undated but contextually 1587) and Bouillon to Henri de Navarre, 20 August 1587; G. Mattingly, *The Defeat of the Spanish Armada* (London, 1959), pp. 146, 149–54.

34   See AEMD, France, 28, *Princes estrangers en France*; D. Parrott, 'Richelieu, the *Grands*, and the French Army', in J. Bergin and L. Brockliss (eds), *Richelieu and His Age* (Oxford, 1992), pp. 136–9; S. Carroll, *Noble Power during the French Wars of Religion: The Guise Affinity and the Catholic Cause in Normandy* (Cambridge, 1998), pp. 14–23, 39, 50–51, 99.

In 1598 the Treaty of Vervins ended the war with Spain and the same year the Edict of Nantes guaranteed freedom of religion for the members of France's reformed churches. With peace at home, the attention of Huguenot soldiers once again turned outwards. Some may have served alongside Catholics in one of two French contingents under the Holy Roman Emperor against the Turks: one recruited in 1597, the other (made up entirely of noble volunteers) in 1599.[35] Huguenots may also have been among the French troops who served in Muscovy in the early 1600s: one French company distinguished itself in the service of Boris Gudunov (*c*.1605); a *corps* of 5,000 Scots, French and Swedish soldiers served the Muscovite government from 1608 to 1611. That the Scots and Swedes would have been Protestants may give a clue about the confessional allegiance of the French.[36] As in the 1570s and 1580s, there is no question that most Huguenot soldiers preferred to fight for fellow Protestants: from 1599, the Netherlands once again drew them.

IV

The surviving rebellious provinces of the Netherlands had in the preceding 15 years become firmly established; their considerable financial muscle would allow the Dutch Republic to punch above its weight and maintain a disproportionate war effort for the next 120 years. Indeed, in the 1590s Dutch troops had aided Henri IV in France, against the Catholic League and its Spanish allies.[37] The republic also, in the 1590s, reorganised its army under the guidance of Maurits van Nassau, Willem van Oranje's son and eventual successor as Commander-in-Chief. Maurits's reforms were administrative, logistical and tactical and made the Dutch army – the *Staatse leger* – a model for the rest of Europe. But the northern Netherlands lacked the population base necessary to recruit enough troops for its military purposes and so the United Provinces made up the difference with mercenaries. English, Scottish and

---

35　See E. Grimeston, *A General Inuentorie of the History of France from the Beginning of that Monarchie ... Written by Ihon de Serres. And Continued [and] Translated out of French into English, by Edward Grimeston* (London, 1607), pp. 876–8; C. F. Finkel, 'French Mercenaries in the Habsburg-Ottoman War of 1593–1606: The Desertion of the Papa Garrison to the Ottomans in 1600', *Bulletin of the School of Oriental and African Studies, University of London*, 55 (1992): 453; Parrott, *Richelieu's Army*, p. 30. Grimeston wrote mostly on the history of Protestants and Protestant states (having himself served in the Dutch army); he may have been interested in this episode, the hero of which in his original (Catholic) sources was the Duc de Mercœur (who had been an ally of the Spanish in the 1590s and was close to the Guise clan of Catholic zealots), because Huguenots also served in Hungary. The fact that there were serious divisions among the French troops in Habsburg employ (Finkel, 'French Mercenaries in the Habsburg-Ottoman War': 459) may also point to the presence of both Huguenots and Catholics.

36　Herd, 'General Patrick Gordon of Auchleuchries', pp. 138–41. The captain of the Frenchmen serving Boris Gudunov was one Jacques Margeret (ibid., p. 139) – the Margerets may have been a Calvinist family as a Paul Margarett was a surgeon in Colonel Bland's Horse in England in 1713: C. E. Lart, 'The Huguenot Regiments', *Proceedings of the Huguenot Society of Great Britain and Ireland*, 9 (1911): 527.

37　Ten Raa and de Bas (eds), *Het Staatsche Leger*, vol. 2, pp. 23, 307 et seq.

German mercenary contingents were key elements of the *Staatse leger* throughout its history.[38] And with the settlement of the Wars of Religion by the Edict of Nantes, French mercenaries, too, became an integral part of the States' army.

In 1596 the States General had sought a 'French noblemen of quality [and] of the religion' to raise a regiment in France whose 'officers and soldiers ... shall profess the religion', but conditions in France made recruiting this regiment impossible.[39] By 1599, circumstances had changed and the Dutch found the men they wanted: a Huguenot infantry regiment numbering some 1,500 men, commanded by Odet de La Noüe-Téligny (who, thus, resumed service in Dutch pay), was shipped into the Netherlands.[40] Téligny and his men distinguished themselves the next year in fierce fighting on the strategically vital island of Bommel.[41] In January 1601, command of the French regiment passed to Henri de Coligny, Seigneur de Châtillon-sur-Loing (grandson of the Admiral de Coligny).[42] In August that year Henri de Coligny-Châtillon commanded a detached, multinational force of 20 companies (of which only six were French) sent to reinforce the besieged fortress of Ostend.[43] The French contingent, which included many 'persons of quality', suffered heavy casualties, including Coligny-Châtillon who, in the autumn of 1601, was decapitated by a canon ball.[44]

Command of the French regiment passed to Léonidas de Béthune, Seigneur de Congy, though that of the Huguenot troops in Ostend seems to have been exercised by Jean de Sau, Coligny-Châtillon's Lieutenant-Colonel. Also commanding was Jacques de Rocques, Baron de Montesquieu, who won the praise of the Governor of Ostend, General Sir Francis Vere, for his 'worth and valour'. Meanwhile, recruiting was stepped up in France to replace the losses – and so successfully were Huguenots enlisted that by the spring of 1602 there were 21 infantry companies, with a total establishment of over 3,000 men. The French regiment was, therefore, split in two,

---

38   Trim, 'Fighting "Jacob's Wars"'; H. L. Zwitzer, *De militie van den staat: Het leger van de Republiek der Verenigde Nederlanden* (Amsterdam, 1991), ch. 3, esp. pp. 39–42.

39   Ten Raa and de Bas (eds), *Het Staatsche Leger*, vol. 2, p. 41 ('*Franchois Edelman van qualiteyt, die religie*'; '*officieren ende soldaten (...) daerse professie doen vande religie*').

40   HNA, *Collectie Aanwinsten* (hereafter Aan.) 879, fols 6v, 11r, SG summary of extraordinary military expenditure, 1599; Ten Raa and de Bas (eds), *Het Staatsche Leger*, vol. 2, pp. 51, 164, 352–3.

41   A. d'Aubigné, *L'Histoire universelle* (3 vols, Maille, 1616–20), vol. 3, p. 526; J. Orlers, *Den Nassauschen Lauren-crans: Beschrijvinge ende af-beeldinge van alle de Victorien, so te Water als te Lande, die Godt Almachtich de (...) Staten der Vereenichde Neder-landen verleent hefte (...)* (Leyden, 1610), p. 129.

42   HNA, *Archief Raad van State* 1226, fols 132r, 135v, *Staat van oorlog* (military budget) for 1601; Ten Raa and de Bas (eds), *Het Staatsche Leger*, vol. 2, pp. 356–7.

43   HMC, *Salisbury*, vol. 11, p. 346, J. Holcroft to Robert Cecil, 16 August 1601; Francis Vere *et al.*, *The Commentaries of Sir Francis Vere*, ed. W. Dillingham (1657), published in E. Arber and T. Seccombe (eds), *Stuart Tracts 1603–1693*, intro. C. H. Firth (New York, 1964), p. 178.

44   Anon., *Histoire Remarquable et veritable de ce qui s'est passé par chacun jour au siege de la ville d'Ostende, de part & d'autre jusques à present* (Paris, 1604), p. 17r ('*personnes de qualité*'), p. 29v; Vere, *Commentaries*, pp. 177, 192, 202; Ten Raa and de Bas (eds), *Het Staatsche Leger*, vol. 2, p. 165.

with Guillaume d'Hallot, Seigneur de Dommarville et de Guichery, Colonel of the new regiment.[45] French companies were rotated in and out of Ostend throughout the three-year siege of the city, until it eventually fell in the autumn of 1604. Command of the Huguenot contingent was exercised in 1602 by Captain Jacques du Fort; in 1603 by Captain Brusse; and in 1604 by Lieutenant-Colonel de Rocques. Huguenots also served the garrison as engineers and gunners.[46] Meanwhile, in August 1603, Léonidas de Béthune had been accidentally killed, while trying to break up a quarrel between members of his regiment and one of the States' English regiments. He was succeeded as Colonel of the first French regiment by Gaspard III de Coligny, Henri's brother and successor as Seigneur de Châtillon. When Guillaume d'Hallot was killed at the Battle of Mulheim (9 October 1605) he was replaced as Colonel of the second regiment by Syrius de Béthune, son of Léonidas.[47]

Thereafter, there was consistently a strong Huguenot presence in the States' army. In 1608–9 the United Provinces negotiated the Twelve Years' Truce with Spain and took the chance to retrench many mercenary units; that the French regiments were kept in pay, with the same number of companies, is testimony to their value to the Dutch army.[48] Gaspard de Coligny-Châtillon was appointed Colonel-General of the Infantry in 1614, an office he held until 1638.[49] In 1613, Syrius de Béthune was replaced as Colonel of the second French regiment by his Lieutenant-Colonel, Jean Antoine de Saint-Simon, Baron de Courtomer; in 1615, a third Huguenot regiment was added, under the command of François de Laubespine, Seigneur d'Hauterive and Marquis de Châteauneuf.[50] Further, the Huguenot regiments are known to have kept their strength up by recruiting in France, so that any dilution of their ranks with locals must have been small – these were, and they remained, French regiments, because Frenchmen constantly enlisted to serve in them.[51]

For the Huguenot nobility, it became virtually the done thing to visit the Netherlands and serve at least a season: from 1600 on with Maurits; and, after his death in 1625, with his brother and successor, Frederik Hendrik, Prince of

---

45   Ten Raa and de Bas (eds), *Het Staatsche Leger*, vol. 2, pp. 164–6; Vere, *Commentaries*, p. 202; HNA, Aan. 879, fol. 30r, SG accounts for extraordinary military expenditure, 1602; *Resolutiën der Staten-Generaal van 1576 tot 1609*, ed. H. Rijperman (14 vols, The Hague: RGP, 1950), vol. 12, *1602–3*, pp. 187, 489, SG warrant, 23 November 1602 and SG to Henri IV, February 1603.

46   Ten Raa and de Bas (eds), *Het Staatsche Leger*, vol. 2, pp. 276–9.

47   HMC, *Dudley and De L'Isle MSS*, vol. 3, pp. 44, 48, William Browne to Robert Sidney, July 1603; *Resolutiën der Staten-Generaal*, vol. 12, p. 517, SG resolution, 14 November 1603; Ten Raa and de Bas (eds), *Het Staatsche Leger*, vol. 2, pp. 83, 166, 367; Parrott, *Richelieu's Army*, p. 29.

48   Ten Raa and de Bas (eds), *Het Staatsche Leger*, vol. 2, p. 164.

49   Ibid., vol. 3, p. 187; Parrott, *Richelieu's Army*, p. 29.

50   *Not* Bertrand de Vignolles, Seigneur de Casaubon – *pace* Parrott, *Richelieu's Army*, p. 29: see Ten Raa and de Bas (eds), *Het Staatsche Leger*, vol. 3, pp. 187–8.

51   For example HNA, Aan. 879, fol. 68v, extraordinary military accounts, 1605; HMC, *De L'Isle and Dudley MSS*, vol. 3, p. 282, Browne to Lisle, 15 June 1606; and this was standard practice for foreign regiments in the *Staatse leger*, see Trim, 'Fighting "Jacob's Wars"', ch. 7.

Orange. Henri IV actively encouraged this. An English colonel with many years in Dutch service observed that the King regularly urged his nobles to gain military experience by serving the Prince of Orange; consequently, 'he made the Low Countries swarm every year for three or four months with his Princes, Nobility and his Gentry'.[52] And the pattern set in Henri IV's reign outlasted him. To be sure, from the late 1610s, Catholics were among the French troops in Dutch pay; but Calvinists predominated.[53] Henri, Duc de Rohan, *colonel-général* of the Swiss Guards, and his younger brother, Benjamin, visited the Netherlands in the summer of 1606 to fight for Maurits. This *did* incur Henri IV's displeasure for France was supposed to be neutral, so one of the *grands* (and an important official of the French army) serving against Spain was extremely provocative. Yet Rohan did not return home until he had seen the campaign season out, leaving only in November.[54] Frédéric-Maurice de La Tour, the new Duc de Bouillon, served in the States' army from 1621 to 1635; his service included holding the important office of Governor of Maastricht, a post occupied during the Spanish siege in 1634. Bouillon's younger brother, Henri de La Tour, Vicomte de Turenne (later the celebrated *maréchal de France*) also started his military career under Maurits van Nassau. Many other young French nobles either did likewise, or served in the *Staatse leger* at some point, including the authors of many influential military treatises published from the 1610s to the 1640s. A strong aristocratic component was typical of the Huguenot units in Dutch pay; so, too, was the presence of sons and grandsons of men who had fought for Willem in the 1570s and 1580s (including La Noüe-Téligny and the grandsons of Coligny). There were particular influxes of such volunteers in 1606–7, when the Dutch Republic was threatened by a great offensive directed by the celebrated Spanish general Spínola and increased its army in response; and in the early 1620s, following the resumption of hostilities between the United Provinces and Spain at the end of the Twelve Years' Truce.[55] The strong family connections and high aristocratic component suggest that, as

52   BL, Royal MS 18.C.xxiii, fol. 74, Lord Wimbledon, 'The Demonstrance of Cavallerye', printed in C. Dalton, *Life and Times of General Sir Edward Cecil, Viscount Wimbledon* (2 vols, London, 1885), vol. 2, p. 329. Henri IV's deliberate encouragement of French service in the Dutch army was also recognised by contemporary Catholic soldiers, for example see BSG, MS 847, fol. 108v, *Articles concernant le service du roy et l'estat et necessité de ses affaires en son armée*, 17 September 1621.

53   Parrott, *Richelieu's Army*, p. 31.

54   Parrott, 'Richelieu, the *Grands*, and the French Army', p. 170; HMC, *Dudley and De L'Isle MSS*, vol. 3, p. 329, Browne to Lisle, 12 November 1606; Ten Raa and de Bas (eds), *Het Staatsche Leger*, vol. 2, p. 83.

55   See Parrott, *Richelieu's Army*, pp. 28–30, 37; Ten Raa and de Bas (eds), *Het Staatsche Leger*, vol. 2, pp. 83, 277, 279 n.31, 364–5; Trim, 'Fighting "Jacob's Wars"', pp. 188, 337–8; HMC, *De L'Isle and Dudley MSS*, vol. 3, p. 282, Browne to Lisle, 15 June 1606; HNA, *Archief SG*, 8043, list of French captains in the 1607 *staat van oorlog*; Koninklijke Bibliotheek, The Hague, MS 133.M.63, entries in *album amicorum* of Bernard ten Broecke; William Crosse, *A Generall Historie of the Netherlands: Newly Revewed, Corrected, and Supplied with Observations Omitted in the First Impression, by Ed. Grimeston. Continued from the yeare 1608 till the yeare 1627 by William Crosse* (London, 1627), p. 1436; *Dudley Carleton to John*

with the Huguenot units of the 1560s, recruiting for Huguenot units in Dutch pay in the seventeenth century was done via affinity connections, including kinship networks and 'extended clienteles'.[56]

V

In the 1620s, the Dutch Republic was on good terms with the French crown which, under Richelieu, was increasingly anti-Spanish. This coincidence of interests meant that when, in 1627–8, English naval squadrons and troops aided the defenders of the great Huguenot stronghold of La Rochelle in the last of the Wars of Religion, they did so against the urging of their Dutch allies. The Dutch supported the French crown against Protestant militants, because civil war in France reduced the support France could lend the republic against the common Habsburg enemy. Nevertheless, the Dutch were no less committed to the Protestant cause ('the common cause' as Protestant writers of all nationalities regularly referred to it) and continued to recruit heavily from among the Huguenots, who, back in France, increasingly faced restrictions on their right to worship. Significantly, for those Protestants in the French army, there were obstacles in the path of promotion.

It is true that Richelieu appointed Coligny-Châtillon, Rohan and Bouillon, and other Huguenot nobles (including Charles de Blanchefort de Créqui and the Duc de La Force), to high command in the French army. Coligny-Châtillon and de Créqui each became a Marshal of France and the former was granted 50,000 *livres* by the Crown in 1636. None had a good record in command of French armies; Viscount Scudamore, English ambassador in Paris, wrote home in 1635 that Coligny-Châtillon and de La Force sought excuses to avoid taking the field. The same two (so a contemporary alleged), when facing an invading Spanish army in 1638, 'stood with arms folded a mile and a half from their enemies and did nothing with twenty-two thousand foot and seven thousand horse'.[57] Thus, it may seem, on the face of it, that elite Huguenot soldiers, at any rate, faced no penalties for their faith.

In fact, however, none of the Huguenots appointed to army command ever received Richelieu's full trust. Although the Duc de Rohan was employed as an army commander by Richelieu in 1635–6, the Cardinal continued to distrust Rohan. In March 1637, Rohan was held responsible for the collapse of the French army in the Valtelline, although David Parrott shows that, in fact, royal officials who starved it of money were more culpable. Parrott also notes that the criticism of Coligny-Châtillon and La Force in 1638 was unwarranted, because their army was much weaker than its establishment strength, so that their cautious strategy had been, 'in the circumstances … entirely justified'.[58] The elevation to army command of Bouillon simply reflected

Chamberlain, 1603–1624: Jacobean Letters, ed. M. Lee, Jr. (New Brunswick, NJ, 1972), p. 305, Carleton to Chamberlain, 11 July 1623.

56   Parrott, *Richelieu's Army*, p. 29.

57   Parrott, 'Richelieu, the *Grands*, and the French Army', pp. 145, 157, 163, 170; BL, Add. MS 35097, fols 5r, 7r, Scudamore reports, 18 September 1635 and early October 1635.

58   Parrott, 'Richelieu, the *Grands*, and the French Army', pp. 157, 163–4 (at 163), 170.

the fact that he was a sovereign prince and could not be ignored. His younger brother, Turenne, one of the most celebrated French generals of the seventeenth century, had to wait until Richelieu's death to receive a full command and be made *maréchal*. As for Coligny-Châtillon's 'gift' from the King in 1636, it was actually a reimbursement (and probably only a partial one) of his own expenditure on the army under his command in Flanders in 1635. Furthermore, his preferment to command of that army reflected the fact that Coligny-Châtillon had been a successful commander of the large (and mostly Huguenot) French contingent in Dutch employ. He also continued to be on good personal terms with the Prince of Orange, so that he was the obvious person for command of an army operating with Frederik Hendrik against the Spanish army of Flanders.[59] It also reflected Coligny-Châtillon's bitter, inherited feud with the Guise clan (dating back to the 1560s), while the appointments of La Force and Créqui also reflected the notorious antipathy between the Guise and the Huguenot nobility in general. Richelieu had his own inherited feud with the Guise and consistently made appointments to high military command in order to keep them marginalized. Richelieu's appointments of Huguenots to senior army rank are revelatory, then, not of charity to Huguenots, but of the Cardinal's acceptance of military reality and his strategy to exalt himself and diminish his rivals.[60]

Increasing religious repression in France led to a gradual but intensified trend amongst the Huguenot nobility of conversion to Roman Catholicism. For many Calvinist nobles, however, especially those who wished to follow the noble's traditional military career, the *Staatse leger* provided an admirable alternative, not least since the States' recruiting increased hand-in-hand with the intensification of the Thirty Years' War (1618–48).

In the spring of 1625 the Dutch took on a fourth French infantry regiment, when a unit commanded by Henri de Nogaret de La Valette, Comte de Candalle, which had been in Venetian service, was taken into the United Provinces' employ. A fifth regiment was added in 1634, under the command of Hercule, Baron de Charnacé. In the mid-1630s the French *corps* commanded by Coligny-Châtillon, serving in the main Dutch field army in Flanders, consisted of all five infantry regiments, plus four cavalry squadrons.[61] This was the high water mark of the Huguenot contribution to the Dutch army; throughout the 1640s, as the war wound down, and then after the conclusion of the Peace of Westphalia in 1648, the *Staatse leger*'s strength was consistently and considerably condensed. The Huguenot regiments were all kept in service, but the unit establishments were reduced.

The Baron de Courtomer had been replaced as Colonel of the second regiment in November 1629 by Isaac de Perponcher, Sieur de Maisonneuve; he was replaced in turn by Charles de Rechine-Voisin, Sieur des Loges, in April 1645. The Sieur d'Hauterive kept command of the third regiment throughout the Thirty Years' War,

---

59   Ibid., pp. 170–71, 145; BSG, MS 3338, fols 8r, 249r, Frederik Hendrik to Coligny-Châtillon, 18 March 1635, and Coligny-Châtillon to Frederik Hendrik, n.d.

60   Parrott, 'Richelieu, the *Grands*, and the French Army', pp. 155–8, esp. 157; Carroll, *Noble Power during the French Wars of Religion*, pp. 124–37.

61   BSG, MS 3338, fols 179v–82v, *Estat des Troupes de l'armée de Messieurs les Estats*.

but in April 1639, Candalle was succeeded as Colonel of the fourth regiment by Philippe-Henri de Fleury de Culan, Sieur de Buat (who was replaced in turn, two years later, by Louis d'Estrades). Charnacé ceded command of the fifth regiment in November 1637 to Louis du Plessis, Sieur de Douchant. Finally, Gaspard III de Coligny-Châtillon was Colonel of the first regiment until his final retirement from Dutch employ in 1638; the command passed initially to Maurice de Coligny, before the Colonel-General's son, Gaspard IV de Coligny-Châtillon became Colonel in 1644.[62] The Perponcher-Maisonneuve and Hauterive families retained command of two regiments into the 1670s.[63]

Huguenot soldiers also served the Dutch outside the *Staatse leger*. In the 1630s there were many French troops in the employ of the Dutch West Indies Company. This private trading company was charged with conducting Dutch operations against the Portuguese and Spanish possessions in the New World; a large garrison in Pernambuco was definitely Huguenot, not just French, as we know from the correspondence of its chaplain, part of which has survived. To serve these Huguenot troops in South America, French churches were built in Pernambuco and Recife.[64]

VI

The Dutch Republic was the biggest seventeenth-century employer of French Protestants up to 1688. Huguenot soldiers did not, however, serve only the States General. In 1610 the United Provinces and France had successfully waged the brief Jülich succession war to install a Protestant (and thus anti-Habsburg) claimant as Duke of Cleves-Jülich; the French corps, which included (though it was not composed only of) Calvinists, had been commanded by Henri, Duc de Rohan. (The Dutch corps also included some 3,000 Huguenots, in the regiments of Coligny-Châtillon and Béthune – the latter under its then Lieutenant-Colonel, de Courtomer). In 1612, Rohan led an ultimately unsuccessful Huguenot rebellion against the regents for Louis XIII and in the 1620s he opposed the Crown again: first in the war, fought mostly in the south, that ended with the Treaty of Montpellier in 1623; then in the celebrated war that revolved around the siege of La Rochelle (1627–8), the defence of which was led by Rohan's brother, Benjamin, Duc de Soubise.[65]

---

62   Ten Raa and de Bas (eds), *Het Staatsche Leger*, vol. 3, pp. 188–90, vol. 4, pp. 246–50.

63   J. Stapleton, 'Forging a Coalition Army: William III, the Grand Alliance, and the Confederate Army in the Spanish Netherlands, 1688–1697', PhD thesis (The Ohio State University, 2003), p. 260n. The Perponcher family ultimately settled in the Dutch Republic, becoming naturalised: ibid., p. 261n.

64   B. N. Teensma (ed.), *Dutch-Brazil* (Rio de Janeiro, 1999), vol. 3 'Vincent Joachim Soler's Seventeen Letters 1636–1643', *passim*, but esp. pp. 7, 84, 124–5.

65   BN, MS Fr. 654, fols 7r–45 (24v–25v), S. Stevin's treatise on Jülich campaign, *c.*1611; Ten Raa and de Bas (eds), *Het Staatsche Leger*, vol. 3, p. 14; Parrott, 'Richelieu, the *Grands*, and the French Army', p. 170.

In the early 1620s, Huguenots fought for the Elector Palatine in his unsuccessful struggle against the Holy Roman Emperor.[66] In the late 1620s and on into the 1630s, others served King Gustavus Adolphus of Sweden, the Republic of Venice, and the Protestant prince and military entrepreneur, Bernhard, Duke of Saxe-Weimar. Among those who served Gustavus Adolphus were the Sieur d'Aurignac, later the author of an influential military book, entitled the *Livre de guerre*. Venice recruited one Huguenot regiment in the mid-1620s, and Rohan and his entourage served the Serene Republic in 1630 – the Duc de Rohan contracted to raise a 6,000-strong corps in France for the Serene Republic's service; in the end, he was unable to meet his obligations, but he and his entourage were in Venetian service through the campaign seasons of 1630 and 1631. Rohan ended his long and varied military career as a gentleman volunteer with Saxe-Weimar, being mortally wounded at the battle of Rheinfelden (28 February 1638).[67]

The Elector Palatine's younger son, Prince Rupert of the Rhine, had taken several Huguenot officers with him to England in the 1640s. By the 1660s and 1670s, individual Huguenot officers had also begun to find employment, if only short-term, in the armies of German and Scandinavian Protestant princes. Others are known to have served, briefly, in Hungary, combating a renewed Turkish threat. This trend reflected the increasing difficulties of both French Calvinists in general, and the Huguenot nobility (with its traditions of military service) in particular, in the face of an ever more repressive religious regime, though not all those who took up service abroad had faced sanction in the French army because of their confessional stance, or at least not directly.[68]

In the 1650s through to the early 1670s, foreign employment of Huguenots seems to have been mostly of individual officers and specialists with the exception of those in Dutch pay. In 1672, Louis XIV invaded and nearly overwhelmed the United Provinces. For a French Protestant, for whom life as a Calvinist in France was ever more difficult, it was a bitter blow to see a traditional ally in trouble. It is notable that numerous Huguenots deserted the French army during the invasion.[69] In its aftermath the Dutch were shaken out of their complacency and realised that citizen militias could not protect them from a large modern army. There was once again a large-

---

66   Probably seconded from the French regiments of the *Staatse leger*: see O. Chaline, 'La bataille de la Montagne Blanche 8 novembre 1620', in L. Bély and I. Richefort (eds), *L'Europe des traités de Westphalie: Esprit de la diplomatie et diplomatie de l'esprit* (Paris, 2000), p. 318.

67   Parrott, *Richelieu's Army*, p. 29, citing Aurignac's *Livre de guerre* (1663); P. Azan (ed), *Un tacticien du XIIe siècle: Le maréchal de bataille d'Aurignac* (Paris, 1904); H. Layard, 'The Duc de Rohan's Relations with the Republic of Venice, 1630–1637', *Proceedings of the Huguenot Society of Great Britain and Ireland*, 4 (1891–3): 218–24, 290; Parrott, 'Richelieu, the *Grands*, and the French Army', p. 170.

68   For example B. Strayer, 'Un "Faux frère": le Sieur de Tillières et les réfugiés huguenots aux Provinces Unies, 1685–1688', *Bulletin de Société de l'Histoire du Protestantisme français*, 150 (2004): 507–16 (at 509), which is to be preferred to the brief account of 'Tellières' [*sic*] in W. A. Speck, 'The Orangist Conspiracy against James II', *Historical Journal*, 30 (1987): 453–62 (at 457–9).

69   Stapleton, 'Forging a Coalition Army', pp. 111, 259–61.

scale employer waiting to recruit Huguenots. Five Huguenot infantry regiments fought against their King during the Franco-Dutch War (1672–8). Although after the conflict these dedicated French regiments were disbanded, many French officers and men remained in the States' service in nominally Dutch regiments. A good example is Jacques-Louis, Comte de Noyelles, who began his military career as an ensign in William of Orange's élite Blue Guards regiment. In 1674 he was promoted Captain in the same regiment and, in 1681, became its Colonel. He eventually rose to the rank of General, becoming a naturalised Dutch citizen.[70]

VII

This survey, hopefully, conveys a sense of the variety of Huguenot military experience before the diaspora of the 1680s and the mass employment of Huguenot soldiers during the Nine Years' War. One element is the role of the nobility, not only as great Captains but also as officers and in the rank-and-file. This is worth emphasising since modern historiography tends to portray mercenaries as being drawn, mostly, from the scum of the earth, albeit sometimes captained by nobles.[71]

It has already been seen that, at the beginning of the Wars of Religion, the Huguenots recruited through aristocratic affinities. A high proportion of noble volunteers ('glittering Frenchmen' in the words of one English observer) was characteristic of Huguenot units at least until the mid-seventeenth century, reflecting wider French practice; as Parrott observes, the French armies that fought the Thirty Years' War were recruited through

> … the clienteles and influence of the nobility, especially the provincial aristocracy. They had access to a system of subcontracting through relatives and lesser noble supporters, who could themselves carry out the local recruitment of units of soldiers.[72]

This recruitment *via* affinities was one of the factors that made the Huguenots attractive to the Dutch.[73] Into the 1680s, kinship and friendship networks provided the basis for much of the recruiting for William III's Huguenot units.[74]

Moreover, Huguenot nobles not only recruited through their *solidarité* connections: they also themselves served in the ranks. Thus, like English and at least some Scottish, Irish and Italian mercenaries, French Protestant soldiers were often nobles or their immediate dependants.[75] This meant that a high proportion of

---

70 Ibid.

71 See discussion in Trim, 'Fighting "Jacob's Wars"', pp. 64–7, 69–71.

72 *Jacobean Letters*, ed. Lee, p. 305, Carleton to Chamberlain, 11 July 1623; Parrott, 'Richelieu, the *Grands*, and the French Army', p. 143; cf. Parrott, *Richelieu's Army*, chs 3, 5.

73 SG resolution, 15 August 1596, quoted in Ten Raa and de Bas (eds), *Het Staatsche Leger*, vol. 2, p. 41.

74 See C. Lougee Chappell, '"The Pains I Took to Save My/His Family": Escape Accounts by a Huguenot Mother and Daughter after the Revocation of the Edict of Nantes', *French Historical Studies*, 22 (1999): 6–7.

75 See Trim, 'Fighting "Jacob's Wars"', pp. 70, 260–86; Dubost, *La France italienne*, pp. 61–4, 242–4; and G. P. Hanlon, 'The Decline of a Provincial Military Aristocracy', *Past*

Huguenot units were members of the second estate, or noblemen, while even those who were not had close ties to the men who made up the élite of the units in which they served.

This remained true right down to the 1690s. As Matthew Glozier observes: 'The story of the Huguenot soldiers who fought under William of Orange in 1688 is essentially that of the Huguenot nobility in exile' (see Harman Murtagh's chapter for amplification of this point).[76] This aristocratic influence partly explains the considerable numbers of Calvinist Frenchmen willing to engage in military service, since war was both the prerogative and the *raison d'être* of the nobleman – particularly of those sub-sets of the nobility, like the country gentry, among which Calvinism was strong. Then, too, there were always great nobles willing either to serve abroad or to go into exile and then serve foreign princes, around whom lesser nobles with their followers could and did cluster. Moreover, the natural ties of affinity and hierarchy helped to provide a basis for organisation, not only of specially recruited units (as with the Huguenots serving the Dutch Republic from the 1570s onwards), but also among the mass of exiles that fled France in various waves, most notably after the revocation in 1685. The relative speed with which an inchoate agglomerate of refugees were mobilised and organised into very capable fighting units in the late 1680s is very striking – that social structure provided a basis for military structures is an important point to bear in mind.

So too, however, is the fact that, as in 1562, many Huguenots were 'deserters' from royal forces. No doubt many of the volunteers who fought for the Dutch Republic, Brandenburg, Britain and other states in the 1690s were no more than angry *émigrés* with a desire for vengeance and an apocalyptic world view.[77] However, many exiles were veterans, who could be readily integrated into new military organisations. In the 1680s and 1690s the proportion of refugees with military experience was probably lower than in the late sixteenth or early seventeenth centuries, simply because the Protestant community had been demilitarised since the 1620s. Nevertheless, the veterans supplied a vital hard core around whom the remainder (who were often kin or clients in any case) could be moulded more readily than if they did not exist. This was true, as we saw, in the 1560s and was equally true in the 1680s. It was surely true in the 120 years intervening. It is interesting to note that the formation of the Jacobite Irish exiles into an effective corps in French pay in the same period owed something to similar dynamics.[78]

In addition, Huguenots were quickly integrated into the army of the Netherlands, in particular, because of the long tradition of service in Dutch pay, with three and four generations sometimes fighting for the United Provinces. As for integration into

---

and Present, 155 (May 1997): 74–8.

76   Glozier, *Huguenot Soldiers*, p. 2.

77   Pierre Jurieu, the great Huguenot theologian of the late seventeenth century, identified the Revocation as the death of the two witnesses of Revelations 11:7–10, and thus an imminent sign of Christ's second coming and the judgement; it also, of course, implied that France (and French Protestants) would be at the centre of the final events.

78   See G. Rowlands, 'An Army in Exile: Louis XIV and the Irish Forces of James II in France, 1691–1698', *Royal Stuart Paper*, 60 (2001).

other armies, tradition is, again, important here. After all, Huguenots had fought alongside English, Scottish, German and Swiss soldiers from the 1560s–1570s all the way down to the 1680s. There was no reason to feel suspicion of or alienation from soldiers of different nationalities. Ethnic diversity was something the Huguenots (and indeed their colleagues of varying national backgrounds) would have taken for granted.

Finally, why did so many Huguenots become soldiers? No doubt for many exiles soldiering was just a job, useful and necessary in staving off starvation. But then, for well over a century, French Protestants had voluntarily exiled themselves precisely to fight. Probably profit was a consideration for many, both financial and honorific. However, it is clear when considering the history of Huguenot soldiering that Huguenot soldiers had a strong preference for serving other Calvinists – or at least for serving against what they would have regarded as anti-Christian enemies.

Huguenots fought for Catholic powers in the 1570s and 1590s, the 1620s and 1670s, but they did so briefly and in small numbers and, in any case, against the Turks – as bad an enemy of reformed Christendom as the Papacy, even to many zealous Protestants. Parrott shows that confessional allegiance helped to determine where French nobles undertook military service in the early seventeenth century.[79] Those Huguenots who served Charles I did so under the leadership of a Calvinist prince, Rupert of the Rhine. Although the Netherlands was by early-modern standards highly pluralistic, rather than a Calvinist society, the Dutch Republic came close to being a Calvinist state and William III of Orange relied greatly on the support of the Reformed church. Similarly, although Calvinism lacked widespread popularity in Brandenburg and Prussia, it was the faith of the Elector and his court.[80] And in Stuart England, although a Calvinist national church was missing, there was widespread commitment to helping Huguenot refugees and a connection with William III. If Calvinist military service was not always confessionally motivated, it was consistently confessionally directed.

There is certainly no question that most Huguenot soldiers were *only* seeking even honourable and profitable employment. Calvinist confessional fervour had been an important part of Huguenot soldiering since the early days of the *guerres de religion* and had always been a substantial element in their battlefield potency. Calvinist psalm-singing is famous, but for the Huguenots it was not just a form of devotional – it was a means of sustaining themselves in the heat of battle. Psalm 68 became known to them as the 'battle hymn' (*psaume des batailles*) because it was a favourite before going into action.[81] But whichever psalm was sung, the religious zeal stood the Huguenots in good stead. Most famously, at the battle of Coutras (1587), just before Henri IV's cavalry charged, the men, as a participant later

---

79 Parrott, *Richelieu's Army*, p. 29.

80 J. Pollmann, 'From Freedom of Conscience to Confessional Segregation? Religious Choice and Toleration in the Dutch Republic', in R. Bonney and D. J. B. Trim (eds), *Persecution and Pluralism: Calvinists and Religious Minorities in Early Modern Europe 1550–1700* (Oxford, Bern, New York, 2006), ch. 4; B. Nischan, 'The Second Reformation in Brandenburg: Aims and Goals', *Sixteenth Century Journal*, 14 (1983): 186–7.

81 Thierry, 'L'homme de guerre', p. 146.

remembered, 'made communal prayer and some sang from Psalm 118'. They were heard in the opposing *compagnies d'ordonnance* and 'many Catholic nobles cried out loud enough to be heard, "They tremble the cowards, they confess themselves"'. But as a Catholic veteran quickly cautioned his fellows: 'When the Huguenots make these sounds, they are ready to charge hard'. And the hard charging of the aristocratic Huguenot heavy cavalry, caught up in religious fervour, swept the much larger Catholic army to destruction.[82]

Thus, a combination of social structure, service history and confessional zeal allowed French Calvinists to be mobilised quickly into very effective members of both Huguenot and foreign armies. When this happened in the Netherlands, England, Ireland, Geneva, Brandenburg and elsewhere in the late 1680s and 1690s, Huguenots were simply following a well-worn pattern. It must also be noted, however, that French Calvinists served in foreign armies, as they thought, to frustrate the tyranny of Antichrist and his adherents. This is alien to a modern, pluralistic society, but it was the very essence of Huguenot soldiering in the sixteenth and seventeenth centuries, and a large part of why Huguenot soldiers were so potent on the battlefield – and so attractive to prospective employers across Europe.

---

82   Aubigné, *L'Histoire universelle*, vol. 3, p. 53; see also Mattingly, *The Defeat of the Spanish Armada*, pp. 139–45.

Chapter 2

Huguenots and Huguenot Regiments in the British Army, 1660–1702
'Cometh the moment, cometh the men'

John Childs

University of Leeds, UK

At the climacteric of the reign of Louis XIV, in 1688–9, when a series of political misjudgements resulted in a Europe-wide war, a brigade was recruited for the British army from amongst French, Protestant refugees.[1] Despite useful service in Ireland between 1689 and 1691, their distinctiveness had been lost by 1699 as the specific political and religious justification for their separate existence dissipated. Thereafter, individual Huguenot soldiers continued to serve in the British army, but the history of the Huguenot regiments was brief. Why, when European armies were mostly polyglot in composition, has their contribution to British military history been generally regarded as distinctive and memorable? The obvious and glib answer is that some of the Huguenot military refugees founded martial dynasties, many of which have endured to the present day. More importantly they were a phenomenon that, within a British and Dutch context, first personified and then institutionalized contemporary political and religious issues.

Since the early years of the 1660 Restoration, a smattering of Huguenots had come to England to take commissions under Charles II. Louis de Durfort-Duras, Marquis de Blanquefort and Earl of Feversham (1640–1709), the nephew of Marshal Turenne, was the most notable. He remained a favourite of James II despite his modest abilities. It was not until the beginning of the acceleration of the campaign of persecution against the Huguenots in the wake of the Peace of Nijmegen in 1678 that significant numbers of Protestant officers in the French army began to look overseas to continue their careers. Until then, Louis XIV had required every officer and soldier, whatever their religion, to man his forces during the War of Devolution against Spain (1667–8) and the Franco-Dutch War (1672–8). Louis retained his large army after the Peace of Nijmegen, both to labour upon the palace, gardens and water works at Versailles and to support the aggressive, militarised diplomacy through which he bullied the Germans, Italians and Habsburgs between 1678 and 1684. Only

---

1 After the Restoration there were separate English, Scottish (until 1707) and Irish (until 1800) military establishments, reflecting the national revenue from which a military unit was maintained. In operational and administrative matters all three combined into a single formation. To some extent after 1600, and most certainly from 1688, the description 'British' army is, therefore, both convenient and accurate.

with the revocation of the Edict of Nantes in 1685 was there a pressing need for Huguenot officers, who refused to convert, to leave France. The more valuable were subjected to considerable pressure to change faith rather than emigrate.

I

In Britain the army of the Roman Catholic King, James II, was scarcely a congenial haven for Huguenot, martial refugees despite the fact that he had gained a favourable impression of their collective military capacity when serving with the French army between 1652 and 1656. This admiration was increased when, during a short period of service with the Spanish army in the Netherlands, he fought against his old comrades, including Turenne. At the Battle of the Dunes in 1658 James was impressed by the conduct of the French army, the Huguenots in particular, as well as the corps from Cromwell's Puritan New Model army.[2] This high opinion of Huguenot soldiers in general, plus his enormous respect for and sense of gratitude towards Turenne, was probably one of the factors accounting for James's continued preferment of Feversham, whom he had first encountered in 1650. Like his brother Charles, King James had acquired a taste for all things French during exile and, after the Restoration, he offered considerable patronage to French army and navy officers and employed a number of French servants. James also chose his professional friends because of their loyalty to him rather than from any religious considerations. In return, he rewarded their fidelity even in the face of proven incompetence.[3] This blinkered advancement by the heir to the throne allowed Feversham to act as the centre of patronage to the trickle of Huguenot military refugees which came into England during the reign of Charles II. When Solomon de Foubert emigrated to England in 1679 'on account of his religion … at the insistence of many gentlemen and nobles' in order to re-create his Parisian military academy off Regent Street in London, he benefited from the support of Feversham and his clique at Somerset House. Henry Foubert, his son, was commissioned cornet of horse in 1685 and later served as *aide-de-camp* to Schomberg in Ireland, attending at the moment of his death at the Boyne. He was promoted to major of horse in 1692 and retired in 1700 to assume the directorship of his father's academy at a salary of £500 per annum.[4] Feversham's nephew, Armand de Bourbon, Marquis de Miremont, became a cavalry

---

2   *The Memoirs of James II, His Campaigns as Duke of York, 1652–1660*, ed. A. Lytton Sells (London, 1962), pp. 255–75. Blanquefort was shot through the thigh at the battle of the Dunes, 4 June 1658 (p. 257).

3   *The Diary of Samuel Pepys*, ed. R. Latham and W. Matthews (10 vols, London, 1970–83), vol. 7, p. 163; J. Callow, *The Making of King James II: The Formative Years of a Fallen King* (Stroud, 2000), pp. 149, 173.

4   The National Archives, Kew (hereafter TNA), PRO SP 29/411, fol. 142, 'The Humble Proposals of Solomon de Fobert, Esq., concerning a Royal Academy for Military Exercises here in London'; *Calendar of Treasury Papers, 1557-1696, Preserved in the Public Record Office*, ed. J. Redlington (6 vols, 1557–1728, London, 1868–89), vol. 3, p. 101, Petition of Solomon Foubert, 13 February 1690; W. H. Manchée, 'The Fouberts and their Royal Academy', *Proceedings of the Huguenot Society of Great Britain and Ireland*, 16 (1938–41):

colonel in 1688. Miremont's brother, Louis, Comte de La Caze, served under Schomberg in Ireland and was killed at the Boyne. In 1686 or 1687, Feversham's Huguenot *ménage* in Somerset House was increased by the arrival of his sister-in-law, the Comtesse de Montgomery, widow of his brother Charles-Henri, plus his sister, Elisabeth, and her husband, Frédéric-Charles de La Rochefoucauld, Comte de Roye et de Roussy, and three of their children: Frédéric-Guillaume, Comte de Marton; Charlotte; and Henriette. Louis XIV had given permission for the de Roye family to leave France for Denmark where Frédéric-Charles was appointed Commander-in-Chief of the Danish army. Unfortunately, his wife, Elisabeth, made some less than flattering remarks about the Queen of Denmark's dress and the whole family had to remove to London and seek Feversham's protection. Frédéric-Charles de Roye is said to have been granted an English peerage as Baron Lifford although this was never gazetted. His son, Frédéric-Guillaume, Comte de Marton and later Earl of Lifford, fought in Ireland and at the Boyne.[5]

The diaspora of the Huguenots took them principally into the Dutch Republic, Brandenburg, Switzerland and England. Most of those who came to England, apart from the few attached to Feversham's circle, did not seek and would not have been awarded commissions in the army of James II. In the first place, James was sympathetic to Louis and his attitude towards the wave of Huguenot refugees spreading across Protestant Europe between 1685 and 1688 ambivalent.[6] Secondly, James did his best to promote Catholic officers in England and Scotland whilst attempting, through Tyrconnel, to refashion the army in Ireland as a wholly Catholic force. Huguenot refugees who fled from the French army and wished to continue to pursue a military career, and those who turned to the sword *faute de mieux*, went mainly into the Dutch Republic and Brandenburg. Some of those who chose the Dutch Republic were retained by William of Orange. Not wishing to offend Louis, the States General declined to pay for these officers and so William funded as many of them as he could from his own personal moneys. A number of Huguenots, 796 according to Baxter,[7] accompanied William of Orange to England in November 1688: some as volunteers; others as officers in the three remaining regiments of the Anglo-Dutch Brigade;[8] and some as officers and *reformadoes* in the Dutch army.[9] It was from amongst these that

---

77–97; C. Dalton, *English Army Lists and Commission Registers, 1660–1714* (6 vols, London, 1892–1904), vol. 2, pp. 15, 125, 206; vol. 3, p. 227.

    5   See ch. 3 of this volume: P. Rambaut, 'A Study of Misplaced Loyalty? Louis de Durfort-Duras, Earl of Feversham (1640–1709)', pp. 51–62; M. R. Glozier, *The Huguenot Soldiers of William of Orange and the Glorious Revolution of 1688: The Lions of Judah* (Brighton, Portland, 2002), p. 96.

    6   R. D. Gwynn, 'James II in the Light of his Treatment of the Huguenot Refugees in England, 1685–6', *English Historical Review*, 92 (1977): 820–33.

    7   S. B. Baxter, *William III and the Defense of European Liberty 1650–1702* (New York, 1966), p. 209.

    8   Glozier, *Huguenot Soldiers*, ch. 4, 'The Huguenots and the Anglo-Dutch Brigade'.

    9   A *reformado* was a supernumerary officer, attached to a regiment and, usually, drawing half-pay. It was normally the practice for *reformadoes* to take regular commissions as these became available through promotion, casualties and purchase, although the process was far from automatic. They took their name from the fact that, in most cases, they had previously

the four Huguenot regiments in the British army were raised. Typical of the breed was Henri de Caumont, Marquis de Rade, who first sought asylum in the Dutch Republic, entering the Anglo-Dutch Brigade as a captain early in 1688. He came to England with William in November, becoming Lieutenant-Colonel of John Cutts's infantry regiment in the following year. On 1 February 1694, Rade was made a full infantry colonel. He died of wounds received in a duel with Colonel Bevil Grenville in the summer of 1695.[10]

The four 'new' Huguenot regiments were the first, formed, foreign units to be included within the seventeenth-century British army. Distinct national corps and regiments from Great Britain had served in European armies throughout the century – Spain, Austria, Sweden, Denmark, France and the Dutch Republic – but this had never been copied on the home establishments. Even during the decade of civil war, 1642–51, the armies had been composed mostly of native soldiers supplemented by remarkably few foreign officers and soldiers, except for those like Princes Rupert and Maurice who had direct family interests.[11] Mercenaries preferred the well-organised structure of warfare that had evolved in Europe as a result of a century of religious conflict. The advent of the Huguenot regiments in 1689 was a novel departure; rather than British subjects constituting corps within European armies, a foreign brigade was formally attached to the British army. In effect, it represented the introduction into the British army of a practice that had existed in the French, Danish and Dutch armies for well over a century. The latter depended on foreign contingents for its basic strength: substantially in excess of 50 per cent of the soldiers in the Dutch army came from Germany, Scandinavia and Britain, including the Anglo-Dutch Brigade, consisting of three English and three Scottish infantry regiments. However, the Huguenot regiments did not fit the later stereotype of the Hanoverian, Hessian or Württemberg mercenaries who did so much of Britain's fighting in Europe during the eighteenth century. Nor did they resemble the numerous mercenary formations, mostly from Germany and Scandinavia, which formed a substantial proportion of the British army during the Nine Years' War. These were all state mercenaries whose length and condition of service was determined by legal, written contracts drawn up between the British and Dutch governments and the rulers of the supplying powers.

The Huguenot regiments were composed of volunteers, not mercenaries, and enjoyed the status of full members of the British establishment and were permanent components of the British army. In addition to the basic point that they dropped like manna from heaven into the lap of William of Orange at a time when he was desperate for troops to meet his rapidly expanding commitments, they also possessed considerable propaganda value. Had the opportunity been more skilfully exploited,

---

been 'reformed' or disbanded from the possession of a regular commission: see TNA, PRO SP Ireland 63/340, fol. 179, Shrewsbury to Schomberg, 24 February/6 March 1690.

10 'Lord Cutts's Letters, 1685', ed. J. Childs, *Camden Miscellany XXX* (London, 1990), p. 411; Glozier, *Huguenot Soldiers*, pp. 35, 79, 81.

11 J. Childs, 'Military Élites in Seventeenth-Century England', in F. Bosbach, K. Robbins and K. Urbach (eds), *Geburt oder Leistung? Elitenbildung im deutsch-britischen Vergleich* (Munich, 2003), pp. 66–7. For foreign soldiers in Britain, 1642–51, see M. Stoyle, *Soldiers and Strangers: An Ethnic History of the English Civil War* (Yale, 2005).

the Huguenots could have been developed into the shock troops of Protestant Europe's indignant reaction to Louis's excess of conversionary zeal, but this potential was lost in the confusion and haste emanating from the Glorious Revolution and the outbreak of general European conflict. Whilst the waves of Huguenot refugees in the 1680s were an international advertisement of Louis's intolerance, had the Huguenot regiments been more carefully nurtured by William they might have spearheaded the revenge.[12]

That these possibilities remained unfulfilled was probably of little consequence because the Huguenot refugees had already served their purpose by accelerating the formation of the League of Augsburg and assisted in its evolution into the Grand Alliance against Louis, thus serving their essential purpose. Thereafter, the Huguenots were basically a military resource although hopes were fostered throughout both the Nine Years' War and the War of the Spanish Succession that the remaining Huguenots in France might destabilise the regime either by revolt or by assisting an invasion of southern France via Piedmont-Savoy. Following recruitment, training and temporary billets in and around London, the Huguenot regiments were dispatched to Ireland as part of the expeditionary force under Friedrich Hermann von Schomberg, a Calvinist and unofficial lay leader of the exiled Huguenots. Having landed at Carrickfergus on 13/23 August 1689, the corps advanced south to spend the rest of the year mouldering in the ill-chosen camp at Dundalk. The War of the Two Kings in Ireland – both a discrete conflict and a subsidiary theatre of the Europe-wide Nine Years' War – was fought to determine the succession to the British crowns and the political future of Ireland, but it was also a civil war between Protestant and Catholic Irishmen. Flanders, the Spanish Netherlands, the bishopric of Liège and the corridor of the Lower Rhine witnessed the principal campaigns between the main armies of France and the Grand Alliance.

Although quickly realizing the potential mischief that could be created by sending James II to Ireland to lead the nationalist insurrection, during 1689 Louis XIV only committed what would now be termed 'military advisers' to Ireland. Not until March 1690 did a small French expeditionary force of 6,000 men arrive at Kinsale and Cork. The subsequent Battle of the Boyne was not, therefore, a confrontation between the major land forces of the Grand Alliance and France. So the Huguenot regiments, the Protestant shock troops of the Grand Alliance, did not engage in the main contest but were committed to a war which, although closely related to international, political and religious issues, was essentially a domestic affair. However, in 1689, there is every reason to think that William, however reluctantly, had come to regard Ireland as the principal theatre in the war with France. If William's aim in November 1688 had been to bring England, with its potential human, financial and material resources, into the Grand Alliance and prevent James II from entering into an association with Louis, then securing that new regime in England was central to the strategy of the Grand Alliance. The major challenge, particularly after the arrival of James II in Dublin in March 1689, lay across the Irish Sea and so it

---

12 Similarly – deploying exiled nationals as the vanguard of retributive re-conquest – William cleverly involved the Protestant remainder of the Anglo-Dutch Brigade in leading his attack on England in November 1688: Glozier, *Huguenot Soldiers*, pp. 83–7.

was into this theatre that William was obliged to commit the majority of his more competent troops. Personally, William thought that Ireland was a sideshow and if the English navy could sever communications between Ireland and France, the Jacobite rebellion would wither and die. Unfortunately, the navy had suffered during the Glorious Revolution and was both weak in numbers of ships and deficient in reliable leadership. Parliament, which was representative of many of the Protestant planters and colonists, calculated that a victory for James II in Ireland, the vulnerable back-door to England since Elizabeth I's reign, would threaten the new regime of William and Mary as well as English economic interests. Parliament also felt certain that the war on the continent would favour Dutch long-term interests: English concerns would be more directly and effectively addressed by dealing first with Ireland. In other words, it was essential to crush the Irish rebellion before England could turn her full weight towards the campaigns on the European mainland. Even William recognised that he could not campaign on the continent whilst leaving an undefeated, Catholic and French-supported Ireland in his rear. Having fully realised the strategic logic, William simply wished to defeat Tyrconnel with minimum disruption to his campaigns in the Spanish Netherlands.[13]

Everywhere in 1689 William of Orange was short of soldiers, but particularly in Britain. Feversham had allowed James II's army to dissolve during the latter stages of the campaign of 1688 leaving William facing grave difficulties. Immediately he needed to raise 10,000 British troops for the armies of the Grand Alliance in the Netherlands, according to the terms of the Anglo-Dutch Mutual Defence Treaty of 1678. Raw recruits and some of the formed units rescued from the shambles of the partial disbandment of James II's army were committed to this corps under Marlborough's command. Mercifully, these constituted only a small portion of Prince Georg Friedrich von Waldeck's field army and they could be nursed into operational health by experienced Dutch and German troops. More pressing was the requirement to raise troops to subdue Jacobite rebellions in Scotland and Ireland, as well as occupy and secure England itself. In these theatres the military effort had to be principally British bolstered by as many Dutch formations as could be spared. Before Schomberg's arrival, Colonels Solomon Richards and John Cunningham had made a pusillanimous effort to give military support to Londonderry. They were followed by Major-General Percy Kirke. Although Kirke had only four battalions with which to tackle Lieutenant-General Richard Hamilton's Irish army besieging Londonderry, he dithered and acted in such a thoroughly indecisive manner that his loyalty to the new Williamite regime was subsequently questioned. These two 'expeditions' illustrated the military problems facing William in Ireland. The British army was weak, undermanned, unused to active operations and commanded by political and courtier officers whose loyalty to the new regime in England was often uncertain, if not two-faced. Schomberg's corps, which William hoped would be

---

13   J. Childs, *The British Army of William III, 1689–1702* (Manchester, 1987), pp. 211–12; *The Life and Letters of Sir George Savile, Bart., First Marquis of Halifax*, ed. H. C. Foxcroft (2 vols, London, 1898), vol. 2, pp. 79–80; D. W. Hayton, 'The Williamite Revolution in Ireland, 1688–91', in J. I. Israel (ed.), *The Anglo-Dutch Moment: Essays on the Glorious Revolution and its World Impact* (Cambridge, 1991), pp. 202–3.

sufficiently powerful to end the Irish war in a single campaign during 1689, thus required stiffening by some reasonably experienced troops commanded by officers who knew their trade and were demonstrably loyal to William of Orange. The new Huguenot regiments, plus two Dutch battalions, were all that was available.

II

During the emergency of the anticipated Dutch invasion in 1688, Armand de Bourbon, Marquis de Miremont, was commissioned on 21 September 1688 to raise a regiment of cavalry.[14] It was not, however, a specifically Huguenot formation and had few French officers, Miremont proving unable to persuade many of his fellow refugees in London to serve in a cause so unworthy as that of James II. Apart from Miremont, only Lieutenants Charles Saint-Clair and Antoine Penetière and the chaplain, John Dubourdieu, were French, the remaining officers being British. Following Feversham's disbandment of James's army at Uxbridge in December 1688, Miremont paraded his regiment and advised his men to declare for William of Orange. This they did, and the regiment was formally disbanded on 3 January 1689. Miremont and some of his men then took service in the Dutch army.

Later, when William realised he must fight James in Ireland, the Prince decided to raise four purely Huguenot regiments. The first of the four new French Protestant units to be recruited on to the Irish establishment (March 1689) was a regiment of cavalry designed to act as a life guard for the Duke of Schomberg. It was principally officered by *reformadoes* from the Dutch army.[15] Following Schomberg's death at the Boyne, Lord Galway assumed command and the regiment fought in Ireland until 1691, Flanders until 1694 and then in Savoy-Piedmont until 1696. It returned to England and was disbanded following the Peace of Ryswick in 1697. On 1 April 1689, three battalions of foot were embodied. Isaac de Monceau de La Melonière had risen to lieutenant-colonel of the *régiment d'Anjou* by 1685 when he left France for the Dutch Republic where he served as a volunteer. The second battalion was commanded by François du Cambon, who had been a French engineering officer until the revocation of the Edict of Nantes in 1685. He transferred to the Dutch army becoming Chief Engineer and Director-General of Fortifications in 1688 in the rank of Major-General. He was killed at the battle of Landen (Neerwinden) on 9 August 1693 and replaced by Frédéric-Guillaume de La Rochefoucauld, Comte de Marton (later Earl of Lifford), who had first entered the English army on 24 September 1688 as Guidon of the Third Troop of the Life Guards, commanded by his uncle, Feversham.

The third battalion was directed by Charles Massue de La Caillemotte until he was killed leading his troops at the battle of the Boyne. He was succeeded by Pierre de Belcastel-Montvoillant, Marquis d'Avèz and Baron de Beaufort, from Languedoc, formerly a volunteer in the Dutch army and a captain in Schomberg's

---

14   P. J. Shears, 'Armand de Bourbon, Marquis de Miremont', *Proceedings of the Huguenot Society of Great Britain and Ireland*, 20 (1958–64): 405–18; Dalton, *Army Lists*, vol. 2, pp. 164–5.

15   Glozier, *Huguenot Soldiers*, pp. 152–4; Childs, *British Army of William III*, p. 132.

Huguenot cavalry regiment. A Huguenot dragoon regiment was raised by Miremont in 1695 on the Irish establishment, but this was disbanded in 1698. Two additional Huguenot regiments were recruited by Galway after he had assumed duties as envoy extraordinary to the court of Savoy-Piedmont in 1694, but they were mostly manned from amongst Huguenot refugees who had congregated around Geneva in Switzerland and were paid from the treasury of Vittorio Amedeo II of Savoy.[16]

Charles Lart estimated that about 3,000 Huguenot officers had to leave the French army. Some 500–600 entered the service of Brandenburg, others gravitated towards Switzerland, but the majority sought positions in the Dutch army.[17] Very many of the field officers and senior subalterns in the four new Huguenot regiments on the English establishment in 1689 had served in the Dutch army, either as volunteers, *reformadoes* or commissioned officers, and their abilities were thus well enough known to William. Not only did many of them enjoy considerable military experience from their previous service in the French army, but they were Protestant and firmly attached to the religion and anti-Louis XIV policies of William and the Dutch Republic. In Britain during the Glorious Revolution and its aftermath, when so many British officials were of uncertain allegiance and could not be trusted, the officers of the Huguenot regiments formed a kernel of political and religious reliability blessed with a certain measure of martial competence. The number of potential and available Huguenot officers was considerable. William had 54 supernumerary officers, or *reformadoes*, attached to his Dutch Blue Dragoons in 1688 and another 34 in his Life Guards. Schomberg's Huguenot regiment of cavalry and the three infantry battalions possessed a total officer establishment of 166, but a host of 'incorporated officers' was attached to every unit.

On 1 July 1689, Schomberg's cavalry regiment was ordered to accept 144 *reformadoes* and each of the infantry battalions 78.[18] An inspection of the regiments in the Dundalk camp on 18/28 October 1689, found considerable numbers of *reformado* officers attached to the three Huguenot infantry battalions: La Melonière's had 117; du Cambon's 122; and La Caillemotte's 101. Of these, 206 were fit and on duty; 144 were sick; and 16 had died. All in all, 418 *reformadoes* were attached to just four regiments, well over double the formal establishment of commissioned officers.[19] Competition for promotion and regular commissions must have been ferocious. Although the Huguenot regiments moved *en masse* from Ireland to Flanders during the summer of 1692, they continued to be inundated with *reformadoes*. According to lists drawn up in 1694, extant in the papers of William Blathwayt, the Secretary-at-War, and Richard Jones, Earl of Ranelagh, the Paymaster-General of the army, Schomberg's regiment of horse, now under Galway, employed an additional major

---

16   Glozier, *Huguenot Soldiers*, pp. 149–58; HMC, *Bath*, vol. 3, p. 7; *The Lexington Papers*, ed. H. M. Sutton (London, 1851), p. 28; G. Symcox, *Victor Amadeus II: Absolutism in the Savoyard State, 1675–1730* (London, 1983), p. 145; C. Storrs, *War, Diplomacy and the Rise of Savoy, 1690–1720* (Cambridge, 1999), pp. 43–4; Dorset County Record Office, Ilchester MS D60/X42, Sir John Trenchard to Galway, 27 February 1694.

17   C. E. Lart, 'The Huguenot Regiments', *Proceedings of the Huguenot Society of Great Britain and Ireland*, 9 (1911): 500.

18   British Library (hereafter BL), Harleian MS 7,439, fols 15–16, 1 July 1689.

19   Dalton, *Army Lists*, vol. 3, pp. 118–20.

whilst each of its nine troops possessed two *reformado* captains, three lieutenants and as many cornets.[20] The regiment thus had 39 commissioned officers but 72 *reformadoes*, drawing half-pay. The three infantry regiments were more modestly endowed. Their establishments allowed for 42 commissioned officers: La Melonière's had 48 *reformadoes*; de Marton's 42; and de Belcastel's 39. However, this still doubled the officer complement of each.

In 1694, a time when the British army was achieving its maximum expansion during the Nine Years' War and qualified officer candidates were at a premium, there were enough spare Huguenot officers to equip five new regiments but do not appear to have been employed. Many, no doubt, were simply too poor to purchase commissions, even at the heavily discounted rates charged in hostilities-only units. All foreigners were actively disliked by the English and the Huguenots, when all was said and done, were French, the most hated category of all. Also, there had been loud complaints in 1692 about William's preference for Dutch, German and Danish general officers and his deep reluctance to promote British subjects.[21] It may be that Huguenot emigration into England continued at quite a high level during the war and those with military qualifications were temporarily lodged within the four regiments before receiving commissions in other corps. Perhaps these *reformadoes* formed a perpetually refilling reservoir of officers, automatically re-stocked by new emigrants? In the absence of muster rolls, it is impossible to know. It remains an unexplained anomaly, but the answer probably lies in an intense hatred of foreign officers, particularly those directly patronised by the increasingly unpopular King William III. The officers of the Huguenot regiments had enjoyed virtually no contact with Britain and had only lodged in England for a few weeks between their arrival from the Netherlands and departure across the Irish Sea. Thereafter, they travelled directly from Ireland to the Netherlands where they were disbanded in 1697 before returning to Ireland. They could not in any sense be regarded as even remotely British and they owed allegiance to William as Prince of Orange rather than King of England. This direct patronage and association with an increasingly loathed monarch cannot have enhanced their own popularity within the army.

Disputes and antagonisms between British and French soldiers commenced as soon as they reached Ireland. As a result of their performance in the Dundalk camp, where they had preserved better health, suffered fewer deaths from disease and demonstrated superior skill in field craft, they were regarded by the British troops as arrogant and insolent. By 1 October 1689, a market had been established in the Dundalk camp to which local people brought produce. Some Huguenot troops left the camp and either bought or seized provisions that were on their way to the market and then sold them to the British soldiers at exorbitant prices. They were rewarded with extra guard duty. Stuck-up, superior and always one step ahead, the Huguenots were loathed by the British. On 2 July 1690, when the army encamped a mile or so south of Duleek following the battle of the Boyne, Colonel du Cambon almost caused an open fight between his French Protestant regiment and Lord Drogheda's English batallion. It was the practice in camp to leave the pasture immediately to the rear of a

---

20   BL, Add. MS 38,699, fols 58–61, 156–61, 177–8; Ilchester MS D. 124, box 278.
21   Childs, *British Army of William III*, pp. 73–7.

regiment's tents as grazing for that formation's horses, usually the officers' mounts in addition to pack and cart horses. Not content with the grass behind his own position, du Cambon tried to requisition Drogheda's grazing as well. The matter 'came so high' that both regiments were loading their muskets ready for a set-to when Drogheda ordered his men to their tents and Lieutenant-General James Douglas stepped in and ordered du Cambon to desist 'from his pretensions'. Drogheda had the good sense to not escalate this incident by telling tales to William.[22] Further evidence for this hatred is shown by the fact that the Huguenots always stood at the rear of the pay queue and their arrears were consistently larger than those for other line regiments.[23] Agnew asserts that one of the reasons for disbanding the Huguenot regiments into Ireland was because of their unpopularity in England, although the fact that they were paid from the Irish establishment may also have been material.[24] Neither, when the army faced disbandment following the Peace of Ryswick, was there any sense of gratitude for political and military services rendered in securing the new order of the English succession. The Disbanding Act of 1699 insisted upon the discharge of all foreigners (those who had not taken citizenship or been denizened) from the English, Irish and Scottish establishments.[25] Between 9 April and 6 July 1699, 211 disbanded Huguenot officers were granted permission to sail from Ireland for the Dutch Republic, most of them in a 'destitute' condition.[26]

William, who maintained a high opinion of the martial capabilities of the Huguenot soldiers throughout the Nine Years' War, wanted to retain the disbanded French officers and soldiers *en bloc* so that they could be rapidly remobilised on the resumption of war with Louis XIV. In addition to trying to save for the future the officers and Protestant soldiers from the four British Huguenot regiments, William also wanted to keep together the two Huguenot regiments that had been serving in Savoy-Piedmont under Galway's leadership. He proposed to extract the Huguenot officers and men who had been fighting with the four British regiments attached to the Imperial armies on the Upper Rhine front and transfer them into the vacancies within the regiments in Savoy-Piedmont. Then, on disbandment, all of these Huguenot troops were to be brought into Ireland to form a body ready for instant re-recruitment.[27] Considering that the Huguenot regiments in Savoy-Piedmont and, probably, the Huguenot officers and men within the British regiments on the Rhine front, had been recruited in Switzerland it is highly unlikely that these men would have contemplated travelling to Ireland. The re-raising of two Huguenot regiments in the Piedmontese army at the beginning of the War of the Spanish Succession also

22   G. W. Story, *A True and Impartial History of the Most Material Occurrences in the Kingdom of Ireland During the Last Two Years* (London, 1691), pp. 25, 90–91.

23   Ilchester MS D. 124, box 276, accounts of Charles Fox and Thomas, Lord Coningsby, Paymasters-General of the Forces in Ireland, January–October 1698.

24   D. C. A. Agnew, *Henri de Ruvigny, Earl of Galway* (Edinburgh, 1864), pp. 81–2.

25   10 William III, c. 1.

26   W. H. Manchée, 'Huguenot Soldiers and their Conditions of Service in the English Army', *Proceedings of the Huguenot Society of Great Britain and Ireland*, 16 (1938–41): 263–5; CSPDom., 1698, p. 384, Robert Yard to Sir Joseph Williamson, 2 September 1698.

27   *Letters of William III and Louis XIV and of their Ministers, 1697–1700*, ed. P. Grimblot (2 vols, London, 1848), vol. 1, p. 129, William III to Galway, 8/18 October 1697.

suggests that William's grandiose plan for Huguenot military migration remained just that. However, a less ambitious form of the experiment went ahead with the foundation of a military colony. Some 590 Huguenot officers, non-commissioned officers and rankers were given pensions on the Irish establishment in order to receive which they had to remain in Ireland.

Lord Galway had been granted the lands of the Jacobite Sir Patrick Trant, in 1696 as part of the Irish forfeitures and he allocated some of these estates around Portarlington in the Queen's County (County Laois) to settle the Huguenots; co-religionist tradesmen and craftsmen in England were encouraged to move to Ireland to provide for the new community. As early as May 1701, the pensions were substantially in arrears and had, effectively, been stopped. The problem was largely solved by the re-recruitment of most of the Huguenot colonists into the British army from June 1702 to fight in the War of the Spanish Succession. Even before England was involved, in the previous April William III had given de Belcastel permission to raise a regiment for the Dutch service from amongst the Huguenot refugees and veterans in England and Ireland. So, not only were the majority of the Huguenot veterans who wished to return to military service accommodated within the expanded army during 1701 and 1702, but the outbreak of Huguenot revolt in the Cévennes brought a further wave of emigration into England, amounting to perhaps as many as 120,000 people, which formed the basis for a reinvigorated Huguenot recruiting pool during the War of the Spanish Succession.[28]

III

Very little is known about the rank-and-file soldiers. In all probability, they were not very militant Protestants and the description 'Huguenot' referred mainly to the officers. On 28 September 1689, a conspiracy was uncovered amongst Schomberg's corps encamped at Dundalk. A captain in a Huguenot infantry battalion (all four of the Huguenot regiments were at Dundalk) was informed by one of his men that four soldiers and a drummer, all of whom were Roman Catholic, planned to desert to the Irish army garrison at Charlemont. They were immediately arrested and the captain who had discovered the information subsequently found amongst the possessions of an accused soldier letters addressed to the Comte d'Avaux, the eyes and ears of Louis XIV and Louvois in Ireland. During interrogation this man revealed that he also had letters from one du Plessis, another Roman Catholic, then serving as a private soldier in one of the Huguenot regiments. Du Plessis had previously been a cavalry captain in

28   *Dublin and Portarlington Veterans: King William's Huguenot Army*, ed. T. P. Le Fanu and W. H. Manchée, Huguenot Society Quarto Series 41 (London, 1946), p. 3 *passim*; W. A. Shaw, 'The Irish Pensioners of William III's Huguenot Regiments, 1702', *Proceedings of the Huguenot Society of Great Britain and Ireland*, 6 (1902): 295–326; Manchée, 'Huguenot Soldiers': 252–3; N. Luttrell, *A Brief Historical Relation of State Affairs, from September 1678 to April 1714* (6 vols, Oxford, 1857), vol. 5, p. 40; J. G. Simms, *The Williamite Confiscation in Ireland, 1690–1703* (London, 1956), pp. 88–9; CSPDom., 1700–1702, p. 326, Lords Justices of Ireland to James Vernon, 17 May 1701; Lart, 'Huguenot Regiments': 502–3.

the French army, but had been obliged to resign his commission having committed a murder. Du Plessis was seized and confessed under 'examination' that he had written to both King James and d'Avaux telling them that there were many Catholics in the Huguenot regiments, promising to bring them over to the Irish army on condition that he might be rewarded by Louis XIV with a commission and a pardon for his crime. Another account says that du Plessis had promised in his letters to d'Avaux to cause the desertion of over 400 Catholic soldiers from the Huguenot regiments and hinted that there were also numbers of native Irishmen amidst the ranks of the Huguenots. Indeed, d'Avaux said that du Plessis carried a list of these 400 in his pocket. King James's answer to du Plessis's letter was brought to the Huguenot lines in the Dundalk camp by a Frenchman who concealed a red and white cross under the folds of his sleeve and clutched a bottle of brandy. By prior arrangement, he promenaded up and down the streets of the Huguenot sector of the camp shouting, 'Brandy wine, brandy wine', until approached by a soldier who said to him, 'God bless you friend, how do you sell your brandy?', whilst simultaneously turning back the brandy seller's sleeve in search of the red and white cross. When this had been satisfactorily accomplished, the letter from James was handed over. This part of the operation proceeded without incident but the brandy seller was apprehended during his return to the Irish camp: he was allowed his freedom in return for informing on du Plessis. Together with his five accomplices, du Plessis was tried, sentenced to death and hanged.

This incident occurred at a critical time for Schomberg's army: sickness was breaking out amongst the soldiers and a week before the Jacobite army had made an aggressive demonstration before the Dundalk position. When Schomberg was informed he ordered a proclamation to be read at the head of every regiment to the effect that all Catholics were to declare themselves. Anyone who did not do so immediately and was later discovered to be Catholic would be instantly executed. Until further notice, no Huguenot was to be allowed to leave the Dundalk camp without a pass. Upon this, 150 surrendered themselves and were sent under escort for England via Carlingford. This new breed of Catholic-Huguenots was not wasted. They were dispatched to the Dutch Republic where they were transferred to the pay of the States General and used to garrison fortresses.[29] The colonels of the three Huguenot infantry regiments, then conducted an investigation into how many Roman Catholics they were harbouring but no more seem to have been found:

> Most of these had deserted the French service this summer and, passing to Holland and thence to England upon report that three French regiments were levying here, had listed themselves in the same, the officers raising their companies in so much haste that they had not time to examine them very strictly.[30]

Recruits were hard to come by at Dundalk and, in all probability, the three Huguenot infantry colonels did not over-exert themselves in the search for secreted Roman Catholics: they were too short of men to indulge in such luxuries. Considering that du Plessis had named 400 potential deserters from the Huguenot regiments and only

---

29   Luttrell, *Historical Relation*, vol. 2, p. 508.
30   *London Gazette*, 2,496, 9/19 October 1689.

150 were uncovered again suggests that the hunt was perfunctory. The Huguenot regiments remained 'unclean'.[31] On 30 June 1690, during the march south towards the Boyne, a chaplain, George Story, reported that there were still Catholics in the Huguenot regiments. Feeling very unwell after drinking contaminated water, a French soldier stumbled out of his column and collapsed on to the side of the road. Fearing for his life he started fingering his rosary beads and muttering Catholic incantations. One of the Protestant Danish soldiers noticed this and promptly shot him dead probably justifying his action, if anybody bothered to enquire, by reference to Schomberg's proclamation.[32]

When the Huguenot infantry battalions and Galway's Horse were redeployed into the Spanish Netherlands in 1693, they became natural magnets for French deserters, both Catholic and Protestant. In preparation for the voyage from Flanders to Ireland in November 1697, the Huguenot colonels dismissed their Catholic soldiers. Their ranks were accordingly 'decimated' by the evictions and as many as 700 Roman Catholics had to leave the regiments.[33] In this, of course, the Huguenot regiments were no different from many other *corps* in contemporary armies, most of which took whatever soldiers they could get from whatever source. Niceties of nationality, religion and motivation were not the concern of the recruiting party. The six 'French' regiments that landed at Kinsale around 12/22 March 1690 to reinforce the Jacobite Irish army consisted of a mixture of Frenchmen, Walloons, Germans and Swiss, some of whom were prisoners-of-war who had been captured by the French in the Spanish Netherlands during 1689. One report says that as soon as these regiments arrived in Dublin, 500 of the so-called 'French' attended Protestant churches. When this French corps marched north from Dublin on 16 June 1690 to join James's assembling field army, a Dublin diarist noted that their ranks were so depleted that they had been recruited with native Irish and, even then, their establishment strength of 6,000 had fallen to 5,000.

The rank-and-file soldiers of seventeenth-century armies and regiments were cosmopolitan and polyglot and the Huguenot regiments were no exception to this rule. Indeed, this was entirely congruent with the whole concept of an early-modern standing army. It was 'professional': in other words, composed of foreigners, riff-raff and mercenaries under the direction of state-appointed aristocrats and gentlemen who, it might reasonably be presumed, would conduct themselves with honour in the interests of their employer. No one expected common soldiers to act honourably. If a regiment bore a national identity in its title then this usually only referred to the majority of its officer complement.[34]

---

31   P. Playstowe, *The History of the Wars in Ireland, betwixt Their Majesties Army and the Forces of the late King James, by an Officer in the Royal Army* (London, 1691), pp. 49–50; *Great and Good News from His Grace the Duke of Schomberg's Camp at Dundalk* (London 1689), p. 1; Dalton, *Army Lists*, vol. 3, pp. 118–20; *Négociations de M. le comte d'Avaux en Irlande, 1689–90*, ed. J. Hogan (Dublin, 1934), p. 495.

32   Story, *A True and Impartial History*, p. 72.

33   BL, Add. MS 9,731, fols 31, 51.

34   J. C. O'Callaghan, *History of the Irish Brigades in the Service of France* (Glasgow, 1870; reprinted Shannon, 1969), p. 8; *The Danish Force in Ireland, 1690–1691*, ed. K. Danaher and J. G. Simms (Dublin, 1962), p. 61; *Great News from Ireland:*

Huguenot soldiers did not serve exclusively in the Huguenot regiments, but were found far and wide in the British army. On 6 June 1694, 52 volunteers for the troop of Major Charles de La Tour, Comte de Paulin, in the Earl of Macclesfield's cavalry regiment, appeared at the Hertford Quarter Sessions before Alexander Weld, JP, to register their voluntary enlistment. Of these volunteers, 11 were Huguenots, no doubt attracted by the fact that Major de Paulin and some other officers of the regiment were also French refugees. C. T. Atkinson lists seven Huguenot officers serving with the Royal Regiment of Dragoons during the Nine Years' War. Colonel Edward Fox's battalion of infantry was transferred to the West Indies in 1699 and disbanded there; 14 of the officers were Huguenot and, having struggled in the Protestant cause throughout the Nine Years' War, petitioned for naturalisation, which was granted. Charles Lart says that, in addition to the officers serving with the Huguenot regiments, a further 800 Huguenot officers fought with the British army during the Nine Years' War. A Jacobite source suggests that, during 1690 and 1691, 736 officers in William's British army were Huguenot.[35] If, at a very rough estimate, about 8,000 officers were required to command the British army during the Nine Years' War, then perhaps as many as 10–15 per cent were Huguenot.[36]

IV

The general disbandment that followed the Peace of Ryswick marked the end of the Huguenot regiments on the British establishment. The experiment was not to be repeated. During the ensuing War of the Spanish Succession numerous Huguenot officers and soldiers were recruited and re-recruited, but dispersed amongst the native regiments. In the Dutch army, however, specifically Huguenot units were formed between 1702 and 1714 but this was in the context of an already-international army. As we have seen above, de Belcastel recruited a battalion for that service from amongst Huguenots in England and Ireland during 1701 and two additional Huguenot infantry *corps* were created in the same year commanded by Henri de Bois-Belland de Monteciel, Chevalier de L'Isle-Marais, and François, Baron de Viçouse. In 1706, a regiment was formed out of French emigrants commanded by

---

Being a Full and True Relation of the Several Great and Successful Defeats, which the Danish and Inniskilling Forces hath lately obtained over a Party of the Irish Rebels at Cliff and Emismack (London, 1690), pp. 1–2; HMC, *Ormonde*, new series, vol. 8, pp. 384–5; A. Starkey, *War in the Age of Enlightenment, 1700–1789* (Westport, CT, 2003), pp. 21–2.

35 C. O'Kelly, *Macariae Excidium, or the Destruction of Cyprus*, ed. G. N. Plunkett and E. Hogan (Dublin, 1896), p. 113.

36 *Hertford County Records: Notes and Extracts from the Sessions Rolls, 1581–1698*, ed. W. J. Hardy (3 vols, Hertford, 1905), vol. 1, p. 417; C. T. Atkinson, *History of the Royal Dragoons, 1661–1914* (Glasgow, 1934), pp. 50, 69n.; HMC, *House of Lords*, new series, vol. 4, p. 367, 10 May 1701; Dalton, *Army Lists*, vol. 3, p. 354; Glozier, *Huguenot Soldiers*, p. 153. Childs, *British Army of William III*, pp. 132–8; Dalton, *Army Lists*, vol. 3, pp. 1–9; *The Parliamentary Diary of Narcissus Luttrell, 1691–1639*, ed. H. Horwitz (Oxford, 1972), pp. 46–9.

reformed officers who had fought in the Cévennes and Catalonia. England bore two-thirds of the cost of this regiment, the Dutch one-third. In 1711, the Dutch formed a two-battalion infantry regiment out of French deserters under the command of Major-General de Seissan.[37] The cost was to be borne equally between the Dutch and English treasuries, but it was disbanded in October 1711 because of the fiscal exhaustion of both countries towards the end of a long and debilitating war. The majority of the redundant soldiers went into the Polish service under Prince Karol I Stanislas Radziwill.[38]

Certainly senior officers and military officials of Huguenot descent have played important roles in British history up to the present day – Marlborough's secretary, Adam de Cardonnel, Field Marshal Lord Ligonier and General Sir Peter de la Billière, amongst them – and Huguenots comprised the largest foreign element in the officer corps of the British army during both the Nine Years' War and the War of the Spanish Succession, but this does not adequately explain the enduring prominence of the fleeting phenomenon of the Huguenot regiments. The most generous interpretation extends their life to ten years from 1689 to 1699 and they are principally remembered for their contribution to the Williamite campaigns in the War of the Two Kings in Ireland between 1689 and 1691. Historians, certainly not contemporaries, have fashioned a somewhat unhistorical prominence for these dragonfly units. As if to reinforce the anti-Catholic, Francophobe and international character of the Glorious Revolution, one of the seminal events in British history ranking alongside the Norman Conquest, the Henrician Reformation, the Civil Wars and the First Reform Act, they have been closely associated with helping to sustain the resultant polity. There have even been suggestions that they embodied the revenge of the Huguenots and allowed emerging exile communities in England to make a vicarious and immediate contribution to their adopted state. However, although they were of the British army, the Huguenot regiments more closely resembled the Dutch troops of William of Orange, their rise and fall reflecting the fluctuations in his popularity in England. The regiments were not, in any sense, English, but Huguenot-Dutch, and barely touched base in England before moving to Ireland and Flanders. Their recruitment was the result of expediency and William's desperate shortage of politically and religiously reliable officers within the British theatre of operations rather than the conscious creation of a specifically Huguenot force for the purposes of political demonstration and propaganda. Without the context of the Glorious Revolution the Huguenot regiments would probably have been relegated to the footnotes of military history. Indeed, even within the parameters of the Glorious Revolution their actual historical significance can be narrowed down to one single event. In Schomberg's camp on the Dundalk marshes the native British troops showed themselves inept, incompetent, untrained, ill-motivated and utterly unfit for service when compared with the Dutch battalions and the four Huguenot regiments. The latter became a

---

37   See Agreement relating to Seissan's command of two French deserter regiments, 1711: BL, Add. MS 61,377, fols 133–4; Establishment for his regiment, 1711: BL, Add. MS 61,318, fol. 16.

38   W. H. Manchée, 'Huguenot Regiments in Holland', *Proceedings of the Huguenot Society of Great Britain and Ireland*, 14 (1930–33): 96–8.

yardstick by which historians have measured the gradual improvement in the quality of the British army.

Chapter 3

A Study in Misplaced Loyalty
Louis de Durfort-Duras,
Earl of Feversham (1640–1709)[1]

Philip Rambaut[*]

Huguenot Society of Great Britain and Ireland

If James II had made a fight for his throne in 1688, two Huguenot generals might have met – opposed in combat on the battlefield. One was Friedrich Hermann von Schomberg, serving William of Orange, and the other Louis Feversham, James II's general. This chapter is concerned with the latter – Louis de Durfort-Duras, Marquis de Blanquefort, later to be the second Earl of Feversham. Born a French Protestant, he would spend most of his life in England, where he became a central figure in the 'French interest' that surrounded Charles II. He would also become Commander-in-Chief of the English army in the reign of the Catholic James II. He was thus a Huguenot who remained steadfastly loyal to a monarch popularly perceived to be a Catholic tyrant. Was his loyalty, therefore, misplaced? This chapter analyses Feversham's life and attempts to answer that question in the context of domestic and international upheavals in Europe in the 1680s. It analyses that career in the context of an international aristocratic soldiering courtly elite, both Catholic and Protestant, for which bonds of loyalty meant quite different things than they do today.

I

Louis de Durfort–Duras was born at Duras, in Gascony, in 1640 and came to England in 1662.[2] He was the sixth son of Guy-Aldonce, Marquis de Duras, and Elisabeth de La Tour d'Auvergne, sister of Henri Turenne, the great Marshal of France. Staunch Protestants at that time, the Durfort family had supported the cause of Henri de Navarre, during the religious wars of the sixteenth century and was favoured by Henri when he became King of France. Together with the illustrious de La Force

---

* The editors were saddened to learn that Philip Rambaut has passed away before he could see this book in its published form. His support for the project was very gratefully appreciated.

1 This is an updated and amended version of a paper first published in the *Proceedings of the Huguenot Society of Great Britain and Ireland*, 25 (1989–93): 244–56, and republished in P. Rambaut and R. Vigne, *Britain's Huguenot War Leaders* (London, 2003), pp. 1–12.

2 J. Clair-Louis, *Pourquoi Louis de Durfort-Duras quitta la France* (Paris, 1964).

family, the Durforts presided over the well-being of many Protestant households in Guienne.[3]

With the assumption of personal rule by Louis XIV in 1661, Louis de Durfort feared for his prospects as a member of a Huguenot military family and, according to Winston Churchill, 'flying from the wrath to come', came to the court of Charles II, entrusted to James, Duke of York, by his uncle, Marshal Turenne.[4] During the years of the Commonwealth, James had served with distinction in the French army under Turenne and had great admiration for him and Huguenot officers generally.[5] After his arrival in England in 1662, Louis received a commission as a lieutenant in the Duke of York's Life Guards. Oddly, his first taste of action in English service was at sea during the Second Dutch War (1665–7). He accompanied the Duke of York in the successful battle of Lowestoft in 1665 and fought bravely.[6] Following his distinguished service at sea, the Duke appointed Louis captain of his Life Guards and after naturalisation that year he became his Keeper of the Privy Purse. Back in England, during a particularly cold spell in London in January 1666, fire broke out in Pump Court, Middle Temple. All water supplies were frozen and barrels of beer were used. Houses were blown up and Feversham received severe head injuries when one collapsed near him.[7] He underwent a trepanning operation on his head, the surgeon using a cylindrical saw. This was successful and, recovering, he was later to be seen playing tennis with the King, Godolphin and John Churchill.

During the next few years, Louis was active in recruiting for the Duke's guards and also made a number of visits to France. On one of these, in 1672, he made arrangements for the transfer of an English cavalry regiment to serve Louis XIV, as part of Charles II's obligations according to the secret articles of the 1670 Treaty of Dover. Later that year he joined the Duke of York in an indecisive action against the Dutch at Solebay in the Third Dutch War (1672–4).[8] Not having achieved command of the sea, an intended Anglo-French seaborne assault upon Walcheren under the Count of Schomberg was abandoned. In January 1673, the Duke of York made available to Louis his estate at Holdenby, or Holmby, in Northamptonshire.[9] At the same time he was ennobled, receiving the title of Baron Duras of Holdenby in the peerage of England. Then Louis and John Churchill, who was ten years his junior, accompanied the Duke of Monmouth and an expeditionary force to assist Louis XIV against the

3   R. Blanc, *Histoire du Pays Duraquois* (*Histoire du château, de la ville, des seigneurs de Duras et de son pays*) (Duras, Eymet, 1979), pp. 67, 72.

4   W. S. Churchill, *Marlborough: His Life and Times* (4 vols, London, 1933–8), vol. 1, p. 96.

5   *The Memoirs of James II: His Campaigns as Duke of York, 1652–1660*, ed. A. Lytton Sells (London, 1962).

6   J. Haswell, *James II: Soldier and Sailor* (London, 1972), pp. 159–64.

7   N. Luttrell, *Relation of State Affairs* (6 vols, Oxford, 1857), vol. 1, pp. 7–8.

8   Ibid., pp. 185–91.

9   'Lord Duras, a valiant gentleman whom his Majesty made an English Baron ... and gave him his seat of Holmby in Northamptonshire': *The Diary of John Evelyn*, ed. W. Bray (London, 1952), p. 387, 24 August 1675; G. Baker, *History of the Antiquities of the County of Northampton* (2 vols, London, 1822–41), vol. 1, p. 197.

Dutch.[10] At the siege of Maastricht, Louis rejoined his brother, Guy-Aldonce de Lorge, who successfully breached the fortifications. He continued to campaign in France until the end of the year. After hostilities ceased, Louis praised the part that John Churchill had played in the actions and wrote that 'Monsieur Turenne is very pleased with our nation'.[11]

In March 1676 Louis married Mary Sondes, the eldest daughter by his second marriage and co-heiress of Sir George Sondes of Lees Court, Sheldwich, Kent, at the church of St James, Sheldwich. The Sondes family had suffered a great tragedy in 1655 when Sir George's younger son by his first marriage, apparently in a fit of jealous rage, killed his elder brother while he was asleep. Sir George took the younger son to Maidstone, where he was tried, sentenced to death and hanged, meeting his end with resignation. After the marriage Sir George was created Baron Throwley, Viscount Sondes of Lees Court and Earl of Feversham, the titles being remaindered to Louis. Lady Mary Duras died after less than a year of marriage and was buried at Throwley. Her father, aged 77, died shortly afterwards. Louis then became the second Earl of Feversham. There followed family squabbles over marriage settlements and inheritances. Louis resorted to litigation, which caused much ill feeling. As a result, he does not appear to have spent any length of time at Lees Court.

Following the marriage of William of Orange and Mary Stuart in November 1677, Charles II changed his policy and supported the Dutch against Louis XIV. Feversham again took part in actions on the continent, serving as Lieutenant-General under the Duke of Monmouth. His part was praised by William of Orange.

For his services during the campaign on the continent, Feversham became Gold Stick in Waiting to the King and, in 1680, Lord Chamberlain to the Queen, Catherine of Braganza, a position he held until her death. In 1685 Charles II, on his deathbed, is said to have expressed a desire to be received into the Catholic Church. His conversion was witnessed by two Protestant Gentlemen of the Bedchamber, the Earls of Bath and Feversham.

II

Feversham was brought up a Calvinist in France and became an Anglican after arriving in England. He was a regular worshipper at the French Church of the Savoy in the Strand and the Protestant Chapel in Somerset House where he lived. To many, although naturalised for some time, he was considered very much a foreigner not to be trusted, especially in the matter of religion. He was described by Macky as a middle-statured, brown man, which was likely, being a Gascon.[12] Gimlette writes that he was 'a high minded nobleman, the house of Stuart proven him a faithful

---

10 For details of continental campaigns where Feversham accompanied Monmouth, see J. N. P. Watson, *Captain-General and Rebel Chief: The Life of James, Duke of Monmouth* (London, 1979).

11 Churchill, *Marlborough*, vol. 1, p. 111.

12 *Memoirs of the Secret Services of J. Macky ... including, also, the True Secret History of the ... English and Scots Nobility, ... and other Persons of Distinction, from the Revolution*, ed. A. R. with marginal notes by Dean Swift, transcribed by T. Birch (London, 1733).

adherent'.[13] He was popular at court, particularly with the ladies, and enjoyed the pleasures of the table. In France, two of his brothers abjured and later became dukes and marshals of France. In 1668 Feversham's sister, Elisabeth, Comtesse de Roye, arranged a meeting of Protestant aristocrats in Paris to discuss various religious doctrines submitted by the Protestant preacher, Claude, and the Catholic Bossuet.[14] Feversham's brother, Guy-Aldonce, and their uncle, Turenne, abjured to the Catholic faith (in 1668), the latter's conversion to Rome doubtless influencing the Duke of York, whose own conversion took place soon afterwards.[15] Feversham's mother, widowed in 1665, remained a firm Protestant until her death at Duras in 1685 and the local Catholic Bishop of Agen did not dare to visit the town while she was alive.

Towards the end of Charles II's reign, Huguenot refugees started to arrive in England, although the largest number was to come during the reign of the Catholic James II. Feversham helped one of them, Isaac de La Croix, a merchant of Calais, to settle in England and obtained for him an appointment as jeweller to Queen Catherine. Feversham and his nephew, Frédéric-Guillaume de La Rochefoucauld, Comte de Marton, were noted by John Evelyn in 1684 while exercising with the 'gallants' at the Huguenot Foubert's riding school in London.[16] In King James's reign, Feversham's nephew, Armand de Bourbon, Marquis de Miremont, Armand's younger brother, Louis, Comte de La Caze, and sister, Charlotte de Bourbon, came to London and were given accommodation at Somerset House.[17]

When James, Duke of York, succeeded his brother as King in 1685, one of his first actions was to make Feversham a privy councillor. Feversham's elder brother, Guy-Aldonce de Lorge, was sent to London by Louis XIV to congratulate James on his succession to the throne. On 11 June 1685, the Duke of Monmouth, in rebellion, arrived at Lyme in Dorset with fewer than a hundred men, but carrying guns and ammunition sufficient to arm 5,000.[18] On hearing the news of the landing, King James sent John Churchill to the west, where he made contact with the rebels. At Taunton, on 19 June, Monmouth proclaimed himself King. That day, Feversham was appointed Commander-in-Chief of the royal army, news which irked John Churchill, who is alleged to have said later: 'I see plainly that the trouble is mine and that the honour will be another's'.[19] The day after his appointment, Feversham proceeded rapidly to the west with an advance guard and was able to deny the important port

13   T. Gimlette, *The Huguenot Settlers in Ireland* (Waterford, 1888), pp. 254–5.

14   J. Favre, *Précis historiques sur la famille du Durfort de Duras* (Paris, 1858).

15   W. A. Speck, *Reluctant Revolutionaries: Englishmen and the Revolution of 1688* (Oxford, 1988), p. 123.

16   *The Diary of John Evelyn*, ed. Bray, p. 4622, 18 December 1684.

17   P. J. Shears, 'Armand de Bourbon, Marquis de Miremont', *Proceedings of the Huguenot Society of Great Britain and Ireland*, 20 (1962): 405–15.

18   D. Chandler, *Sedgemoor* (London, 1985).

19   E. Hyde, Earl of Clarendon, *The Correspondence of Henry Hyde, Earl of Clarendon, and His Brother Laurence Hyde, Earl of Rochester; With the Diary of Lord Clarendon from 1687 to 1690, Containing Minute Particulars of the Events Attending the Revolution and the Diary of Lord Rochester During his Embassy to Poland in 1676*, ed. S. W. Singer (2 vols, London, 1828), vol. 1, p. 141.

of Bristol to the rebels. He was followed by the bulk of the royal army and artillery and was joined by Churchill on 26 June. At Bath, Feversham sent out patrols to find out where the bulk of the rebel forces was and instructed his patrols 'not to return till they had been shot at'. Monmouth had camped around Philip's Norton. Advancing towards the town, Feversham's forces met heavy musket fire and suffered casualties. Feversham had to re-group and bring up artillery before the rebels could be beaten back. Heavy rain had prevented his musketeers from being effective and, as the weather was so bad, the action was not taken to a conclusion. Monmouth, realising he was now outnumbered and with promised help from Cheshire and Scotland not materialising, retired to Bridgwater.

Feversham followed the rebels and drew up his forces near Weston Zoyland, three miles from Bridgwater. Fearing that Monmouth might move north towards Bristol, Feversham posted a party of horse to watch that road. At 11 p.m. on 4 July he rode through the camp checking that all sentries and guards were in position. Having satisfied himself that every precaution had been made against a night attack, Feversham returned to Weston Zoyland at 12.45 a.m. At 1.15 a.m. he received a report that there was no activity on the road towards Bristol. Feversham then returned to a camp bed at Weston Court, leaving Churchill in charge during the night. It was about this time that Monmouth led his forces out of Bridgwater on the road to Bristol, but, after about two miles, the rebels turned right towards the royal army. Surprise was lost when an outpost gave the alarm. Churchill immediately took charge and orders were given to awaken Feversham, who at once rode to the camp and gave orders that the royal troops were not to stir without an order.[20] It was later written maliciously that he was aroused only with difficulty and then took much time making sure his wig and cravat were straight, even complaining that the looking-glass provided was too small.

The royal troops stood firm and, firing wildly in the dark, the rebel forces were soon short of ammunition and in disarray. At first light Feversham gave orders for the cavalry to charge. The rebels were overwhelmed and then cut down by the pikes and bayonets of the infantry. It was all over by 5 a.m. Monmouth fled the field and was later captured, brought to London and beheaded. Leaving Colonel Percy Kirke to round up the rebels, Feversham returned to London with three battalions of the guards. Stopping at Glastonbury, where six rebels were hanged, he sent Churchill ahead to convey the news of Monmouth's defeat to the King.

Many were unable to give full credit to Feversham for his success; he was still considered a foreigner who, according to Lord Macaulay, was 'ignorant of the laws and careless of the feelings of the English'.[21] All typical of what Samuel Smiles called the 'sour native heart growing jealous' when Huguenots were successful. As a reward for his success, Feversham was given England's highest honour, the Order of the Garter.[22]

---

20   HMC, *Stopford Sackville* (London, 1904), vol. 1, 'Lord Feversham's March, 20 June–6 July 1685'. The MS also includes Feversham's despatches to the King in French.

21   T. B. Macaulay, *History of England* (4 vols, London, 1848–61), vol. 1, p. 610.

22   A Gascon ancestor, Gaillard de Durfort, was similarly honoured in 1463 by King Edward IV. Gaillard de Durfort, Seigneur de Duras et de Blanquefort (d.1481), KG no. 193

III

Feversham had now been a widower for nearly ten years and the task of finding a suitable wife was undertaken by his friend, Sir John Reresby. In the summer of 1688 Reresby called at Welbeck, the home of the Duke of Newcastle, to recommend Feversham as one suitable for the hand-in-marriage of his daughter, Lady Margaret Cavendish. Negotiations lasted over a year and were unduly protracted as the Duke and Duchess held different views on Feversham's suitability and, being estranged, were unable to communicate with each other except in writing. The Newcastles did not consider Feversham had sufficient land for his portion of a marriage settlement though he had great credit, but Reresby was under the impression that Newcastle would have preferred the Duke of Berwick, King James's natural son. The negotiations failed and Feversham remained a widower for the rest of his life.[23]

At the time, Feversham was joined in London by his sister-in-law, the Comtesse de Montgommery, his brother Charles-Henri's widow. Another arrival was his sister, Elisabeth, along with her husband, Frédéric-Charles de La Rochefoucauld, Comte de Roye et de Roussy, and the rest of their children – Charlotte and Henriette. Protestants, the de Royes had been given leave by Louis XIV to go to Denmark, where Frédéric-Charles became Commander-in-Chief of the Danish army, receiving the Order of the Elephant. In 1686 he had to leave Denmark as a consequence of an act of *lèse-majesté* on the part of his wife, who was overheard making fun of the Queen's dress.[24] In England, the Comtesse de Roye was made a Lady-in-Waiting to Queen Mary of Modena, which required her husband to receive an English title. Frédéric-Charles styled himself Lord Lifford. (The honour was never gazetted, which would have been proof of royal assent.) Throughout this period the Huguenot de Bourbons, de Royes and the Comtesse de Montgommery lived with Feversham in Somerset House.

During his reign, James II doubled the size of the standing army and reviewed it annually at Hounslow Heath, which became a social event of some importance. In 1688 the King, when dining there with Feversham in June, was startled by the outbreak of cheering in the camp. Feversham told him: 'it was nothing but the joy of the soldiers at the acquittal of the Bishops'. Seven had been on trial for refusing to announce the King's 1687 Declaration of Indulgence, popularly perceived as opening the door to Roman Catholic influence. 'Nothing', said the King, 'and you call it nothing?'[25] He then rode back to London in silence. It now became apparent to many that there were plots to remove the King and replace him with the Protestant

(inv *c.*1463): P. de Commynes, *Mémoires*, ed. J. Calmette and G. Durville (3 vols, Paris, 1924), bk 10, pt 4; Y. Durand, *La Maison de Durfort à l'Époque Moderne: Fontenay-le-Comte* (France, 1975); R. Aldrich, *The Register of the Most Noble Order of the Garter, from Its Cover in Black Velvet, Usually Called the Black Book: With Notes Placed at the Bottom of the Pages*, ed. J. Anstis (2 vols, London, 1724).

23   J. Reresby, *The Memoirs of ... Sir John Reresby ... Containing Several Private and Remarkable Transactions, from the Restoration to the Revolution inclusively*, ed. J. J. Cartwright (London, 1875), pp. 375–86.

24   Favre, *Précis historiques*, p. 128.

25   Macaulay, *History*, vol. 2, p. 384.

William of Orange. These became more widespread when the Queen gave birth to a son, James Francis. Feversham was to take an oath attesting to the validity of the birth, to counter the warming pan myth. Not until October did James seem to appreciate the danger of an invasion from Holland and in that month appointed Feversham to be Lord Lieutenant of Kent, ordering him to withdraw all horses and oxen well inland from the coast to prevent their use by a hostile force.

Following a disastrous sortie, which was turned back by gales, and aided by a favourable wind, William of Orange's second attempt to invade England succeeded when he landed at Torbay on 5 November. His army amounted to 14,000 all told. In opposition the royal army was 40,000 strong (including garrisoned troops in fortresses and recently enrolled men who could not readily assist James's cause), many of whom were deployed on the east coast, where a landing had been expected. William's invasion force, with Schomberg as second-in-command, consisted of a well-disciplined cosmopolitan and partly mercenary collection of fighting men from Holland, England, Scotland and Scandinavia, with many Huguenots. Some 54 officers in the Dutch Blue Dragoons and 34 officers in the Dutch Life Guards were Huguenot.[26] Catholics served in both armies in roughly equal numbers.[27]

The King was alerted when the Dutch fleet was sighted moving down the Channel. He offered the leadership of his army to Feversham's brother-in-law, Frédéric-Charles de Roye but, aware since his arrival in England of the feeling of the army against the French, put the suggestion aside. He remained an advisor to the King, supporting James's feeling that he must defend the capital.[28] 'He could not', he said, 'command an army not one word of whose language he could speak'.[29] His objection was nonsensical, since most armies had multi-lingual regiments, and very often a foreign commander: his grasp of Danish is far from certain. But it was a good diplomatic move as he may (rightly) have doubted his influence over the King; for example, he advised James to keep the army near London, but was overruled.[30] Feversham was then given the task of opposing the invader with Churchill, promoted to lieutenant-general, as second-in-command. At once 26 squadrons of cavalry and ten dragoons were sent to the west, some going to Marlborough and others to Warminster and Salisbury. Remembering the importance of Bristol from his experience in the Sedgemoor campaign, Feversham, sent forward Sir John Fenwick to destroy the strategic bridge over the Avon at Keynsham. The Huguenot earl then moved with the bulk of the foot soldiers and artillery to Salisbury. Arriving there on 13 November he learned that Lord Cornbury and others had deserted. Visiting his troops at Warminster he had to reassure many who feared that if James overcame

---

26 J. Childs, *The British Army of William III, 1689–1702* (Manchester, 1987).

27 P. Earle, *The Life and Times of James II* (London, 1972), writes that 'there were probably more Catholics in William's army than in James's', p. 187.

28 Archives du ministère des affaires Etrangères, Quai d'Orsay (Paris), *Cahiers Politiques Angleterre* 167, Barrillon to Louis XIV, 25 November 1688; G. Burnet, *History of My Own Times*, ed. M. J. Routh (6 vols, Oxford, 1723–24), vol. 3, p. 331; J. Miller, *James II: A Study in Kingship* (London, 1989), p. 200.

29 Churchill, *Marlborough*, vol. 1, p. 288.

30 R. Beddard, *A Kingdom Without a King: The Journal of the Provisional Government in the Revolution of 1688* (London, 1988), p. 23.

William he intended to destroy the Protestant religion and especially the Church of England, telling them the King, 'had as much kindness for them as they could desire and that he would establish the Church of England as much as any Protestant prince could'.[31]

The King arrived at Salisbury on 19 November and Feversham acquainted him with the unrest which existed in the higher command of the army which, in the west, still outnumbered William's by two to one. The King now seemed to have lost his sense of resolve and his physical decline was apparent. He was 55 and, suffering from continuous nose-bleeds, became temporarily ineffective. Churchill, Kirke, Trelawny and the Duke of Grafton pledged their loyalty to him, but Feversham in private begged the King to arrest them and others and 'clap them up', as he was convinced they would desert at a suitable opportunity.[32] Pointing out that the 'private men were steady', he went so far as to suggest that he suspected officers should be replaced by the most trustworthy sergeants.[33] The King could not bring himself to believe that so many senior officers could desert, particularly as they had just pledged their support. On 23 November he held a council of war. Supported by Feversham and de Roye, he decided to withdraw the army towards London as a further landing was expected on the east coast along with an uprising in the capital by William's supporters. Already anti-Catholic feeling was being whipped up there. The decision to withdraw was opposed by Churchill; Kirke, in the field, refused to obey the order. The King commanded Kirke's arrest, but he was soon released by Feversham, whose common sense prevailed in this instance.

That night (23 November) Churchill and the Duke of Grafton deserted to William, who was at Axminster. On arrival there, Churchill was greeted by Schomberg with sarcasm so cutting that he never forgot it. 'Sir', said the old Marshal, 'you are the first deserter of the rank of Lieutenant-General I ever saw.'[34] For Churchill, loyalty was a slippery concept, but his defection was frowned upon by Schomberg, who himself had served Louis XIV loyally despite their different religious persuasions. As such, it might seem that Churchill showed misplaced loyalty and Schomberg was right to criticise his lack of professional soldierly ethics. There were further desertions, including the King's daughter, Anne, and her husband, Prince George of Denmark. James remarked: 'Help me, even my children have deserted me.'[35] Feversham,

---

31   Ibid., p. 23 n. 12.

32   T. Bruce, Earl of Ailesbury, *Memoirs*, ed. W. E. Buckley (2 vols, Westminster: Roxburgh Club, 1890), vol. 1, pp. 184–5; J. Lowther, Viscount Lonsdale, *Memoir of the Reign of James II* (York, 1808; reprinted London, 1846), pp. 59–60.

33   C. Dalton, *English Army Lists and Commission Registers, 1661–1714* (6 vols, London, 1892–1904).

34   However, there is some doubt about the veracity of this tale; Winston Churchill went so far as to call it Jacobite propaganda, citing the fact that Churchill later commissioned a portrait of Schomberg: Churchill, *Marlborough*, vol. 1, p. 265 n. 1. The story was first related in the *The Life of King James the Second, King of England, etc., Collected Out of the Memoirs Writ of His Own Hand*, ed. J. S. Clarke (2 vols, London, 1816). The portrait was later in Earl Spencer's collection and is the one reproduced in Sir H. B. Butler and C. R. L. Fletcher, *Historical Portraits, 1660–1700* (Oxford, 1909), p. 258.

35   Macaulay, *History*, vol. 2, p. 517.

now retreating towards London with the bulk of the army, was at his wits' end, his superiors unable to make decisions, his capable lieutenants – Churchill, Kirke and others – having abandoned the colours. He was in an unenviable position. Having experience of the campaigning in the west in 1685, Feversham might well have had a chance against William, were it not for the actions of others about him. However, William's army was a far more formidable force than Monmouth's and probably had substantially greater public support; and James was psychologically shattered by mid-November 1688. There was little or no fighting in the campaign apart from a skirmish near Wincanton where 14 soldiers were killed. The King's most loyal (but impotent) supporters were now his two Huguenot generals, Feversham and de Roye. Both they and James himself were protégés of Marshal Turenne. According to Winston Churchill: 'They were immune from the passions which shook England. The King could count on their fidelity however his own subjects might behave.'[36]

With William steadily advancing and all crumbling about him, James handed a letter to Feversham's sister, the Comtesse de Roye, on 10 December for delivery to her brother at Uxbridge.[37] In it he said he had sent the Queen and Prince of Wales abroad and that he proposed to leave the country. The letter continued to relate that if he could have relied on the loyalty of his army he would have had 'one blow at it'. However, he himself could not take the risk and thanked Feversham and other officers and soldiers who had been loyal to him, and told them not to expose themselves 'by resisting a foreign army and poisoned nation'.[38] Feversham read the King's letter aloud to his troops, which drew tears from most of them. A council of war concluded that since the King did not expect them to resist the invading army, he intended that his army should be disbanded. Accordingly Feversham immediately dismissed them. He then wrote to William of Orange saying:

> Sir, having received a letter from His Majesty with the unfortunate news of his resolution to go out of England, I thought myself obliged, being at the head of his army and having received orders, to make no opposition against anybody, to let your Highness know it, with the advice of the officers here, as soon as was possible, to hinder the effusion of blood. I have ordered already to that purpose all troops under my command, which shall be the last order they shall receive from me.[39]

Feversham then received orders from the Lords spiritual and temporal to prevent further hostilities. Returning to London he learned that the King had already left for Dover. At Faversham (in Kent) James was recognised, detained and insulted by ruffians. Hearing this, the Council of Regency, which had just been set up, sent Feversham, with an escort of Life Guards and Grenadiers, to rescue James and bring him back to London. Feversham arrived at Faversham on 16 November, having left the escort at Sittingbourne. He then rescued James and brought him back to

---

36 Churchill, *Marlborough*, vol. 1, p. 289.

37 R. Vigne, 'Huguenots at the Court of William and Mary', in C. Wilson and D. Proctor (eds), *1688: The Seaborne Alliance and Diplomatic Revolution* (London, 1988), p. 117.

38 *The Life of James II*, ed. Clarke, vol. 2, p. 250.

39 Ibid., p. 250 n.

Sittingbourne. With the full escort they proceeded to Rochester where James instructed Feversham to ride post-haste to William requesting a meeting in London.

On arrival at Windsor, Feversham was not received by William but at once imprisoned in the round tower at Windsor Castle. William's anger was doubtless caused by Feversham's action in disbanding the army which he had hoped to take over intact. William sent a message to the King demanding that there should be a formal surrender of all troops loyal to him and that all Catholics should be removed from the army. James himself was to go to Ham House near Richmond. When the King returned to London from Rochester his arrival was surprisingly acclaimed by the crowd. At once he went to Somerset House to obtain news about Feversham. He was told by the Comte de Roye that he was imprisoned in Windsor Castle. Being extremely concerned, he complained to William's envoy, Willem Frederik van Nassau-Zuylestein, but Feversham was not released. James now returned to Whitehall and, after he retired for the night, Dutch Guards surrounded the palace. He was awakened early and instructed to go to Ham House, but he refused. Later, escorted by Dutch Guards, he went to Rochester on William's instructions and was allowed to escape to France, arriving in Calais on Christmas Day.

On 18 December, the day James left London, William and Schomberg drove down Piccadilly in the rain and London was soon full of soldiers of many nationalities, including Huguenots. Two days later William called at Somerset House to visit the Queen Dowager, Catherine of Braganza. He found her pensive and unoccupied and asked why she was not playing basset that night. She replied that she had not been able to play for some time, as Lord Feversham, who always kept the bank for her, was still imprisoned. William took the hint and Feversham was released the next day, 21 December 1688.

IV

Feversham's military career was now over. Loyal to the end, he had backed a loser. He was not, however, alone in his support for the defeated king. Other supporters included Samuel Pepys and William Penn, for whom James had released 1,200 Quakers from prison in 1686. Nine bishops, five of whom had been imprisoned in 1688, and 400 clergy remained loyal to James and were to lose all as Non-Jurors. The Jacobite cause remained strong for many years to come among all classes in England. However, Feversham's relatives were quick to change their allegiance. His nephew, Armand de Bourbon, Marquis de Miremont, placed his cavalry regiment at the service of William. It was sent to Holland. Armand's younger brother, Louis, Comte de La Caze, served under Schomberg in Ireland and was killed at the battle of the Boyne. The Comte de Roye's son, Frédéric-Guillaume, also fought in the battle of the Boyne. He was ennobled by William, bearing the titles of Earl of Lifford and Baron Clonmel. He later became a general in Queen Anne's reign. His father, the Comte de Roye (himself styled Lord Lifford), retired to Bath, where he died in June 1690.

It was at the time of the battle of the Boyne that Queen Mary II asked that prayers be said for the success of her husband in Ireland. (He was, of course, fighting her father there.) At Somerset House the Queen-Dowager, Catherine, had forbidden the recital of prayers at the Protestant chapel where Feversham, 'looking as pale as death', explained to her that it had been his decision that the prayers were not said. A deliberate untruth, as he was concerned for the future of the services there.[40] Indeed, at Somerset House, Feversham was often thought to be harbouring Jacobite sympathies. Several searches were made, but no plotters were found. Queen Catherine departed for Portugal in 1692. Feversham was given £10,000 a year to maintain her household staff. It was then suggested to Feversham that 'by reason of the great obligation he had to James Stuart, he should retire to Holland'. This he refused to do, emphasizing his right as a Peer of the realm and the need to manage Queen Catherine's affairs. This he did until she died in 1705. During the years he was Lord Chamberlain to Queen Catherine, he received many favours from her, including the Mastership of St Catherine's Hospital, worth £1,000 a year. This, according to Agnes Strickland, led to his being called 'King Dowager', suggesting more than a professional relationship.[41] The alleged partiality of Catherine for Feversham was strongly denied by Queen Mary of Modena.

During the reign of Queen Anne, Feversham was able to live comfortably with his relatives at Somerset House and participate in the social life of the court. In 1702 Queen Anne asked the Huguenot Earl and other Garter knights to advise her how she should wear the garter herself. He also helped in drawing up the rules governing the procedure and etiquette for installing new knights. He was now a man of considerable means, having an estimated income of £8,000 a year. He banked at Hoare's Bank, close to Somerset House. His bank statements still exist and show that in 1707 he held a credit balance of £13,500. Narcissus Luttrell, writing in 1709, says: 'Yesterday on 8 April, Louis Feversham, who was General of King James' army, Chamberlain to the Queen-Dowager and Knight of the Garter, died of the gout in his stomach, aged about 70.'[42] He was buried in a vault at the French church of the Savoy in the Strand. In his will he left rings to his sister, Lady Lifford, his nieces, Lady Charlotte de Roussy and Lady Strafford, the residue going equally to his nephews, the Marquis de Miremont and the Earl of Lifford.

Feversham's titles were devolved on his brother-in-law, Baron Rockingham, who, in 1714, became Baron Throwley, Viscount Sondes and Earl of Rockingham; the title of Earl of Feversham being in abeyance. The French dignity of Marquis de Blanqufort devolved on the Duc de Duras and the Barony of Duras of Holdenby became extinct. The bodies of Feversham, his nephew, de Miremont (who died in 1732), and his niece, Charlotte de Bourbon-Malauze, who died in the same year as her brother, were taken from the vault at the French church at the Savoy and re-interred in one grave at the North transept of Westminster Abbey in March 1739.[43] There are no visible markings on the tomb which, according to the abbey's burial

---

40 Vigne, 'Huguenots at the Court of William and Mary', p. 116.

41 A. Strickland, *Lives of the Queens of England: From the Norman Conquest* (16 vols, London, 1840–48).

42 Luttrell, *Relation of State Affairs*, vol. 6, p. 428.

43 *Westminster Abbey Registers*, ed. J. L. Chester (London, 1875; reprinted London, 1976), p. 355.

book, is 'even with the north corner and touching the plinth of the iron rails of the Duke and Duchess of Newcastle, three feet deep'. Unable to unite in life, the Newcastles and Feversham were almost united in death.

Though steadfastly Protestant throughout his life, Feversham proved loyal to a Catholic monarch and suffered for his choice. Yet he never regretted the association and considered it to be right. He was loyal to James II, a Catholic King, in the same way that Schomberg had been to Louis XIV in France. But while Schomberg was eventually pushed out of his loyalty, Feversham never took the easy or advantageous option accepted by contemporary figures such as Churchill. As members of an international soldiering elite, both Feversham and Schomberg might be counted as the norm for such notions of loyalty; Churchill was the exception, and Schomberg's derogatory comments about his behaviour must be understood in that context. Thus Feversham's loyalty was by no means misguided, simply because he backed the losing side. Nor can it be considered immoral for a Huguenot to support a friend and patron whose cause was just according to all the precepts of 'divine right' kingship common at the time. In this context, Feversham made what he considered to be the correct and honourable choice. It was a decision, moreover, for which he seems to have been respected by his contemporaries and is one which should be remembered when considering the actions of the Huguenots as a group in exile.

Chapter 4

'The Good Lord Galway'
The English and Irish Careers of a
Huguenot Leader[1]

Randolph Vigne
Huguenot Society of Great Britain and Ireland

The Reverend David Agnew, the only biographer of Henri de Massue, Marquis de Ruvigny, Earl of Galway subtitled his book 'a filial memoir'.[2] He lists in the index 23 'encomiasts', among them, such contemporaries as King William III, the Duke of Marlborough and Lord Godolphin and later writers like Archdeacon Coxe and Dr Weiss.[3] At one point he writes: 'It is remarkable how at every stage in Lord Galway's course we hear his praises sounded.' The soubriquet 'the good Lord Galway' he quotes from a letter of Bishop Hough's to Galway's cousin and great friend, Rachel, Lady Russell, but notes that 'Dean Swift differs in his estimate'. Agnew's own description of Swift as 'that reckless and starving pamphleteer', in marked contrast with his customarily moderate tone, indicates the passions aroused by Galway's role in the last 35 years of his long life, as a subject and servant of William and Mary, Anne and George I, and from 1689 as the devoted leader of the Huguenot refugees.[4]

It is not the purpose here to balance the columns of praise and blame and suggest a verdict, but to point to these antitheses as examples of the tenor of Galway's public life as exiled soldier, diplomat, administrator and Huguenot leader. This was one of intense shocks, peaks followed by troughs, 'triumphs and disasters' which impostors he treated just the same, outwardly at least.

They run through his exile, six or seven years of which he spent in Ireland, and it will be necessary to tell briefly the story of those exile years since, rather more than

---

1   This chapter was originally a paper delivered at Trinity College, Dublin, during the launching of the Irish Section of the Huguenot Society of Great Britain and Ireland, 23 November 1987.

2   D. C. A. Agnew, *Henri de Ruvigny, Earl of Galway, a Filial Memoir with a Prefatory Life of His Father the Marquis de Ruvigny* (Edinburgh, 1864). References below are, unless otherwise stated, from the same author's *Protestant Exiles from France in the Reign of Louis XIV* (3 vols, London, 1871; second edition) which contains a revised version of the former.

3   *Private and Original Correspondence of Charles Talbot, Duke of Shrewsbury*, ed. W. Coxe (London, 1821); C. Weiss, *History of the French Protestant Refugees* (2 vols, Edinburgh, 1854).

4   Agnew, *Protestant Exiles from France*, vol. 2, p. 149.

does his time in Ireland, so many examples of these antitheses occurred in them. The contradictory judgements of his character and personality can be seen in the picture by the court 'detective', John Macky, set against the 'differing estimate' annotated by Swift in his copy of Macky's book (in italics):

> Lord Galway, Lieutenant-General, the son of Mr Ruvigny, who was ambassador from the French court to King Charles II, had a regiment of horse given to him at the Revolution, was sent to command under the Duke of Savoy in the last War, and on that Prince's making peace with France, was sent commander in chief to Ireland and created a Peer. He is one of the finest gentlemen in the army, with a head fitted for the cabinet as well as the camp; is very modest, vigilant and sincere; – *in all directly otherwise* a man of honour and honesty, without pride or affectation; wears his hair, is plain in his dress and manners, towards sixty years.[5]
>
> *A deceitful, hypocritical, factious knave – a damnable hypocrite of no religion.*[6]

Swift's last barb is hardest to understand, since Henri de Massue de Ruvigny, already 37, came to England in 1685 as an exile in the cause of religion with his aged father, mother and brother Pierre, Sieur de La Caillemotte. The word 'refugee', coined at the time of the *grand refuge* resulting from the revocation of the Edict of Nantes, does not apply as they left in spite of the pleas of Louis XIV that they stay. Their estates and fortune in France remained intact, and, for a time, they retained the friendship of the King, to whom father and son had in turn represented the Protestants of France as Deputy-General, the son through the worst of the persecution until after the Revocation itself.[7]

The father was the closest friend of Turenne, and the son learned his soldiering in Germany under that greatest of Louis XIV's generals.[8] Turenne abjured his Protestant faith: the de Ruvignys did not. The old Marquis had left his ambassadorship at Charles II's court partly because of pressure to build an embassy chapel, where Catholic services would have been held which he should have been obliged to attend.[9] The first French Protestant services in Greenwich, where the family were given quarters in a Royal residence, were held in the Anglican parish church.[10]

Galway did not himself play a major part in Huguenot church affairs, but was served by a succession of chaplains and in his early period as Commander-in-Chief in Ireland (both before and after his service in Piedmont, *pace* Macky) actively sought the unifying of the conformist and non-conformist Huguenot congregations

---

5   J. Macky, *Memoirs of the Secret Services of J. Macky ... including, also, the True Secret History of the ... English and Scots Nobility, ... and other Persons of Distinction, from the Revolution*, ed. A. R. with marginal notes by Dean Swift, transcribed by T. Birch (London, The Hague, 1733).

6   J. Swift, *Miscellaneous and Autobiographical Pieces and Marginalia*, ed. H. Davis (Oxford, 1962), p. 261.

7   First use of OED is as 'refugie' in 1685 (Burnet): Agnew, *Protestant Exiles from France*, vol. 1, pp. 129, 147.

8   *Véritables Œuvres de M. de Saint-Evremond, publiées sur les Manuscrits de l'Auteur* (5 vols, London, 1706), vol. 2, p. 252.

9   Agnew, *Protestant Exiles from France*, vol. 1, p. 135.

10   *The Diary of John Evelyn*, ed. A. Dobson (3 vols, London, 1908), p. 397.

in Dublin, and stood as *parrain* at baptisms at several Huguenot churches in London and Dublin.[11] In Piedmont he also convened a synod and served as an elder.[12] Among the letters written in his regiment is one of 1717 thanking a distinguished Genevan theologian for a sermon brought to him by one of Galway's godsons, the young *proposant* having been introduced four years earlier to the theologian by Galway.[13] A man 'of no religion', would scarcely have acknowledged so constantly the Calvinist faith or have suffered greatly for its sake.

I

Galway's early years in England were under the shadow of the old Marquis at Greenwich and in London. He had clearly resumed the contacts he had already built up in France and on his own diplomatic visits to England on behalf of Louis XIV. One of these had been to meet the 'patriotic party' in Parliament and to work on Danby's influence on Charles II, thought in France to be against Louis's interests.[14] His link with Danby's opponents was their leader, Lord Russell, whose wife, born Rachel Wriothesley, was his first cousin, daughter of the old Marquis's sister, also Rachel, who, as Countess of Southampton at the court of Charles II, was known as 'the beautiful and vertueuse Huguenot' (*la belle et virtueuse Huguenote*). The meetings with Russell and his friends were interpreted by T. B. Macaulay and others as attempted bribery (but, according to Barillon, the French ambassador, he offered them money and they took it).[15] But the slightness of the evidence precludes even a guess at the truth. The incident is a foretaste of the long succession of alleged failures, wrapped in misunderstandings, which were to darken his years in exile. Equally so was his attempt to intercede with Louis XIV on behalf of Russell, sentenced to death after the Rye House Plot. Louis gave him a letter to Charles, who told Barillon: 'I do not want to prevent what M. de Ruvigny came here to do, but my Lord Russell will have his neck slit before he arrives.'[16]

Rachel Wriothesley's marriage to William Russell linked Ruvigny with the new Whig family network which was to dominate English government during his life in exile. The widowed Lady Russell's highly moral published letters, which ran into many editions through the nineteenth century, contain frequent references to her Huguenot cousin. In January 1689 we find her helping him raise money for the release of a party of Huguenot pastors and *proposants* 'taken going into Holland and

---

11   T. P. LeFanu, 'Archbishop Marsh and the discipline of the French church of St Patrick's, Dublin, 1691', *Proceedings of the Huguenot Society of London*, 12/4 (1920): 20–1; Huguenot Society Quarto Series 26, pp. 33, 35; 29, pp. 63, 75; 42, p. 16.

12   Agnew, *Protestant Exiles from France*, vol. 1, pp. 145–7.

13   Bibliothèque Publique et Universitaire, Geneva (hereafter BPUG), Turretini Coll., fol. 135.

14   Agnew, *Protestant Exiles from France*, vol. 1, pp. 145–7.

15   T. B., Macaulay, *The History of England from the Accession of James II* (4 vols, London, 1848–61), vol. 1, pp. 228–9.

16   Agnew, *Protestant Exiles from France*, vol. 1, pp. 145–7.

made slaves in Algiers'.[17] This mission was, it seems, successful, as were so many of the efforts he was to make for the Huguenot refugees, whose leader he had become as Deputy-General in 1679, and was to remain throughout his life, as if the post had never lapsed.

Early efforts he made on behalf of the refugees are recorded in a series of letters written between 1688 and 1691 probably to Jacques Muisson, a *conseiller* of the Paris *parlement*, who had fled to Amsterdam, to whom he addressed also business, family and religious matters. Two of the letters relate to the battle of the Boyne, at which his younger brother La Caillemotte, aged 37, was fatally wounded.[18] The old Marquis had died the year before, and the second Marquis proceeded in 1691 to Ireland, extending himself at last beyond the family and refugee stewardship which had occupied him since leaving France.

Typically, he cared also for the sons of Captain Brasselay of Schomberg's regiment who had survived the 'sickly season' at Dundalk which decimated Schomberg's army in 1690, only to die at Windsor on his return to England. They were sent to school at Eton that year, their fees being paid by the Royal Bounty in the name of Henri de Ruvigny.[19]

II

He took command of Schomberg's Horse, leaderless since the death in action of the Commander-in-Chief, securing at its head the victory at Aughrim which was to decide the war for William. In the same crucial moment, the advantage being with James's forces, his French general, Saint-Ruth, fell dead, struck by a cannon ball and 'Ruvigny's cavalry delivered a magnificent charge and swept the enemy away'.[20]

From the victory at Aughrim followed all Henri de Massue de Ruvigny's honours and appointments. His conduct at Aughrim had justified William's elevating him to the status of the other continental soldiers and statesmen – Friedrich Hermann von Schomberg, Godard van Reede van Ginkel, Arnold Joost van Keppel, Hans Willem Bentinck and many lesser men who could offer the Crown long experience, training, professionalism and above all, loyalty. The opening couplets of the 'True-born Englishman' are too often quoted alone: the three that follow make Defoe's point, as does Galway's extensive correspondence with William, conducted with a frankness and intimacy that shows William in his best light:

We blame the King that he relies too much
On strangers, Germans, Huguenots and Dutch

---

17 *Letters of Rachel, Lady Russell*, ed. Lord J. (later Earl) Russell (2 vols, London, 1853), vol. 2; Agnew, *Protestant Exiles from France*, vol. 1, p. 149.

18 Huguenot Library, de Ruvigny letters; see *Proceedings of the Huguenot Society of London*, 17: 244–61.

19 Bodleian Library, Oxford (hereafter Bod. Lib), Rawlinson Coll., A306, 129, 180, 212, 267.

20 Macaulay, *History of England*, vol. 3, p. 624; R. H. Murray, *Revolutionary Ireland and its Settlement* (London, 1911), p. 217.

And seldom does his great affairs of state
To English councillors communicate.
The fact might very well be answered thus –
He has too often been betrayed by us;
He must have been a madman to rely
On English Godolphin's fidelity;
The foreigners have faithfully obeyed him,
And none but Englishmen have e'er betrayed him.[21]

Ginkel, who was made Earl of Athlone and Baron Aughrim, and Schomberg's second son, created Duke of Leinster, moved on, respectively, to Flanders to lead William's forces, and to Piedmont as allied commander. After a brief visit to England de Ruvigny, who became Viscount Galway, returned to Ireland as Commander-in-Chief, effective from February 1692. Isaac Dumont de Bostaquet, who had fought with Galway at Aughrim, and sailed from 'Olihec' in Anglesey with him describes the arrival of their yacht in Dublin's river on 3 November 1691. In quarters on 'the quay before Essex bridge' (*'le Quai pre de pont d'essex'*), Galway received the Lords Justices, Chancellor, Mayor and Aldermen, while his Huguenot officers lodged happily for a month with a Huguenot citizen of Dublin, in 'Copraly' (Copper Alley). Galway was besieged by officers claiming arrears in pay and took great pains to settle the many young people without subsistence to whom he gave refuge in his house.[22]

Dumont de Bostaquet narrated Galway's travels to military establishments at Athlone, where he tried to alleviate the poverty and starvation with private charity, Limerick, Cork and finally Waterford where his staff joined him for the dispatching of infantry regiments and cavalry to England, after suitable public ceremony and dinners. Dumont de Bostaquet notes the General's search for possible places to settle the Huguenot refugees whom he clearly saw as ideal settler material for Ireland, as he saw Ireland, as an ideal territory for their settlement. He had three categories in mind: the Dumont de Bostaquets and many other families of his officers and *aides*, the civilian refugees who had swarmed about his father in Greenwich, and the vastly greater number still in France, in the King's galleys, or in Geneva and elsewhere. Correspondence on this subject, concerning also the 'breaking' of the Huguenot regiments and provision for their officers and other ranks, is with William Blathwayt, Secretary-at-War, and George Clarke at the Horse Guards, written from Dublin Castle, Kinsale and 'Corak' (Cork).[23]

Until 1698 Galway's grand plan to settle in Ireland the refugees in the Swiss cantons – perhaps all the refugees – was negotiated by Henri de Mirmand, whose lack of confidence in it negated Galway's enthusiasm. He saw that William could not divert resources from his great mission, to defeat Louis XIV, even if able to

---

21   *The Earlier Life and the Chief Earlier Works of Daniel Defoe*, ed. H. Morley (London, 1889), p. 213.

22   *Mémoires inedites de Isaac Dumont de Bostaquet, gentilhomme Normande*, ed. M. Richard (Paris, 1968); *Memoirs of Isaac Dumont de Bostaquet: A Gentleman of Normandy*, ed. D. W. Ressinger, Huguenot Society New Series 4 (London, 2005).

23   British Library (hereafter BL), Add. MS 9,718, fols 81–232.

overcome the English parliament's characteristic rejection of a scheme that might advance Ireland.[24] The long-term prospects resulting from filling Catholic Ireland's forfeited estates with staunch Calvinists favoured the scheme at the time, but did not save it. The report by de Sailly to Galway made it clear that they were misled by the evacuations due to the war and thought large areas of the country were uninhabited.[25]

It was intended, says Agnew, that Galway himself 'should reside permanently in Dublin'.[26] The Catholic nobleman and exiled man of letters Saint-Evremond jested to the Huguenot Marquis de Miremont of the temptations and 'the delights of Dublin, the abundance of the country, the bountiful fish' that Galway was offering him, corrupting, with presents, the Duchess de Mazarin and himself 'by whisky, and me by the Strawberries of Ireland'.[27]

Ruvigny's estates in France had been confiscated by Louis XIV after he had joined in the campaign against James II in Ireland. His fortune was, much later, given by Louis to the Marquis de Harlay who had long held it in trust. The Earl of Portland, Ambassador Extraordinary in Paris in 1698, on William's orders, interceded with Louis, to no avail.[28] Galway reminded William in 1692 that 'when I took leave of you, you assured me of your goodwill, and you have told me several times, even before I entered your service, that you wished to do me a kindness and would recompense me for what I had lost in France by giving me something to the value of £25,000 sterling'. He had asked for the estate of James's Irish viceroy, Tyrconnel, but accepted that it was to go to 'a person whose service merits recompense'. Instead 'I beg you to give me that of Sir Patrick Trant', or 'if you have absolutely resolved not to give any more lands in Ireland, I pray you grant that I may be keeper of it'.[29]

And so it was, his occupation as 'custodian' being converted to full ownership after three years. The story of Portarlington has been looked at closely in recent years and, all in all, it repeats the light and dark of Galway's days.[30] The grand design of a commercial and industrial centre became a collection of small holdings and private residences for the families of the officers and men who had fought with him, its main product being education at its several schools to which the Irish Protestant gentry and middle classes sent their sons. The lives of its citizens did not to any extent fit

24 A. de Chambrier, 'Projet de colonisation en Irelande par les refugiés français, 1692–9', *Proceedings of the Huguenot Society of London*, 11/3 (1901): 370–432; A. de Chambrier, *Henri de Mirmand et les réfugiés de Révocatoin de l'Édict de Nantes, 1650–1721* (Neuchâtel, 1910), *passim*; *Proceedings of the Huguenot Society of London*, 9/4 (1911); 267–9; *Mémoires inedites de Isaac Dumont de Bostaquet*, ed. Richard, pp. 267–9.

25 R. Vigne, '"Le Projet d'Irlande": Huguenot migration in the 1690s', *History Ireland*, 2/2 (Summer, 1994).

26 Agnew, *De Ruvigny*, p. 49.

27 *Véritables Œuvres de M. de Saint-Evremond*, vol. 5, p. 217.

28 CSPDom., 1698, p. 256.

29 Ibid. 1691–2, p. 550.

30 R. Hylton, 'The Huguenot Settlement at Portarlington, 1682–1775', in C. E. J. Caldicott, H. Gough and J. P. Pittion (eds), *The Huguenots and Ireland* (Dublin, 1987), pp. 297–320.

Smiles's idyllic picture of 'military refugees in their scarlet cloaks sitting in groups under the old oaks in the market place, sipping tea out of their small china cups'.[31] It was rather 'divided by religious controversy, haunted by a sense of transition and insecurity', not least by the plight of so many over delays in military pension payments, endemic in those days.[32] And more so, indeed, by Galway's own loss of title in 1700, when the Act of Resumption took away his estates at Portarlington and Clanmaliere. They were sold to the Hollow Sword Blade Company but the leases of their houses and gardens he had granted to the Huguenot settlers at Portarlington were subsequently confirmed by Act of Parliament, after two years of uncertainty.[33]

The year before, William had both warned and reassured Galway, who had expressed himself to the King as 'uneasy at the proceedings of the Parliament (in London) against the foreigners', agreeing that 'you have too much cause to be so, though as yet nothing has passed about you and I have good reason to hope you will be left undisturbed'. William clearly felt himself a victim of the 'ignorance and malice prevailing here beyond conception', since it was also 'not to be conceived how people here are set against the foreigners: you will easily judge on whom this reflects'.[34]

The parliamentary attacks went on and the King, again with the intimacy which Galway seemed to inspire, explained 'I have not written to you all this winter, by reason of my vexation at what passed in Parliament and because of the uncertainty I was under to know what to send you'. It was not only the Huguenots of high station like Galway who were the sufferers from English xenophobia: 'It is not possible to be more sensibly touched than I am, at my not being able to do more for the poor refugee officers who have served me with such zeal and fidelity. I am afraid the good God will punish the ingratitude of this nation.' He was still able to assure Galway, however, that he was

> perfectly satisfied with your conduct, and hope now you will be left undisturbed, since in the last Parliament nothing was said to you, though you were much threatened. I fear the commission given here by the Commons, for the inspection of the forfeitures, will give you a great deal of trouble, and me none less, the next winter; assuredly on all sides my patience is put to the trial.[35]

The Act of Resumption was duly promulgated on 2 April 1700 and William wrote to Galway that 'your being deprived of what I gave you with such pleasure was not the least of my griefs' and promised to recompense him with 'marks of my esteem and friendship'. The same letter advised him that his service as Lord Justice, effectively

---

31 S. Smiles, *The Huguenots ... in England and Ireland* (London, 1869; third edition), p. 300.

32 Hylton, 'The Huguenot Settlement at Portarlington', p. 303.

33 G. L. Lee, *The Huguenot Settlements in Ireland* (London, 1936), p. 144; Agnew, *Protestant Exiles from France*, vol. 1, p. 181.

34 *Letters of William III and Louis XIV and Their Ministers: Illustrative of the Domestic and Foreign Politics of England, from the Peace of Ryswick to the Accession of Philip V of Spain, 1697 to 1700*, ed. P. Grimblot (2 vols, London, 1848), vol. 2, pp. 247–9.

35 Ibid., p. 334.

ruling Ireland, with the young Marquis of Winchester, his fellow Lord Justice, and Lord Chancellor John Methuen in lesser roles, was also at an end, as the Duke of Shrewsbury was to replace them as viceroy.[36] He was to continue in command of the forces in Ireland. We do not have Galway's reply, but William received it with the words: 'Of all the proofs you have given me of your attachment to my service, I do not reckon as the least the spirit of resignation you evince to me with respect to your office in Ireland.'[37]

Macaulay distinguished between the land grants to politicians or favourites and to 'warriors who had been sparingly rewarded for great exploits achieved in defence of the liberties and the religion of our country'. Unlike 'the predominant faction, drunk with insolence and animosity ... Athlone was a Dutchman – Galway was a Frenchman – and it did not become a good Englishman to say a word in favour of either'.[38]

Galway saw himself as an Englishman by adoption and well understood the limitations of that status. When one Eyres wrote libellous letters about him to Robert Harley and the Speaker in 1698 he wrote to Secretary of State James Vernon that he was much obliged to learn that they were not to be minded, adding: 'although I feel that such accusations are beneath me, I know that one who has the misfortune not to be a natural-born Englishman should be well satisfied if he is not obliged to justify himself.'[39]

III

William's 'mark of esteem and respect' was the Colonelcy of the Blue Dragoons Regiment, the most elite unit of his Dutch foot-guards, in succession to the Duke of Württemberg, with the rank of General in the Dutch army.[40] His military career had gone on, but the zenith – Aughrim – was never repeated. Recalled from Ireland in 1692, he and Meinhard von Schomberg, Duke of Leinster, set about training and equipping an expeditionary force to be landed at Brest or Saint-Malo. 'The expedition was not advised by him', wrote Agnew, 'nor in his opinion was it advisable.'[41] Apart from a small landing at Ostend, no invasion took place, and Mary (the King was in Flanders) and her ministers were more preoccupied with the threatened invasion the other way, which was scotched at La Hogue. The abandonment of the landing in northern France has been ascribed to the Whig Admiral Edward Russell's unwillingness to carry out Tory orders, which factor might have inspired more couplets from Defoe,

---

36 On Methuen, see A. D. Francis, *The Methuens and Portugal, 1691–1708* (Cambridge, 1966)

37 *Letters of William III. and Louis XIV and Their Ministers*, ed. Grimblot, p. 424.

38 Macaulay, *History of England*, vol. 5, p, 272.

39 CSPDom., 1698, pp. 201–2.

40 N. Luttrell, *A Brief Historical Relation of State Affairs* (6 vols, Oxford, 1857), vol. 4, p. 660; Agnew, *Protestant Exiles from France*, vol. 1, p. 177.

41 Ibid., p. 153.

justifying William's reliance on 'Germans, Huguenots and Dutch' rather than the factious English.[42]

Galway's Whig friends and family connexions had a high opinion of his character and abilities, as indeed did King William. Lady Russell writes of his 'sincere heart and honest mind'.[43] The 'ignorance and malice' against foreigners in high places was intense: reaching a peak in the speech of Sir John Knight, MP for Bristol, vilifying the bill for the Naturalisation of Foreigners in 1694. He complained of the Egyptian plague, for frogs were

> even in the chambers of Kings. For there is no entering the Courts of St James's and Whitehall, the palaces of our hereditary Kings, for the great noise and croaking of the Froglanders. [He ended] let us first kick the Bill out of the House, and then Foreigners out of the kingdom.[44]

With his patent integrity and his military and diplomatic record, Galway was willingly defended by the family network, which was powerful and extensive. His aunt, the Countess of Southampton, was sister-in-law to Lord Spencer, whose son became Earl of Sunderland, grandfather of the statesman Sunderland married to Marlborough's favourite daughter, Anne. Marlborough's other daughters married the son and heir of his political ally Lord Godolphin, and Ralph, Duke of Montagu, whose Huguenot connexions began with his ambassadorship to Paris before the Revocation. Lady Southampton's daughters, Galway's first cousins, linked him, through their own, their children's and grandchildren's marriages directly with the Dukes of Beaufort, Bedford (the second Duke was Lady Russell's brother-in-law, the third her son), Bridgewater, Devonshire, Portland and Rutland, the Earls of Essex and Gainsborough, all of whom transmitted their share of the Massue de Ruvigny heritage. Of his connexions by marriage, Sunderland, Godolphin and Marlborough were, with the King, his greatest supporters.

In Flanders in 1693, commanding the cavalry, he covered the English retreat at Landen, and 'kept at bay, almost unsupported, the entire force of the French cavalry'.[45] The story of his momentary capture by the French, and release on being recognized, is told by Saint-Simon, who fought in the battle, and suggests a relationship which does not bear out the view that, like Macaulay on the Huguenots at the Boyne, he was 'animated by a spirit peculiarly fierce and implacable' and was 'thirsting for the blood of the French'.[46] An 'inextinguishable hatred of the House of Bourbon' may have 'glowed in the bosoms of the persecuted, dragooned, expatriated Calvinists of Languedoc', but Galway was not one of this mind, being part of the international Huguenot elite, who had transferred his allegiance from a Catholic to a Protestant monarch.[47] Voltaire ascribes to him 'true refugee hatred of the country that had driven him out', but nowhere is this expressed in Galway's voluminous

---

42 D. Ogg, *England in the Reigns of James II and William III* (Oxford, 1957), p. 372.
43 Lady Russell, *Letters*, vol. 2, p. 200.
44 Agnew, *De Ruvigny*, p. 214.
45 Weiss, *History of the French Protestant Refugees*, p. 245.
46 Macaulay, *History of England*, vol. 3, p. 625.
47 Ibid., p. 426.

correspondence, which contains so many references to the sufferings and succour of the persecuted and refugee Huguenots, but none of the crimes of their Catholic countrymen or monarch.[48]

From Flanders he went to Piedmont in command of the British force seeking, with the allies, to invade France from the south-east and as Envoy to Vittorio Amedeo II, Duke of Savoy. Three thankless years trying to keep the alliance together ended in failure, with the Duke completing his secret negotiations with the French and signing a treaty which totally destroyed allied plans for a combined operation. Was he, as more recent historians than Macaulay judge, 'outmatched in diplomacy' by Vittorio Amedeo?[49] He wrote to Shrewsbury that he had, to quote the published summary, 'long foreseen this misfortune, and wishes the King had withdrawn him from hence. Has been of little service here, as he was aware of His Royal Highness's intentions and was coldly looked on in consequence.'[50] Shrewsbury's letter on the subject contained not a hint of reproach for what his biographer William Coxe called Galway's 'blindness' and seems to admit shared responsibility for the Duke of Savoy's damaging defection.[51] He used the same letter to express special goodwill to the humiliated envoy by advising Galway that 'the King does not think fit' that an Order in Council 'obliging him (and the other Ambassadors) to confine his Extraordinaries within the rules', to which Galway had objected, 'should in this present conjuncture reach your Lordship'.[52] The Convention of Vigevano was indeed a heavy blow to William's hopes, and Galway has carried the guilt.

He rejoined the forces in the Netherlands in 1696 and returned to England in January 1697, the long war at last ending with the Peace of Ryswick. The Huguenot writer Misson Maximilien described his homecoming:

> The Earl of Galway, a brave and noble gentleman, if ever there was one in the world, is their leader, their friend, their refuge, their advocate, their support, their protector. When he arrived from Turin some days ago, his house was so crowded every morning that for a quarter of an hour after his rising it was scarce possible to get so much as to the bottom of the staircase.[53]

He had continued his efforts for the refugees throughout his time in Savoy, corresponding with Geneva and London in his own hand, and through his secretary, Elie Bouhéreau, about their needs and his schemes for their resettlement in Ireland.[54] He maintained for three months at least over 80 refugees in Vevey, with only ten adult males among them: the ledger, in his own hand, is still extant.[55] He wrote

---

48   'Siècle de Louis XIV', in *Oeuvres completes de Voltaire* (69 vols, Paris [Kehl], 1784–9), vol. 20 (1785), p. 429; Agnew, *Protestant Exiles from France*, vol. 1, p. 155.

49   Ogg, *England in the Reigns of James II and William III*, p. 381.

50   HMC, *Buccleuch and Queensberry* (2 vols, London, 1903), vol. 2, pt. 1, p. 359.

51   *Correspondence of Charles Talbot, Duke of Shrewsbury*, ed. Coxe, p. 260.

52   HMC, *Buccleuch and Queensberry*, vol. 2, pt. 1, p. 361.

53   H. Misson de Valberg, *Memoirs and Observations in his Travels over England* (London, 1721; French edition, The Hague, 1698).

54   BPUG, Turretini Coll., fol. 487.

55   *Bulletin de société de l'histoire de Protestantisme française*, 9: 419–65.

from London, shortly after his return, to '*Monsieur Duroure, capitaine d'Infanterie dans le regiment du collonel Hamilton à Emmerick* [Mr Duroure, Captain of the infantry in the regiment of Colonel Hamilton at Limerick]', sympathizing with his wounds, advising him to sell his company, and reassuring him that his case had gone to the very top: 'I spoke of your affair to the King, to my Lord Albemarle before Mr Keppell, and to your Colonel'.[56]

IV

His appointment as Lord Justice came the same year, as did his earldom and promotion to lieutenant-general, all of them emphatic condonations of the Savoy *débâcle*. His duties were heavy and he seems to have carried them out assiduously, despite the post-Limerick bitterness in the body politic – though widespread attribution of the penal laws to his Protestant vengefulness has been ably answered in recent work.[57] He had no part in the Treaty of Limerick nor in its damaging later insertion. He could not have been the anti-Catholic zealot his enemies labelled him, as he remained the firm friend of Saint-Evremond (whose executor he was at the latter's death in 1693). He showed practical generosity to the sons of Lord Clanmalire, former proprietor of the O'Dempsey lands at Portarlington, sending them to school at Eton, and to Catholic individuals like 'Redmond Morris, gent., who went to France and has been in arms under the French King' on whose behalf he wrote to Albemarle to allow him to return to Ireland.[58]

He was the servant of the English parliament, rather than of the Irish, and of the King, who, as with the Act of Resumption in 1700, had to subordinate his wishes to parliamentary action on many issues, often to his great dislike. If the penal laws were the work of Protestant Irish against their Catholic compatriots, the legislation aimed at crippling the growing trade in woollen cloth was purely in the interest of England, though aided and abetted by a majority in the Irish parliament. It must have been fortuitous that only Irish frieze, such as he had sent to Saint-Evremond five years before, was exempt from the effective banning, in 1698, of woollen exports.

Galway worked hard to develop linen manufactures to take its place, sending for a French weaving expert, of whose efforts he wrote 'If the King approves the suggestion we are making through Mr Crommelin I hope that we shall establish the linen manufacture more firmly.'[59] The problem, again, was not with the King: 'I am much mortified', he wrote to Vernon,

---

56   Vignoles–Duroure papers, correspondence 26A, Huguenot Library (London).

57   P. Kelly, 'Lord Galway and the Penal Laws', in Caldicott *et al.* (eds), *The Huguenots and Ireland*, pp. 239–84.

58   G. E. Cokayne's *The Complete Peerage* lists no sons of the third Viscount Clanmalire, however (p. 549 n. 59); Agnew (*Protestant Exiles from France*, vol. 2, p. 162 n.), correcting Luttrell, has them as grandsons of the Earl of Clanrickard: CSPDom., 1698, p. 202.

59   Ibid., p. 162.

by the vote of the Commons and I fear that your House will resent the unceremonious way in which our Commons dealt with the Linen Bill. However, if there were any hope that the English Commons would leave the matter alone, I am convinced we might establish the linen manufacture there in a short time, and to advantage, for both the soil and the people are admirably suited.[60]

More intractable than the Irish or English Commons over wool or linen were the Bishops in the Irish House of Lords, who blocked toleration of Presbyterians, already granted to French Calvinists and Quakers. Galway felt that the Ulster Presbyterians were 'now trying to compel the government to oppose them openly' because of the lack of support they had received.[61] Yet he counselled patience and moderation towards them, as their loyalty could be crucial should Scotland rebel, or the Jacobites invade. It took 20 years for Protestant Ireland to extend to Presbyterians what was taken for granted by non-conforming Huguenots and Quakers, though still denied to the Catholic majority.

Added to Ruvigny's difficulties over Portarlington was a ceaseless demand from the Members of Parliament for the disbanding of the regiments, mainly Huguenot, which had fought under Schomberg and Ginkel ten years earlier. One of his many letters about the latter expresses at once his concern, his predilection for Ireland as a home for his men, and his sensitivity to Irish feelings about their bounty. He wrote to Vernon that he was inclined to do all he could for Captain Gignoux of Colonel Buchan's regiment,

> but fail to understand what charm London has for him. He could live here with his family cheaper and would be more sure of his pay. The People here would also be better pleased; they complain of the absence of those to whom they give so much money. Persuade him to come here if you can.[62]

His concern did not end there. Two years later he wrote to Vernon, recalling his recommendation that Gignoux come 'to this country for a small pension' and continuing, 'the poor fellow died two or three days ago leaving a widow and seven children. I am writing to Mr Blathwayt on their behalf: please give us your assistance. The pension was 3s [per day]: could you not save two for the family?' The same letter reported the death of Monsieur Gally with the request that his 5s a day 'might do for Monsieur de La Pesne'.[63] On behalf of the officers of the Huguenot regiments he ceaselessly appealed to Vernon and Blathwayt, from Dublin Castle (once from Laughlinstown), sometimes at length when he had a close personal connexion, as with 'Mr de Bostaquet, aged pensioner receiving five shillings a day' and his son ('the little boy, and my godchild').[64]

---

60 Ibid., p. 235.
61 J. C. Beckett, *Protestant Dissent in Ireland* (London, 1948), p. 35.
62 CSPDom., 1697, p. 29.
63 Ibid., 1699, p. 251.
64 BL, Add. MS 9,718, fol. 81, Galway to Blathwayt, 12 February 1700.

His papers contain a few references to his care for 'other ranks'.[65] Evidence of his connexion with the Royal Hospital, Kilmainham, the Duke of Ormonde's 1680 Dublin foundation (predating the Chelsea equivalent by two years), exists in his presentation in 1697 of his full-length portrait still hanging in the great hall. His name was perpetuated until the nineteenth century in Galway Walk, a footway linking Watling Street with Kilmainham.[66] But his commitment spread far beyond his comrades in arms, to others for whom he felt responsible, above all to the Huguenot community at large. In 1700 he corresponded with Vernon about the relief funds for Vaudois and Palatinate refugees as well as for the Huguenots in Boston and Virginia. The sum in question, about £3,800, wrote Vernon, 'we understand by Lord Galway ... will be paid in Ireland in sterling or in bills drawn on Whitehall', using the balance of funds raised for the relief of the Vaudois in earlier years.[67]

Galway's scorn for the charms of London adds to the impression of a stern, joyless old Calvinist. Saint-Evremond's letters have left us clues to a private life of a different character. They depict a connoisseur, a lover in his youth and a philosopher. He wrote to the Huguenot, Pierre Silvestre, one of the King's physicians and an architectural adviser of the Duke of Montagu, on the landscaping of Boughton in 1700:

My Lord Galway, an expert in all things, said to me that the waterfall at Boughton is most perfect and the most complete that he ever saw; that there are larger ones at Versailles and Chantilly; but that, if he had to give a model of these kinds of works, he would give the waterfall at Boughton to the prejudice of all others.[68]

Saint-Evremond's only published letter to Galway congratulates him on his colonelcy of the Blue Guards and then discourses on wine, referring to the wine merchant they have in common, Monsieur de Puisieux: 'You were formerly a lover, and perhaps believe that the term 'lover' is profane [He ends:] Your very humble and very obedient servant, and little subaltern philosopher'.[69]

Galway's official duties in Dublin were well carried out, according to Lord Chancellor John Methuen, who told Shrewsbury:

The people in general seem reasonable and will be convinced when they see the Government intend the King's service only and not their own. My Lord Galway's prudence and application to business and the Marquis [of Winchester] his good intention and easy humour please all people, and keep them very well together; which gives them an advantage no Government here hath yet held.[70]

He increased the measure of praise soon after:

---

65   Ibid., fol. 134 (list of corporals under Lord Galway's command), fol. 198 (request for payments to NCOs and Miremont's Dragoons).

66   N. Burton, *History of the Royal Hospital, Kilmainham* (Dublin, 1834), p. 214.

67   CSPDom., 1700, p. 307.

68   *Oeuvres de Saint-Evremond*, ed. R. de Planhol (3 vols, Paris, 1927), vol. 3, p. 211.

69   Ibid., pp. 248–9.

70   HMC, *Buccleuch and Queensberry*, vol. 2, pt. 1, p. 483.

My Lord Marquis [of Winchester] really exceeds my expectation and applies himself to
business more than I could have imagined ... My Lord Galway is certainly an extraordinary
man in every respect; and the country are generally very satisfied and pleased with
everything they do.[71]

Others were critical, certainly those in the Presbyterian interest:

He had little experience in political affairs, and scarcely any knowledge of the country he
governed; and though sincerely desirous of discharging his high trust to the satisfaction
of the King, and for the welfare of the people of Ireland, his administration was far from
proving successful or popular.

So wrote J. S. Reid, nineteenth-century historian of the Presbyterian church in
Ireland.[72] Galway himself suffered from intrigues and enmities about the castle.
Lampoons were circulated in 'some verses made in My Lord Galway's time against
some who were not thought so much his friends as they should be'.[73] Swift took a hand
on the other side, but his verses referring to 'Lord Collway' and 'Lord Dromedary'
(Drogheda, whose imminent arrival as Lord Justice makes 'Lord Collway's folks ...
all very sad') are harmless enough, compared to his other execrations.[74] Governing
mostly alone, despite Methuen's fine words to Shrewsbury, he was plagued too by
money shortages. He complained to Vernon:

I am constantly here and I support the greater part of the cost of government ... I am
reduced to borrowing and thanks to my position and my good reputation I have been able
to raise some money, but as I have no funds my credit will not last long.

His regiment, like the other Huguenot units, had been 'broke' and he had lost
£1,600 from that source. His emoluments were down to £2,648. The same letter,
characteristically, asked for funds for the Marquis d'Arzilliers, another noble
Huguenot refugee, serving as English ambassador in Geneva, without funds.[75] He
suffered also from the number of 'hangers on' about him, as Vernon told a petitioner
on behalf of a young officer seeking a place in Ireland.[76]

In July 1700 a misfortune befell Galway, then 52, which was to cause him untold
suffering in the years left to him. He told Vernon that he had had 'a severe attack of
gout, the first I have ever had. I am beginning to walk ...'[77] Perhaps his recall nine
months later seemed providential: in the quiet of Rookley, the Hampshire country
estate he had acquired at King's Somborne near Winchester, he could garden, write
and read, enjoy some social life with Lady Russell nearby at Stratton Park and look
after his deteriorating physical state. In February 1702 he wrote from Rookley

---

71   Ibid., p. 491.

72   J. S. Reid, *History of the Presbyterian Church of Ireland* (Belfast, 1867), p. 458.

73   HMC, *Marquess of Ormonde*, vol. 8, p. 272.

74   *The Poems of Jonathan Swift*, ed. H. Williams (Oxford, 1958), p. 70.

75   CSPDom., 1699, p. 139.

76   Ibid., p. 235.

77   Ibid., 1700, p. 91.

warmly to his successor – Shrewsbury having pleaded ill health, the viceroyalty had fallen to the Duke of Ormonde.[78]

He had performed some final duties for King William in 1701, travelling to Het Loo with Marlborough and conducting an embassy to the Elector of Cologne. Nine days after his letter to Ormonde from Rookley, the King was dead, and Rookley must have seemed secure as a home for his remaining years. Only two years later he was called into public life again, to enter Queen Anne's service abroad for a seven year stretch in which he was put through the Job-like trials that have given him his place in history.

V

Those seven years in which he commanded the English army in Spain and served later as ambassador and military commander in Portugal, where again he led his troops in battle, left him a semi-invalid, dropsical and racked with gout, his arm shot off below the elbow at Badajoz in October 1705. After the stump was healed, though he had to be lifted on to his horse like a child, he fought on, only to lose his right eye from sabre cuts at the battle of Almanza on 25 April 1707.[79] His wounds were terrible, his bodily pains almost unbearable. He constantly pleaded to be allowed to come home, but his indispensability in holding together the uneasy alliance in Spain obliged Godolphin and Marlborough, controlling events from London and Flanders, to deny his wishes.[80]

He was faced too with endless dissension, not only among the Austrian, Dutch and Portuguese soldiers and officials around him but among his own officers, especially from the eccentric, ungovernable Lord Peterborough. Though constantly seeking to undermine his authority, Peterborough was recommended by Galway, who seems to have been a man without jealousy, as his successor when at last he was allowed to relinquish his command.

His footnote in the history of Europe, sadly, is as the French general who was disastrously defeated in April 1707 at Almanza, the key battle of the campaign. The French, under the English Duke of Berwick, James II's illegitimate son, humiliatingly defeated the English led by the Frenchman Galway. Galway's culpability will always be a matter for debate.[81] There is no lack of historians who have blamed him for Almanza, and among his contemporaries Peterborough led the pack in the Lords demanding his acceptance of guilt. Marlborough and the Whig leaders stood by him.

---

78 HMC, *Ormonde*, vol. 7, p. 762b.

79 W. S. Churchill, *Marlborough: His Life and Times* (4 vols, London, 1933–8), vol. 3, p. 43

80 *The Marlborough–Godolphin Correspondence*, ed. H. L. Snyder (3 vols, Oxford, 1975), vol. 2, p. 734.

81 See, for example, *A Detection of the Earl of Gallway's Conduct at Almanza ... in the Following Original Letters Writ by M. Schonenberg, the Dutch Ambassador at Lisbon, to the States; the Count de Noyelle, the Dutch General in Spain, to M. Schonenberg; Brigadier Drinborn (who was in the battle) to Count de Noyelle; the Count of Cordona, Governour of the Kingdom of Valencia* (London, 1711).

'I find Lord Galway in very bad circumstances', wrote Marlborough in June 1707, 'For my own part I think him incapable of being guilty: but if there be no confidence, the consequences must be fatal.'[82] He did allow himself the view that 'it appears that the enemies were very much stronger than Lord Galway, which makes it strange that by choice they should go to attack them in a plain'.[83] Defoe perpetuated the story that Galway had been fed false information by Irish agents of the enemy.[84] All agreed that the flight of the Portuguese cavalry from the field proved fatal, though their infantry fought on. Galway countered the charge that they should not have been given the right wing with the sober fact that they would not otherwise have fought at all.[85]

In that life of contrasts, the disaster of Almanza can be set against the judgement of a writer who will be read by generations whose historians will alternate in their views. Winston Churchill thus describes the aftermath of 'this savage battle, the accounts of which are both scanty and obscure':

> Considering how destructive was the defeat of Almanza, the rally and front presented by Galway were praiseworthy indeed. Crippled, wounded, beaten, discredited, distrusted in the vilest manner, a foreigner hated in England, an intruder in a Spanish brawl, he never for a moment ceased to wage war upon the enemy. He gathered together the fragments of his shattered army; he yielded no post without stubborn fighting, and, in October, after five months of apparently hopeless struggle, he was still at the head of a coherent force of upwards of 15,000. [He ends:] There is nothing known about Galway that is not to his honour.[86]

From March 1708 Galway endured his last 18 months in the Peninsula, as envoy extraordinary and commander-in-chief in Portugal. His lowest point came when, deserted again by the Portuguese cavalry, he was heavily defeated at the Caya, wounded, his horse shot under him, his *aide-de-camp*, Lord Henry Powlett (son of his fellow Lord Justice Winchester, now Duke of Bolton) captured and, according to Peterborough's very partisan biographer, he himself 'wandering about for a night alone, with difficulty avoiding capture'.[87] Abel Boyer recorded Galway's 'capacity and courage' in the action.[88]

More than two years before, Godolphin had written to Marlborough: 'My poor old Lord Galway continues so very pressing to retire and come home that I really think it would be too great a barbarity to refuse it to him.'[89] Marlborough's view

---

82 *The Marlborough–Godolphin Correspondence*, ed. Snyder, vol. 2, p. 727.

83 Ibid., p. 734.

84 D. Defoe, *The Memoirs of Capt. George Carleton, an English Officer who Served in the Two Last Wars against France and Spain ... Containing an Account of the Conduct of the Earl of Peterborough, etc.* (London, 1728; reprinted 1854), p. 386.

85 Agnew, *Protestant Exiles from France*, vol. 1, p. 211.

86 Churchill, *Marlborough*, vol. 3, p. 264–5.

87 F. S. Russell, *The Earl of Peterborough and Monmouth: A Memoir* (2 vols, London, 1887), vol. 2, p. 124; see also Agnew, *Protestant Exiles from France*, vol. 1, p. 304.

88 A. Boyer, *The History of the Reign of Queen Anne, Digested into Annals* (11 vols, London, 1703–13).

89 *Marlborough–Godolphin Correspondence*, vol. 2, p. 727, 1 November 1706.

at that time was that 'should he leave that service everything there must turn to confusion'.[90] The war had not been won, English hopes had begun to die, a patched up peace was in sight, and Galway was at last free – though not yet for an honourable retirement. He had first to appear at the bar of the House of Lords with his second-in-command, Lord Tyrawley, who had led the left wing at Almanza. They were interrogated before two lengthy debates, both of which ended in divisions that went against them, on strictly party lines. His censure was much modified by the fact that he had acted according to a council of war.[91]

The general public were, as usual, less engaged, and, paradoxically, Galway, in the hour of his humiliation, found not only his friends firmer than ever, but the general public for the first time on the side of what one pamphleteer called the 'aged General, maimed and covered with wounds, by birth a foreigner, by sentiments and inclinations an honest Englishman'.[92]

VI

He was allowed less than four years of rural peace at Rookley, where his public activities were few, and mostly in the Huguenot refugee interest. He worked for the release of Huguenot *galèriens*, and presented to the new king, George I, a loyal address from the French Protestant refugees of London, and another from those Huguenots who had been released from the galleys through English pressure. The new king assured him of his protection, and was soon to do more.[93] The Prince and Princess of Wales presented to the French church at Portarlington a splendid communion set by the Huguenot goldsmith David Willaume, and a new church bell recording the gift *'promovente illustrissimo Comite Henrico de Galloway'* (a gift from the illustrious Henry, Earl of Galway). In August 1715 he was appointed to his last public office – to be Lord Justice in Ireland for a second term, and again with a young and untried Peer, the Duke of Grafton (whose father, one of Charles II's offspring, had been killed at Cork, serving under Marlborough, in 1690).

Joseph Addison, disappointed of his hopes of a secretaryship, recorded that Galway had set off ahead of Grafton 'and as his Lordship's marches are but slow, it is probable that the Duke of Grafton may overtake him … The Duke of Grafton is a perfectly good-humoured man', he added, 'and we would have been too happy might he have learned the arts of government under such an associate as I could have wished him.'[94] Galway, despite his increasing physical problems and deafness, applied himself with vigour in the two parliamentary sessions ahead.

90   Ibid., p. 734, 9/20 November 1706.

91   Agnew, *Protestant Exiles from France*, vol. 1, p. 211.

92   J. Withers, *Secret History of the Late Ministry* (London, 1715). Cited in Agnew, *Protestant Exiles from France*, vol. 1, p. 211.

93   Ibid., p. 214.

94   *The Works of the Late Right Honourable Joseph Addison, Esq.: Including the Whole Contents of Bishop Hurd's Edition, with Letters and Other Pieces Not Found in any Previous Collection; and Macaulay's Essay on His Life and Works*, ed. G. W. Greene (third edition, ed. Thomas Tickell) (6 vols, New York, 1856), vol. 1, p. 86.

The major issues were, as in 1700, agriculture – the Tillage Bill, which would free so much land from raising cheap wool for the English market – and toleration of the Presbyterians, whose loyalty was needed more than ever with the Jacobites in arms in Scotland. The Tillage Bill, the 'only way', said the Lords Justices, 'left to the gentlemen of the country to improve their estates while they were under such hard restrictions of trade', was thwarted by the English parliament, probably, wrote Froude, due to 'the detestable opinion that, to govern Ireland conveniently, Ireland must be kept weak'.[95]

Despite the continued blocking of toleration measures by the Church of Ireland bishops, and continuing Catholic disaffection, the Scottish rising had not spread to Ireland. The Prince of Wales was made Chancellor of Trinity College, Dublin, with much expression of loyalty to the House of Hanover. With the failure of the Tillage Bill, Galway and Grafton wrote to Stanhope, in January 1716, of their concern that, despite the constant denials of the King's friends his enemies had been proved right, since 'all the marks they had been given of duty and affection would not procure one bill for the benefit of the nation'.[96]

He promoted education and welfare for the Irish poor but lacked support.[97] By contrast, the schools Galway had himself founded in Portarlington flourished, as did some of his unremitting work for the refugee families.[98] In September 1716 he persuaded the Lords of the Treasury to settle more Palatines in Ireland. 'Considering the use these poor people are towards improving the manufactures and strengthening the Protestant interest in Ireland it will be a charity very beneficial to the public.'[99] His work for deserving families in need included non-Huguenots. He urged the Treasury to pay a long overdue pension to John Walker, son of the late Bishop of Derry, and Governor of Londonderry, killed at the Boyne ('the papers have lain before the Lords of the Treasury for some time past'), since 'I have a particular regard for that good man and the welfare of his family.'[100]

VII

Galway's health was bad. In May 1716 Lady Russell wrote: 'I beseech God to give the consolation of his Holy Spirit to enable you to struggle with bodily pains: your resignation I have no doubt of.'[101] A few months later, a position having to be found for Viscount Townshend, who had fallen from grace in London, Galway and Grafton were recalled and the viceroyalty resumed. In retirement in England he was given

95   Lord Justices to Stanhope, 22 May 1716, quoted in J. A. Froude, *The English in Ireland in the Eighteenth Century* (3 vols, London, 1872–4), vol. 1, p. 223.

96   Ibid., p. 446.

97   Ibid., pp. 659–60.

98   S. Lewis, *Topographical Dictionary of Ireland: Comprising the Several Counties, Cities, Burroughs, Corporate, Market and Post Towns, Parishes and Villages* (2 vols, London, 1837), vol. 2, p. 465.

99   CSPDom., 1714–19 (London, 1883), p. 231.

100 Ibid., p. 141.

101 Lady Russell, *Letters*, vol. 2, p. 208.

a final task: the first governorship of the 'Hospital for Poor French Protestants and their Descendants residing in Great Britain', founded in 1718 and still flourishing, the repository of a great part of the English Huguenot tradition, its directors having also founded a century ago the Huguenot Society, now 'of Great Britain and Ireland'. His portrait was given to *La Providence*, as the Hospital soon became known (another copy hangs at Corsham Court, the Methuen family seat in Wiltshire).

La Providence was established in London, in the parish of St Luke's, and its officers and 38 directors, leaders of the Huguenot community, asked Galway only for his patronage. From Rookley and from Lady Russell's house, Stratton Park, near Micheldever, he continued to care for his officers of long ago. In August 1717 he wrote again to Captain François Duroure, assuring him of his support in seeking the reinstatement of his pension of 5 shillings *per* day, clearly recalling that he had been 'wounded by a cannon ball while commanding the premier detachment', 26 years before.[102] He had, Agnew writes, tried to have these pensions transferred to the wives, who would otherwise be penniless as widows, but Parliament's charity to the Huguenots had not improved, and his move had been rejected, with loss of pensions by many veterans.[103] We may believe what he told Duroure, also still awaiting payment for the company he had sold: 'I can never be negligent of that which was done by you to render service.'[104]

Galway's charity to scholars and pastors continued to the end. His last known letter, from Lady Russell's at Stratton in August 1719, concludes correspondence about the support for a young Vaudois trainee for the pastorate in Piedmont, following on another Vaudois protégé, Giraud.[105]

He died at Stratton on 3 September 1720 and was buried in Micheldever churchyard, 'the grave never closing over a braver or more modest soldier'.[106] His was a life of great reverses and glories, contradictions and paradoxes. A French Protestant exile had three times ruled Catholic Ireland, with constructive sympathy. A heroic cavalry leader who had triumphed over England's enemies was slighted by the English, who took from him the estate granted him in compensation for that which he had lost in France by fighting for them. As Commander-in-Chief in Spain he had lost the key engagement of the campaign, the disastrous battle of Almanza, was made to answer for this before Parliament and yet, though earlier ridiculed as the French general beaten by an English one, was acclaimed by the public as a hero, and closely supported throughout by the military genius of the age. Galway was a patently honourable and virtuous man in a society whose standards of public and private morality were low. He had given up high office, estate and fortune in his native land for his Protestant faith, yet was accused, by Dean Swift, of being 'of no

---

102 Vignoles–Duroure papers, Galway to F. Duroure, 10 August 1717.

103 Will of The Right Honourable Henry de Massue, Earl and Viscount of Galway, and Baron of Port Arlington in the Kingdom of Ireland, 7 December 1720: Prerogative Court of Canterbury, Shaller Quire Numbers: 246–269, 11/577; Agnew, *Protestant Exiles from France*, vol. 1, pp. 186–7.

104 Vignoles–Duroure papers, Galway to F. Duroure.

105 Bod. Lib., Rawlinson Coll., C933, 114–20, p. 133.

106 Robert Dunlop in *DNB*.

religion'. A Calvinist of plain dress and manners, most of the small details of his interests reveal a lover of wine, women, landscaping and philosophy, and come from the Catholic epicure Saint-Evremond, who wrote, implying a necessity to do so: 'I will dispute with everyone that regard and friendship which one must have for you. I respect the virtue, good qualities, philosophy, and capability [you possess] in all things.'[107]

The lowest point in his long life was probably his Iberian tribulations, yet among many bequests to godchildren, servants and the poor (the bulk of his estate having been left to Lady Russell), his will, dated three days before his death, allowed £300 to

> Domingo Roca of Alicant in Spain, gent. [who] did formerly buy a certain number of mules in Spain by my order, but for the public use … if the government shall not pay and satisfy the said Domingo Roca for the said mules within two years of my decease.[108]

We must hope that his executors, or the Treasury, settled this debt of honour incurred by such an honourable man despite the snakes-and-ladders that went on beyond the grave: his fortune was in South Sea stock ('where he made great mischief', wrote a disappointed beneficiary). Only two-thirds was recovered, six years later.[109]

He left no heir to his titles but, collaterally, his French marquisate was claimed by later generations, who settled in England. A holder in the twentieth century was a prominent Roman Catholic and a leader of the vestigial Jacobite League in England, thus adding posthumously to the contradictions that beset Henri Massue de Ruvigny during his long and turbulent life.

---

107 *Oeuvres de Saint-Evremond*, ed. de Planhol, vol. 3, p. 249.

108 Agnew, *Protestant Exiles from France*, vol. 1, p. 243.

109 E. B. Vignoles, 'The MS Memoirs of Pierre de Cosne', *Proceedings of the Huguenot Society of London*, 9/3 (1911): 539.

Chapter 5

'Janisaries, and spahees and pretorian band'
Perceptions of Huguenot Soldiers in Williamite England[1]

David Onnekink
Universiteit Utrecht/Universiteit Leiden, The Netherlands

During the Glorious Revolution a large number of Huguenots joined the Dutch *stadhouder*'s army and provided it with an important numerical and moral impulse.[2] They formed a key element in William's international invasion army and were regarded by many as saviours of the Protestant religion in England. However, soon they were also considered to be foreign mercenaries, esteemed by an increasingly unpopular king who tried to build up a standing army. The Huguenot regiments serving in the army of William III have enjoyed a good reputation among historians, earning praise for their bravery, battlefield skills and religious fervour, but little attention has been paid to the negative allusions to their reputation.[3] Moreover, most studies have mainly concentrated on the military contribution of the regiments, rather than on their symbolic role in the Williamite cause.

The King-*Stadhouder* would suffer criticism from various corners during the 1690s. Jacobites attempted to completely discredit the Williamite regime, whereas Country ideologists were critical of the centralising tendencies of William's government as a result of the war. They could draw from various discourses and traditions to support their case, but two of these stood out. Firstly, the standing army had often been regarded as a threat to English liberties as it could become an instrument by which an absolute king could subject the nation. Control over the standing army had been one of the contributing factors leading to the Civil War in 1642 and nearly so in 1688, and would become the object of parliamentary debate again immediately after the Nine Years' War. Secondly, drawing from a long tradition of xenophobia, William was criticised for being a Dutchman introducing an alien style of government, by many seen to be prejudicial to the English interest. William

1   I would like to thank Tony Claydon and Charles-Edouard Levillain for their comments, and Kate Delaney for editing the text. Any shortcomings remain my own.

2   M. R. Glozier, *The Huguenot Soldiers of William of Orange and the Glorious Revolution of 1688: The Lions of Judah* (Brighton, Portland, 2002).

3   For example C. E. Lart, 'The Huguenot Regiments', *Proceedings of the Huguenot Society of London*, 9 (1911): 515–16.

had difficulties legitimising his kingship, and slating foreigners became a way of criticising the King himself. These two main rhetorical strands came together in the verbal attacks on William's foreign soldiers, who had come to epitomise the evils of the King-*Stadhouder*'s regime. This chapter seeks to explore the identification of the Huguenot soldiers with the government of William III, and to provide an analysis of the tension in this image of the Huguenots, as saviours of the Protestant religion on the one hand, and foreign mercenaries on the other.

I

Immediately after the Revolution the Huguenot soldiers were received with acclamation and respect, especially the aged Duke of Schomberg, who was naturalised and made a Knight of the Garter on 3 April 1689, and appointed Master of the Ordnance and General of all William's forces.[4] He was the only foreigner, apart from the Earl of Portland, to become a privy councillor.[5] Schomberg was praised in Parliament in early 1689. Sir Robert Howard, in a debate on 24 April, described him as 'one of the greatest captains in the world', and reminded his fellow MPs that he 'has had his estate and pensions all seized in France, and he has waved all things in this world to serve you and his religion'.[6] Although the Duke commanded universal respect, not everyone concurred with a proposal to lavishly reward the Huguenot officer.

Robin Gwynn has admirably narrated the history of French immigration in England throughout the seventeenth century, mapping the vicissitudes of their reception.[7] After 1685 sympathy ran high for the Huguenots, not just for the sake of their own misfortunes, but also because it highlighted the problems England itself was experiencing. If a Catholic king such as Louis XIV could establish absolutism and persecute Protestants, might not James II do the same in England in the near future? Although Huguenots brought in skills and capital that could be utilised, the English also had deep reservations about the influx of competing foreign labourers. It seems that their coming incited mixed feelings among the English population.

The Huguenot soldiers arriving with William were seen to be supporting the maintenance of the liberties and Protestant religion of England, but were also criticised for being foreign mercenaries. The favour shown by King William to his foreign officers amplified such sentiments. There was no doubt that William had a particular

---

4   On Schomberg, see M. R. Glozier, *Marshal Schomberg, 1615–1690: 'The Ablest Soldier of His Age': International Soldiering and the Formation of State Armies in Seventeenth-Century Europe* (Brighton, Portland, 2005).

5   D. C. A. Agnew, *Protestant Exiles from France in the Reign of Louis XIV* (Edinburgh 1866), p. 62.

6   *Cobbett's Parliamentary History of England. From the Norman Conquest, in 1066, to the Year 1803 etc.* (12 vols, London, from 1809), vol. 5, p. 234.

7   R. Gwynn, *Huguenot Heritage: The History and Contribution of the Huguenots in Britain* (Brighton and Portland, 2001).

esteem for his Dutch friends,[8] but also the Huguenots in his entourage. A number of highly acclaimed Huguenot officers such as Henri Massue de Ruvigny, later Earl of Galway, and the Duke of Schomberg were well regarded by the King. Schomberg's son, Meinhard, the third duke, became acquainted with William's favourite, the Earl of Portland, and rented his house on Pall Mall.[9] The Huguenot commanders were thus identified with the King-*Stadhouder*'s regime, and were sometimes part of his most intimate circle. Portland, employed a number of Huguenots rather than Englishmen in his service,[10] and the Scottish High Commissioner, the Duke of Hamilton, had appointed a French refugee as his page.[11] These connections fostered the impression that William's entourage consisted of foreigners, either Dutch or French.

Antipathy against foreigners was first expressed in pamphlets questioning the motives of the invaders. Jacobite pamphleteers in particular bitterly accused the Huguenot soldiers of betrayal and ungratefulness; whereas many had been received by James II when they had to flee France, they forsook him in 1688:

> Nor has the compassionate and merciful king been requited as he ought and deserved by the French refugees, to whom he made his kingdoms both an asylum and sanctuary, and his own treasure, and the wealth of his people, a fund of succour and subsistence, when they knew not where with safety to hide their heads, nor how to get bread to preserve them from starving; but notwithstanding all the 'Hossanahs' they gave him at first, they were many of them in a little time the forwardest to cry 'Crucify him'; and, contrary to all the measures of discretion and prudence, as well as of rebellion, and have taken arms in great numbers for supporting the usurper.[12]

Nathaniel Johnstone's notorious Jacobite pamphlet *The Dear Bargain; or, A true Representation of the State of the English Nation under the Dutch* (1690) as well blamed the 'French refugees, who had been so charitably received, and liberally relieved here', for betrayal, as they were now fighting James in Ireland.[13]

The most visible manifestation of Williamite rule and the influx of foreigners was the standing army. It is difficult to determine how many Huguenots were serving, as many contemporary sources speak of 'Dutch troops' even when German or French regiments are referred to. Huguenots had continued to serve in the army and a number

---

8   See. D. Onnekink, '"Dutch Counsels": The Foreign Entourage of William III', *Dutch Crossing*, 29 (2005).

9   Agnew, *Protestant Exiles*, pp. 85–6.

10   On Portland's relation with Huguenots, see D. Onnekink, *The Anglo-Dutch Favourite: The Career of Hans Willem Bentinck, 1st Earl of Portland (1649–1709)* (Aldershot, 2007).

11   National Archives of Scotland, GD 406/1/6451, Duke of Hamilton to his wife, 2 November 1689. Gaspard Chambon, formerly a surgeon in France, and Pierre Lacoste, were two Huguenots who served Hamilton: R. K. Marshall, *The Days of Duchess Anne: Life in the Household of the Duchess of Hamilton, 1656–1715* (Edinburgh, 2000), pp. 67–8. Thanks to Matthew Glozier for the latter reference.

12   'Whether the Preserving of the Protestant Religion was the Motive unto, or the End that was Designed in the late Revolution' (1695), in *A Collection of Scarce and Valuable Tracts*, ed. W. Scott (13 vols, London, 1809–14), vol. 9, pp. 552–3.

13   N. Johnstone, 'The Dear Bargain; or, a true Representation of the State of the English Nation under the Dutch. In a Letter to a Friend', in *Collection*, ed. Scott, vol. 10, p. 361.

of vacancies in the fleet were reserved for French Protestants.[14] Under William as king, England employed a multitude of auxiliary troops, mostly Scandinavian and German, but only the French Protestants formed part of the English Establishment as such. John Childs estimated that some 1,000 of them served in the English army, 700 of whom were part of a Huguenot regiment, the remaining 200–300 were scattered over the ordinary English regiments.[15] Separate French regiments were created before the Irish campaign: three infantry units under Colonels François du Cambon, Pierre Massue de La Caillemote and Isaac Monceau de La Melonière (all three of whom had accompanied William during the invasion of 1688) and two of cavalry commanded by Schomberg and his son.[16] The cavalry regiments were made up of Huguenots formerly serving in the Dutch Blue and Red Guards. The regiments of Schomberg and La Caillemotte were taken over by Henri Massue de Ruvigny and Pierre de Belcastel respectively after the Battle of the Boyne. In 1695 Armand de Bourbon, Marquis de Miremont, raised a regiment of dragoons in Ireland. Ruvigny also raised two regiments consisting of Huguenots in Piedmont, paid for by the Duke of Savoy, Vittorio Amedeo.[17]

II

The 'invaders' were initially well received and regarded as well-behaved. Narcissus Luttrell, the parliamentary diarist, who witnessed a regiment of French Protestants marching through London, thought them 'well mounted and accoutred'.[18] In January 1689 Sir John Reresby was still an exception when he wrote that 'The streets were filled with ill looking and ill habited Dutch and other strangers of the Prince's army'.[19] By March 1689, however, the Dutch Blue Guards, containing large numbers of Huguenots, became increasingly unpopular. Resentment over foreign soldiers was mounting, especially concerning their conduct during the Irish campaign. Nathaniel Johnstone complained that the foreign troops were much better off than the English soldiers in Ireland, many of whom fell ill: 'most of the surgeons and others, who were at last ordered to attend the sick, were Dutch or French, strangers to the English constitution'.[20] Interestingly, the accusation was refuted by Comte d'Avaux – now marching with the Franco-Jacobite forces in Ireland – who observed that the French refugees in Ireland suffered equally from disease.[21] Another pamphleteer thought

14 See CSPDom., 1696, p. 29, Trumbull to Lords of the Admiralty 28 Jan. 1696.

15 J. Childs, *The British Army of William III 1689–1702* (Manchester, 1987), pp. 133–4.

16 Lart, 'The Huguenot Regiments': 490; Glozier, *Huguenot Soldiers*, p. 118.

17 Childs, *The British Army*, pp. 132–3.

18 N. Luttrell, *A Brief Historical Relation of State Affairs from September 1678 to April 1714* (6 vols, Oxford, 1857), vol. 3, p. 60.

19 22 January 1689: *Memoirs of Sir John Reresby: The Complete Text and a Selection from his Letters*, ed. W. H. Speck (London, 1991).

20 Johnstone, 'The Dear Bargain', in *Collection*, ed. Scott, vol. 10, p. 364.

21 G. van Alphen, *De Stemming van de Engelschen tegen de Hollanders in Engeland tijdens de Regeering van den Koning-Stadhouder Willem III 1688–1702* (Assen, 1938), p. 94.

that William neglected his English troops, but made sure his foreign troops 'were fat and well liking'.[22] The author of *A True and Impartial Narrative* complained that Dutch and Huguenot troops were treated better by the Anglo-Dutch king: 'the most of the soldiers are 12 or 13 weeks in arrears for very subsistence ... while the Dutch and foreigners, in the same service, are punctually paid'.[23] In actual fact the Huguenots were paid last and often in arrears.[24]

Jacobites such as Johnstone were not the only ones to criticise William's evident predilection for foreign troops. William Sherlock, a non-juror, wrote: 'I believe English people will not be better pleased with Dutch, or German, or any foreign soldiers, than they are with their own countrymen.'[25] Moreover, he thought, 'English soldiers will not be extremely pleased to see themselves disbanded, or sent into other countries to hazard their lives, while their places are taken up by foreigners, who live in ease, plenty and safety'.[26] Sherlock's arguments resonated in the House of Commons during the debates on the Naturalisation Bill in the 1693/4 session and were picked up by Country MPs. Sir John Knight, a fierce opponent of the Court, for instance, rhetorically asked: 'Can any man hope to persuade me, that our forefathers would have brought foreign soldiers into England, and pay them, and naturalize them likewise, and at the same time send the English soldiers abroad to fight in a strange land, without pay?'[27]

Discontentment about foreigners in the army had been expressed in Parliament by Knight as early as 1689, but it was not until 1692 that a dispute erupted about foreign officers, led by disgruntled officers including the disgraced Earl of Marlborough. The immediate cause was the role of General Solms, who had reputedly sacrificed English troops during the battle at Steinkirk.[28] On 21 November 1692 the Commons debated on foreign officers in the English army. The opposition argued that English officers should be in charge because they were naturally more loyal and deserved to be employed by their own government. It would also enhance the coherence and efficiency of a national army. Paul Foley thought that 'This summer there was a mighty confusion in the English army; orders were given in Dutch, and French to the English, who understood neither Dutch nor French.'[29] The Paymaster-General of the army, the Earl of Ranelagh, reported to the House that although two German generals held the highest command, the offices of lieutenant-general and major-general were equally split between English and foreigners; amongst the officers of lower rank English commanders held a clear majority. The Huguenot officers with the highest rank were Schomberg (general of the cavalry), Ruvigny (major-general)

22 'Remarks upon the present Confederacy, and late Revolution in England, &c' (1693), in *Collection*, ed. Scott, vol. 10, p. 507.

23 'A True and Impartial Narrative of the Dissenters' New Plot etc.', in *Collection*, ed. Scott, vol. 9, 1692.

24 Childs, *The British Army*, pp. 135–6.

25 W. Sherlock, 'A Letter to a Member of the Convention', in *Collection*, ed. Scott, vol. 10, p. 188.

26 Ibid., p. 188.

27 Speech of Knight, printed in *Collection*, ed. Scott, vol. 10, p. 593.

28 C. Rose, *England in the 1690s: Revolution, Religion and War* (Oxford, 1999), p. 39.

29 *Cobbett's Parliamentary History*, pp. 715–21.

and La Melonière, De l'Estang and Boncours, who were now brigadiers. It should be noted that several foreigners, such as the Huguenots Schomberg and Ruvigny, or Portland and Athlone, were in fact naturalised.[30] MPs in opposition, like Foley and Sir Thomas Clarges, lost the debate for now, as even Sir Edward Seymour plausibly argued that the foreign officers had more experience.[31] The only foreign officer who was singled out for misbehaviour and arrogance was the German Count Solms, and even the King himself seemed discontented with his conduct.[32] The fact that it was a German officer who was first attacked should serve as a reminder that it was not primarily the Huguenots that figured large in the anti-Williamite propaganda, but rather the Dutch, and to a lesser extent, the German and Danish soldiers.[33]

The officers' protests were widely supported by Country MPs, such as Robert Harley and Paul Foley, suspicious of a large standing army. The most commonly heard grievance was that the foreign Huguenot soldiers contributed to William's designs to establish a standing army in England, with which he could impose a military dictatorship. Their French origin also made more plausible the accusation that William was attempting to establish himself as an absolute monarch in the French style.

Sherlock argued that William would 'keep up a standing army to quell such discontents ... and this will raise and increase new discontents, for it alters the frame of our constitution from a civil to a military government, which is one of the great grievances we have complained of'.[34] Jacobite pamphleteers would even go further, suggesting that the new government attempted to become 'absolute and arbitrary' and would enslave the English by bringing in foreign troops: Danes, Dutch and French. These troops would also be in a position to observe ports; because they were quartered in towns and got to know the roads, they posed a threat to vital security interests, as they would be able to take state secrets abroad. Moreover, Johnstone expressed concern over

> The putting the highest offices of trust and importance into the hands of [William's] own mercenary foreigners, who have no other interest or being but what depends on his fortune, like so many *bashaws*, or *beglerbegs*, upon the Grand Seignior; such as Schomberg, and Huson, Benting, Solmes, &c. All these and their janisaries, are pretended for the reduction of Ireland, and subduing of Scotland; but their last service and reward will be the enslaving of England.[35]

The Bill of Naturalisation likewise led one pamphleteer to believe that Huguenot soldiers were an instrument of William to enslave the English nation:

---

30   *Letters of Denization and Acts of Naturaliation for Aliens in England and Ireland, 1603–1700*, ed. W. A. Shaw (Lymington, 1911), *passim*.

31   *Cobbett's Parliamentary History*, pp. 715–21.

32   Ibid., p. 719.

33   Childs, *The British Army*, p. 136.

34   Sherlock, 'A Letter to a Member of the Convention', in *Collection*, ed. Scott, vol. 10, p. 188.

35   Johnstone, 'The Dear Bargain', in *Collection*, ed. Scott, vol. 10, pp. 374–5.

The consequence of this latter bill, if it pass, may more effectually enslave us to the French Huguenots and foreigners than ever we can expect from the transmarine arms. We shall then find the provident care of the Commons, in having the new-voted troops to consist of, and be officered by the king's natural-born subjects only, by this naturalization transferred to these foreigners, who must be janisaries, and spahees and pretorian band. These shall then be armed, and the only people confided in, to prevent the fear of any English desertion.[36]

The theme of a foreign king enslaving the English nation with the help of his foreign mercenary troops persistently came up in pamphlets. *The Substance of King William's Second Discourse to his Cabinet Council* presents William arguing with his parliament. If the Commons do not give him the means to conduct the war, he shall bring English soldiers to Holland, and foreign troops to England:

For by this means I shall overawe Holland by my own subjects there, and England by foreigners here, and either make them give me what money I want by way of parliament, or else set up my title of conquest, and take it where I shall see fit.[37]

William was supposed to do this with the help of refugee regiments in particular:

To strengthen myself more, I can arm the French Huguenots of whom we have here good store, and fetch over the Vaudois, if I find Savoy inclinable to make peace. I fear I must be forced to this, for I find the English an inconstant and head-strong nation, and false to their kings, nor otherwise to be ruled long but with a rod of iron.[38]

This theme was explored in great detail in *A Supplement to His Majesty's most Gracious Speech*. It first referred to examples in the past when foreigners had entered the country. Even when they had been brought in for support they had turned against the English and enslaved the country. In the past 'Lord Dane' had subjected the English, now the Dutch were bringing with them regiments of Danes and French refugees. This argument was also employed by others; one poet hoped to be saved 'from the French, the Dane, and the nasty *Myn-heer*'.[39]

The following section of *A Supplement* is of particular interest and rather unusual, as it alludes to a specific danger of the influx of armed Huguenots:

It is not unknown to you, how great a number there are of French refugees in and about this city, who are in full union with their brethren in the army; nor what military authority and power the Duke of Leinster [Schomberg's son], their countryman, hath in this kingdom; nor can it be doubted but he hath great authority and influence over them, and manages them according to such methods and councils as may best answer the ends which are driven at: That accordingly most of the French refugees, who are able to bear arms, are

---

36 'A True and Impartial Narrative', in *Collection*, ed. Scott, vol. 9.

37 'The Substance of King William's Second Discourse to his Cabinet Council', in *Collection*, ed. Scott, vol. 10, p. 590.

38 Ibid.

39 'A Litany Recommended to the Ecclesiastical Commissioners', in *Political Ballads of the Seventeenth and Eighteenth Centuries*, ed. W. Walker Wilkins (2 vols, London, 1860), vol. 2, p. 15.

actually armed and listed under distinct officers, and of whom the said duke is chief; that there have been several sums of money distributed to them, and some in particular by the said duke, in all probability to supply themselves with weapons to use upon such occasions as they shall be called to, when opportunity serves.[40]

French refugees were supposed to be buying small pistols – rather than muskets for battle – and threats had been made. Lastly, Huguenots entered England almost weekly, ostensibly to be sent to Ireland, but they stayed, 'no doubt, to augment their forces and strengthen the confederacy'.[41] A similar conspiracy was suspected by the author of *A True and Impartial Narrative*, observing that,

> the Duke of Leinster, a naturalised foreigner, is already dignified with the title of general; the French Huguenots, as is well known, are daily and nightly disciplined in their houses or out-fields, in small bodies, to learn the use of arms; *reformadoe* officers to command them are in readiness; and granting commissions for the new levies is only suspended till that bill pass. We shall then see those refugees soon strut in their buff and feathers.[42]

The features of such a Huguenot-Williamite plot resembled the Jacobite conspiracies; Huguenots would gather weapons in secret before coming out in the open and enslaving the nation. The fact that the most prominent Huguenot, the Duke of Leinster, held the highest military command in England whilst William was in Flanders, added some plausibility to the scheme. The ubiquitous fear of popery, normally connected with Jacobitism, was now projected upon French refugees, in which the older association of French influence with Catholicism was employed. If the plot seemed improbable, it touched upon the continuous fear of French invasion.

Applying the charge of Catholicism to French Huguenots was problematic, but was somewhat facilitated by discoveries of Catholics among French immigrants. The French regiments, therefore, formed a potential security risk. Charles Lart pointed to a conspiracy of a number of Catholic French in William's army in Ireland to betray the camp to James in 1689. The plot being discovered, the leaders were executed whilst the rest were imprisoned and returned to the continent, where a number of them apparently made their way to St Germain.[43] Huguenot soldiers in Ireland sometimes deserted to the Catholic enemy.[44] The Traitorous Correspondence Act of 1691 stipulated: 'That the French Protestants shall hold no correspondence with France, without a license from a Secretary of State', recognising the possibility of treason amongst French immigrants.[45] Several pamphleteers could therefore question the extent to which the Huguenot regiments really did form the Protestant and zealous core of William's army. Especially once operating in Flanders, they attracted French deserters, many of whom were actually Catholics,

---

40   Ibid.

41   'A Supplement to His Majesty's most Gracious Speech' (1693?), in *Collection*, ed. Scott, vol. 10, p. 615.

42   'A True and Impartial Narrative', in *Collection*, ed. Scott, vol. 10, pp. 462–3.

43   Lart, 'The Huguenot Regiments': 497.

44   Glozier, *Huguenot Soldiers*, p. 124.

45   HMC, *House of Lords 1690–1692* (London, 1892), p. 447.

most of these had deserted the French service this summer, and passing to Holland, and thence to England upon the report that three French regiments were levying there, had listed themselves in the same, the officers raising their companies in so much haste that they had not time to examine them very strictly.[46]

These Catholics were dismissed when the Huguenot regiments returned to Ireland after the war.[47] Some eighty Catholics had already been removed from du Cambon's regiment in Ireland.[48]

The foreignness of the Huguenots thus made it easier to target the standing army as something unnatural, and Huguenot soldiers became a twofold metaphor in a powerful confluence of anti-French and anti-army rhetorics. However, the Country opposition was split because of a curious paradox. Richard Hampden embraced the typical country-whiggish anti-standing army attitude by arguing to his fellow MPs: 'I think it is for your interest to have foreigners rather than natives, for thereby your own men will not be bred soldiers and so prevent the fear of a standing army, which I am against.'[49] Thus in his view foreigners were a necessary bulwark against the abuse of a standing army. His views were not shared by other Country Whigs such as Foley, but on balance the Whigs were more favourable to Huguenots than were the Tories. The Tories in particular suspected the Calvinist Huguenots of Whiggish sympathies, not without good reason.[50] An anonymous pamphlet on the *Avis aux Réfugiés sur leur prochain retour en France* (Opinion of the refugees on their next return to France), attributed to Pierre Bayle, even associated the French Huguenot influx with a 'spirit of revolt' (*esprit de révolte*) and endorsed absolute government.[51] In 1692 Jacques Abbadie, a former client of the Duke of Schomberg, wrote his *Defence of the British Nation* in response to the *Avis*. Whereas Bayle criticised the Glorious Revolution, Abbadie defended its principles and the role that Huguenot soldiers had played in it.[52] Still, Tories must have been particularly sensitive to such accusations. Unlike Court Tories, Country Tories such as Sir Thomas Clarges were rather concerned about the influx of foreigners. Thus, Whigs and Tories were divided, also internally, about their opinions on Huguenots. Nevertheless, Country Tories and Whigs often united in their criticism of the foreign officers and the standing army, forging a powerful union in Parliament.

The Huguenot regiments were not without defenders, either from French Protestant circles, such as Abbadie, or pamphleteers commissioned by the Court. One reply to Sherlock's pamphlet downplayed the number of foreign soldiers who were, moreover 'brought over to deliver us, and cannot presently be returned back

---

46   Quoted in J. Childs, *The British Army of William III 1689–1702* (Manchester, 1987), p. 135.

47   Childs, *The British Army*, p. 135.

48   Lart, 'The Huguenot Regiments': 490.

49   Quoted in Childs, *The British Army*, p. 75.

50   Rose, *England in the 1690s*, p. 109.

51   M. Yardeni, 'The Birth of Political Consciousness among the Huguenot Refugees and their Descendants in England (c. 1685–1750)', in Vigne and Littleton (eds), *From Strangers to Citizens*, p. 407.

52   Agnew, *Protestant Exiles*, p. 225.

to Holland'.[53] One of the more prominent and able defenders was John Somers, a lawyer and as Lord Chancellor one of William's most trusted Whig *junto* ministers. According to him, the mere fact that William employed foreign soldiers, of which there were not even many, did not signify any covert design, as it was common practice at the time among all the princes of Europe:

> Does the French king mistrust his own subjects because of his joining with them several foreign nations, as Switzers, Italians, and both English, Scotch, and Irish upon occasion; the true reason of this common practice is, that an army consisting of forces of different nations, is upon this account more formidable than it would be if it consisted of mere natives, that both those foreigners, and the natives, fighting through emulation, leave no stone unturned to outdo one another.[54]

Moreover, according to Somers, William could not trust his English troops: 'Is it not then more advisable now, and I am sure those that love their religion and the present interest will be of my opinion, to make use of this juncture of foreigners, together with the natives, to keep a little in awe the hidden Jacobites?'[55] Indeed, it may very well be the case that William thought it wise to have non-English troops in Ireland and England during his absence. It is clearly no coincidence that William appointed Huguenot commanders, such as Schomberg and then Galway, in Ireland rather than Englishmen. Many soldiers were raw recruits, as William distrusted his English veterans to fight against James in Ireland in 1689.[56] This rendered the role of the Huguenot regiments relatively more important.

Despite debates over the Huguenot regiments, they certainly did not have to bear the brunt of criticism. The main reason, of course, was that they had been the victims of an oppressive Catholic regime. Another reason may have been that many Huguenot soldiers, unlike the Dutch and Danish, really did regard England as their adopted country. Many English observers, likewise, regarded the Huguenots as an integral part of the native army; in April 1690 Narcissus Luttrell spoke of an encounter between '*our* forces commanded by Colonel Calimote [La Caillemotte]' and Irish troops.[57] Another reason why Huguenot soldiers may have been much less unpopular than the Dutch might be the fact that many of them fought abroad in the Nine Years' War, either in Ireland or Flanders and naturally did not incite xenophobia among the native English population. The King had instructed the Huguenot regiments to go to Ireland as early as the spring of 1689.[58] They served there until the end of the Irish campaign, and were transferred to Flanders in the summer of 1692.[59] They were often

---

53   'An Answer to the Author of the Letter to a Member of the Convention', in *Collection*, ed. Scott, vol. 10, p. 193.

54   J. Somers, 'A Vindication of the Proceedings of the late Parliament of England' (1689), in *Collection*, ed. Scott, vol. 10, pp. 260–61.

55   Ibid.

56   Lart, 'The Huguenot Regiments': 490.

57   Luttrell, *Brief Historical Relation*, vol. 2, p. 26 [emphasis added].

58   HMC, *House of Lords 1689–1690* (London, 1889), p. 174.

59   Luttrell, *Brief Historical Relation*, vol. 2, p. 516.

seen as Protestant heroes, especially those who fought in the Huguenot regiments under Charles, second Duke of Schomberg, and later Galway, in Piedmont.

III

Resentment towards foreign soldiers was most bitter during the anti-standing army debates after the Peace of Ryswick. By then most officers were English; in fact only the Huguenot Duke of Leinster, Schomberg's son, held high command.[60] When in December 1697 Parliament launched its first assault on the government in order to reduce the army, William worriedly confided to the Earl of Galway, then Lord Justice of Ireland: 'I am very sad to find here things so extremely animated against the poor refugees; that struck me, but you know that these kind [of things] pass here easily.'[61] To save the Huguenot regiments – hitherto operating in the Low Countries – Portland and Galway had concocted a plan to transport them to Ireland, hoping this would keep them out of the clutches of the disgruntled MPs. Expecting antipathy towards his foreign troops, William spread rumours in London in September 1697 that regiments of French Protestants and Dutch soldiers would be disbanded. Meantime, on 18 October he approved of Galway's plan to keep up troops in Ireland.[62] In November 1697 William ordered many French refugees, including the regiments of Galway, La Melonière, Marton, Belcastel and Puissar, to go to Ireland. Almost 600 officers travelled directly from Flanders to Ireland where many received pensions.[63] The struggle between King and Parliament over the standing army continued in the next session as his decision was being challenged. 'Perhaps the greatest squabble', Secretary of State James Vernon wrote to the Duke of Shrewsbury in September 1698, 'may be about some French regiments, which have been kept, as it were, concealed in Flanders, and all of a sudden are going for Ireland.'[64] William's desire to maintain the Huguenot regiments was obviously inspired by his respect for their loyalty, but also for their capacity and experience, and they had been praised and recommended by their superiors.[65] A French report from February 1698, probably meant for the French ambassador to London, Comte Tallard, noted that the French

---

60   'A List of Seven Thousand Men, appointed by his Majesty, in his late Proclamation to be the Standing Forces of this Kingdom 1699', in *A Second Collection of Scarce and Valuable Tracts etc.*, ed. J. Somers (4 vols, London, 1750), vol. 4, p. 246.

61   William to Galway, 6 December 1697, *Correspondentie van Willem III en van Hans Willem Bentinck, Eersten Graaf van Portland*, ed. N. Japikse (RGP 23, 24, 26, 27, 28; 5 vols, The Hague, 1927–33), vol. 28, p. 450.

62   L. G. Schwoerer, *'No Standing Armies!' The Antiarmy Ideology in Seventeenth-century England* (Baltimore, London, 1974), p. 163.

63   Childs, *The British Army*, p. 136.

64   Quoted in Van Alphen, *De Stemming van de Engelschen*, p. 265n. Cf. the Portland–Galway correspondence in Nottingham University Library, Welbeck Manuscripts Pw A 1114–17 and Childs, *The British Army*, pp. 194–6.

65   See Agnew, *Protestant Exiles*, p. 291.

refugee soldiers in England were very unpopular, but 'the new king will lose a great support if he is obliged to disband the regiments which he has formed of them'.[66]

An Act of Parliament declared that all foreigners would be dismissed from the army on 26 March 1699.[67] The House of Commons reserved £35,000 for the disbandment of the three remaining regiments of Huguenot infantry and cavalry in Ireland.[68] Luttrell wrote that 12 soldiers in every company were to be dismissed, and that it was generally thought all Huguenot regiments would be disbanded completely, and the soldiers given land.[69] In February 1699 some 75 French officers travelled to London, in an attempt to get naturalised. Galway had feared that the journey of many Huguenots to London would only stiffen English bias against French soldiers, but later endorsed their initiative. In the spring of 1699, however, most Huguenots were forced to sail back to the United Provinces with the Dutch Blue Guards.[70] Some 200 Huguenot officers among them were reported to be in a 'destitute' condition.[71] In June 1699 William wrote to Galway of his being 'sensibly touched ... by my not being able to do more for the poor refugee officers, who have served me with so much zeal and fidelity'.[72]

The disbandment of Huguenot regiments was inspired by several accusations prevalent amongst English soldiers and MPs. Illustrative was the effort of one Huguenot officer in Cork to defend the regiments against allegations of an English officer in Dublin who supported the disbandment. The Huguenot officer argued that he wanted to return to his home country, but could not do so, and was, therefore, content to stay on half-pay, and disbanded soldiers would be pleased to join established regiments. He refuted the allegation that Ireland had been flooded by thousands of Huguenots, saying there were 1,500 at most. 'It is reported', he continued, 'that we are so filled with papists who would have betrayed Duke Schomberg's army at Dundalk, when the most diligent scrutiny cannot produce one professed papist among us.' He concluded that these reports 'rise from designing papists or bigoted Jacobites'.[73] In Parliament as well the plight of Huguenot soldiers was the subject of heated debate. Sir Christopher Musgrave thought that the Commons should not 'give way for strangers to be in place'.[74] Sir Richard Cocks thought otherwise, saying 'they are better Englishmen than the Jacobites, the papists and other discontents'. Apparently

---

66 *Letters of William III, and Louis XIV and of their Ministers etc. 1697–1700*, ed. P. Grimblot (2 vols, London, 1848), vol. 1, p. 248.

67 Van Alphen, *De Stemming van de Engelschen*, p. 268; CSPDom., 1699–1700, pp. 43–4, 65, 68.

68 Luttrell, *Brief Historical Relation*, vol. 4, p. 486.

69 Ibid., p. 300.

70 See W. H. Manchée, 'Huguenot Soldiers and their Conditions of Service in the English Army', *Proceedings of the Huguenot Society of Great Britain and Ireland*, 16 (1938–41): 263–5; W. A. Shaw, 'The Irish Pensioners of William III's Huguenot Regiments, 1702', *Proceedings of the Huguenot Society of Great Britain and Ireland*, 6 (1902).

71 Quoted in Childs, *The British Army*, p. 136.

72 William to Galway, 1/11 June 1699, quoted in Agnew, *Protestant Exiles*, p. 122.

73 CSPDom., 1698, pp. 397–9.

74 *The Parliamentary Diary of Sir Richard Cocks, 1698–1702* ed. D. W. Hayton (Oxford, 1996), pp. 15–16.

the debate centred specifically on Huguenot soldiers, as Cocks continued: 'Sir, these men have no country unless you give them one; they have fought against their natural prince for us, they have shed their blood and spent the best of their time to preserve our lives, liberties and fortunes.'[75] In the House of Lords, the Commons' aversion towards Dutch regiments was shared, although the peers were more sympathetic to the plight of French refugee soldiers, as the Brandenburg envoy, Bonnet, reported in February 1699.[76]

One of the reasons why the Huguenot regiments had become compromised was their settling in Ireland.[77] Galway had founded Huguenot settlements in Ireland, and acted as their patron after his appointment as Lord Justice of Ireland in February 1697. Galway's lands in France had been forfeited, but he was compensated with the Portarlington estate in 1696.[78] These settlements were encouraged by the government in Dublin. In a letter to the Lord Lieutenant of Ireland, the Duke of Shrewsbury, the Lords Justices expressed their belief that 'colonies of French refugees would be very beneficial to the country, and especially for the English interest'.[79] Lobbyists defending the Huguenot interest, such as the Baron de Virazel, were well known in Westminster.[80] The French refugees received dispensation to establish their own churches in Ireland.[81] A good example is a grant of forfeited land, where a Jesuit chapel made way for a place of worship for French Protestants in the spring of 1697.[82]

The Huguenot settlements were not uncontroversial, and tension had been building for some time; in the summer of 1697 a pamphlet appeared in Ireland entitled *A Ballad against the French Protestants* and caused uproar, a prelude to the fierce debates that were to follow in subsequent years.[83] After the war the opposition in Parliament insisted on an investigation of William's Irish grants, and a Commission of Inquiries was set up to look into the forfeitures. Even before the end of the Irish campaign in 1691 William had sought ways to use the spoils of war to reward his loyal subjects. Most of those acquiring forfeited lands had fought in the Irish campaign or had been involved in Irish politics.[84] The Huguenots obtained a sizeable part of the Irish forfeitures. Galway received over 36,000 acres. 'In consideration of the many good and faithful services', the Marquis of Puissar was rewarded with almost 31,000 acres. Together they held more than 10 per cent of the total Irish forfeitures.[85] A report was made up listing a number of Huguenots receiving grants of land in

---

75 Ibid., p. 16.

76 Van Alphen, *De Stemming van de Engelschen*, p. 257.

77 For example CSPDom., 1694, pp. 51–2.

78 Agnew, *Protestant Exiles*, p. 119.

79 Lords Justices to Shrewsbury, 15 June 1697, CSPDom., 1697, p. 197; Cf. Capell to Shrewsbury, 3 January 1696, CSPDom., 1696.

80 CSPDom., 1696, pp. 5–6.

81 Proposal Galway, 21 July 1692: rejected, CSPDom., 1695 add.

82 CSPDom., 1697, pp. 113–14.

83 Minutes of the Lord Justices, 20 July 1697: CSPDom., 1697, pp. 258, 274.

84 Arnold Joost van Keppel, Earl of Albemarle, was the only one who had no connection with Ireland.

85 HMC, *House of Lords, 1699–1702* (London, 1908), pp. 34, 36.

Ireland as a reward for their services during the Irish campaign. The grants were thought excessive and would have to be utilised to support the Treasury. The harsh report of the Commission, however, must be regarded in the light of the mounting opposition against William's government. Two commissioners were reportedly anti-Huguenot, and a third, John Trenchard, was known for his pamphlet against William's standing army.[86] But the report was controversial, and at times three out of seven commissioners refused to sign the findings.[87] The Irish Resumption Bill annulled most of the grants made by the King, but an exception was made for the estate of the Earl of Athlone, who had considerably contributed to the war in Ireland, and the Earl of Galway, whose Portarlington estate harboured many Huguenot veterans.[88] But Galway in a way embodied the foreignness of William's army and entourage, and in 1700 the King was forced to replace him as lord lieutenant with the Duke of Shrewsbury.[89]

The xenophobia reached its climax with John Tutchin's venomous pamphlet *The Foreigners*, published in 1700, which neatly summed up the grudges of the 'true-born Englishmen'.[90] Not specifically targeted at Huguenots – Tutchin was taken into custody in August for criticising prominent politicians – the pamphlet succinctly captured the xenophobic mood in post-Ryswick England.[91] The Huguenot soldiers were defended by Daniel Defoe. In *The True-Born Englishman*, he praised Schomberg, and continued: 'We blame the king that he relies too much/ On strangers, Germans, Huguenots, and Dutch/ The fact might very well be answered thus/ He has often been betrayed by us/ He must have been a madman to rely/ On English gentlemen's fidelity'.[92]

The 1701 Act of Settlement banned foreign elements from the King's councils and army, but the beginning of the War of the Spanish Succession reignited the debate on French officers. In 1701 the Earl of Rochester, Lord Justice of Ireland, forced the Huguenots, who were on half-pay, and had to await orders in Ireland, to serve in the West Indies.[93] The Huguenots did not wish to leave Ireland and complained to the King. To Agnew, Rochester was a 'semi-Jacobite' who loathed the adherents to William's cause, but Rochester, a High-Church Tory, also associated the Huguenots with the Whigs.[94] Although William had wanted to maintain the Huguenot regiments in 1702, they were not retained as they were now too controversial. Those who knew better could only repeat what many experienced officers and MPs had already

---

86 J. G. Simms, *The Williamite Confiscation in Ireland, 1690–1703* (London, 1956), p. 98; H. Horwitz, *Parliament, Policy and Politics in the Reign of William III* (Manchester, 1977), p. 255.

87 Van Alphen, *De Stemming van de Engelschen*, pp. 277–9; Horwitz, *Parliament*, p. 263; Simms, *Williamite Confiscation*, p. 106.

88 Simms, *Williamite Confiscation*, pp. 88–89.

89 Luttrell, *Brief Historical Relation*, 27 June 1700.

90 J. Tutchin, *The Foreigners: A Poem* (London, 1700).

91 Luttrell, *Brief Historical Relation*, vol. 4, p. 676.

92 D. Defoe, *The True-Born Englishman and Other Writings*, ed. P. N. Furbank and W. R. Owens (London, 1997), p. 53, *vs* 1026–32.

93 See Lart, 'The Huguenot Regiments': 524–9.

94 Agnew, *Protestant Exiles*, pp. 291–2.

observed during the Nine Years' War, namely that the Huguenot regiments were well trained and highly motivated. But by then the mood had turned decisively against William III and his foreign officers. Just after the King's death, in May 1702, Colonel Henry Mordaunt (whose regiment contained a number of Huguenots) told his fellow MPs that 'though he loved his own countrymen very well he could not but own that these Frenchmen behaved themselves very well nay better than the English'.[95] But it was to no avail, and the Commons concurred with one MP who argued

> that the foreigners could not raise men, the people did not understand gibberish, and that the question was no more but to prevent foreigners not born of English parents from having command of our forces in England and that they could not think England safe under the command of foreign officers.[96]

IV

Perhaps the most tragic result of the Huguenot's identification with William's cause was that the Huguenot regiments ultimately became its victims. During the parliamentary debates concerning the standing army in 1698 and 1699, many MPs were sympathetic to the plight of the homeless Huguenots, but were unable to distinguish them formally from the hated Dutch Blue Guards. Moreover, they wished to have no visible foreign presence in the English army. This is evident in the discussions concerning measures to expel foreigners. Following the Disbanding Act, in the spring of 1699 a number of foreigners had asked for a bill of naturalisation.[97] Bonnet suggested that these naturalisations would be easily granted, because the Commons mainly objected to Huguenot regiments, not so much individual French soldiers.[98] Therefore, officers from Huguenot regiments would find it more difficult, because the aim of the measure had been to disband their units.[99] What seems clear is that there was a great deal of sympathy for the Huguenots, but not for the Huguenot regiments as such, for as the 'pretorian band' of the King-*Stadhouder* they symbolised the hated foreign standing army.[100]

The Huguenot regiments then were perceived to embody several interrelated dangers to English liberties. Firstly, they were part of William's soldiery, whom he kept after the peace had been established, and, therefore, were seen as contributors to a design of the King to keep a standing army designed to awe his subjects. Secondly, in a curious twist the association with France also touched a snare with traditional anti-French sentiments, in which French refugees could be seen as instruments to be used by William to establish an absolute and arbitrary government, similar to Louis XIV's in France. Thirdly, in a way they were associated with popery, which could be made somewhat plausible by the fact that some French soldiers appeared to

---

95   Hayton, *Diary*, p. 279.
96   Ibid.
97   Childs, *The British Army*, p. 136.
98   Van Alphen, *De Stemming van de Engelschen*, p. 268.
99   Ibid.
100 Agnew, *Protestant Exiles*, p. 291.

be Catholics. Fourthly, as foreign soldiers their presence was considered a security risk, whereas moreover the spectre of a Jacobite plot was cleverly utilised to allude to a possible French scheme instead. Lastly, they were mixed together with other foreigners and symbolised the foreignness of William's reign in general, as expressed in the Act of Settlement. John Childs has already observed this transformation of the Huguenot regiments in English public opinion; the Huguenots used to be the most obvious victims of Louis XIV, and were living symbol of the international alliance against Catholic France, but by 1702 they were associated rather with the vices of Williamite rule.[101]

More generally, the position of the Huguenot soldiers in England during the reign of King William highlighted the paradoxical complexities of the Englishmen's loyalties and identity, which were both in flux. What was the essence of Englishness and English liberties when a foreign king, aided by foreign mercenaries, was asked to protect these? Was loyalty due to the banished king who had reigned by divine right or to a monarch whose claim to the throne might be doubtful but who defended the true religion? If the Huguenot soldiers reminded the English that the defence of Protestantism was the task of all believers in Europe, it was still hard to accept that among William's army that fought Catholic France there were French soldiers, some of whom were thought to adhere to the Catholic religion. As such, the debate on French soldiers in England during this decade could also be regarded as a struggle for the English to redefine their own identity, religion and loyalty in changing political circumstances.

---

101 Childs, *The British Army*, p. 137.

Chapter 6

Schomberg, Ruvigny and the Huguenots in Ireland
William III's Irish War, 1689–91

Harman Murtagh
Irish Commission for Military History

In the latter part of 1688, just as the Nine Years' War commenced, Louis XIV was badly outmanoeuvred by his most inveterate enemy, William of Orange, who seized the English throne in the Glorious Revolution.[1] Louis reacted by sending his ally, the deposed King James II, to Ireland in March 1689. He calculated that the support of the Irish Catholics, who had raised a large army, would give James a reasonable chance of restoration. At the very least the intervention in Ireland would sufficiently threaten the stability of William's new regime to divert his military resources from operations in mainland Europe, thereby easing pressure on the French armies.[2] To strengthen James's war effort, Louis sent eight convoys of officers, troops, money, arms and munitions to Ireland in 1689–91.[3]

I

William's focus was on the continent, and he was slow to respond to the developing situation in Ireland. However, he could not ignore James's arrival there and Louis's involvement. In the summer of 1689 an expeditionary force was prepared in England. Its command was given to Friedrich Hermann von Schomberg (1615–90), who had been second-in-command to William of the Dutch force that had invaded England to topple James.[4] Of Anglo-German parentage, Schomberg's military career

---

1 S. Baxter, *William III and the Defense of European Liberty 1650–1702* (New York, 1966), pp. 222–43; J. R. Jones, *The Revolution of 1688 in England* (London, 1972); J. Childs, *The Army, James II and the Glorious Revolution* (Manchester, 1980), pp. 168–202.

2 J. G. Simms, *Jacobite Ireland 1685–91* (Norfolk, 1969); H. Murtagh, 'The War in Ireland, 1689–91', in W. A. Maguire (ed.), *Kings in Conflict: The Revolutionary War in Ireland and its Aftermath 1689–1750* (Belfast, 1990), pp. 61–92.

3 *Franco-Irish Correspondence December 1688–February 1692*, ed. S. Mulloy (3 vols, Dublin, 1983–4), vol. 1, pp. xlii–xliii.

4 CSPDom., 1689–90, p. 188. For details of Schomberg's career, see J. Kazner, *Leben Friedrichs von Schomberg, oder Schoenburg* (2 vols, Mannheim, 1789); *Allgemeine Deutsche Biographie* (55 vols, Munich, 1875–1912), vol. 32, pp. 260–62; C. de Courcelles, *Dictionnaire*

had commenced in the Thirty Years' War under the Protestant general Bernhard von Saxe-Weimar. After a short spell in Holland, he entered the French service in 1651, gaining renown and rapid promotion under Marshal Turenne. In the 1660s, with Louis XIV's secret support, he commanded the Portuguese in their struggle against Spain, overcoming immense logistical, military and political difficulties to win a series of victories, which sealed Portuguese independence. Schomberg's next employment was in England in 1673 as commander of an expeditionary force intended for an abortive invasion of Holland. Returning to France, he achieved considerable success against the Spaniards with the inexperienced Roussillon army. In 1675 he was created a marshal of France, and for the campaign of 1676 given the senior command in Flanders under Louis himself. However, at Valenciennes, he dissuaded Louis from making an attack that had the potential to destroy William of Orange's army. Reservations about his excessive prudence on this occasion, coupled with growing distaste for his Calvinism, may have accounted for the series of lesser appointments, which marked the remainder of his career in France.

Schomberg's employment abruptly ended in 1685 with the revocation of the Edict of Nantes. Having resisted a personal attempt by Louis to persuade him to abjure his Protestant faith, he retired to Portugal before moving to Brandenburg where the 'Great Elector' gave him command of his army until 1688, when he was released to join William of Orange. Despite his mercenary career and several changes of nationality, it is fair to regard Schomberg as a Huguenot. Almost certainly this would have been his own preference. The bulk of his military career had been in French service. He had become a naturalised French subject, taken a Huguenot wife and bought an estate near Paris. He shared exile and (eventually) confiscation of property with other French Protestants, and he was regarded as the unofficial general of the numerous Huguenot military *émigrés*, using his influence to find them military employment in Brandenburg, Holland and England.[5] In Ireland his

---

historique et biographique des généraux français. Depuis le onzième siècle jusqu'en 1823 (9 vols, Paris, 1820–83), vol. 9, pp. 135–7; G. E. Cokayne, *The Complete Peerage* (12 vols, London, 1910–59), vol. 11, pp. 522–7; D. C. A. Agnew, *Protestant Exiles from France in the Reign of Louis XIV* (3 vols, London, 1871, second edition); J. Childs, 'The English Brigade in Portugal, 1662–1668', *Journal of the Society for Army Historical Research*, 53/215 (Autumn 1975): 135–47; C. F. Duperrier-Dumouriez, *Campagnes du Maréchal de Schomberg en Portugal, 1662–1668* (London, 1807); J. Childs, 'A Patriot for Whom? "For God and for honour": Marshal Schomberg', *History Today*, 38 (July 1988): 46–51; J. Childs, *The Army of Charles II* (London, Toronto, 1976); J. Lynn, *The Wars of Louis XIV 1667–1714* (London, New York, 1999); G. Burnet, *History of his Own Time* (2 vols, Dublin, 1724; reprinted 1734); revised article by R. D. and H. Murtagh in *Oxford Dictionary of National Biography* (Oxford, 2004), 'Schomberg'. See also M. R. Glozier, *Marshal Schomberg, 1615–1690: 'The Ablest Soldier of His Age': International Soldiering and the Formation of State Armies in Seventeenth-Century Europe* (Brighton, Portland, 2005).

5   The number of Huguenot military *émigrés* remains uncertain: at the time of the revocation of the Edict of Nantes in 1685 the theoretical peacetime strength of the French army was about 165,000, of which at most 10 per cent were Protestants. From 1685 a royal ordinance made clear that Protestants were no longer welcome in the army. They were offered a bounty to convert, but few, it seems, did so; one estimate is that at least 3,000

partiality to the Huguenots was notorious. It was said that of his seven or eight *aides-de-camp* there, only one could speak English, and Schomberg told William that the Huguenot soldiers were worth twice the number of any other troops.[6] In England Schomberg was appointed commander of the land forces, given £100,000 by Parliament, conferred with the Order of the Garter and created a duke.[7] There was little appreciation in England of his cautious disposition. But in his 74th year he was physically and mentally fit, and the expectation was that under a Protestant soldier of such experience and reputation, the expeditionary force would have little difficulty in overcoming the Irish Jacobites.

William's concern about the loyalty of the English army made him reluctant to employ it on any significant scale against James in Ireland. Instead, much of Schomberg's force was comprised of regiments newly raised for the expedition in England, supplemented by the Irish Protestant defenders of Derry and Enniskillen. Most of the British soldiers were new to military life, or at least lacking in combat experience. To compensate for these deficiencies, two veteran Dutch battalions were included, together with four regiments of Huguenots. Although a large number of Huguenots had participated in the invasion of England, the regiments raised for Schomberg's expedition to Ireland were the first specifically French Protestant units in William's service. Each of the infantry regiments was a single battalion of 13 companies, while the cavalry regiment comprised nine troops.[8] The House of Commons was informed that the youngest and strongest of the refugees were ready to lay down their lives in defence of the Protestant religion and against the enemies of England.[9] For the Huguenots, the new units were a much-needed opportunity for honourable employment, as well as a chance to cross swords with Louis XIV. However, at about 170 the establishment of officers was insufficient for all that sought places.[10] Those that accompanied William to England were favoured for appointment

---

officers left the army, although Marshal Vauban, who was in a strong position to know, put the figure at only 600 officers and 12,000 soldiers. Incidentally, there is evidence that during the near continuous wars of the latter half of Louis XIV's personal reign, Protestant soldiers and even officers continued to be found in the armies of France: C. E. Lart, 'The Huguenot Regiments', *Proceedings of the Huguenot Society of London*, 9 (1909–11): 480, 482; J. A. Lynn, *Giant of the Grand Siècle: The French Army 1610–1715* (Cambridge, 1997), pp. 435–6.

6   CSPDom., 1689–90, pp. 201, 401.

7   He was already a Portuguese count and grandee by 1668, and there is considerable debate about whether he also received a French dukedom and peerage: Glozier, *Marshal Schomberg*, ch. 4 'Portugal'.

8   J. Childs, *The British Army of William III, 1689–1702* (Manchester, 1987), pp. 132–3.

9   *Journals of the House of Commons*, vol. 10, p. 103.

10   The standard establishment was three commissioned officers *per* infantry company (captain, lieutenant and ensign) and four *per* cavalry troop (captain, lieutenant, ensign and quartermaster). In addition each regiment would have had a small headquarters staff of major, adjutant, chaplain, surgeon and (in the infantry) quartermaster. The colonel and lieutenant-colonel of each regiment were also company or troop commander. Matthew Glozier's figure of 14 officers per infantry regiment in 1689 takes into account only the company commanders and is not, therefore, correct for the whole: M. R. Glozier, *The Huguenot Soldiers of William*

over members of the existing English refuge. William, himself a Calvinist, was well disposed towards the Huguenots, who brought to his cause military experience and ideological commitment, together with propaganda value as victims of Louis's absolutism.[11] He allowed about 500, for whom there were no appointments on the establishments, to attach themselves to the regiments as *incorporés*, or reformed officers, an arrangement whereby they received some pay while on active service, but held no command.[12] Eventually a thousand or more Huguenots are estimated to have held commissions in William's British forces, a majority of whom would have served in some capacity in Ireland.[13]

Schomberg was colonel of the nine-troop cavalry regiment, which was otherwise led by its lieutenant-colonel, Etienne de Casaubon. The infantry colonels were Isaac de La Melonière (d.1715), François du Cambon (k.1693) and Pierre Massue, Comte de La Caillemotte (k.1690). All three had accompanied William to England. La Melonière was a former lieutenant-colonel of the Anjou regiment in the French army. Du Cambon had been an engineer in the French army and was later Chief Engineer and Director-General of Fortifications in Holland. La Caillemotte was a younger son of the aged Marquis de Ruvigny et Raineval, the former *député general* of the Huguenots at the French court, who was one of the most respected of the refugees' London leaders and said to have been influential in the decision to raise the Huguenot regiments.[14] A number of other Huguenots served elsewhere in the army. The chief engineers were successively Charles Le Goulon, whom Schomberg found unsatisfactory, David Nolibois, who was killed at the siege of Killeshandra in April 1690, and François Philiponneau de La Motte.[15] Amongst several other Huguenot engineers to serve with the Williamite forces, Jean Goubet deserves particular mention for his cartographical survey of Irish fortifications, which is a valuable resource for scholars.[16]

The cavalry troopers were described as French gentlemen. However, as was common with most armies of the time, recruitment to the rank-and-file of the infantry was less select, with Swiss, Germans and Flemings brought in to make up

---

of Orange and the Glorious Revolution of 1688: The Lions of Judah (Brighton, Portland, 2002), p. 65.

11   G. C. Gibbs, 'The European Origins of the Glorious Revolution', in Maguire (ed.), *Kings in Conflict*, pp. 14–15.

12   For lists of regimental officers in Ireland, see C. Dalton, *English Army Lists and Commission Registers, 1661–1714* (6 vols, London, 1892–1904), vol. 3, pp. 26, 81–2, 118–20, 181, 205; for a list of *incorporés*, see National Army Museum, Chelsea, MS and TS, fols 1801–38, 8303–97. Useful biographical notes on many officers are to be found in Glozier, *Huguenot Soldiers*, pp. 149–59.

13   Childs, *British Army of William III*, p. 134.

14   Agnew, *Protestant Exiles from France*, vol. 1, p. 98; vol. 2, p. 1.

15   R. Loeber, 'Biographical Dictionary of Engineers in Ireland, 1600–1730', *Irish Sword*, 13 (1977–9): 30–31, 237, 251–2; F. J. Hebbert, 'The Memoirs of Monsieur Goulon', *Journal of the Society for Army Historical Research*, 69/279 (Autumn 1991): 161–5.

16   Loeber, 'Engineers in Ireland': 237; National Library of Ireland, MS 2,742.

the strengths.[17] There was considerable embarrassment in the autumn of 1689 when nearly 200 recruits turned out to be Catholics, some of whom were found to be in communication with the Irish.[18] Six were hanged and 200 sent back to England. In 1690, just after the battle of the Boyne, where they had taken casualties, the total strength of the four French regiments, including *incorporés*, was 2,800 officers and men, or about 8 per cent of the army, but in 1689 they formed about 15 per cent of Schomberg's smaller force.[19] The Huguenot cavalry was armed with sabres and pistols; the infantry had up-to-date flintlock muskets and swords, but were without bayonets, pikes or (until 1691) *chevaux-de-frise* – arrangements of spiked poles used as protective screens – which left them vulnerable to cavalry attack.[20] Jan van Wyck's Boyne paintings apparently show a Huguenot regiment clothed in grey coats, bearing two colours (or regimental flags), one blue and the other white, each with a white overall cross and a first canton *semée* of gold *fleurs-de-lis*.[21] La Caillemotte's and La Melonière's battalions were issued with *surtouts* (probably overcoats) by the autumn of 1689, but du Cambon's men had none, which left his regiment with more sick men.[22] *Gris blanc* (dull white) is mentioned as the uniform colour of *surtouts* supplied to de Belcastel's (formerly La Caillemotte's) regiment in 1691.[23] The contractors who supplied the uniforms when the regiments were first raised were still unpaid almost a year later.[24] The soldiers' pay was soon in arrears: Schomberg informed William in January 1690 that a £1,000 was due to each of the French regiments.[25] By the summer of 1691, du Cambon's men were complaining that they had received only 70 days' pay in the preceding 18 months; and the treasury books and papers contain many references to arrears and petitions for money, especially in relation to the reformed officers.[26] A novel welfare arrangement applied to the Huguenot regiments provided for deductions from their subsistence for the support of their wives and families in England.[27]

---

17 Lart, 'Huguenot Regiments': 484, 498; *The Danish Force in Ireland 1690–1691*, ed. K. Danaher and J. G. Simms (Dublin, 1962), p. 123; CSPDom., 1689–90, pp. 269–70, 510.

18 G. Story, *A True and Impartial History of the Most Material Occurrences in the Kingdom of Ireland During the Last Two Years* (London, 1691), pp. 24–5. Reports that the regiments contained French deserters are in *Négotiations de M. le comte d'Avaux en Irlande, 1689–90*, ed. J. Hogan (Dublin, 1934), pp. 495, 522, 543, 578, 604. However, the practice of indiscriminately recruiting rank-and-file, regardless of their religious affiliation, was not easily suppressed: in 1697, 700 Roman Catholics had to be purged from the regiments prior to their demobilisation: Childs, *British Army of William III*, p. 135.

19 Story, *Impartial History*, pp. 95–7.

20 *Calendar of Treasury Books, 1689–92* (hereafter CTB), pp. 136, 145, 272; CSPDom., 1689–90, p. 207.

21 Stephen Ede-Borrett, 'A Huguenot Regiment?', *Journal of the Society for Army Historical Research*, 70/283 (Autumn 1992): 204–5, n. 1351.

22 Dalton, *English Army Lists*, vol. 3, p. 119.

23 CTB, 1689–92, p. 1113.

24 Ibid., pp. 672, 830.

25 CSPDom., 1689–90, p. 401.

26 Ibid., 1690–1, p. 493.

27 CTB, 1689–92, pp. 735, 820, 876, 1013, 1429.

Desertion was always a factor in seventeenth-century warfare, and the Jacobites made sporadic attempts to persuade the Huguenots to change sides.[28] But the loyalty of the refugees to William was strong and they had little confidence in any reconciliation with Louis, La Caillemotte declaring in 1689, 'we have nothing in France, but the liberty to breathe the air'. The French officers in the Jacobite army displayed a mixture of attitudes towards their Williamite counterparts. Captain Le Bourgey of du Cambon's regiment, who was captured at the siege of Limerick in 1690 and later exchanged, was loud in his praise of the courtesy and good treatment he had received from Major-General de Boisseleau, the French Catholic governor of Limerick, and the other enemy French officers in the city.[29] On the other hand Saint-Ruth, who commanded the Jacobite army in 1691, had a reputation – at least amongst the Williamites – as a persecutor of Protestants, and there was a rumour, which proved unfounded, that he would give no quarter to French heretics in Ireland.[30] After the surrender of Galway a number of Huguenot officers spoke at length to d'Usson, one of the French generals on the Jacobite side, and told him of the unhappiness of their exile.[31] D'Usson reported to Louvois that he viewed the group with great sadness, prudently adding that he had shown his disapproval of their conduct by remaining silent during the interview.

II

Schomberg's forces, including the Huguenots, landed in Belfast Lough in August 1689. Although, with the addition of the Ulster Protestants, his army was nearly 20,000 strong, the campaign which followed was a disaster. Schomberg set out for Dublin, but his offensive came to a halt at Dundalk where he was confronted by an Irish force under James.[32] Despite strong pressure in letters from William, Schomberg, with his customary caution, declined battle.[33] In November, as the weather worsened and sickness ravaged his army, he abandoned the campaign and withdrew to winter quarters in the north. Almost a third of his men died, mainly of dysentery or pneumonia.[34] Undoubtedly Schomberg bore some of the responsibility for the *débâcle*. Always a methodical soldier, he had been unable to adjust to the improvisations needed for campaigning in Ireland. He over-estimated the capability of the Irish army at this time, and with a more aggressive and daring campaign could probably have defeated James. Nevertheless, there was also truth in his complaints

---

28 Story, *Impartial History*, p. 34; CSPDom., 1690–91, pp. 235–6; *A Jacobite Narrative of the War in Ireland 1688–1691*, ed. J. T. Gilbert (Dublin, 1892; reprinted Shannon, 1971), pp. 251–3.

29 *Mémoires inédits de Dumont de Bostaquet, gentilhomme, Normand*, ed. C. Reid and F. Waddington (Paris, 1864), p. 290.

30 Agnew, *Protestant Exiles from France*, vol. 1, p. 150.

31 *Franco-Irish Correspondence*, ed. Mulloy, vol. 2, p. 395.

32 J. G. Simms, 'Schomberg at Dundalk, 1689', *Irish Sword*, 10 (1971–2): 14–25.

33 CSPDom., 1689–90, pp. 287–8, 313.

34 K. P. Ferguson, 'The Organisation of King William's Army in Ireland, 1689–92', *Irish Sword*, 18 (1990–91): 67.

of inadequate supplies, bad transport, inexperienced troops, incompetent officers, poor artillery and deficient medical services.[35] Responsibility for these shortcomings rested, at least in part, with William's government. In the face of angry complaints from the House of Commons, it was politically expedient to scapegoat the Irish command. John Shales, the incompetent commissary-general of provisions, was arrested, and Schomberg heavily criticised. His relationship with William deteriorated. Although ill, he was not granted the permission he sought to convalesce in England, where, presumably, he might have made a defence.[36] His reputation, perhaps not altogether fairly, was severely damaged. As a contemporary predicted, his handling of the Irish campaign had 'caste such a mist upon him that the remainder of his life will not be able to dissipate'.[37] Ireland had proved 'a bridge too far' for the old French marshal.

The rest of the Huguenots, meanwhile, had acquitted themselves well. After suffering their first casualties at the capture of Carrickfergus, they were less affected by sickness at Dundalk, where, unlike the English, they had built huts for shelter.[38] Hospitals to tend the sick were serviced by French doctors.[39] La Melonière, with the French infantry, covered the retreat from Dundalk.[40] In October a detachment of grenadiers from his regiment won great praise for their spirited defence of a fort near Sligo, which they surrendered only after their provisions were exhausted.[41] The favourable terms offered by the Jacobites allowed them to march out with their arms and baggage. Sarsfield, the famous Irish leader, made an attempt to persuade them to change sides, but only one responded, only to desert again the next day with his new horse. Captain de Saint-Sauveur, the commander of this company, later died of fever at Lisburn.[42] Over the winter La Caillemotte and du Cambon, with detachments from their regiments, participated in the investment of the isolated Jacobite garrison at Charlemont, which did not surrender until May 1690.[43] The Huguenots were disliked by the rest of the army, and Schomberg thought it prudent to keep the English and French officers apart.[44] La Caillemotte attributed the bad feeling to envy of the

35 Story, *Impartial History*, pp. 41–6; CSPDom., 1689–90, pp. 231, 251, 261–2, 276–8, 283–4.

36 Ibid., pp. 320, 347, 372.

37 Ibid., p. 382.

38 R. Parker, *Memoirs of the Military Transactions ... from 1683 to 1718* (London, 1747), p. 15.

39 *Diary of Thomas Bellingham: An Officer under William III*, ed. A. Hewitson (Preston, 1908), p. 86.

40 Ibid., p. 95.

41 Story, *Impartial History*, pp. 33–4.

42 Camille de Saint-Sauveur was commissioned an infantry captain by William in the Netherlands in 1686: 'Letter Book of Moreau – Polish Ambassador at The Hague, 1687–1688', in *Townshend Papers*, vol. 3: BL, Add. MS 38,494, fol. 14.

43 CSPDom., 1689–90, pp. 534, 566; 1690–91, p. 5; *Franco-Irish Correspondence*, ed. Mulloy, vol. 1, pp. 340, 342, 391.

44 Agnew, *Protestant Exiles from France*, vol. 2, p. 232.

Huguenots' professionalism, but an English view was that the French were insolent and over-greedy in seizing provisions.[45]

For the campaign of 1690, William came to Ireland. He was greatly displeased at having to absent himself from the war on the continent, but with James in his rear, the consolidation of his position in the British Isles had become the overriding necessity, and he took the view that without his personal direction nothing would be achieved. Extensive preparations were made for the campaign, and particular care taken to address the deficiencies, which had been so evident in 1689.[46] This in itself was something of a vindication of Schomberg. New commissaries took over from Shales, and a bread-supply contract was placed with the Pereira brothers of Amsterdam. An artillery train was brought in from Holland. Wagons to the number of 550 and 2,500 draught horses supplied the army's transport, and a marching hospital and a fixed hospital addressed its health needs. Army strength was raised to 37,000, including significant contingents of Dutch and Danish professionals. A major role in the negotiations leading to the provision of the Danes was played by Frédéric-Henri, Marquis de La Forest-Suzannet, a Huguenot who had become Danish envoy in London and who, subsequently, served in Ireland as major-general of the Danish cavalry.[47] About 50 other Danish officers were Huguenots, and the French Protestants were also well represented in the officer corps of the Dutch and English regiments.[48] They were also present in the rank-and-file of at least some non-Huguenot regiments, but the numbers remain unknown. Meinhard von Schomberg, the Marshal's son who had left the French service with his father, was appointed general of the cavalry.[49]

Like Schomberg before him, William marched south for Dublin, and on 1 July 1690 was confronted by James and the smaller Jacobite army of Irish and French troops at the River Boyne, the only substantial natural obstacle before Dublin.[50] William's opening move was to send Meinhard von Schomberg upstream with about 10,000 men to threaten the Irish flank in the vicinity of Rosnaree. This drew the bulk of the Irish army to the west, leaving the Williamite forces to focus their main attack at Oldbridge and the fords downstream from it, where they had overwhelming superiority. The Huguenot regiments of La Caillemotte and du Cambon followed the Dutch Guards across the river in this sector shortly after 10 o'clock in the morning.[51] Their commitment to battle at such an early stage was a tribute to William's

---

45   CSPDom., 1689–90, p. 269; Story, *Impartial History*, pp. 25, 27.

46   Simms, *Jacobite Ireland*, pp. 136–7; Ferguson, 'King William's Army in Ireland': 68–71.

47   *Danish Force in Ireland*, ed. Danaher and Simms, pp. 7, 11.

48   Ibid.; Dalton, *English Army Lists*, vol. 3, *passim*; Childs, *British Army of William III*, pp. 132–8. I am grateful to Vivien Costello for suggesting this figure, which is based on her examination of the officer rolls of the Danish corps in the National Library of Ireland, microfilm P2836.

49   G. Story, *A Continuation of the Impartial History of the Wars of Ireland* (London, 1693), p. 28.

50   G. A. Hayes-McCoy, *Irish Battles: A Military History of Ireland* (London, 1969; reprinted Belfast, 1990), p. 224.

51   Ibid., p. 231.

appreciation of their quality. Schomberg encouraged them with the words: 'Forward, my friends, gather your courage and resentment; there are your persecutors.'[52] If he intended the term persecutors to refer to the French infantry brigade on the Jacobite side, it was true only in a general sense. King Louis's Frenchmen were not at Oldbridge, but were part of the force James sent upstream to counter Meinhard von Schomberg. At no stage did the Williamite and Jacobite French regiments confront each other directly.[53] The Irish infantry was driven off, but as the Williamites deployed on the south bank they came under pressure from the cavalry of the Irish right wing. The Huguenot battalions, lacking defensive weapons, could not prevent the Irish squadrons breaking through their ranks and inflicting casualties.[54] La Caillemotte was mortally wounded in the thigh, but, we are told, continued to encourage his men as he was carried back across the river, calling out: 'Go forward, my children, go forward; to glory, to glory!'[55]

Schomberg had crossed the ford to rally the faltering Williamites, probably the Dutch Guards. On the south bank he became involved in the *mêlée* with the Irish cavalry. Surrounded by his *aides* and wearing his blue garter sash, he made a prominent target and was cut twice in the head by the Irish troopers before being killed by a carbine bullet in the neck.[56] It was thought by some to have been a stray shot from his own side, but two Jacobite accounts attribute the deed to a supernumerary officer of the Irish Horse Guards, who was quickly also killed.[57] However, the Irish cavalry was eventually repelled as more infantry, including La Melonière's regiment, crossed the river to consolidate the Williamite position at Oldbridge. A mile downstream at Drybridge William crossed with the left wing of his horse, including the Huguenot cavalry regiment.[58] In the vicinity of Donore, south of the river, the two French squadrons were involved in confused fighting in broken ground and lost more than 20 officers killed or wounded.[59] The casualties included the two squadron commanders, de Casaubon and de Belcastel, both of whom were wounded, the latter fatally. Eventually the Irish were driven back, and their retreat became a rout as they converged on Duleek.

Of more than 50 contemporary accounts of the battle of the Boyne, three are by Huguenot soldiers, who took part in the engagement. The best known is that of Isaac Dumont de Bostaquet, Seigneur de La Fontelaye, an *incorporé* with Schomberg's

---

52   Ibid.; Story, *Impartial History*, p. 85; Parker, *Memoirs*, pp. 20–21; *Mémoires inédits de Dumont de Bostaquet*, ed. Read and Waddington, p. 271, n. 1.

53   H. Murtagh, 'Huguenot Involvement in the Irish Jacobite War, 1689–91', in C. E. J. Caldicott, H. Gough and J.-P. Pittion (eds), *The Huguenots and Ireland: Anatomy of an Emigration* (Dublin, 1987), p. 231.

54   Story, *Impartial History*, pp. 80, 82; *Danish Force in Ireland*, ed. Danaher and Simms, p. 42.

55   Lart, 'Huguenot Regiments': 494.

56   Story, *Impartial History*, p. 82; *Mémoires inédits de Dumont de Bostaquet*, ed. Read and Waddington, p. 271.

57   *The Life of James II*, ed. J. S. Clarke (2 vols, London, 1816), vol. 2, p. 400; *Jacobite Narrative*, ed. Gilbert, p. 102.

58   *Mémoires inédits de Dumont de Bostaquet*, ed. Read and Waddington, pp. 272–3.

59   Ibid., p. 273.

Horse, who crossed the Boyne at Drybridge with the left wing of the cavalry, led by William, and took an active part in the fighting at Donore.[60] A second account is by Gidéon Bonnivert, a cavalry trooper in the force that accompanied Meinhard von Schomberg to Rossnaree.[61] The third is that of Jean-François de Morsier, a Swiss Protestant who served initially in one of the Huguenot regiments, before transferring to the Dutch Guards in whose ranks he crossed the Boyne in the initial attack at Oldbridge.[62]

Bonnivert and de Morsier are exceptional in being accounts of late seventeenth-century warfare by private soldiers. Dumont de Bostaquet, although higher on the social scale, held no significant command and likewise offers a worm's eye view of events. This is in contrast to most other accounts, which are by commentators, observers or commanders, the latter frequently being amongst the most confused. All three Huguenot accounts are very clear, honest and literate. Although fairly dispassionate, they possess the immediacy of direct involvement. Together, they contribute significant detail to our factual knowledge of the battle. For example, Bonnivert's reference to 'a very fine plain' is critical topographical information towards identifying the precise location at which Meinhard von Schomberg's force crossed the river. While Bonnivert is more matter-of-fact, a sense of belonging and pride in their respective units' achievements is discernible in the accounts of both Dumont de Bostaquet and de Morsier.[63] The universal private soldier's incomprehension of the grand schemes of his generals is well captured by de Morsier's recollection of the Dutch Guards' advance: 'I asked many time what did our manoeuvre mean and if we were going to attack the enemy in this formation. My lieutenant replied that he knew nothing, others replied likewise.'[64] Dumont de Bostaquet gives a vivid glimpse of mounted combat and makes references to the role and fate of many of the Huguenot personalities that participated. His account is also useful for the rest of the 1690 campaign after the Boyne.

Huguenot jubilation at the Williamite victory was tempered by their disproportionate share of the casualties and the loss of Schomberg. William was reported to have shown no emotion, when he first heard of the Marshal's death.[65] This was in the heat of battle. Afterwards, he was reported to have wept on being informed of the details and to have declared he had lost a father.[66] Since coming to

---

60   CTB, 1689–92, pp. 735, 820, 876, 1013, 1429.

61   G. S. (ed.), 'Two Unpublished Diaries connected with the Battle of the Boyne', *Ulster Journal of Archaeology*, 4 (1856): 77v95.

62   'Journal de Jean-Francois de Morsier' in A. Jullien (ed.), *Soldats Suisses au service étranger* (12 vols, Geneva: Jullien, 1908–95), vol. 7 (1915), pp. 96–101. This source is referred to in Pádraic Lenihan's *1690: Battle of the Boyne* (Stroud, 2003), *passim*. Lenihan's book is by far the best modern account of the battle of the Boyne.

63   G. S. (ed.), 'Two Unpublished Diaries connected with the Battle of the Boyne': 77–95.

64   Ibid.: 77–95. See also *Leven and Melville Papers. Letters and State Papers chiefly Addressed to George Earl of Melville, Secretary of State for Scotland, 1689–1691*, ed. W. L. Melville (Edinburgh, 1843), 459–61n.

65   G. Clarke, 'Autobiography' in HMC, *Leyborne-Popham* (London, 1897), pp. 272.

66   Jean Payen de La Fouleresse to King Christian V of Denmark, 2 July 1690: *Notes and Queries*, series 5, 7 (14 July 1877): 23. La Fouleresse was a Danish diplomat. However, his

Ireland, however, the King had treated the marshal coldly and pointedly ignored his advice. In the council of war before the battle, Schomberg had advocated a flanking movement to the west that might have enveloped the Jacobite army and brought about its annihilation.[67] Instead William (who was an indifferent general) had focused his main effort in a frontal attack that ultimately allowed the Irish to escape. William's hostility deeply affected Schomberg and, it was even suggested, might have encouraged him to seek an honourable death on the battlefield: certainly he had neglected to don armour on the day.[68] His body was brought off from where he fell by Captain Henri Foubert, one of his *aides-de-camp*, and ten days later, after the Williamites had occupied Dublin, he was buried in St Patrick's Cathedral. It was remarkable that he was given no state funeral, and no monument marked his grave until Dean Jonathan Swift and the cathedral chapter erected a stone to his memory in 1731.[69] The day after the battle the nearby town of Drogheda surrendered to La Melonière, and three weeks later du Cambon negotiated the capitulation of Waterford.[70] Command of La Caillemotte's regiment was given to its lieutenant-colonel, Pierre de Belcastel, Marquis d'Avèze (k.1710), a native of Languedoc, described as an officer of 'rigorous integrity, prudence and bravery'.[71]

III

James now fled from Ireland and returned to France. William might have ended the war by offering the defeated Irish leaders reasonable terms. Instead, in a surprising lapse for such an accomplished statesman, he overestimated the extent of his victory and was persuaded by the Irish Protestants to demand unconditional surrender. Left with no alternative, the Irish Catholics re-entered the struggle with renewed determination. Sarsfield surprised and destroyed William's train of heavy artillery as it approached Limerick, and the assault on the city was a costly failure. De

---

name suggests that he was French and, therefore, probably a Huguenot, although this remains unconfirmed. Like those of the Huguenot soldiers mentioned above his account is rich in detail, but in other respects it differs from theirs in being very much that of an observant and well-informed diplomat who was moving in circles close to the Williamite high command.

67   J. G. Simms, 'Eye-witnesses of the Boyne', *Irish Sword*, 6 (1963–4): 18, 25.

68   Clarke, 'Autobiography', pp. 271–2; *Mémoires inédits de Dumont de Bostaquet*, ed. Read and Waddington, p. 271.

69   Its Latin inscription, penned by Swift, extols the Marshal's greatness, but is critical of the parsimony of his descendants who failed to contribute towards the cost of the monument's erection: Glozier, *Marshal Schomberg*, p. 150.

70   Story, *Impartial History*, p. 89; *A Letter from an English Officer in His Majesty's Army in Ireland Giving a True Account of the Progress of Affairs in that Kingdom: Together with what Past at the Surrender of Waterford and Duncannon: And of His Majesty's March Towards Limerick. Dated July 29th, 1690* (London, 1690).

71   Dalton, *English Army Lists*, vol. 3, p. 120; Agnew, *Protestant Exiles from France*, vol. 1, p. 187; Glozier, *Huguenot Soldiers*, p. 153. He is to be distinguished from the officer of the same surname who served in Schomberg's Horse and was mortally wounded at the Boyne. Another member of the family, Daniel de Belcastel-Montvoillant, Seigneur de Campagnac, was a captain in La Melonière's regiment.

Belcastel was wounded, and his regiment suffered 150 casualties in an attack on a redoubt.[72] On the same occasion a small supporting detachment of Huguenot cavalry was wiped out. On 27 August the French *incorporés* spearheaded the Williamite grenadiers in a major attempt to storm the small breach which William's depleted artillery had made in the Irish fortifications.[73] Beforehand du Cambon had argued that the assault was premature and urged its delay, but his advice was ignored.[74] After several hours of hand-to-hand fighting, the Williamites were driven from the breach with heavy losses, including almost 200 French officers.[75] Most of the Huguenot casualties were *incorporés*, although Cambon's regiment, which formed part of the supporting infantry, was said to have been left with only six officers (presumably of its establishment cohort) who were fit to serve.[76] One of those wounded on that day was Paul Rapin de Thoyras, a Huguenot lieutenant in an English regiment, who later won renown with his *History of England*, which ran to many editions in the eighteenth century.[77] Some of the wounded French officers were sent to Bath to convalesce.[78] William was obliged to raise the siege, and he returned to England, accompanied by Meinhard von Schomberg, whom he created Duke of Leinster.[79] The Huguenot regiments remained in Ireland and subsequently participated in Churchill's successful autumn campaign, which captured Cork and Kinsale.[80] Du Cambon acted as engineer-general at this time, deputising for La Motte, who had been wounded at Limerick.[81] Their winter quarters were in south Leinster.[82]

For the 1691 campaign, Henri Massue, second Marquis de Ruvigny, joined the army in Ireland as a major-general and colonel of the Huguenot cavalry regiment.[83] The death at the Boyne of his brother, La Caillemotte, seems to have impelled him to take a commission from William, although the consequence was the confiscation of the family estates in Picardy and Champagne, which, despite leaving France in 1685, his father and he had been allowed to retain. In his youth the younger Ruvigny

---

72   *Mémoires inédits de Dumont de Bostaquet*, ed. Read and Waddington, pp. 284–5; *Danish Force in Ireland*, ed. Danaher and Simms, pp. 70–71.

73   Ibid., p. 73.

74   Story, *Impartial History*, p. 128.

75   Ibid., pp. 128–31; *Danish Force in Ireland*, ed. Danaher and Simms, pp. 73–4.

76   Lart, 'Huguenot Regiments': 492–3.

77   *The History of England by M. Rapin de Thoyras*, ed. N. Tyndal (4 vols, London, 1743), vol. 1, p. ix.

78   CSPDom., 1690–91, p. 375.

79   Ibid., p. 314.

80   Story, *Impartial History*, pp. 120–21, 134; J. G. Simms, 'Marlborough's Siege of Cork, 1690', *Irish Sword*, 9 (1969–70): 115.

81   *Danish Force in Ireland*, ed. Danaher and Simms, pp. 71, 87.

82   Ibid., p. 80.

83   For details of his career, see D. C. A. Agnew, *Henri de Ruvigny, Earl of Galway: A filial memoir, with a prefatory life of his father, le marquis de Ruvigny* (Edinburgh, 1864); Agnew, *Protestant Exiles from France*, vol. 1, pp. 144–219; article by R. D. in *DNB, compact edition* (1975), pp. 1344–5; Caldicott *et al.* (eds), *The Huguenots and Ireland*, pp. 205–54, 297–320; Cokayne, *Complete Peerage*, vol. 5, pp. 612–3; CSPDom., 1685–1702, *passim*; Dalton, *English Army Lists*, vols 3, 5 and 6, *passim*; article by H. Murtagh, *Oxford Dictionary of National Biography*, 'Ruvigny'.

had served under Marshals Schomberg and Turenne before succeeding his father as *député général* of the Huguenots at Louis XIV's court. In exile he continued to be an influential spokesman and benefactor of the refugees. From 1691 he succeeded Schomberg as the leading Huguenot soldier of the era, emerging from the Irish war with an enhanced military reputation, although his subsequent career suggests that he was a competent rather than a gifted military commander.

The Huguenot regiments were reinforced and re-equipped. In June they marched up from Cashel with the Danes to join the main Williamite army, now commanded by the Dutch general, Godard van Reede van Ginkel, for the attack on the Jacobite stronghold of Athlone. There, on the first day of the siege, a lieutenant from du Cambon's regiment was killed leading the successful assault on the east side of the town.[84] Ten days later the west town was overrun after a dramatic attack across the Shannon in which Huguenot detachments participated and La Melonière was one of the commanders. This was followed on 12 July by the battle of Aughrim in County Galway, which, though not as well known as the Boyne, was probably the decisive engagement of the war and certainly the bloodiest.[85] The Williamites were guided to the battlefield and probably provided with a map of the ground by the Trench brothers of Ballinasloe, said to have been of Huguenot ancestry.[86] In the engagement the Huguenot infantry, brigaded together in the front line under La Melonière, took part in a general advance of the Williamite left wing.[87] The Irish position on Kilcommodon Hill was strong, and their determined resistance halted the Williamites and beat them back in several places. However, the Huguenots held the ground they had taken behind *chevaux-de-frise* – the defensive equipment they had lacked at the Boyne – and defended themselves in a declivity that, from the intensity of the fighting there, is still known as Bloody Hollow.[88] De Belcastel was again wounded, and the French infantry suffered 176 casualties in all.[89] The Huguenot cavalry was divided between the left and right wings. La Forest-Suzannet was one of the generals on the left, where the French squadron, sword in hand, made a spirited charge which virtually wiped out a troop of Irish lifeguards.[90]

In the end it was Ruvigny who secured victory for the Williamites. On the right wing he led a force of cavalry, including a squadron of his own regiment, along a narrow causeway near Aughrim Castle into the heart of the Irish position.[91] It was fortunate for the Williamites that his thrust coincided with the death from a cannon shot of the Jacobite commander, the Marquis de Saint-Ruth. Irish resistance began to crumble and crucially the cavalry on their left wing abandoned the field. This enabled the Williamites to roll up the Jacobite left flank, inflicting thousands of

---

84 Story, *Continuation*, pp. 97–8.

85 Hayes-McCoy, *Irish Battles*, pp. 70.

86 Richard le Poer Trench, second Earl of Clancarty, *Memoir of the Le Poer Trench Family* (Dublin, 1874), pp. 1–5.

87 The line of battle is given in Story, *Continuation*, facing p. 124.

88 D. Murtagh, 'The Battle of Aughrim', in G. A. Hayes-McCoy (ed.), *The Irish at War* (Cork, 1964), p. 65.

89 Story, *Continuation*, p. 139; CSPDom., 1690–91, p. 445.

90 *Danish Force in Ireland*, ed. Danaher and Simms, pp. 121–3.

91 Story, *Continuation*, p. 133; *Jacobite Narrative*, ed. Gilbert, pp. 141–7.

casualties on the beleaguered infantry of the Irish centre as the battalions broke and fled. After the victory Ginkel came to the head of the Huguenot cavalry to praise the regiment for its contribution, and there he publicly embraced Ruvigny in gratitude for his conduct and courage.[92]

The Williamites went on to invest Galway, where du Cambon's was one of the regiments sent across the River Corrib to prevent relief being sent in from the north.[93] The city's capitulation was followed by the second siege of Limerick. Hostilities in Ireland ended in October with the signing of the Treaty of Limerick, 'in form a compromise, in fact ... a Williamite victory'.[94] With King James and the Irish Catholics defeated, William was now secure on his throne, and the ascendancy of the Irish Protestants assured for several generations. But victory had been won at a heavy price in blood and money. Louis XIV had mounted a successful diversion in Ireland for a relatively modest investment and, as a bonus, he acquired the bulk of the battle-hardened Irish Jacobite army – for which the Williamites provided the transport to France – at the end of hostilities.

Throughout the war in Ireland the Huguenots had proved brave and resourceful soldiers, who contributed substantially to the Williamite victory. The two Schombergs, Ruvigny and La Forest-Suzannet had all held high commands and Huguenots were central to the army's engineering strength. The four Huguenot regiments gave the refugees an identifiable collective profile, which was further highlighted by their deployment in the forefront of some of the most hazardous operations and their consequent casualties. The input of Huguenots in other regiments, Dutch, English and Danish, was probably equally important, if less obvious. Although the English parliament proved ultimately neither gracious nor grateful in respect of the Huguenot contribution, nonetheless the good account they had given of themselves in Ireland was probably an important factor in maintaining the pride and cohesion of the refugees and consolidating their position as a respected immigrant minority in both England and Ireland. The soldiers were not rewarded with grants of confiscated Irish land, but the pensions paid to them acknowledged in some measure their contribution to the success of the Glorious Revolution and gave them and their dependants some level of economic security.

IV

In 1692 the Huguenot regiments were transferred to the continent where they continued on active service until the Peace of Ryswick in 1697. The English parliament then forced William to reduce the size of the army, insisting that it should contain none but the King's native-born subjects. The Huguenots were brought back to Ireland for demobilisation.[95] Ruvigny, created Earl of Galway for his part at Aughrim, was in charge of the Irish government at the time. He arranged pensions for officers and

---

92   *Mémoires inédits de Dumont de Bostaquet*, ed. Read and Waddington, p. 303.

93   Story, *Continuation*, p. 162.

94   Simms, *Jacobite Ireland*, p. 267.

95   K. Ferguson, 'The Army in Ireland from the Restoration to the Act of Union', PhD thesis (University of Dublin, 1980), pp. 55–6.

non-commissioned officers and settled a number at the midland town of Portarlington, where he had been granted a large estate.[96] Their position was unaffected when the English parliament overturned the grant to Ruvigny in 1700. Over 400 Huguenot pensioners were living in Ireland in 1702, and some of the pensions were still being paid until the middle of the eighteenth century.[97] Of the four regimental colonels who survived the war, du Cambon was promoted brigadier-general in 1693, only to be then discharged from the army following complaints from his junior officers over improper pay stoppages and mismanagement. He was soon reinstated and was then killed at the battle of Landen later that year.[98] De Belcastel, promoted brigadier-general in 1696, transferred after the demobilisation to the Dutch service, where he rose to the rank of lieutenant-general before his death in action in Spain at the battle of Villaviciosa in 1710.[99] La Melonière was promoted major-general in 1692, serving in Flanders until 1697.[100] In retirement he settled in London, where he died in 1715.[101] Ruvigny served twice as a lord justice and twice as commander-in-chief in Ireland. He held commands in Flanders and Piedmont in the 1690s, and in the Peninsula during the War of the Spanish Succession, where he was heavily defeated at the battle of Almanza in 1707. This and other setbacks during his career suggest that he was no more than a competent soldier at best, and that he lacked any exceptional talent for high command, such as that possessed by his outstanding contemporaries: Marlborough, Prince Eugène, Luxembourg or Villars. However, throughout his life he was solicitous for the welfare of the Huguenot exiles, being described as 'their head, their friend, their refuge, their advocate, their support [and] their protector'.[102] Minus an arm and an eye he had lost in the wars, he died in retirement in England in 1720.

---

96 R. Hylton, 'The Huguenot Settlement at Portarlington, 1692–1771', in Caldicott *et al.* (eds), *The Huguenots and Ireland*, pp. 297–315. The process had already started in 1692 with the settlement at Portarlington of aged and disabled Huguenot veterans.

97 Ferguson, 'The Army in Ireland', p. 55.

98 Dalton, *English Army Lists*, vol. 3, p. 119; Glozier, *Huguenot Soldiers*, pp. 156–7.

99 Ibid., p. 153.

100 Dalton, *English Army Lists*, vol. 3, p. 118.

101 Glozier, *Huguenot Soldiers*, p. 155.

102 Agnew, *Protestant Exiles from France*, vol. 1, p. 162.

Chapter 7

Huguenot Soldiers in Dutch Service
'A good Captain to disperse the royal troops'

Matthew Glozier and David Onnekink

University of Sydeny/Universiteit Utrecht/Universiteit Leiden, The Netherlands

Historians studying the influx of Huguenot émigrés in Dutch society have shown little interest in their military activities, and have rather focused on their intellectual, economic and cultural contributions. Specialised studies have rather ignored the Huguenot soldiers in Dutch service,[1] and consequently there is little attention paid to them in more general works on Dutch politics in the late seventeenth century.[2] This is probably also partly the result of the relative lack of attention until recently to military history in Dutch historiography.[3] It is also an acknowledgement that most Huguenot soldiers spent very little time in the Netherlands, though they often remained in Dutch pay for years. And yet Huguenots played an important part in the army of the United Provinces during the late seventeenth century, in particular after

---

1   See, for instance, H. P. H. Nusteling, 'The Netherlands and the Huguenot Emigrés' and P. J. A. N. Rietbergen, 'William of Orange (1650–1702) between European Politics and European Protestantism: The Case of the Huguenots', both in J. A. H. Bots and G. H. M. Posthumus Meyjes (eds), *La révocation de l'édit de Nantes et les Provinces-Unies* (Amsterdam, Maarssen, 1986). For a specific study of the Huguenots in Dutch, see W. E. J. Berg, *De réfugiés in de Nederlanden na de herroeping van het Edict van Nantes. Eene proeve van onderzoek naar den invloed, welken hunne overkomst gehad heeft op handel en nijverheid, letteren, beschaving en zeden* (8 vols, Amsterdam, 1845).

2   For example W. Troost, *William III, the Stadholder-King: A Political Biography* (Aldershot, 2005) and J. I. Israel, *The Dutch Republic: Its Rise, Greatness and Fall 1477–1806* (Oxford, 1995).

3   The standard account of the army of the Dutch Republic is J. W. Wijn, F. J. G. ten Raa and F. de Bas (eds), *Het Staatsche Leger 1568–1795* (11 vols, Breda, The Hague, 1911–64). For recent interest on the Dutch army in this period, see, for example, the work of Olaf van Nimwegen: *De Subsistentie van het Leger. Logistiek en Strategie van het Geallieerde en met name het Staatse Leger tijdens de Spaanse Successieoorlog in de Nederlanden en het Heilige Roomse Rijk 1701–1712* (Amsterdam, 1995); *De Republiek der Verenigde Nederlanden als Grote Mogendheid. Buitenlandse Politiek en Oorlogvoering in de Eerste Helft van de Achttiende Eeuw en in het Bijzonder tijdens de Oostenrijkse Successieoorlog (1740–1748)* (Amsterdam, 2002); *'Deser landen chrijchsvolck'. het Staatse leger en de militaire revoluties (1588–1688)* (Amsterdam, 2006); R. Fagel and D. Onnekink (eds), *Oorlog en Samenleving in de Nieuwe Tijd* (Maastricht, 2005). On the Huguenots in the Dutch army, see M. R. Glozier, *The Huguenot Soldiers of William of Orange and the Glorious Revolution of 1688: The Lions of Judah* (Brighton, Portland, 2002).

the revocation of the Edict of Nantes. Their numbers, discipline and zeal substantially reinforced the army of the Dutch Republic at a crucial moment in its history when invasion loomed from various sides in 1688. This chapter does not aspire to give an exhaustive overview of Huguenot soldiers in Dutch service, but rather to highlight some essential features of their commitment and professional contribution by way of providing a provisional sketch of the their significance and role in the army of the United Provinces. The Nine Years' War forced the Dutch to strike abroad as well, and this chapter will close with two case-studies; Huguenot soldiers played an important part in the Dutch invasion of England in 1688, and were part of an expeditionary force in Piedmont in the early 1690s.

I

It has traditionally been accepted that many of the Huguenot refugees who fled France, in the decade of the Revocation (and especially those who went to the Netherlands), directly entered military employment in their place of refuge. However, scant evidence exists for this assertion between the Revocation and the Glorious Revolution of 1688. Despite a tradition which insists that they were employed eagerly, William of Orange was prevented from accommodating the majority of them.

In fact, most of the Huguenots associated with Dutch service before the 1690s served in but a few regiments, when in 1688 William issued commissions to 54 officers in his Blue Guards. Another 34 refugees joined his Life Guards.[4] Foreshadowing this event, between 1686 and 1687 almost 300 Huguenot refugees were attached on slender means to Dutch regiments. The assertion that the principle Dutch fortresses 'were used as so many *depôts* for such officers and soldiers as continued to take refuge in Holland', is true only in so far as some groups of Huguenot gentlemen could be found in each in the 1680s.[5]

Of those Huguenot refugees that attained military employment in the Netherlands before William's invasion, it has been said:

> [They] formed a body ready drilled, either to fight the cause of freedom on the battlefield, or to guide public opinion by means of the press. Whilst six hundred *gentilhommes* were induced to swell the Prince's body-guard, four regiments of soldiers were enrolled.[6]

One barrier to their immediate employment in the Netherlands was the fact that French drill differed from the Dutch version. Huguenots seeking military employment would first have had to serve as volunteers, in order for them to learn Dutch drill, before

---

4   C. E. Lart, 'The Huguenot Regiments', *Proceedings of the Huguenot Society of London*, 9 (1911): 480–81; J. Childs, *The Army, James II and the Glorious Revolution* (Manchester, 1980), p. 175.

5   For example, after escaping to the Netherlands in 1687, Dumont de Bostaquet found his brother-in-law, Lieutenant David de Moncornet, in garrison at Maastricht: Glozier, *Huguenot Soldiers*, p. 64; S. Smiles, *The Huguenots: Their Settlements, Churches, and Industries in England and Ireland* (London, fourth edition 1870), pp. 201–3.

6   G. Masson, *The Huguenots: A Sketch of their History from the Beginning of the Reformation to the Death of Louis XIV* (London, New York, 1882), pp. 154–5.

they could be employed in the Dutch army.[7] However, very few refugee Huguenots appear to have been immediately or eagerly employed in Dutch service. And while a few, including Dumont de Bostaquet, were lucky enough to find themselves among the 100 men accommodated by William in 1687, most refugees were forced to cool their heels, without military employment, until the eve of William's embarkation for England.

Only when it became clear that the Prince's aims would be backed, or at least tolerated, by the majority of the reluctant regents, was he in a position to facilitate the rapid creation of a number of Huguenots to be attached to existing Dutch regiments. Each of their new companies was to be manned exclusively by French Protestants. Two companies of French cadets – volunteer gentlemen and future officers – had indeed been raised as early as 1686, but they contained no more than 50 Frenchmen each.[8] They were paid for by the province of Holland. Furthermore, William III did maintain almost 300 Huguenot officers on pensions in 1686 (193)[9] and 1687 (100).[10] But they were few enough in number for the Polish ambassador to The Hague, Antony Moreau, to name each of them in his correspondence to John III Sobieski, King of Poland.[11] Their number was small by comparison to later pension

---

7   T. Pluncket, *The Character of a Good Commander: Together with a Short Commendation of the Famous Artillery (more properly Military) Company of London: also a Brief Encomium on the Duke and Worthy Prince Elector of Brandenburg: Lastly, Plain Dealing with Treacherous Dealers: Whereunto is Annexed the General Exercise of the Prince of Orange's Army* (London, 1689).

8   The first company of cadets was commanded by Charles de Cosne de Chauvernay, while the second was commanded by Daniel de Rapin. An additional company, in the service of Groningen, was commanded by Antoine de Houx, Seigneur d'Espinoles. Jean Guichard, Marquis de Peray, was appointed in his stead by the provincial States of Groningen to command all French refugee soldiers, as colonel: Ten Raa and de Bas (eds), *Het Staatsche Leger*, vol. 6, pp. 216–17. Daniel was the cousin of the Huguenot historian Paul Rapin de Thoyras, who joined him in this regiment of cadets *c.*1687: H. Trevor-Roper, 'A Huguenot Historian: Paul Rapin', in I. Scouloudi (ed.), *Huguenots in Britain and their French Background, 1550–1800* (London, 1987), p. 6.

9   'Letter Book of Moreau – Polish Ambassador at The Hague, 1687–1688', in *Townsend Papers*, vol. 3: British Library, Additional Manuscript (hereafter BL, Add. MS) 38,494, fols 13–18. The 193 Huguenot officers maintained from 7 February 1686 included two colonels, two lieutenant-colonels, two majors, eight captains of Horse, 11 *reformé* captains of Horse, eight lieutenants of Horse, 16 *reformé* lieutenants of Horse, three cornets, 29 captains of Foot, 30 lieutenants of Foot, 40 *reformé* lieutenants of Foot and 42 reserve lieutenants of Foot.

10   Ibid.: The 100 Huguenot officers maintained from 30 July 1687 included four captains of Horse, six *reformé* captains of Horse, seven lieutenants [*sic*] of Horse, nine cornets, 12 captains of Foot, 21 *reformé* captains of Foot, 27 lieutenants of Foot and 14 *entrepues* (volunteers).

11   Moreau was a fellow refugee who later asked Abel Tassin d'Alonne to recommend him to the Earl of Portland as tutor to his son, Lord Woodstock, 'in case he needed a secretary or steward to accompany him' on his Grand Tour: Abel Tassin d'Alonne to Hans Willem Bentinck, Earl of Portland, The Hague, 8 May 1703: University of Nottingham MS Pw A 317/1–2; *Correspondentie van Willem III en van Hans Willem Bentinck, eersten graaf van Portland*, ed. N. Japikse (5 vols, RGP, 1927–33), vol. 2, no. 24, pp. 542–5.

lists that groaned with the veterans of his Irish campaign (1689–91).[12] These efforts can in no way be construed as representing a general swelling of the Dutch army with Huguenots before 1688.

Though proportionately few of the Huguenots who fled to the Netherlands around the time of the Revocation were immediately commissioned, they found in the Dutch Republic a number of resident Huguenots already holding commissions in the Dutch army. Indeed, Huguenots were a prominent part of the Dutch army before the 1680s, and links between William III, some of his closest Dutch friends, and the Huguenot soldiers who served in the Netherlands, were strong before the Revocation.[13] Many Dutchmen served in predominantly French regiments in the Netherlands, whose genesis lay in the Franco-Dutch wars of the 1670s. There were many French soldiers scattered throughout the Dutch regiments of the United Provinces' army. A small number of these Frenchmen were Roman Catholic, but the majority of them were Huguenots.[14] In this way a number of prominent Huguenots served William of Orange and the Dutch Republic throughout the last quarter of the century.[15]

There are many instances of the permeation of Huguenots throughout the regiments of the Dutch army before 1685. Indeed, French Huguenots could be found serving in its most prestigious regiments throughout the 1670s and 1680s.[16] On the eve of the Glorious Revolution, many of the Dutch Republic's allied regiments also contained veteran French soldiers.[17] The army of Brandenburg, for example, employed many Huguenot soldiers, losing those it could not accommodate to the Dutch army when Marshal Schomberg entered openly into Netherlands service in 1688.[18] The fate of

---

12   *Inventaire des Archives Wallonnes*, ed. J. W. Verburgt (Leiden, 1950), 'A. Pièces concernant les synods Wallons: III. Pièces diverses – Liste des pensions des Officiers Français refugies, d'apres la resolution des Etats Generaux. 1683–1689. 1697. 1698. 1700. 1717'.

13   For example, long before 1685, Hans Willem Bentinck had established himself in the Huguenot regiment of Paul de La Baye du Theil. First raised in 1672, the regiment contained both Dutch and French officers. Bentinck was appointed lieutenant-colonel of the regiment in 1677, when he succeeded Paulus van Alkemade. In 1683 he was replaced in that position by Louis Mirleau d'Illiers, Marquis de Rhodes, and in 1687, Rhodes was succeeded by yet another Huguenot, Pierre Solbert de Marsilly: Glozier, *Huguenot Soldiers*, p. 58.

14   Ten Raa and de Bas (eds), *Het Staatsche Leger*, vol. 6, pp. 239, 242; W. H. Manchée, 'Huguenot Soldiers and their Conditions of Service in the English Army', *Proceedings of the Huguenot Society of London*, 16 (1938–41): 234, 265.

15   W. A. Shaw, 'The Irish Pensioners of Huguenot Regiments', *Proceedings of the Huguenot Society of London*, 6 (1901): 304; Ten Raa and de Bas (eds), *Het Staatsche Leger*, vol. 6, p. 233.

16   Het Nationaal Archief The Hague (hereafter HNA), *Commissieboek*, 1681–91, fol. 315; Ten Raa and de Bas (eds), *Het Staatsche Leger*, vol. 6, pp. 190, 297, 300.

17   Two of the four Hanoverian regiments attached to the Dutch army were commanded by Huguenots. By 1694, the First Regiment of Hanoverian infantry in Holland was commanded by Colonel du Pont, and the Second Regiment by Major-General Louis de Saint-Pôl des Estangs: Ten Raa and de Bas (eds), *Het Staatsche Leger*, vol. 6, pp. 374, 361–4.

18   See. R. Wiebe, 'Untersuchung über die Hilfeleistung der deutschen Staaten für Wilhelm III von Oranien im Jahre 1688', PhD thesis (Georg-August University, Göttingen, 1939).

the large number of Huguenots who remained in Brandenburg is treated at length in other chapters of this volume.[19] According to Vauban, 600 officers and 12,000 soldiers in total of Huguenot origin were serving in 'enemy armies'. When Vauban addressed Louvois on the matter, he talked of the 'quantities of fine feathers [in our caps] which deserted the kingdom ... [and now] are cruelly unchained against France and the person of the King' (*quantités de bonnes plumes qui ont déserté le Royaume ... se sont cruellement déchaînées contre la France et la personne du Roi meme*).[20] During the Nine Years' War, 17 French Protestant regiments were serving in the Allied armies.

Shortly before his forces departed the Netherlands for Britain in 1688, William of Orange made a request for volunteers to accompany him, from among Dutch-based Huguenots. The Huguenot refugee Isaac Dumont de Bostaquet says that William invited the ablest among the French gentlemen to join with him in the invasion. Dumont de Bostaquet was one of a large number of Huguenots who responded eagerly to the invitation, and he was one of the few successful applicants, securing a captain's position in the Blue Dragoons. It was only at this late stage that 54 Huguenots were incorporated into the Blue Dragoons regiments. The available data on post-Revocation Huguenot refugee employment in the Dutch army, confirms the fact that Huguenots appeared in the Blue Dragoons and in William of Orange's Life Guards only on the eve of the Glorious Revolution.[21]

In all, 88 Huguenots were appointed to the Blue Dragoons and the Life Guards. Clearly, post-Revocation Huguenot refugees did not constitute a large or significant group of commissioned officers in the Dutch army in the period between 1685 and the Glorious Revolution of 1688. John Childs has estimated that William commanded more than a thousand Huguenot officers, constituting 10 per cent of his entire officer corps. This can be taken as a relevant comment only *after* 1688, when that Prince was in a position to offer commissions in a sprawling Anglo-Dutch force to the vast majority of these soldiers.[22] While the significance of the post-Revocation refugees in the Dutch army belongs to the decade of the 1690s, it is clear that unnamed multitudes

---

19   E. Amburger, *Die Anwerbung ausländischer Fachkräfte für die Wirtschaft Rußlands vom 15. bis ins 19. Jahrhundert* (Wiesbaden, 1968); M. Kohnke, 'Das Edikt von Potsdam zu seiner entetehung verbreitung und uberlieferung', *Jahrbuch für Geschichte des Feudalismus*, 9 (1985): 241–75; J. P. Erman and P. C. F. Reclam, *Mémoires pour servir à l'histoire des Réfugiés François dans les États du Roi* (9 vols, Berlin, 1782–99), vol. 1; A. Ruiz, 'Une famille Huguenote du Brandenburg au XVIIIe siècle: Les Theremin', *Revue d'Allemagne*, 14/2 (1982): 217–28; T. Schmidt and H. Schnitter, 'Die Hugenotten in der Brandenburgisch-Preussischen armee', *Militärgeschichte*, 24/3 (1985): 233–9; M. Magdelaine, 'Le réfuge: Le role de Francfort-sur-le-main', *Bulletin de la société de l'histoire du Protestantisme française*, 131/4 (1985): 485–94; U. Janssens, 'Jean Deschamps (1709–1767) and the French colony in Brandenburg', *Proceedings of the Huguenot Society of London*, 23/4 (1980): 227–39.

20   S. Le Prestre de Vauban, 'Mémoire pour le rappel des Huguenots' (Paris, October 1689), quoted in Nusteling, 'The Netherlands and the Huguenot Emigrés', p. 30n.

21   This is based, primarily, on the Dutch commission books; see the references to these throughout the footnotes of this chapter.

22   J. Childs, *The British Army of William III* (Manchester, 1987), p. 134.

of rank-and-file level refugees accompanied William to Britain in his 1688 invasion force. Their number is evidenced by the speedy creation of the Huguenot regiments for William's Irish campaign. Nevertheless, this later 'Dutch' force still required an international advertising campaign to fill its ranks, and the services of competent recruiters such as William's agent in Geneva, the Marquis d'Arzilliers.

By contrast, it is claimed that in Britain James II did 'not disdain the Huguenot contribution' to his army.[23] The establishment of Miremont's Horse, and the fact that some Huguenots served in the Royal Dragoons and under Lord Dover in the Life Guards seems to support the notion of the King's appreciation of the Huguenots' worth as competent and potentially loyal soldiers. Ironically, Lord Dover, the Roman Catholic commander of the Fourth Troop of the Life Guards, is said to have sold half the available commissions to refugee Huguenots: 'For if a Turk had come, the 50 guineas had been acceptable to that Lord, the Captain'.[24] But then, Huguenots could drive hard bargains, and Henri de Foubert (son of Solomon, who established a gentleman's academy in London in 1679) secured his cornetcy in the Life Guards with a payment of £500.[25] Having said this, it is also clear that the Fourth Troop harboured a number of committed Roman Catholics and others deeply loyal to the King. One of the most significant of these men was Patrick Sarsfield, who was among William's most implacable opponents in Ireland.[26]

Stephen Saunders Webb has highlighted the speed with which the Huguenot officers of the Fourth Troop became devoted subordinates to John, Lord Churchill, the executive officer of the Life Guards.[27] The lack of control exercised by King James over the personnel of the Fourth Troop of his Life Guards is demonstrated by the fact that it not only contained ostensibly loyal Huguenots, but also housed some violent Whigs.[28] The Huguenots of the Life Guards later followed Churchill

23   R. H. Whitworth, '1685 – James II, The Army and the Huguenots', *Journal of the Society for Army Historical Research*, 63 (1985): 136.

24   S. S. Webb, *Lord Churchill's Coup: The Anglo-American Empire and the Glorious Revolution Reconsidered* (Syracuse, NY, 1995), p. 108.

25   T. Bruce, Earl of Ailesbury, *Memoirs of Thomas, Earl of Ailesbury: Written by Himself*, ed. W. E. Buckley (2 vols, Edinburgh, 1890), vol. 1, pp. 128–9; J. Childs, *The Army of Charles II* (London, Toronto, 1976), pp. 65–6.

26   There was a fairly even mix of latent Williamite and Jacobite soldiers in the Fourth Troop in the years immediately preceding William's invasion: J. Kinross, *The Boyne and Aughrim: The War of the Two Kings* (Gloucestershire, 1997), p. 31.

27   Whitworth, '1685': 130; Ailesbury, *Memoirs*, vol. 1, pp. 130–31; G. Arthur, *The Story of the Household Cavalry* (2 vols, London, 1909–26), vol. 1, p. 202; F. Hare, Bishop of St Asaph and Chichester, *The Conduct of the Duke of Marlborough during the Present War* (London, 1712), p. 12; Webb, *Lord Churchill's Coup*, p. 108.

28   One of these was Richard Savage, Viscount Colchester. This nobleman left Lord Churchill's direct command in the Third Troop in order to take a commission in the Fourth – presumably with the intention of consolidating anti-Jacobite feeling within the corps. Colchester eventually became lieutenant-colonel of the Life Guards. He was also the representative of the 'Treason Club', being one of the first of James II's officers to desert to William when the Prince arrived in 1688: he took 60 veterans of the Life Guards with him: Webb, *Lord Churchill's Coup*, p. 178; Dalton, *Army Lists and Commission Registers, 1661–1714*, vol. 2, pp. 75, 115, 228–9; Kinross, *The Boyne and Aughrim*, p. 31.

into the service of William of Orange. They did not, however, create, foster or even significantly aid Churchill's so-called 'conspiracy in the army'.[29] The Huguenots who joined the Fourth Troop were professional gentlemen officers in search of a livelihood, commensurate with their religious faith and social status. They were not, as the British king feared, plotters or committed republicans. Based on the evidence of their later actions, it is difficult to see any political profile at all among Huguenots employed in the English army before 1688.

The example of Lord Dover's Life Guards troop reinforces the problem that faced James II in ensuring the support of his army. However, his attempt to introduce Catholics into his armed forces does not represent a desire to Catholicise the army as a whole. What it does demonstrate is the King's desire to staff his forces with trustworthy and dependable subjects upon whom he hoped he could rely. Even on the eve of the Glorious Revolution, no more than 1,000 out of 18,000 soldiers, or less than 10 per cent of the English army, was Roman Catholic.[30] The number of Huguenots employed elsewhere in James's army was meagre by comparison even to this small figure. Besides those already mentioned, Edward Fox's infantry regiment contained some Huguenot officers, and there were six Frenchmen in the Royal Dragoons and a further nine in the Earl of Macclesfield's Horse.[31]

The notion that the Huguenots were, at least outwardly, loyal officers was similarly the reason for the sometimes-generous royal support of their academies for gentlemen in London, run by men such as Foubert, Mestre and d'Agard.[32] However, based on the evidence of a 1683 letter from refugee officers to Charles II, Bernard

---

29   Webb, *Lord Churchill's Coup*, p. 108; Whitworth, '1685': 130; Ailesbury, *Memoirs*, vol. 1, pp. 130–31; Arthur, *The Story of the Household Cavalry*, vol. 1, p. 202; Hare, *The Conduct of the Duke of Marlborough*, p. 12.

30   Whitworth, '1685': 136.

31   Macclesfield maintained close associations with some Huguenots and Abraham de Moivre dedicated to the Earl his *Annuities upon Lives* (London, 1725): Childs, *The British Army of William III*, p. 134; G. C. Gibbs, 'Huguenot Contribution to England's Intellectual Life, and England's Intellectual Commerce with Europe, *c*.1680–1720', in Scouloudi (ed.), *Huguenots in Britain*, pp. 29, 40 n. 62. Colonel Edward Fox raised a Regiment of Marines in 1702 whose duties were to assist in working and fighting the ships and the defence of ports for the British Fleet. Fox's Marines were part of an amphibious force dispatched in 1704 to the Spanish coast to attack and destroy Spanish dockyard facilities, but it failed to achieve anything either at Barcelona or Cadiz. Knowing that he would have to justify his poor performance upon returning home, Fox landed 5,000 men at Gibraltar on 22 June. To the surprise of all involved the force was opposed by only 500 Spaniards of whom only 150 were regular soldiers: the fortress surrendered two days later.

32   Solomon de Foubert (d.1696), received £100 from Charles II towards the establishment of his academy in Sherwood Street, Piccadilly, in 1679; it helped 'lessen the expense the nation is at yearly in sending children into France to be taught military exercises'. Both d'Agard's academy in the Savoy, Strand (established *c*.1680), and Mestre's in Long Acre, next to the White Hart Inn, maintained a valued emphasis on mathematics and its application to geography and navigation, long neglected by similar English establishments: T. Murdoch (ed.), *The Quiet Conquest: The Huguenots 1685 to 1985* (London, 1985), p. 94.

Cottret says that the 'Huguenot element in the English army was conspicuous'.[33] In truth, it was anything but conspicuous. Like many historians of the Revocation and Glorious Revolution, Cottret failed to perceive the difference between these scattered groups of French gentlemen refugees in Britain before 1688, and the large bulk of Huguenots who entered Britain at the time of William III's invasion. A brief survey of the military careers of some of the signatories of the 1683 petition to Charles II is enough to demonstrate the relative obscurity of all but a very small number of them. Of 19 original signatories, only four later appear on record in Britain as being in any way connected with the army. One of the four – Monsieur Le Picard – retired from Britain to the Netherlands, where he was taken on by William as a cavalry officer.[34] The other three gentlemen – Pierre du Quesne, and Messieurs d'Arques[35] and de Jouisse[36] – later obtained commissions from William in the Netherlands.[37]

The evidence presented by the careers of these French Huguenot gentlemen suggests that they all left Britain before 1688, returning via the Netherlands at the time of the Prince's invasion. This seems to support contemporary reports of Dutch army recruiters operating in Britain before the invasion.[38] At least one British army officer, Humphrey Oakover, firmly believed that Aernout van Citters, the Dutch ambassador in London, was recruiting both Britons and Huguenot refugees resident in Britain, for service in the Netherlands before 1688.[39] Based on these suspicions, King James may well have feared among his French Protestant officers in Britain (what he thought to be) the 'latent republicanism' of the Huguenots as a group. In practice he had little to worry about on this point, as the number of Huguenot officers holding commissions in Britain during his reign was demonstrably small and of little significance.[40]

Before 1688, the armies of the Dutch Republic and Britain contained a number of Huguenot officers. Some of them had been employed before the Revocation, and they, like the small number of their compatriots who joined them before the Glorious Revolution, enjoyed a well-deserved reputation as competent professional soldiers. Consequently, the few post-Revocation Huguenot soldiers employed anywhere before 1688 can scarcely be described as a 'conspicuous' element in either Britain

---

33   B. Cottret, *The Huguenots in England: Immigration and Settlement,* c.*1550–1700* (Cambridge, 1985), p. 216.

34   Michel Le Picard de Boison: 'Letter Book of Moreau – Polish Ambassador at The Hague, 1687–1688', fol. 13.

35   Possibly Jacques Larquier de Borda, an infantry captain in the Netherlands in 1687, or Louis d'Asquier de Rival, an *entrepue* in the same year: ibid., fols 15, 18.

36   Possibly Jean Louis de Jossaut, a *reformé* infantry lieutenant in the Netherlands in 1687, or Edouard de Leuse de Liverne, a cavalry lieutenant [*sic*] in 1686: ibid., fols 14, 18.

37   *Dublin and Portarlington Veterans: King William III's Huguenot Army*, ed. T. P. Le Fanu and W. H. Manchée, Huguenot Society Quarto Series 41 (London, 1946), p. 34; Shaw, 'The Irish Pensioners of Huguenot Regiments': 303; Lart, 'The Huguenot Regiments': 521.

38   BL, Add. MS 41,805, fols 42–3.

39   Ibid.

40   Among other evidence, witness the scarcity of French (and specifically Huguenot) names in the English army commission books 1685–8: C. Dalton, *English Army Lists and Commission Registers, 1661–1714* (6 vols, London, 1892–1904).

or the Netherlands. Even in the Dutch Republic, it was circumstances beyond their control that conspired to thrust Huguenots into a position of prominence. The Glorious Revolution of 1688, and William's Irish campaign in particular – not the few years between the Revocation and the Revolution – was the making of the Huguenots as an international military group in Dutch service.

A leading figure among them, who accompanied William to Britain as his second-in-command, was Friedrich Hermann von Schomberg.[41] A truly international figure, Schomberg, of Geman descent, felt at home in both England and France, having married a French Huguenot lady, while maintaining strong links with members of his English mother's family.[42] After the Revocation, he departed French service (on 11 March 1686) on good terms with Louis XIV, and retired to Portugal, but, soon thereafter, applied for employment to the Elector of Brandenburg. On 24 May 1687 Louis XIV instructed his Minister of State for War, Louvois, to support Schomberg's entry into the service of the Elector of Brandenburg.[43] Attempts to seduce or buy Schomberg into Dutch service soon followed.[44] Louis XIV's regret at losing a loyal servant and a good general was genuine. However, the French king's good-will towards Schomberg evaporated upon the death of the Elector Friedrich Wilhelm (on 9 May 1688) whose successor, Friedrich III, was anti-French. His father's death left the new Elector free to pursue a strongly anti-French policy, in which Schomberg participated.[45]

Schomberg departed Brandenburg to serve William and the Dutch Republic when William concluded an agreement with the Elector Friedrich in September 1688.[46] This new appointment freed Schomberg to act directly against Louis's interests in Europe. The Marshal took with him only those Huguenot refugees who had not already secured employment in Berlin, leaving behind a significant number that had.[47] Many more remained to fight under the Elector Friedrich in several notable actions, playing no role in William's invasion.[48]

41   C. Rousset, *Histoire de Louvois et de son administration militaire* (4 vols, Paris, 1864–5; sixth edition 1879), vol. 4, p. 115.

42   *Letters from George Carew to Sir Thomas Roe: Ambassador to the Court of the Great Mogul, 1615–1617*, ed. J. MacLean (London, 1840), pp. 6, 21, 41; G. E. Cokayne, *The Complete Peerage*, ed. G. H. White (8 vols, London, 1887–98; reprinted 12 vols, London, 1910–59), vol. 11, pp. 522–3; M. R. Glozier, *Marshal Schomberg, 1615–1690: 'The Ablest Soldier of His Age': International Soldiering and the Formation of State Armies in Seventeenth-Century Europe* (Brighton, Portland, 2005), ch. 7 'Revocation'.

43   Rousset, *Louvois*, vol. 4, p. 115 n. 1.

44   Glozier, *Schomberg*, pp. 115–16.

45   Rousset, *Histoire de Louvois*, vol. 4, p. 115 n. 1.

46   H. L. King, *Brandenburg and the English Revolution of 1688* (Oberlin, London, 1914), pp. 17–24; J. R. Jones, *The Revolution of 1688 in England* (London, 1972), p. 207; J. Childs, 'A Patriot for Whom? "For God and Honour": Marshal Schomberg', *History Today*, vol. 38 (July 1988), pp. 47; Glozier, *Marshal Schomberg*, p. 123.

47   Archives du Ministère des Affaires Etrangères, Paris, *Cahiers Politiques Hollande* 156 (hereafter AMAECPH), September–December 1688, *despatches d'Avaux*, fols 302–18, d'Avaux to Louis XIV, 28 October 1688.

48   Glozier, *Schomberg*, p. 116.

II

It would be difficult to disentangle the history of the Huguenot refugee soldiers from the fortunes of the Protestant religion and international tensions during the late 1680s. Especially after the revocation of the Edict of Nantes and the accession of James II in 1685 there was anxiety amongst Protestants. The French ambassador in The Hague, Antoine Mesmes, Comte d'Avaux, warned Louis XIV that the Revocation had caused strong resentment amongst Dutch regents, almost all of whom had commercial or family ties with French Protestants who had suffered from the consequences.[49] The fleeing Huguenots that ended up in Protestant countries, mainly England, Brandenburg and the United Provinces, were natural supporters of the Protestant cause. Those in Holland were generally thought to be loyal and committed to the policy of the Prince of Orange,[50] who acted as a benevolent patron and provided commissions and pensions for almost 300 Huguenots.[51] Dumont de Bostaquet, for instance, related his generous reception in Holland by William's favourite, Hans Willem Bentinck, and served as a lieutenant in the *Stadtholder's* army.[52]

Although many foreign soldiers served in the Dutch army, the Huguenots attracted the attention of foreign ambassadors. D'Avaux, most notably, took a keen interest in the movements of French Protestant refugees in the United Provinces, in particular those of the Huguenot officers. On the eve of the Glorious Revolution the Ambassador sent a list of Huguenot soldiers in Dutch service to Versailles and made a point of the fact that all the principal officers save two would join William in the invasion of England.[53] The British ambassador, the Marquis d'Albeville, estimated that there were 500 French soldiers who participated in the operation.[54] D'Avaux could refine this number and counted 556 infantry, 180 cavalry and 60 volunteers, all dispersed over the Dutch battalions. In 1686 the Polish ambassador, Moreau, listed some 300 French soldiers and officers in Dutch pay, specifically mentioning that they were Calvinist refugees.[55]

---

49   J. A. de Mesmes, Comte d'Avaux, *The Negotiations of Count d'Avaux, Ambassador etc.* (4 vols, London, 1755), vol. 4, p. 50.

50   R. Gwynn, 'The Huguenots in Britain, the "Protestant International" and the defeat of Louis XIV', in R. Vigne and C. Littleton (eds), *From Strangers to Citizens: The Integration of Immigrant Communities in Britain, Ireland and Colonial America, 1550–1750* (Brighton, Portland, 2001), p. 421.

51   Nusteling, 'The Netherlands and the Huguenot Emigrés', *passim*; *Negotiations of d'Avaux*, vol. 4, pp. 30, 50.

52   *Mémoires d'Isaac Dumont de Bostaquet sur les temps qui ont précédé et suivi la révocation de l'édit de Nantes Normande*, ed. M. Richard (Paris, 1968), p. 152.

53   AE CPH 156, fols 286, 302–3, d'Avaux to Louis XIV, n.d. (probably October 1688), memorial of d'Avaux listing the officers.

54   BL, Add. MS 41,816, fol. 219, despatch Albeville, 6 October 1688.

55   BL, Add. MS 38,494, fols 13v–18v.

The total of 796 soldiers which d'Avaux mentions was not an insignificant number in an invasion army of some 12,000.[56] The Ambassador understood, however, that the Huguenot soldiers would not just reinforce the army numerically; they also boosted the Williamite cause, as they seemed to accentuate its Protestant nature. It was surely no coincidence that the majority of Huguenot soldiers joined the invasion forces, rather than staying behind to protect Dutch borders. The Ambassador, who invariably considered William an a-religious cynic, suggested that the Prince exploited the religious factor, Protestantising the army on the eve of the invasion by ridding it of Catholic officers on the advice of Bentinck and Calvinist ministers. The latter must have argued that these could not join in a Protestant enterprise.[57] According to an anonymous Catholic cornet in Bentinck's regiment, the latter was a 'passionate enemy of our religion'.[58] D'Avaux also accused the Grand Pensionary, Gaspar Fagel, of delivering a 'pathetic harangue' in the Holland States Assembly against Louis's dealing with the Huguenots, making Protestantism 'a pretext' and thus acting under a 'cloak of religion'.[59]

Jan Rietbergen has shown how William was not averse to presenting himself as the hero of his Huguenot soldiers, a champion of European Protestantism.[60] Jonathan Israel has argued that William fostered the perception that his intervention in England was for the sake of Protestantism. He did so by presenting his army not so much as an invasion army from the States General, but rather as an international army commanded by a godly prince.[61] When the invasion army entered Exeter days after the landing at Torbay it was headed by 200 English cavalry, followed by 200 black soldiers from Dutch Surinam, 200 Laplanders, 50 gentlemen with the banner 'God and the Protestant Religion' followed by William himself on a white palfrey.[62] Thus, William strengthened his case by entering as a godly prince, together with an international delegation of Huguenots, Dutch and Danes, and under the banner of Protestantism. At his landing in Belfast in the spring of 1690, William emphasised the image of a godly army that was to confront the enemy. Tony Claydon argued

---

56   AE CPH 156, fol. 318, d'Avaux to Louis XIV, 28 October 1688. For a new assessment of the size and composition of William's force, see J. Stapleton, 'Forging a Coalition Army: William III, the Grand Alliance, and the Confederate Army in the Spanish Netherlands, 1688–1697', PhD thesis (The Ohio State University, 2003).

57   AE CPH 156, fol. 237, d'Avaux to Louis, 7 October 1688.

58   'Mémoires de Monsieur de B. ou anecdotes, tant de la cour du prince d'Orange Guillaume III, que des principaux seigneurs de la République de ce temps', in *Bijdragen en Mededelingen betreffende de Geschiedenis der Nederlanden*, ed. F. J. L. Krämer (92 vols, The Hague, 1898; reprinted 1977–94), vol. 19, p. 124.

59   D'Avaux to Louis XIV, 20 September 1688, quoted in *Negotiations of d'Avaux*, vol. 4, p. 177.

60   Rietbergen, 'William of Orange', p. 45.

61   J. I. Israel, 'The Dutch Role in the Glorious Revolution', in J. I. Israel (ed.), *The Anglo-Dutch Moment: Essays on the Glorious Revolution and its World Impact* (Cambridge, 1991), p. 120 *et passim*.

62   'A True and Exact Relation of the Prince of Orange's Publick Entrance into Exeter', in *A Second Collection of Scarce and Valuable Tracts etc.*, ed. J. Somers (4 vols, London, 1750), vol. 3, pp. 419–20.

that when William publicly thanked the Duke of Schomberg – half-English, half-German Huguenot Protestant – for his services, he emphasised the international Protestantism that was central to his campaign.[63] Although William knew very well how to exploit the propaganda value of some of his army units, there were as yet no separate Huguenot regiments. The reason appears to have been that William had in fact tried to create independent French regiments, but was prevented from doing so by the States.[64] Instead, the Huguenots were dispersed amongst William's Red and Blue Dragoons and the Life Guards regiments.[65]

It is indeed striking that the expeditionary army had such a distinctive Protestant character; among the troops were English exiles, Brandenburgers, Swedes (commanded by a son of the Swedish king) and Swiss contingents.[66] The Huguenots were commanded by Lieutenant-General Willem Frederik van Nassau-Zuylestein, a favourite of William III.[67]

William's employment of Protestant imagery and rhetoric does not preclude the genuine religious fervour of many of the soldiers involved in the operation, nor can the religious zeal of the Huguenots be downplayed as a factor of importance. A well-known account of the events of 1688 was provided by John Whittle, a chaplain in William's army who depicted the invasion as a grand Protestant enterprise.[68] Indeed, to the French historian Jules Michelet it was precisely this Protestantism that provided victory; although the Huguenot element might have been small, it formed the moral core of William's army:

> Fortunately William's army was firm. It was strengthened precisely by that Calvinist element which is repudiated in England; I want to say by our Huguenots ... I by no means believe that well-endowed England ... does not acknowledge nobly, the share that our Frenchmen have in its deliverance.[69]

The significance of religious affiliations was also underlined by the Dutch ambassador in London, van Citters, who wrote to the States General that 'those who think to know best are of the opinion that the King's [James II's] army will not effectively consist of 12,000 troops, from which the Protestants should be deducted, of whom it is thought that when it comes to it none will take up their arms' against the Prince of Orange.[70]

---

63   T. Claydon, *William III and the Godly Revolution* (Cambridge, 1996), p. 141.

64   *Negotiations of d'Avaux*, vol. 4, pp. 18–30; Lart, 'The Huguenot Regiments': 480.

65   *Dublin and Portarlington Veterans*, ed. Le Fanu and Manchee, p. 3; AE CPH 156, fol. 287, d'Avaux to Louis XIV, October 1688.

66   A. van der Kuijl, *De Glorieuze Overtocht. De expeditie van Willem III naar Engeland in 1688* (Amsterdam, 1988), p. 42.

67   Ibid., p. 43.

68   J. Whittle, *An Exact Diary of the Late Expedition of His Illustrious Highness the Prince of Orange into England, etc.* (London, 1689).

69   Quoted in W. Cunningham, *Alien Immigrants to England* (London, 1897), p. 244.

70   BL, Add MS 17,677, fol. 529, Citters to States General, 7 December 1688; Israel, 'The Dutch Role', pp. 124–5.

The image of the Prince of Orange as a Protestant hero was also cultivated by the Huguenots themselves. Pierre Jurieu, for one, a leading figure among the refugees, held William in very high regard.[71] It was a Huguenot artist, Daniel Marot, who made a propagandistic engraving based on a sketch from Bentinck on the composition of the invasion fleet.[72] Clearly, a substantial number of Huguenots fled France and participated in military service in the hope of being part of an international crusade against Catholicism. Dumont de Bostaquet, for instance, perceived the march to London in the autumn of 1688 as that of a victorious Protestant army advancing to defeat the Catholic tyrant.[73] William, the new Gideon, led his small army, guided by Providence, to victory and defeated a numerically superior enemy. 'One has never seen such a small army march so gaily and with so much confidence', Dumont de Bostaquet wrote of their religious fervour.[74] However, unlike Bostaquet many Huguenots were otherwise destitute individuals who were being offered an opportunity to take service when international tensions dictated the expansion of armies.

III

Largely as a result of their zeal Huguenot soldiers also served in Anglo-Dutch forces beyond the pale of Protestant Europe. Their role in Savoy-Piedmont was singular and of particular note. At the same time as his forces invaded Ireland William III fostered the plan for an invasion of France via Dauphiné in conspiracy both with the itinerant pastor of the *désert*, Claude Brousson, and his envoy to the Swiss cantons, Thomas Coxe, from November 1689 via the so-called Lindau Project.[75] Though William first prompted Brousson to formulate a scheme, he thought it 'scarce practicable', but understood that its success would depend on a speedy dispatch of King James's forces from Ireland.[76]

On his own initiative, Brousson wrote to Henri de Mirmand, Seigneur de Roubiac et Vestric, praying for the Dutch Republic to send 'a good Captain to disperse the royal troops'.[77] However, another active Huguenot, the Marquis de Miremont, and

---

71   F. R. J. Knetsch, 'Pierre Jurieu: Theologian and Politician of the Dispersion', *Acta Historiae Neerlandica*, 5 (1971): 213–42, 228.

72   Reproduced in Van der Kuijl, *De Glorieuze Overtocht*, p. 64.

73   D. W. Ressinger, 'Good Faith: The Military and the Ministry in Exile, or the Memoirs of Isaac Dumont de Bostaquet and Jacques Fontaine', in Vigne and Littleton (eds), *From Strangers to Citizens*, p. 454.

74   *Mémoires d'Isaac Dumont de Bostaquet*, ed. Richard, p. 199.

75   C. Storrs, 'Thomas Coxe and the Lindau Project', in A. de Lange (ed.), *Dall'Europa alle Valli Valdesi* (Turin, 1990), p. 199; H. Bosc, 'Le Maréchal Montreuil et la défense du Littoral Méditerranéen pendant le guerre de Camisards (mars–novembre 1703)', *Bulletin de la société de l'histoire du Protestantisme française*, 112 (1966): 6; C. Bost, *Les prédicants protestants des Cévennes et du Bas-Languadoc, 1684–1700* (2 vols, Paris, 1912; reprinted Montpellier, 2001), vol. 2, p. 515.

76   HMC, *Finch*, vol. 3, p. 17, Nottingham to Carmarthen, 17 February 1691.

77   Brousson to Miremont, 26 August 1689. Cited in F. Teulon, 'François Vivent, prédicant cévenol', PhD thesis (University of Paris, 1946), pp. 56–7, 66, 69; HMC, *House*

his militant circle, continually advocated an armed invasion led by William III to restore Protestants' rights in France.[78] Brousson would make similar overtures to Schomberg's son, Charles, and enthusiasm for the scheme was strong internationally. It even attracted Brousson's son, Barthélemy, an officer in the Dutch army. In response, the pastor wrote to friends in Holland, imploring them to 'remember my son always, and share your pious remonstrances with him'.[79]

In Switzerland, the Marquis de Miremont helped raise a number of Huguenot regiments, along with those channelled into Geneva via Schaffhausen and Lindau in Germany. By 1 July 1689, there were 14 companies of French Huguenots in Dutch pay and seven Piedmontese, equalling 1,100 men, under the command of Solomon Blosset de Loches. Two other refugee commanders, Jacques de Julien and Gabriel Malet, arrived via Geneva, Chablais and Aosta with 1,400 men. By October 1690 the Huguenot force in Savoy numbered 3,000 (with 700 remaining from Henri Arnaud's expedition to relieve the Vaudois, 800 under Blosset de Loches, 800 under Lieutenant-Colonel Julien, 400 under Lieutenant-Colonel Malet, and 200 dragoons with Colonel Balthazar).[80]

Miremont's second regiment, called Miremont's Dragoons, started its life as Balthazar (or Barthazar's) regiment in Dutch pay in Piedmont.[81] Balthazar was probably Swiss, but his officers were mostly Huguenots. The unit spent some time on the Dutch establishment and some on the English and, sometime between 1693 and 1695 it came under the leadership of Miremont.[82] Evidence of this change of command comes in the form of Major Charles Couteau's petition (probably dated 1699 or 1700), and typical of the experiences of so many Huguenot soldiers. He stated that he had served as major of the regiment of Balthazar from 1690 to the 1697 Peace of Ryswick.[83] His wife and three children were living in Morges (Vaud) in Switzerland, but he also supported three children of his brother, escapees from persecution in France. His mother and father had been put to death in France and he had only his pension on the Irish establishment and so begged permission to go to live with his family, holding himself ready to serve King William at the first order which he would receive either through the King's minister at Bern or through the Marquis d'Arzilliers at Geneva.

---

of Lords, 1690–91, p. 170; N. Luttrell, *A Brief Historical Relation of State Affairs* (6 vols, Oxford, 1857), vol. 2, p. 172.

78   Teulon, 'François Vivent', pp. 56–7.

79   Letter from Brousson printed in L. Rauzier-Fontayne and S. Maurs, *Claude Brousson* (Geneva, 1948), p. 199.

80   Jacques de Julien (b.1660), formerly a page to William of Orange: M. Bokhorst, *Nederlands-Zwitserse betrekkingen voor en na 1700* (2 vols, Amsterdam, Paris, 1930), vol. 1, p. 176.

81   The Balthazar/Barthazar/Miremont Dragoons regiment was raised in Switzerland in 1690 from the Huguenot refugees there and was sent to Piedmont where it served from 1691 to 1695. Afterwards it went to Flanders and entered into English pay from 1 March 1695/6. It was disbanded in Ireland in March 1699.

82   G. C. Boeri, *The Army of the Duke of Savoy 1688–1713* (Turin, n.d.).

83   BL, Add. MS 9,718, fol. 201.

On 28 May 1690, the Vaudois signed a treaty with Vittorio Amedeo II, allowing the Duke to wield his Protestant Vaudois subjects (in collusion with their Huguenot allies) against Louis XIV. When the Duke of Savoy joined the Alliance powers, these units were attached to his army.[84] The Dutch States General was to pay a third of the money designed to subsidise the Duke and the Allies' designs on France.[85] It was even thought (in July 1690) that they might establish an independent Protestant state, to act as a buffer between Louis XIV and Savoy.[86] Count de La Tour, Savoyard minister to The Hague, suggested the idea, though it was not mentioned in the treaty between Savoy and the Swiss cantons, or in his instructions from Vittorio Amedeo II. William had to work hard to overcome the Duke of Savoy's distrust of the Huguenots as former subjects of the French king.[87] Ultimately, the Duke's fears were confirmed; three Huguenot commanders – Julien, Montbrun and Malet – returned to France and became Catholics, though this is said to have been due, in part, to disputes within the Huguenot regiments.[88] Schomberg's death at the Boyne threw the plan into confusion, and nothing was effected.[89] The Allies had to work hard to keep the force together for a further six months; they called for the appointment of a Protestant of international standing to lead them, a prince of Brandenburg or a Schomberg.[90]

On 15 November 1690, Schomberg's successor, Charles, took his seat in the House of Lords and was almost immediately, thereafter, appointed to command the Dutch forces in Savoy, with the rank of lieutenant-general. Plans were put forward in early-1691 to raise three Huguenot battalions, under the Marquis de Miremont, Henri-Laurent de Montbrun and Hector du Puy de Montauban, for a projected invasion

---

84   Storrs, 'Thomas Coxe and the Lindau Project', p. 211.

85   Vittorio Amedeo to Govone, 6 May 1690, quoted in A. Pascale, *La valli durante la Guerra dirimpatrio dei Valdesi* (Turin, 1967), pt. 2, pp. 919–53; treaties in J. M. Solar de La Marguérite (ed.), *Traités publics de la royale maison de Savoie, avec les puissances étrangères: depuis la paix de Château-Cambrésis jusqu'à nos jours* (8 vols, Turin, 1836–44, 1861), vol. 2, pp. 121–31; G. Symcox, *Victor Amadeus II: Absolutism in the Savoy State, 1675–1730* (London, 1983), p. 105.

86   See *Het Archief van den Raadpensionaris Antonie Heinsius, 1683–97*, ed. H. J. van der Heim (3 vols, The Hague: RGP, 1867–80), vol. 1, p. 200, Heemskerk to Fagel, Vienna, 5 August 1690; C. Storrs, 'Machiavelli Dethroned: Victor Amadeus II and the Making of the Anglo-Savoyard Alliance of 1690', *European History Quarterly*, 22/3 (1992): 362, 374.

87   Archivo di stato, Turin, *Lettere ministri*, Olanda (hereafter AST/LM), m. 3, de La Tour to St Thomas, The Hague, 2 October 1693; C. Contessa *et al.* (eds), *La Campagne di Guerra in Piemonte (1703–1708) el'assedio di Torino (1706)* (9 vols, Turin, 1908–33), vol. 1, p. 244, Vittorio Amedeo to Sales, 16 October 1703. Cited in C. Storrs, *War, Diplomacy and the Rise of Savoy, 1690–1720* (Cambridge, 1999), p. 53.

88   Haag, *La France Protestante*, vol. 6 (Julien in 1694: pp. 101–2), vol. 7 (Montauban in December 1698: p. 190; Malet: p. 456); Weiss, *Histoire des réfugiés protestants*, vol. 2, p. 198; Storrs, *War, Diplomacy and the Rise of Savoy*, p. 53 n. 171.

89   W. C. Utt and B. E. Strayer, *The Bellicose Dove: Claude Brousson and Protestant Resistance to Louis XIV, 1647–1698* (Brighton, Portland, 2003), p. 57.

90   AST/ Imprese militari/ m. 1/43/6, Coloma's project, 27 June 1690; Storrs, 'Machiavelli Dethroned': 356.

of France under Charles's overall command.[91] King Louis responded to Savoy's coolness by declaring war on the duchy.[92] By 1692, an Alliance force blockaded Casale, while Schomberg invaded Dauphiné, at the head of a force of Huguenots, but including detachments from the Spanish army of Lombardy and artillery from the Duke of Savoy.[93] They took Guillestre and Gap and when Embrun fell to them on 15 August 1692, it threw Dauphiné into panic, due in part to Schomberg turning over the government of the place to Huguenots; hopes were high for some attack to be launched into the heart of France.[94] Schomberg addressed the inhabitants of Embrun, claiming that he would re-establish the Edict of Nantes, but would respect the privileges of the Catholic Church too.[95] Enthusiasm ran so high that one Huguenot soldier stated: 'We will be unhappy indeed if we are not delivered in six months.'[96] But disputes among the leadership of the invasion force, coupled with the failure of the locals to rise in numbers strong enough to carry it forward, led to a retreat back across the Alps as autumn came on.[97]

Savoy was in crisis and Schomberg's army marched back into a country overrun by the forces of Louis XIV, under the command of Marshal Catinat.[98] His return briefly checked the progress of the French army, but the second Duke of Schomberg was far from happy with the general quality of the men he commanded. In his eyes, the campaign was mismanaged by William's allies. In 1693 his force was rapidly drawn into a pitched battle on the plains of Marsaglia. Schomberg commanded in person the left wing of the central part of the army that, on 4 October, was defeated and Charles mortally wounded.[99] He would have been left for dead on the battlefield

---

91   AST/LM/Olanda, m. 1, Vittorio Amedeo to Filibert, Comte de La Tour, 8 April 1691; Storrs, *War, Diplomacy and the Rise of Savoy*, p. 53.

92   Storrs, 'Machiavelli Dethroned': 400.

93   AGS Estado 3417/48, Leganos to Carlos II, Turin, 30 June 1692; Storrs, 'The Army of Lombardy (I)': 388. HNA/SG/8644/241, 243, Vittorio Amedeo to Fagel, Turin, 6 and 13 June 1692; Storrs, *War, Diplomacy and the Rise of Savoy*, p. 58.

94   Symcox, *Victor Amadeus II*, p. 111.

95   Marquis de Saporta, 'Les derniers représentants de la famille de Mme de Sévigné en Provence', *Revue des Deux-Mondes* (1879); Weiss, *Histoire des réfugiés protestants*, vol. 1, p. 184; A. Mailhet, 'Les protestants du Diois et des baronnies en 1692, pendant l'invasion du Dauphiné', *Bulletin de la société de l'histoire du Protestantisme française*, 58 (1909): 7.

96   W. C. Utt, 'L'itinéraire sinueux du pasteur Clarion', *Bulletin de la société de l'histoire du Protestantisme française*, 177 (1971).

97   For example, the Spanish commanders were horrified at the idea of taking winter quarters in Dauphiné: AGS Estado 3417/106, Leganos to Carlos II, Genoa, 12 October 1692; C. Storrs, 'The Army of Lombardy and the Resilience of Spanish Power in Italy in the Reign of Carlos II (1665–1700) (Part II)', *War in History*, 5/1 (January 1998): 19. At least some booty had been taken: see the agreement for the payment of contributions by the community of Guillestre in *Documents inédits relatifs à l'histoire et toppographie militaire des Aples: la campagne de 1692 dans le Haut Dauphiné*, ed. E. A. de Rochas d'Aiglun (Paris, Grenoble, 1874).

98   *De Briefwisseling van Anthonie Heinsius, 1702–1720*, ed. A. J. Veenendaal (19 vols, The Hague: RGP, grote serie, 1976–2001), vol. 2, p. 509.

99   According to one account Schomberg was taken prisoner but exchanged for his father's old friend, the Grand Prior de Vendôme, who was wounded in the thigh: HMC,

had not his faithful Huguenot servant, Monginot de La Salle, carried him to nearby Turin.[100]

As soon as the disaster at Marsaglia was known in England the Huguenot Earl of Galway was appointed, in November 1693, commander-in-chief of the Anglo-Dutch force in Piedmont. He was also to be William III's envoy extraordinary for England and Holland at the court of Turin. His arrival was a comfort to the large number of Huguenots serving there in William's army, but Galway's duties turned out to be more diplomatic than military. The Earl soon discovered that Vittorio Amedeo had entered into secret negotiations with France so that all he could do was to ensure a small degree of freedom of worship for the Vaudois Protestants. When the Duke of Savoy publicly announced his treaty with France, Galway had just enough time to withdraw his forces into Milan and capture the French subsidy sent by Louis XIV to Vittorio Amedeo II. Most of the Huguenots who had been part of Schomberg's force in Savoy returned to the Netherlands or Britain and, as a result, in 1694, 510 Huguenot officers burdened William III's military budget. Like many officers during a time of peace, they were placed on half-pay and those few who remained in Savoy fared little better.

In England in 1694 (despite hopes of yet another attempt by Miremont to invade France), 11 Huguenot officers joined the cavalry troop of Major Charles de La Tour, Comte de Paulin, in the Earl of Macclesfield's regiment.[101] One reason for the attraction of Paulin's company may be the fact that he was related to Meinhard, third Duke of Schomberg. Having been captured by the Jacobites in Ireland while serving as a cornet in Galway's Horse during the Irish Wars, he was sent by their commander, the Marquis de Saint-Ruth, to be ill treated in France. In response one of William's generals was determined to see his own French Catholic prisoners hanged.[102] It is difficult to say whether this militant attitude was shared by the Count and his Huguenot soldiers, but it seems likely. The vast majority of Huguenots remained in the four extant regiments that had been created in 1689.[103]

Downshire, vol. 1, pt. 1, p. 434; J. Abbadie, *La Mort du Juste ... Sermon [occasioned by the death of Charles, second Duke of Schomberg]* (London, 1693).

100 *Memoires of the Transactions in Savoy During this War. Wherein the Duke of Savoy's Foul Play with the Allies, and his Secret Correspondence with the French King, are [Demonstrated]*, ed. J. Savage (London, 1697), p. 72 *et passim*. It is most unlikely that this man was Etienne Monginot de La Salle, the well-known Paris doctor who was 66 in 1693. However, it may be one of his sons, Etienne, Paul or Jacques, all of whom were naturalised in England on 31 January 1690: O. Douen, *La Révocation de l'Edit de Nantes à Paris* (3 vols, Paris, 1894), vol. 3, pp. 224–9.

101 Macclesfield had served under Turenne in France and married there. His wife was Jeanne, daughter of Pierre de Civille de Sancourt, a Huguenot nobleman from Rouen in Normandy. The Earl was a firm friend of the Huguenots: CSPDom., *King William's Chest* 15, no. 8, Dubourdieu to Earl of Shrewsbury, ?April 1694: CSPDom., 1694–95, p. 122.

102 HMC, *Fourth Report* (London, 1874), pt. 1, pp. 320–1, Ginkel to Lord Coningsby, 9 July 1691.

103 *Hertford County Records: Notes and Extracts from the Sessions Rolls, 1581–1698*, ed. W. J. Hardy (3 vols, Hertford, 1905), vol. 1, p. 417; BL, Add. MS 9,731, fol. 31, Bellasise to Blathwayt, 3 November 1697.

With the re-entry of the Duke of Savoy into the alliance of nations leagued against Louis XIV, and the events of the War of the Spanish Succession (1701–13), plans of Anglo-Dutch Huguenot forces attacking France were revived. When, however, a projected expedition of the refugees into the south of France was deferred many among them were enrolled in Swiss regiments that fought for the Dutch in Piedmont and the Spanish Netherlands, and took their fight with Louis to other nations united against their old homeland. Others returned secretly to the most agitated parts of Languedoc to foment insurrection.[104] The Marquis de Miremont, proposed to find recruits for the Dutch in francophone Switzerland, where there were 'a quantity of [French] foreigners, itinerants, extremely dishevelled and consequently suitable to be made soldiers of so they can eat'.[105] As late as 1703, the Marquis announced that he would revive the Camisard revolt in the Cévennes with 6,000 or 7,000 refugees and carry weapons into the heart of France. He said it need not cost a great deal of money and he was a native of Languedoc and knew the region well.[106]

In this new epoch of the civil war in the Cévennes in the south of France in 1704, Miremont took his body of militant Dutch-paid refugees to Piedmont where, under the orders of the Duke of Savoy, he was to watch for an opportunity to advance into Languedoc. He was active in sending agents to gather advance intelligence, and eager to the degree of neglecting to arrange their passports.[107] Miremont said that Britain's monarch, Queen Anne, was determined to support the Camisards, a fact confirmed to the Marquis in conversation with Prince George of Denmark, the royal consort, and David Flotard, the Huguenot agent in The Netherlands.[108] The Dutch Grand Pensionary, Anthonie Heinsius, hoped to see raised a 'fine corps' of men, but Colonel de Belcastel regretted to inform him that Miremont was mistaken; he would not find in Switzerland or Germany the required number of refugees, and the Colonel himself had had trouble getting permission from the canton of Bern to raise 3,000 Huguenot recruits, with whom it was intended he should join the Duke of Savoy, and then work in co-operation with Miremont for the invasion of France.[109]

---

104 L. H. Boles, *The Huguenots, the Protestant Interest and the War of the Spanish Succession, 1702–1714*, American University Studies 9, History 188 (New York, 1997).

105 G. de *Lamberty, Mémoires pour servir à l'histoire du XVIII siécle, contenant les négociations, traitez, resolutions et autres documents authentiques concernant les affaires d'état* (14 vols, Amsterdam, The Hague, 1731–40), vol. 3, p. 237; A. Verdeil, *Histoire du canton de Vaud* (4 vols, Lausanne, 1849–52), vol. 2, p. 339.

106 *De Briefwisseling van Anthonie Heinsius*, ed. Veenendaal, vol. 2, p. 222, no. 574, Miremont to Heinsius, London, 14 May 1703. See instructions as envoy to the Cévennes, 1703: BL, Add. MS 29,590, fol. 245.

107 His pastry-chef, Monplaisir, and Dalbiac, a subaltern in his regiment, were detained for lack of a passport: *De Briefwisseling van Anthonie Heinsius*, ed. Veenendaal, vol. 2, p. 425, no. 1087, Sparre to Heinsius, Sas de Gendt, 27 August 1703.

108 Ibid., p. 451, no. 1142, Miremont to Heinsius, London, 11 September 1703.

109 *The Correspondence 1701–1711 of John Churchill, first Duke of Marlborough, and Anthonie Heinsius, Grand Pensionary of Holland*, ed. B. van 't Hoff (The Hague, 1951), p. 100, no. 164, Heinsius to Marlborough, The Hague, 11 March 1704; *De Briefwisseling van Anthonie Heinsius*, ed. Veenendaal, vol. 3, pp. 345–6, no. 953, Belcastel to Heinsius, Turin, 19 September 1704.

Miremont clearly intended to use Huguenot veterans left over from William's campaigns in Ireland and Portugal to augment his troops in Piedmont.[110] However, he never achieved a successful invasion of France and the Huguenots he commanded remained in Savoy or moved on to other areas of refuge. Times had changed and, almost 20 years after the Revocation, the generation of refugees who had supplied so eagerly William's invasion force in 1688 now faltered.

IV

William III was by far the most enthusiastic host of Huguenot soldiers in the decade of the Revocation. Yet he was prevented from capitalising on his desire (and their wish) to employ the Huguenots to strike at King Louis. The unexpected event of the Glorious Revolution changed this and the late acquiescence of the Dutch regents to his designs ensured that Huguenots would play a prominent role in the 1688 invasion and subsequent campaigning in Ireland, Piedmont and the Peninsula throughout the Nine Years' War. The vast majority of the Huguenots who ended up on the English and Irish establishments (military budgets) as half-pay *reformé* officers or pensioners started their service in Dutch pay. Throughout the 1690s the Dutch Republic subsidised Huguenot soldiers across Europe. Often these men remained directly in Dutch pay. Fittingly, William was their point of reference, whether as King in Britain or *Stadtholder* in the Netherlands. Significantly, they were his loyal troops throughout his reign, a fact that harmed him in Britain and left Dutch- and British-based Huguenots without a powerful patron after 1702. Their role in Dutch service has, as a result, been less considered because it was so dispersed; they were rarely in the Dutch Republic, but were dispersed abroad in its service (to say nothing of those who aided Netherlands' interests in the Dutch East India Company).

What William gained from the Huguenots' loyalty was a mixed advantage. While he benefitted from their propaganda value as persecuted Protestants, he was forced to consider their (sometimes impetuous and unrealistic) plans for invading France. Huguenot *grands*, such as the Marquis de Miremont – arguably the most fiery man among them – compromised William's overall strategy while, simultaneously, affecting the Prince's foreign policy. Despite this, the Huguenots helped reinforce the 'grand vision' of internationalist Williamite foreign policy more than any other group. Their commitment to returning home on their own terms, like their creation of a militant self-identity in exile, dictated that they would perpetuate a Williamite vision beyond the Prince's grave. Miremont's failure to effect anything to aid the Camisards says much about the value of William's personal support for Huguenot schemes.

Fittingly, this chapter really highlights the unique and fleeting interaction between William and Huguenot soldiers in the last twenty years of his life. More than anything else it elucidates not 'Dutch' policy or designs, but Williamite ones. In England and Brandenburg there can be little doubt that Huguenot soldiers had some sense that they served a new land and its interests, rather than themselves. By contrast, in

---

110 Ibid., p. 354, no. 975, van Vrijbergen to Heinsius, London, 23 September 1704.

the Dutch service they seem never to have progressed to this stage, maintaining all along that their loyalty was to William, Calvinism and international Protestantism in that order. For this reason they were seldom physically located in the Netherlands, but dispersed across Europe, fighting in the Dutch and predominantly Williamite interest. In effect Huguenot soldiers maintained in Dutch service throughout the 1690s that status they first achieved in 1686, when William attempted to pension as many of them as he could manage in order to keep them as a solid reserve to back his plans. In this atmosphere it should not be surprising that the Huguenot soldiers in Dutch service saw so little of the Netherlands. In truth they seem to have felt little regard for it beyond the person of the *Stadtholder* and the benefit the United Provinces could be to their own plans.

Chapter 8

Au Réfugié
Huguenot Officers in The Hague, 1687

Dianne W. Ressinger
Huguenot Society of Great Britain and Ireland

Isaac Dumont de Bostaquet (1632–1709) was not a typical officer in the service of William III as Huguenot soldiers marked time in 1687 and 1688 in Holland before their invasion of England. He was distinctly not a military man either by inclination or by experience. However, his memoirs are a fine source of first-hand information on the assemblage of William's forces in the Netherlands in 1687 and their preparation in the autumn of 1688 for the descent on England.[1] Memoirs of Huguenot officers are in short supply, and Dumont provides an eyewitness account of complex events. Though Dumont de Bostaquet cannot be considered a typical officer for many reasons, much of what he tells the reader is informative about conditions among William's newly recruited French officers.

I

On the eve of the departure of William's forces in 1688 Dumont was a man of 55 who had been three times married, was the father of 19 children by his three noble wives, and belonged to what is now thought of as the leisured class. His only real military experience had lasted less than two years beginning in his twentieth year, which he spent in the service of the young Louis XIV during the tumultuous period

---

1 All quotes from Dumont have been translated into English by the author in her annotated English-language version of the 1864 Charles Read and Francis Waddington edition of the memoirs of Isaac Dumont de Bostaquet: *Memoirs of Isaac Dumont de Bostaquet: A Gentleman of Normandy*, ed. D. W. Ressinger, Huguenot Society New Series 4 (London, 2005). The earlier work in French was published as *Mémoires inédits de Dumont de Bostaquet, gentilhomme Normand, sur les temps qui ont précédé et suivi la Révocation de l'Edit de Nantes, sur le refuge et les expéditions de Guillaume III en Angleterre et en Irlande*, ed. C. Read and F. Waddington (Paris, 1864).

For a review of the Read and Waddington edition of the Dumont de Bostaquet memoirs, see 'Mélanges', *Bulletin de la société de l'histoire du Protestantisme française*, 13 (1865). The original manuscript is housed at the Royal Irish Academy, Dublin, as MS 12N17. A new edition of the French text has also appeared: *Mémoires d'Isaac Dumont de Bostaquet, gentilhomme normand, sur les temps qui ont précédé et suivi la Révocation de l'Édit de Nantes, sur le refuge et les expéditions de Guillaume III en Angleterre et en Irlande*, ed. M. E. Richard (Paris, 2002).

of the Fronde (1648–52). From October 1652 until the summer of 1654, just after Louis's coronation in June, Dumont served in the regiment of the (Protestant) Duc de Longueville who with his treacherous wife had been much involved in the plots and counterplots of the Fronde.[2] Dumont's loyalty was always with the King.

Dumont had enjoyed the classical education of a Huguenot gentleman at the Protestant academies of Saumur and Caen as well as the training of a nobleman in the riding academies of Paris and Rouen where he learned the use of arms. But the use to which he had put his education and training was as a country gentleman living on his estates in Normandy: Bostaquet and La Fontelaye. He had left the service of the King after the 'breaking of the regiments' following the 1654 campaign in Lille, and since no new regiments were being formed his mother decided that it was time for him to marry; his family's choice fell upon Marthe de La Rive, the daughter of a wealthy mercantile family of Rouen. It was clearly a marriage of advantage for him, since he received the enormous dowry of 50,000 *livres*, and he plainly states that he did not love her. He was 24, she was 21 years old; they married in June 1656 at Grand Quevilly, the great Protestant *temple* near Rouen. He soon came to appreciate Marthe's many good qualities which, unfortunately, he does not enumerate.[3]

One of the many misconceptions about Dumont's life is that he was a battle-hardened 'old soldier' at the time of the 1688 descent on England.[4] This error was first made by the editors of his memoir, Charles Read and Francis Waddington, in 1864, and has often been repeated. They conflated the titles of Dumont's great-grandson, also named Isaac Dumont (1765–1847), with those of 'our' Isaac (1632–1709). The younger Isaac had extensive military service and was described as an 'old Musketeer of the first company of the King's guard' (*ancien mousquetaire de la première compagnie de la garde ordinaire du roi*). In fact, the Dumont discussed in this chapter was a family man who chose to stay at home tending to his estates, and enjoying the life of a country nobleman. His family connections were vast and included virtually every noble family of Normandy.[5] Many of his relatives were in the service of Louis XIV in spite of their Protestant faith, though some of them were denied advancement because of it, and most left or escaped from France after the revocation of the Edict of Nantes in 1685.[6]

---

2   *Dumont de Bostaquet*, ed. Ressinger, pp. xvii, 31, 295.

3   Ibid., pp. 46–7, 300.

4   Ibid., pp. xix, xx.

5   E. Drigon, Comte de Magny, *Nobiliaire de Normandie* (2 vols, Paris, 1863–4).

6   Including Jean de Fourniers, Baron de Neufville, commissioned *ritmeister* (captain) in Holland on 24 May 1686 at a salary of 650 florins a year. His wife was the daughter of Catherine Hébert (David Brossard de Grosmesnil's second wife) and her first husband, Noël Hamel. Thus she was the step-sister of Dumont's third wife, Marie Brossard de Grosmesnil. Madame de Neufville accompanied Marie in her flight from France in spring 1688. Each of Marie's uncles, brothers and sisters was known by a different territorial title, among them: de Grosmesnil, de Monthue, de Prouville, d'Augeville, de Béquigny, du Quesnel, d'Heusecourt. The surname in each case was Brossard: see 'Les officiers français en service hollandais après la Révocation pendant la période 1686–1689', ed. T. A. Boeree, *Bulletin des Eglises Wallonnes*, 4/1 (1928): 1–65 (29).

The Revocation was the pivotal event in Dumont's life. Determined at first to hold out against the threat of dragoons being sent to his home, he felt forced, out of concern for his pregnant wife and several daughters whom he wished to protect, to sign his abjuration. Filled with shame and remorse, he agreed to receive instruction in the Catholic faith. Though the rest of his family was forced by dragoons to abjure, they continued to worship at home as they always had, in the manner of the Reformed church, although of course they had no minister other than Dumont himself. Of this difficult period he writes:

> I felt extreme indifference toward everything which had previously engaged my affection … we were all equal in our crime and we no longer enjoyed the tranquillity of soul which had previously been ours. God seemed to withdraw from us … I constantly brooded on my withdrawal into myself, but the flesh fought against the spirit and I feared abandoning my large family.[7]

During the two years following the Revocation Dumont's position was precarious indeed. He was constantly searching for a way to get his family out of France and had attempted to send his youngest daughter to Holland without success. Authorities suspected him of complicity in every successful escape, and not always without reason. He was seen by powerful Catholics as an influential man whose good example would encourage others to follow him. Meanwhile, he 'was painted as the author of all plans for escape by sea'.[8] Before he had completed his own plans to take his family to Holland, his sister and mother decided to try and reach Holland from the northern coast of France near Dieppe in early 1687.

Dumont was forced to flee unexpectedly from his home in Normandy in the spring of 1687 following this unsuccessful escape attempt of his mother, sister and several other members of his family. He had not intended to escape himself until late summer of 1687, but he was caught up and wounded in a skirmish with coastal guards. In his hastily accomplished exile he was forced to abandon his 13 living children and his pregnant wife, Marie Brossard de Grosmesnil. He left France severely wounded, with virtually no money and no hope of supporting the few members of his destitute family who would soon follow him, including his 8-year-old daughter, Judith-Julie, who was sent to him in Holland in September 1687, and his wife, Marie, and three year-old son who joined him there in March 1688.[9] The infant born after his departure he was never to see – too young to accompany her mother, she was left in France in the care of relatives. Many of his family, including his sister, several nieces and his

---

7   *Dumont de Bostaquet*, ed. Ressinger, pp. 107–8.

8   Ibid., p. 110.

9   Dumont's daughter, Judith-Julie, had recently been lowered over the sea wall at Dieppe into a waiting boat destined for Holland where father and daughter were reunited. She later married Antoine Ligonier de Bonneval, chaplain to the regiment of Jacques Laumonnier, Marquis de Varennes (a godson of Louis XIV), and was later attached to that of the Duke of Schomberg in Ireland. Antoine was a kinsman of Jean-Louis de Ligonier, later Field Marshal the Rt. Hon. Earl Ligonier: C. E. Lart, 'The Huguenot Regiments', *Proceedings of the Huguenot Society of London*, 9/3 (1911): 522.

80-year-old mother, were imprisoned, tried and later sentenced to convents for the 'New Catholics' as a result of their attempt to escape from France.[10]

This is the traumatic background to the events in The Hague in December 1687 that are the focus of this chapter, and to set the scene, it is important to look at the situation from the point of view of a newly arrived and well-connected if poor Huguenot. Dumont was far from lonely – he writes that 'Rotterdam had become almost French because so many of the inhabitants of Rouen and Dieppe had sought refuge there'.[11] Holland was replete with first-class scientists, religious leaders (many of them expatriate *pasteurs* from France), refugee Protestant officers from French regiments, lawyers and artists.[12] Dumont wrote the section of his memoirs dealing with his life in The Hague later (in September of 1688), about nine months after the events described in this essay and shortly before he embarked with William of Orange in October for the descent on England. That he spent eight full pages telling the story that this chapter enumerates, in three long paragraphs, illustrates its importance in his mind. When compared with other momentous events in his life, these eight pages assume real importance in their detail and length-of-telling. He takes less than one full page to describe the death of his second (and most beloved) wife, Anne Le Cauchois de Tibermont, and barely five pages to describe the fire which completely destroyed his *château* at La Fontelaye and its contents. He even includes actual bits of dialogue in the telling of this tale, which was truly unusual in his writing.[13]

Dumont had arrived in The Hague in mid-June 1687. Within days of his arrival he called upon his powerful relative, Daniel Tassin de Torsay, who had been in the service of the States General of the United Provinces of the Netherlands since the early 1650s.[14] Dumont had paid a visit to Colonel Tassin de Torsay and had relied upon him for assistance while in The Hague as a young man at the time of his uncle Abraham Dumont's death there in 1653. De Torsay is the man Dumont consistently called (though he spelled it incorrectly) 'my generous relative de Torcé'.[15] Daniel Tassin de Torsay commanded in person an infantry regiment in the Dutch army until 1678, after that he was promoted to the rank of Major-General and, finally, Lieutenant-General in 1704.[16] He was distantly related to Dumont through the de La Haye, Dupuis and Morel families.

In 1687 Major-General Tassin de Torsay was a Huguenot soldier of enormous influence in the Netherlands, in part due to his family connection to William of

---

10   *Dumont de Bostaquet*, ed. Ressinger, pp. 132–4.

11   Ibid., p. 143.

12   'Liste des pasteurs des Eglises Réformées de France réfugiés en Hollande', *Bulletin de la société de l'histoire du Protestantisme française*, 7 (1858): 426–34.

13   *Dumont de Bostaquet*, ed. Ressinger, pp. 154–66.

14   For details of his career, see H. Ringoir, *Hoofdofficieren infanterie van 1568 tot 1813*, Bijdragen van de Sectie Militaire Geschiedenis 9 (The Hague, 1981).

15   *Dumont de Bostaquet*, ed. Ressinger, p. 148.

16   M. R. Glozier, *The Huguenot Soldiers of William of Orange and the Glorious Revolution of 1688: The Lions of Judah* (Brighton, Portland, 2002), p. 58; P. Minet, 'Huguenots in the Marlborough Wars', *Proceedings of the Huguenot Society of London*, 27/4 (2001): 485–96.

Orange. His brother, Charles Tassin d'Alonne, was married to one Johanna Silfvercrona who bore a son in 1646; the boy was her love-child by William II, Prince of Orange. This child, Abel Tassin d'Alonne, was, therefore, the illegitimate half-brother of William III.[17] Abel Tassin d'Alonne had a fine career as secretary to Queen Mary II and later as private secretary to William in England.[18] Jean Rou, in his memoirs, speaks of de Torsay's 'nephew', d'Alonne, at some length and mentions a letter which he received from the Major-General, naming d'Alonne as his nephew.[19] D'Alonne had no children, but when he died in 1723, he left wills in both England and Holland naming cousins of the Damin, Brunier, Joly, Silfvercrona, Van Cralingue, Willocquauw and de Guickery families. He also left money to establish schools for the instruction of 'young children of negro slaves' in the West Indies.[20]

De Torsay introduced Dumont to William III and arranged for him to apply for a commission as Captain in a Dutch cavalry regiment. Dumont's papers were far from in order – proof of his service to the Duc de Longueville in 1652–3 had burned in a fire at his château at La Fontelaye and he had never been given a copy of his commission by the French duke. He says that 'a few days after my arrival there was a third promotion of officers for which many had waited a long time'.[21] He was accepted, in spite of his lack of proof of experience, as a *capitaine réformé*, or half-pay *reformado* Captain, and subscribed his oath of loyalty to the States General on 19 June:

> We all took an oath of loyalty to the Council of State, which I did with all my heart, after which we were given our commissions. Captains who came directly from actual service had a pension of 700 *livres* and the others, as *réformé*, 520 *livres*. They reduced all the officers of the preceding two promotions to almost the same wages in order to find the

17   H. J. H. Siccama, *Aanteekeningen en verbeteringen op het in 1906 door het historisch genootschap uitgegeven register op de journalen van Constantijn Huygens den zoon* (Amsterdam, 1915); C. Droste, *Overblyfsels van geheugenissen* (2 vols, The Hague, 1728), vol. 2, pp. 427, 442; *Correspondentie van Willem III en van Hans Willem Bentinck, eersten graaf van Portland*, ed. N. Japikse (5 vols, The Hague: RGP, 1927–33), vol. 1, pt. 1, p. 422; D. C. A. Agnew, *Protestant Exiles from France* (2 vols, London, Edinburgh, eighth edition 1886), vol. 2, p. 80.

18   The grant to him of Pickering Castle is just one indication of the high esteem in which he was held by his half-brother, William III: see copy of the grant by William III to Abel Tassin d'Alonne of Pickering Castle and other lands; 18 May 1697: Nottingham University, MS Pw A 312/1–2; Abel Tassin d'Alonne to Hans Willem Bentinck, first Earl of Portland, The Hague, 5 February 1706: ibid., Pw A 319/1–2; Abel Tassin d'Alonne *vs*. William Bellamy, Robert Hart: Castle, honour, or manor of Pickering, and manor of Scalby, parcel of the duchy of Lancaster. Touching a schedule of rents payable to said honour, and rents paid since the death of Catherine late Queen Dowager, 7 Anne: TNA, PRO E 134/7Anne/Mich14.

19   *Mémoires inédits et opuscules de Jean Rou (1638–1711), avocat au parlement de Paris*, ed. F. Waddington (2 vols, Paris, The Hague, 1857), vol. 2, pp. 157–200.

20   Will of Abel Tassin of The Hague, Holland, 12 December 1723: Prerogative Court of Canterbury, PROB 11/594, Richmond Quire Numbers: 226–72.

21   *Dumont de Bostaquet*, ed. Ressinger, p. 162.

necessary funds for us. We were not received until the month of July, although we were paid from 19 June. Orders were distributed for garrisons and we all separated.[22]

Thus Dumont and many other officers were commissioned at the end of June 1687 and signed the oath of loyalty to the States General of the United Provinces and Prince William after having read it aloud with the second and third fingers raised, after which he was presented with his commission as *réformé* cavalry Captain.[23] Several days after this 'the President d'Aufègues delivered my orders, signed by His Highness [William], to remain in garrison in The Hague'.[24] He states that 'it would be difficult to describe the fineness of all the officers which I was discovering at each moment'.[25] Soon after he received his commission he completed his *reconnaissance* in a public declaration at the Walloon Church in The Hague on 29 June, which eased his feeling of sin and remorse for having abjured his faith in Dieppe in late November 1685.

Dumont at least was fortunate enough to have resurrected his prospects abroad through military service, met the Prince of Orange, and been accepted as a cavalry officer within a few days of his arrival in The Hague in mid-June 1687. That his treatment was preferential, considering his qualifications, is clearly due to his connection to Daniel Tassin de Torsay, though it is also clear that he must himself have been a man of considerable personal magnetism and forcefulness.

By December Dumont had been in The Hague for six months. His daughter Judith-Julie had been with him since early September and though she was chiefly cared for in the household of Daniel Tassin de Torsay and that of his step-daughter, Mademoiselle de Vanderhaven, she often boarded with her father at an inn called *Au Réfugié*. In September Dumont's friend and relation, Paul Thierry de La Motte-L'Alie (hereafter called La Motte) also arrived in The Hague from the garrison at Breda. He and Dumont decided to share quarters at *Au Réfugié*, the inn where many French officers newly commissioned by William were also living. The two men were from the same region, distantly related, and they had also been together in the service of Louis XIV in 1652–3 when they had been briefly imprisoned at Ostende (then under Spanish rule) after their ship was blown off course and they were arrested by the Governor of the city.

II

On 15 December 1687, a number of officers were dining together at *Au Réfugié* when an argument took place on the subject of the bravery (or lack thereof) of a certain Etienne de Casaubon, a former Captain from the French *régiment de Boulonnais*. He came to The Hague after December 1687, and later commanded one of the eight

---

22   Ibid., p. 151.

23   Ibid.

24   Ibid., pp. 151–2.

25   Letter to King of Poland, 20 January 1688, enclosing two lists of pensions paid to French Reformed Officers: 'Letter Books of Moreau, Polish Ambassador at The Hague 1687–88', *Townshend Papers*, vol. 3: BL, Add. MS 38,494, fols 13–18.

companies of Schomberg's French Horse, serving throughout the Irish campaigns of the 1690s. This argument took place between Etienne de Dampierre-Monginot,[26] who had previously been imprisoned in the Bastille and forced to abjure his Protestant faith, and Daniel Prondre de La Godinière, who spoke in praise of Casaubon. Dampierre had the last word with further harsh comments about Casaubon.

Dumont's friend, cousin and fellow boarder La Motte took offence at Dampierre's criticism of Casaubon's bravery, defending him to Dampierre with strong words. Dumont rather sanctimoniously writes that he tried to discourage gossip among the officers and suggested to La Motte that they should conduct themselves circumspectly in a country in which they were guests – as refugees they ought to act with wisdom and forbearance. La Motte, however, angrily threatened to attack Dampierre.

For a day or two all went well until Dumont invited La Motte to attend Prince William's *levée* at Honselaarsdijk Palace. La Motte declined the invitation, saying that he preferred to sleep late. Dumont writes that the two officers then said their prayers together 'as usual'. Meanwhile, Dampierre was most aggrieved – 'wounded to the heart', Dumont says – by this damaging disagreement on the subject of Casaubon's bravery. He met with fellow officers for a discussion of the argument. In the conversation which followed, in the chamber of Captain de La Croix, Dampierre wondered why La Motte had been so sharp with him and so staunch in his defence of Casaubon.[27] All present tried to calm him, calling it 'much ado about nothing'.

What is not evident when reading Dumont's account of this dispute is the web of family relationships present among the officers involved in the incident; this becomes clear only when the ancestry of the officers and the origins of their titles are explored. All of those who met in the chamber of La Croix and later supported him were allied to the powerful Muisson family. The family network is not readily apparent because territorial titles rather than surnames were in general use.[28]

---

26   Born in Paris in about 1666 he was the son of another Etienne de Dampierre-Monginot and had been in the Marquis de Varennes's *regiment de la marine* in France, but was later incorporated into La Caillemotte's infantry regiment in Ireland as a captain, paid from 1 July 1689. He received a pension until 1717, having served in both Holland and Ireland: *William Blathwayt Papers*, The James Marshall and Marie-Louise Osborn Collection, Beinecke Rare Book and MS Library, Yale University; G. H. Jones, 'Index of Huguenot officers in the service of the British Crown', unpublished Index from British MS material (hereafter Jones Cards), 'Dampierre-Monginot'; H. Wagner, 'Pedigrees', unpublished genealogical charts on deposit at Huguenot Library, London University (hereafter Wagner Pedigrees), 'Durant de Breval', 'Dampierre'.

27   Henri-David de La Croix, a former captain in the *régiment d'Enghien*, son of David de La Croix, Sieur de Merval, Counsellor and Secretary to the King. He was born in Normandy in 1658 and baptized at Charenton in Paris on 7 April. He was imprisoned in the Bastille from March until June 1686 and later married at the Swallow Street Chapel, London, in 1696 his first cousin Madeleine Le Coq, the daughter of Théodore Le Coq de Saint-Léger and Madeleine Muisson: Wagner Pedigrees, 'Muisson', 'de La Croix'; Jones Cards, 'de La Croix'.

28   Members of the important Protestant family of Muisson were long-time residents of The Hague and associated with both Louis XIV and William III. Almost all of the men named as having had a part in this story of a duel in The Hague were related in one way or another to the Muisson family. The will of Jacques Muisson, Sieur de Toillon, further

When Dumont arrived back at *Au Réfugié* the next morning after William's *levée*, he went to La Motte's room and opened the door in order to awaken him. As he approached, down the stairs came La Croix, who also boarded at the inn. The two men clasped hands and Dumont assumed that La Croix was about to join La Motte and himself upstairs in Dumont's room where they were accustomed to meet in the mornings. When he entered his own room Dumont found his daughter, Judith-Julie, writing a letter to her mother who was still in France. Judith–Julie went back downstairs where Dumont heard La Croix ask how she was feeling – she soon came back to tell her father that 'her cousin', La Motte, was still dressing. Dumont began writing his own letter to his wife as he was waiting for his two brother officers. This is what happened next in Dumont's words:

> As I was waiting for my friend to come into my room, a Captain of cavalry named Saint-Cyr[29] came in, horrified, and told me with sorrowful exclamations that La Motte was dead. His astounding news nearly knocked me over – I could not believe it and could not learn from him who had killed [my friend]. He told me that we must remove the body further into the woods. I dressed quickly and ran to inform Monsieur de Torsay of this unhappy event, and he advised me to get a carriage quickly in order to move the body. Saint-Cyr and I looked in several places for a carriage and as we were having one harnessed I saw

---

clarifies these relationships. Muisson's father, Henri, Sieur de Toillon, was married in 1635 to Péronne Conrart, sister of Valentin Conrart (1603–75), a founder and permanent secretary of the *Académie Française*. Henri Muisson had been Secretary of State for Finance to Louis XIV. His son, Jacques Muisson (b.1646), had served as councillor to the *parlement* of Paris. After the Revocation he fled to The Hague where he died in 1697. His wife, Anne, was the daughter of Antoine de Rambouillet, Sieur de Sablière. In Jacques's will, written in 1690, he names Anne as guardian to his children until they reach their majority and also as his executrix. In order to assist her he names François Morin, Seigneur de Sendat, and Jacques de Dompierre, Seigneur de Jonquières, 'my brothers-in-law'. He goes on to say that he is *not* naming (but in the process identifying) his other brothers-in-law, Adam de La Basoge, Baron d'Heuqueville, and Théodore le Coq, Seigneur des Moulins et de Saint-Léger, 'because they do not ordinarily reside in The Hague'. Correspondence from his widow, Anne, to Ezéchiel Spanheim in December 1697 reveals the plight of a refugee widow. In her letter to Spanheim, late Brandenburg ambassador to France, Anne reveals that after her husband's death, in October 1697, she was in need of assistance in getting money out of France. Her husband had left her everything, but she writes *'au nom de Dieu, Monsieur, tâchez de me payer ... du moins une partie'*: 'La famille Muisson', *Bulletin de la société de l'histoire du Protestantisme française*, 12 (1865): 306–9; Wagner Pedigrees, 'Muisson', 'Dompierre'.

29 Isaac de Soumain de Saint-Cyr received a commission as captain in Holland on 29 July 1687 at a salary of 700 florins: 'Les officiers français en service hollandaise', ed. Boeree: 36.

Messieurs du Petit-Bosc[30] and de Sailly[31] [who] ... suggested that I leave the carriage for fear that the driver would betray us. We thought he was right and went back to where the body was – I could not see it without the utmost melancholy – my friend, dead when I least expected it.[32]

The officer, Saint-Cyr, was sent to fetch the surgeon who found the dead man lying in the woods upon his face, his sword drawn. He turned La Motte on his back, returned his sword to its sheath and put his hat upon his knees which is how the body was later found by others, making it appear that La Motte had been murdered because his sword seemed not to have been drawn.

The officers who were connected to the events of December 1687 were of noble origin, but from diverse backgrounds, and most had enjoyed considerable military success in France.[33] They had left their homes under an extraordinary variety of circumstances and joined William III's forces. They had loyally served Louis XIV, but were looked upon by many as deserters from their regiments in France in shifting their allegiance to William; many of the officers had already been in Holland for

---

30   Daniel Legrand du Petit-Bosc, Seigneur de Maubuquet in the parish of Illeville-sur-Montfort, Normandy. He was destined to be Dumont's neighbour at Portarlington in Ireland. Le Fanu identifies him as the 'Petit-Bosc' who took leases on a number of holdings at Portarlington which he sublet to old comrades. The register of the church there shows that he was extremely active as an *ancien*, often acting as witness to baptisms, marriages and deaths. His brothers were Jean Legrand du Petit-Bosc and Josias Legrand du Petit-Bosc, Sieur de Vimaré: *Dublin and Portarlington Veterans, King William III's Huguenot Army*, ed. T. P. LeFanu, Huguenot Society Quarto Series 41 (London, 1946), p. 43; R. P. Hylton, 'Dublin's Huguenot Community, 1662–1701', *Proceedings of the Huguenot Society of Great Britain and Ireland*, 24 (1985); T. P. Le Fanu, 'French Veterans at Portarlington', *Journal of the Kildare Archeological Society*, 11/4 (July 1933): 177–98; J. S. Powell, *Portarlington* (York, second edition 1994). Among the houses Petit-Bosc built was Arlington House on King Street in Portarlington, which survives, though it is currently threatened with demolition. It is across the street from the site of Isaac Dumont de Bostaquet's house, which no longer stands. Daniel Legrand described himself as 'ruined by doctors and drugs' in his 1714 pension statement, but he lived the longest of the early Huguenot settlers at Portarlington. He died at the age of 95 in 1737: F. Waddington, *Le Protestantisme en Normandie depuis la Révocation de l'Edit de Nantes jusqu'a la fin du dix-huitième siècle: 1685–1797* (Paris, 1862), p. 12; *Registers of the French Church of Portarlington, Ireland*, ed. T. P. Le Fanu, Huguenot Society Quarto Series 19 (Dublin, 1908); T. P. Le Fanu, 'Dumont de Bostaquet at Portarlington', *Proceedings of the Huguenot Society of London*, 14 (1929–33): 214; Jones Cards, 'Petit-Bosc', 'Vimaré du Petit-Bosc'.

31   Michel de Bures de Sailly, brother of Charles de Bures de Béthencourt, later served as a lieutenant in La Melonière's infantry regiment in Ireland, received a pension and retired, like his brother, to Portarlington where he died in 1713. He should not be confused with Charles Perrault de Sailly who was associated with establishing the Huguenot colony of Manakin in Virginia as well as with Lord Galway's attempt to bring 600 Huguenot refugees from Switzerland to Ireland in the 1690s: Jones Cards, 'de Sailly'; *Registers of the French Church of Portarlington*, ed. Le Fanu, see index.

32   *Dumont de Bostaquet*, ed. Ressinger, pp. 161–2.

33   Ibid., pp. 159–66.

some time when Dumont arrived in June.[34] It is easy to imagine how tempers and patience ran short as time passed and they waited in The Hague and other Dutch cities with an uncertain future ahead of them. There would be nearly another year of idleness before William's fleet set sail for the descent on England in October 1688.

A duel was one of the (perhaps inevitable) results of tensions at this time. This study of the participants, revealing marriages, surnames and titles, shows how closely they were allied and how they supported one another along family lines. The families involved include the well-known Le Coq de Saint-Léger,[35] Conrart, Muisson, de La Croix, Morin, Thierry and other surnames. Their bonds continued throughout the eighteenth century with marriages amongst their children and grandchildren. A comparison of two extant sources for such people, the Jones Cards and Wagner Pedigrees held by the Huguenot Library in London, to records available in France through departmental archives and other sources makes it possible to identify the officers and provides a comprehensive picture of the multiple interconnections among their families.[36]

The 1687 duel seems to indicate that among the refugee officers, morale was not always good during this period of inactivity when their futures were uncertain. Wanting action, they dwelt in confined living quarters with nothing to do, like any member of the international officer corps, regardless of his religion or national affiliation. Fear was combined with emotional and financial insecurity to make life difficult for them, but duels among the refugees anywhere after the Revocation are almost unknown. Tension arose from the fact that they were refugees and according to military law considered to be deserters from their French regiments, many of them felt that they were still subject to oaths of loyalty to Louis XIV. Conflicts arose between those who held that a French officer must never lack respect for his former sovereign and those who were bitter in their blame of 'Louis the Persecutor'. One of William's reasons for having the officers take an oath of loyalty to the States General was to break their last ties of loyalty to Louis.

In the immediate aftermath of the La Motte–La Croix duel, Dumont's account has a great deal to do with how the incident was both perceived among and handled by fellow officers and officials in The Hague. Gossip was rampant among the officers and the news spread like wildfire; officials and the surgeon, Rongeat, arrived to dispose of the body without delay. Dumont himself went to consult as many officers

---

34   'Les officiers français en service hollandais', ed. Boeree: 7–65.

35   Théodore Le Coq, Sieur de Saint-Léger, born in Normandy in 1635. He had been an *ancien* at Charenton and was banished from France because of his 'too lively and proud spirit' and his refusal to abjure his Protestant faith. He married Madeleine Muisson, sister of Jacques Muisson de Toillon. The Saint-Légers were one of the notable families who settled at Greenwich. John Evelyn called him 'a French refugee who left great riches for his religion; a very learned, civil person': *Diary of John Evelyn*, ed. Austin Dobson (London, 1908), p. 417; Wagner Pedigrees, 'Muisson'; R. Vigne, 'In the Purlieus of St Alfege's: Huguenot Families in Seventeenth- and Eighteenth-century Greenwich', *Proceedings of the Huguenot Society of Great Britain and Ireland*, 27/2 (1999): 257–73.

36   See R. Gwynn. *Huguenot Army Officers in the Service of the Crown in the Late Seventeenth and Early Eighteenth Centuries*, unpublished index of the G. H. Jones cards collected in the Huguenot Library, London University.

1   Friedrich Hermann von Schomberg, engraving by De Larmersin (*c*.1675–84).
     © Private Collection

The Right Hon.ble Lewis Earle of Feversham, Viscount Sonds Baron of Holdenby & Throwley, Captain of his Ma.ties first Troops of Guards, Lord of y.e Bed-Chamber to y.e King, Lieuten.t Gen.ll of his Ma.ties Armie, K.nt of y.e most noble Order of y.e Garter, & Chamberlain to y.e Queen Dowager.

I Riley pinx.   I Smith ex.   I Beckett fe.

2   Louis Duras, second Earl of Feversham, mezzotint by Isaac Beckett after John Riley (*c.*1681–88). © National Portrait Gallery D1913

3   Henri de Ruvigny, Earl of Galway, portrait in oils. © By kind permission
The French Hospital

4   Amaury de Farcy de Saint-Laurent, portrait in oils (*c.*1700). © Evangelisch-
reformierte Kirchengemeinde, Celle

5   Louis August du Verger de Monroy, Seigneur de Bessé et de Paisay, portrait
in oils (*c.*1730). © Bomann Museum, Celle

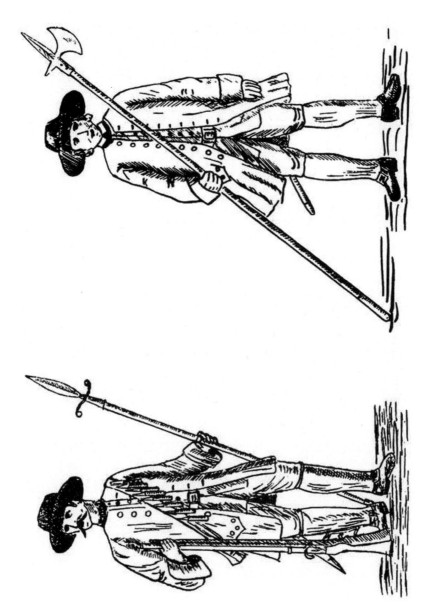

6   Sergeant and officer of the La Motte-Chevallerie regiment, Celle, engraving (c.1700). © Bomann Museum, Celle

7   Jean Louis Ligonier, first Earl Ligonier, portrait in oils by Sir Joshua Reynolds (1755). © National Army Museum FDA1989-08-152

of importance as he could find. All those involved were concerned lest they be seen as acting dishonourably, and wanted to avoid dishonour in William's eyes as well as publicity for their friends and relations. The entire incident was handled as quietly as possible. It is obvious that friendships were important to the men who were for the most part separated from their families. Dumont writes: 'Foreign countries make for strong commitments and one is tightly bound to friends one finds there, particularly those who are relatives as well as friends.'[37] Reinforcing this important aspect of his social connections, Dumont went immediately to inform Madame de Sommelsdijk, a fellow Huguenot and leader of society in the city.[38] At Madame de Sommelsdijk's home he met Isaac de La Melonière, a prominent name among the Huguenot officers abroad and later in Ireland.

There is much that is unclear about this incident which took place at the inn *Au Réfugié* and the nearby woods somewhere on the outskirts of The Hague. It is possible that Dumont himself wanted things left unclear in the account which he was writing, after all, only months after the event. He had to live with these same officers for the foreseeable future – his livelihood depended upon it. Dumont seems unsure whether a duel had actually taken place between the two men, though he suspected it and it seems clear enough that this is what had happened. The other officers were most anxious that it be seen as a duel rather than as murder. They wished to gain lenient treatment for the obvious perpetrator, La Croix, who would otherwise be seen as a murderer. Though his journal was a private document, perhaps Dumont feared discovery and repercussions for fellow officers if he were to die in action and his memoir be read by others. His future was uncertain. He never intended his journal for publication, though he expected that his children would read it.

Loyalty was customary among brother officers, but reasons for their mutual protection beyond such expected loyalty become clear when the identities of the officers involved are known and their family relationships revealed. These relationships form a tangled web, and Dumont himself started rumours to excuse their behaviour – he implied that romantic entanglements existed and even helped to spread tales of the malicious things the dead man, La Motte, had said on the subject of Dampierre. By contrast, Dumont also recorded that he had overheard plans for reconciliation between the two men. Meanwhile he took La Motte's body and had it buried in the New Church in The Hague and informed the dead man's relatives in France of recent events. La Motte's relatives happened to include former

---

37 *Dumont de Bostaquet*, ed. Ressinger, p. 156.

38 Marguerite, the daughter of Saint-André du Puy-Montbrun (1600–73). She married, in 1664, Cornelius Aerssen van Sommelsdijk (1637–88), who went to Surinam in 1683 where he died. They employed the Huguenot, Jean Rou, as tutor for their children in The Hague in 1680. In his memoirs Rou gives many details of life in both the Ruvigny and Sommelsdijk households, though his comments about both Monsieur and Madame de Sommelsdijk are far from complimentary. Rou also had many dealings with Abel Tassin d'Alonne. Sommelsdijk's sister was married to Hendrik van Nassau-Ouwerkerk (1640–1708), who was related to William and served as his Master of the Horse and major-general of cavalry. He accompanied William to England in 1688 and was later field marshal in Holland and deputy *stadhouder* in 1693: *Mémoires inédits et opuscules de Jean Rou*, ed. Waddington, vol. 2, pp. 157–200.

(Catholic) neighbours of Dumont's who lived at the château d'Imbleville within three kilometres of La Fontelaye.[39]

Dumont's main concern was to protect his friend's memory from publicity and dishonour and his body from possible desecration. Privately Dumont believed, sadly, that his friend and cousin, Paul Thierry de La Motte L'Alie, had brought about his own death by his poor judgement and rash behaviour. Nevertheless, Dumont tried repeatedly to defend his friend's reputation. He writes:

> Sieur Morin[40] declared that La Croix had spoken of trying to put things right with Dampierre ... and also that La Motte had said many hateful things about Dampierre and even threatened to put a sword through him – and finally they [La Croix and La Motte] had come to blows. This intelligence went around quickly and everyone who lived in our inn was questioned, including myself. After all of the legalities had been taken care of, the case was put before the council of war who wished to act in our favour. They ordered that the body should be given to relatives, which was a great comfort to me. Wasting no time, I had him buried unceremoniously that night. I took two carriages and five or six Captain friends of mine and went to the New Church, and there he rests, awaiting the Resurrection ... Monsieur de Torsay was kind enough to advance the money for the funeral expenses, for which I reimbursed him from the two months of La Motte's salary which I received from the treasurer ... I had no interest other than safeguarding the body of the dead man from the harshness which publicity would bring; I did not claim to have been involved.[41]

When William III was informed of the affair he was extremely angry and it was thought for a time that he would make an example of La Croix in order to discourage further violence among the officers in this period of enforced idleness. Dumont writes that the officers banded together to make it seem as though it had been a chance encounter between the refugees, La Motte and La Croix. Here is how the matter ended, in Dumont's words:

> I was convinced that La Motte had brought the affair on himself and I was not opposed to clemency for La Croix, though I did reply to an accusation that he made to His Highness [William], charging La Motte with being a rebellious and difficult man. I tried to defend his memory in the strongest terms possible. A request to respond to this charge in his defence was sent to me because I was a relative. After I had replied, the affair was sent to the council of war and when they met, His Highness pardoned La Croix. Afterwards his relatives asked me to sign an act of reconciliation with them, which I agreed to do. Sieur Morin asked if I might be appeased if La Croix himself would come to ask for my friendship, which I could certainly not refuse him. He came to see me and present his compliments. He had written in advance, and we saw each other without speaking of the deed. I believe I did my duty in this business, both for the dead and for the living. The belongings of the deceased man were seized by the tax collector and they stayed there at

---

39   The Baudry d'Imbleville family had always been Catholic.

40   François Morin, Sieur de Sendat (sometimes written 'Scudat'), was married to Marie Muisson and they were the parents of Marie, who married La Croix, who killed La Motte: Wagner Pedigrees, 'Muisson'.

41   *Dumont de Bostaquet*, ed. Ressinger, p. 164.

the request of the ... Sieur de La Motte's brother-in-law [Vaudemont], to whom I had sent his death record.[42]

III

The Hague was the centre of a close-knit French society in which refugee officers, and even some women (such as Madame de Sommelsdijk), had a great deal of influence. Dumont specifically asked for Madame de Sommelsdijk's support in avoiding public disapproval and dishonour to his dead friend, La Motte. Certainly the exiled Huguenot ministers also had tremendous authority among the supportive circle Dumont found in Holland along with other well-known Huguenot figures, who he often encountered.

Their tenuous position in exile is revealed by the refugee officers' fear of reprisals from brother officers as well as from those above them in rank. William III insisted on rigorous discipline and demanded an enquiry into what had happened. Dumont and his friends also feared reprisals in the form of publicity and desecration of the dead man's body such as might have occurred in France. Betrayal by such people as the carriage driver hired to move La Motte's body was a very real threat.

The main strength and interest of this story is its revelation of conditions amongst the unoccupied officers in The Hague. Gossip was rife and tempers quick. It is also of interest to learn that despite the gossip and occasional violence at least some of the Huguenot officers were in the habit of praying together on a nightly basis. It is clear that the officers had a strong sense of honour and loyalty and that they co-operated to protect one another. Living conditions in The Hague were reasonably comfortable and some of the children who had been sent out of France dwelt with their fathers in rented quarters. However, among the temporarily idle officers, violence and disagreements of all sorts was a constant menace.

The refugee officers were in close communication with their families in France: not only with their own immediate relations, but with whole extended family and community networks. The news which Dumont received from his wife (and surely this was true for most absentee husbands) was always upsetting and discouraging to him throughout this period until she was herself able to get out of France with another of their children in the spring of 1688, almost a year after her husband's escape. She was forced to abandon Madeleine, the baby daughter she had borne under most difficult conditions after Dumont's flight. He was never to see this daughter although she was later able to emigrate to Portarlington, the Huguenot colony in Ireland, some time after her father's death there in 1709.[43]

---

42   Ibid., p. 159–66. Etienne Quièvremont, Sieur de Vaudemont, from Dieppe, married Françoise Thierry, the sister of Paul Thierry de La Motte: Wagner Pedigrees, 'Muisson', 'Thierry'.

43   The extent of family ties and inter-relationships among the officers has seldom been explored, mainly due to language difficulties and the vagaries of indexing, in French, Dutch and English. Spelling inconsistencies are typical of the period, exacerbated by Dutch and English interpretation of French names and titles. These factors present problems in determining officers' surnames and relating them to their territorial titles. Since most officers and other

refugees of noble origin were known by these territorial designations rather than their surnames, connections are not easily made; surnames quickly fell into disuse in exile. Some sources for further investigation of their relationships exist in the form of unpublished material at the Huguenot Library in London: see V. Costello and R. Flatman, 'British and Irish Sources for Huguenot Officers', unpublished paper for conference *Huguenot Soldiering* (London, 2001); M. Glozier, 'Huguenot Soldiers in Great Britain, The Netherlands, Brandenburg-Prussia, and Russia, c.1672–1740', unpublished biographical index from MS material (Sydney, 2001); Gwynn, *Huguenot Army Officers*; R. P. Hylton, 'The Huguenot Settlement at Portarlington, 1692–1771', MA thesis (Virginia Union University, Richmond VA, 1982).

Chapter 9

The Refugees in the Army of Brandenburg-Prussia

'those unfortunate banished people from France'

Helmut Schnitter
University of Potsdam

On 31 December 1685 the Elector Friedrich Wilhelm wrote to his highly esteemed Field Marshal, Georg von Derfflinger:

> You also are aware how great is the sympathy which we have for those unfortunate banished people from France of the Protestant religion and that we are engaged in the work of forming a new cavalry regiment and a new infantry regiment [from amongst their number].[1]

On 29 October 1685, the Elector had issued the Edict of Potsdam, which encouraged Huguenots to settle in his territories. Its terms promised, among other things, to cover the cost of establishing Huguenot communities in his dominions.[2] The establishment of Huguenot families in Brandenburg began before the Revocation, though it was only after 1685 that five Huguenot agents were charged with the mission of resettling French refugee families.[3]

The Elector's letter to Derfflinger alludes to an important occurrence in Prussian military history, the incorporation of Huguenot army officers into the Great Elector's army. Their new Commander-in-Chief established a number of separate army units composed entirely of the immigrant French soldiers.[4] Amongst the circumstances which heightened his enthusiasm for the Huguenot regiments was their capacity

---

1   K. W. von Schöning (ed.), *Das General-Feldmarschalls Dubislav Gneomar von Natzmer auf Gannewitz Leben und Kriegshalten* (Berlin, 1838), p. 52.

2   M. Kohnke, 'Das Edikt von Potsdam zu seiner entetehung verbreitung und uberlieferung', *Jahrbuch für Geschichte des Feudalismus*, 9 (1985): 241–75; A. Flick, 'Huguenot Research in the Hanover Area', *Huguenot Families*, 3 (September 2000): 9–14; W. Beuleke, *Die Hugenotten in Niedersachsen*, Quellen und Darstellungen zur Geschichte Niedersachsens 58 (Hildesheim, 1960).

3   J. P. Erman and P. C. F. Reclam, *Mémoires pour servir à l'histoire des Réfugiés François dans les États du Roi* (9 vols, Berlin, 1782–99), vol. 1, pp. 127–41; M. R. Glozier, *The Huguenot Soldiers of William of Orange and the Glorious Revolution of 1688: The Lions of Judah* (Brighton, Portland, 2002), pp. 43–4.

4   G. Lehmann, 'Die brandenburgische Kriegsmacht unter dem Großen Kurfürsten', in *Forschungen zur Brandenburgischen und Preußischen Geschichte*, ed. R. Koser, O. Hintze

to replace a departing contingent of auxiliary troops which Brandenburg-Prussia was obliged to supply for the Imperial campaign against the Ottoman Empire in Hungary.[5]

In the autumn of 1685, many of Louis XIV's officers, who had left France for religious reasons, presented themselves at the Elector's palace in Berlin. It was, however, only feasible for a few of them to become long-term residents in the city. 'In the first instance, not all officers could be enlisted', observed Charles Ancillon in a contemporary report. 'Therefore for a period they obtained an allotted subvention and could settle themselves wherever they wanted, either in an urban or rural area.'[6] Although Berlin was the capital city and was fortified, it nonetheless only had a small garrison and lacked sufficient military openings to accommodate all the newcomers. Two ways of incorporating the Huguenot refugees suggested themselves: the strengthening of existing regiments and the establishment of new ones. However, both these solutions could only be implemented in the provinces where new garrisons could be set up in areas necessitating military exigencies such as securing borders, territories and supply routes. The vast majority of Huguenot officers, therefore, once more departed from Berlin (inasmuch as they had reached Berlin in the first place), armed with commissions from the Elector for companies in different parts of the realm.[7]

I

Brandenburg's military development sustained a durable legacy from this immigration. An examination of the contemporary military *status quo* clearly illustrates this. Brandenburg was one of the territories which repeatedly served as a battleground during the Thirty Years' War and suffered greatly from the consequences of war. Trade, commerce and agricultural production only recovered slowly. The military potential of this German territorial state was also badly hit by the war. After the Peace of Westphalia of 1648, Friedrich Wilhelm, who came to power in 1640, only had at his disposal a small number of military units, mostly garrison troops. The control he exercised over the army was, and initially remained, limited. The old war commanders retained full authority over their regiments which they themselves financed and, therefore, owned. This gave the colonels full control of their units

and A. Naudé, Verein für Geschichte der Mark Brandenburg (54 vols, Leipzig, 1888–1943), vol. 1, p. 502.

5   See P. Wilson, *German Armies: War and German Politics, 1648–1806*, Warfare and History (London, 1998), pp. 68–73.

6   C. Ancillon, *Histoire de l'etablissement des francois refugiez dan les etats de son altesse electorale de Brandenbourg* (Berlin, 1690). Republished in German as *Geschichte der Niederlassung der Réfugiés in den Staaten seiner kurfürstlichen Hoheit von Brandenburg*, Geschichtsblätter des Deutschen Hugenotten-Vereins 15/8 (Berlin, 1939), p. 45.

7   Lehmann, 'Die brandenburgische Kriegsmacht', p. 502.

and in consequence they secured a strong position in relation to the ruler of the electorate.[8]

The establishment of a battle-ready army was hampered above all by the complicated problem of financing it. The Elector had few means and the provincial diet (representative body) was reluctant to provide money. In 1653 the Elector succeeded for the first time in concluding an agreement with the regional legislative assembly whereby he would receive for a period of some years, sufficient funds to sustain a small fighting force. In return he had to guarantee the rights and privileges of the Brandenburg nobles and confirm that he would not interfere with their control over the peasants.[9]

A larger army was only built up during the First Northern War (1655–60). In this war the Elector initially supported Sweden and then Poland. This yielded him the sought-after sovereignty of the duchy of Prussia at the Peace of Oliva of 1660. Afterwards the development of the Brandenburg army was distinguished by a fluctuating numerical strength – recruitment at the beginning of a war or in times of tension, followed by large-scale disbandment at the conclusion of peace. Nevertheless, Friedrich Wilhelm gradually succeeded in limiting the power of the old commanders and establishing his own authority. He appointed and promoted officers and made the troops swear an oath of allegiance to him. Councils of war and commissioners were charged at his behest with the organisation, payment and sustenance of the army.[10]

The military success in the war against Sweden – the victory at Fehrbellin in 1675 and the campaigns in Pomerania, Rügen, and Prussia to the Baltic – contributed substantially to the Elector's military strength and prestige. At the conclusion of peace in 1679 (just as in 1660) units were no longer entirely disbanded, rather the staff officers and some numerically reduced companies were retained. This enabled regiments to be speedily brought up to a full complement after recruitment in times of conflict or at the outbreak of war and meant that they could be battle ready within a short time.[11]

During the last decades of the seventeenth century the Brandenburg army did not fundamentally differ from the mercenary armies of other states, in terms of its framework and organisational structure. The soldiers were recruited or press-ganged and were subject to stern discipline and severe military justice. They received pitiful remuneration and were billeted in civilian quarters. The officers were predominantly recruited from the nobility of Brandenburg-Prussia, but also nobles from France, Sweden, Poland and other German states periodically served in the army of the electorate. There were officers of *bourgeois* and farmer origin who rose up to the rank of General and were ennobled, for example Joachim Hennings von Treffenfeld and the aforementioned Georg Derfflinger. The social boundaries amongst officers,

---

8   C. Jany, *Geschichte der Königlich Preußischen Armee bis zum Jahre 1807* (5 vols, Berlin, 1928–37), vol. 1, p. 274.

9   See E. J. Feuchtwanger, *Prussia: Myth and Reality, the Role of Prussia in German History* (Chicago, 1970), p. 26.

10   Jany, *Geschichte der Königlich Preußischen Armee*, pp. 297 et seq.

11   Ibid.

non-commissioned officers and (ordinary) soldiers were still open and fluid after 1648, and it was only later, specifically under the soldier-king Friedrich Wilhelm I (1713–40) that these distinctions would become strongly defined and inflexible.[12]

It was in the arena of the aspiring power politics of Austria, France, the Netherlands and Sweden that the army of the electorate developed. Noticeable influences on military strategy in Brandenburg-Prussia came above all from Sweden and the Netherlands. In 1656 Friedrich Wilhelm adopted the Swedish articles of war and he was guided by a Dutch-Swedish prototype in his organisation of the army. The Great Elector had become familiar with the Netherlands army as a young man. During the Dutch Republic's war of independence against Spain (1568–1648) the Princes of Orange had carried out military reforms which were a key factor in their victory over the then reputedly unbeatable Spanish. Many politicians and soldiers looked on with astonishment at the success of the Netherlanders whose troop formations were still considered to give them 'unrivalled mastery of the art of war' during the Thirty Years' War.[13]

Towards the end of the seventeenth century, absolutist France's influence became predominant militarily and in international politics. The French army had developed itself into a well-organised power instrument of the Crown. It was coordinated by a military organisational system which was underpinned by *intendants* (military administrators).[14] In wars against neighbouring states the army pinned numerous victories onto its banners. French officers, master fortification builders, military engineers and officials, therefore, easily found employment in foreign countries, whose rulers perceived the Sun King's army as a model for military organization.

II

Already before the revocation of the Edict of Nantes in 1685, a considerable number of officers and generals (nearly all of them Protestant) left France and took military service in other armies. Amongst these was Pierre de La Cave, who came to Brandenburg and was promoted Colonel in 1654, participated in the war against Sweden and became a Major-General in 1669.[15] François, Comte du Hamel, who was a Colonel at the battle of Fehrbellin (1675) and participated in the Pomeranian campaign, reaching the rank of Lieutenant-General in 1690. Hamel was in fact Roman Catholic. However, the regiment commanded by him had a Protestant chaplain and after 1685 experienced an influx of Huguenots. Henri de Briquemault, Baron de Saint-Loup, entered the Brandenburg service in 1680 and in 1684 became Commandant of the Lippstadt garrison in Westphalia. In 1683 he established a

---

12 See Feuchtwanger, *Prussia: Myth and Reality*, p. 44.

13 F. Mehring, *Gesammelte Schriften*, ed. T. Höhle, H. Kock and J. Schleifstein (15 vols, Berlin, 1964–73), vol. 8, p. 337.

14 See D. Baxter, *Servants of the Sword, French Intendants of the Army, 1630–70* (Urbana IL, 1976).

15 Pierre de La Cave (b. 24 December 1605 – d. 8 May 1679 at Pillau): E. and E. Haag, *La France protestante ou vies des protestants français qui se sont fait un nom dans l'histoire* (10 vols, Montpellier, 1992), vol. 6, pp. 171–2.

cuirassier (heavy cavalry) regiment. It originally had six mounted companies, but with the influx of Huguenots this rose to ten companies by 1686. Briquemault spearheaded the establishment of French colonies in the Westphalian towns of the electorate, where the companies of his regiment were also stationed.[16]

The greatest influx of Huguenot army personnel occurred during the years 1685 to 1688. Almost 600 officers and non-commissioned officers along with more than 1,000 soldiers came to the Elector's territories and were incorporated into his army.[17] Friedrich Wilhelm – and his successor Friedrich III (after 1701 King Friedrich I) – were able to establish a standing command *cadre* from these Huguenot immigrants. It formed a 'nucleus' that could be increased whenever further expansion of the army and military administration was required, even though some of the officers only remained in the army for a short time. A high proportion of the refugees were veteran soldiers and amongst the young men there were pupils of the French Cadet schools. In contrast to the scions of many Brandenburg and Pommeranian noble families who entered into army service with scant general knowledge, the refugee officers brought a higher level of education and were in many cases acquainted with the military literature of the time, for the most part written and published in French.[18]

Already in 1587 the Huguenot officer, François de La Noüe, had compiled his *Discours politiques et militaries* ('Political and Military Discourse'), in which he argued for the systematic and methodical education of officers.[19] This publication was still being widely distributed in the seventeenth century and stimulated literary debate. Another key military textbook which was imbued with a Huguenot influence was *La conduite de Mars* ('The Conduct of Mars', who personified war) which was published in The Hague in 1685 and rapidly circulated in other countries.[20] An adapted German translation appeared in Dresden in 1690 under the title *Der tapfere und Verständige Kriegsofficier* ('The Brave and Wise Officer of War').[21]

What consequences did the incorporation of Huguenot refugees have on the Brandenburg army? The vast majority of Huguenots were merchants, tradesmen or followed similar civilian callings and they settled in urban areas where they established segregated colonies with their own legal status. This was of limited relevance to the

---

16   von Schöning (ed.), *Das General-Feldmarschalls Dubislav Gneomar von Natzmer*, p. 53. Henri de Beauvais-Briquemault, Baron de Saint-Loup (d. 16 August 1692), was progressively a major-general, governor of Lippstadt and a lieutenant-general in Prussia: Haag, *La France Protestante*, vol. 2, pp. 130–36.

17   M. Philippson, *Der Große Kurfürst Friedrich Wilhelm von Brandenburg* (3 vols, Berlin: Cronbach, 1897–1903), vol. 3, p. 85. He states that by June 1687 there were already 611 noble refugees of whom the majority had been officers in France.

18   See J. A. Lynn, *Giant of the Grand Siècle: The French Army, 1610–1715* (Cambridge, 1997).

19   F. de La Noüe, *Discours politiques de militaries* (Basle, 1587).

20   G. de Courtilz de Sandras, *La conduite de Mars* (The Hague, 1685).

21   See M. Jähns, *Heeresverfassung und Völkerleben* (Berlin, 1885), p. 259; M. Jähns, *Geschichte der Kriegswissenschaften vornehmlich in Deutschland* (2. vols, Munich, Leipzig, 1889–90); H. Delbrück, *Geschichte der Kriegskunst im Rahmen der politischen Geschichte* (4 vols, Berlin, 1900–20), vol. 4, p. 257; W. Rüstow, *Geschichte der Infanterie* (2 vols, Nordhausen, 1864), vol. 2, p. 134.

soldiers. As a rule they had to move to wherever there were garrisons and these were widely distributed, almost evenly over the whole of the Lower Rhine district of the state as far as Memel. The preferred destinations of the Huguenot incomers were garrisons being developed in the west of the electorate where some French officers and generals had already established their own coterie before 1685. Needless to say, refugee officers and soldiers did not have the special rights accorded to the civilian settlers who could make use of 'colony laws'; instead they were subject to military jurisdiction. Senior officers of great age who could no longer be incorporated in the army received a pension from the Elector.[22]

The units into which the majority of refugees were incorporated included:[23] (a) the Varennes infantry regiment with 16 companies (over 800 men) garrisoned in Soest, Werden (Ruhr), Bielefeld and Herford; (b) Briquemault's *cuirassier* regiment with 10 companies stationed in Lippstadt, Minden, Cleves and Ravensberg; (c) the Briquemault infantry battalion which had a permanent strength of five companies with 750 men; (d) the Cournaud battalion with five companies stationed at Alt- and Neustadt Brandenburg (Havel) with a strength of about 190 men.[24]

In accordance with the model of the French *mousquetaires du roi* (King's musketeers of the *maison du roi* established by Henri IV in 1600), the Great Elector established two companies of Huguenot noblemen, the *grands mousquetaires* (almost 120 men altogether) which had their garrisons in Prenzlau and Fürstenwalde. Each of these nobles had at least the rank of Second-Lieutenant and received pay of ten *Talers* with an additional four *Talers* for an orderly which was very high for the time. The company commanders included the Elector, who presented the Frenchmen with horses and uniforms, and Marshal Schomberg. These privileges are an indication of the value in terms of courtly political representation which was accorded to the Huguenot musketeers. One company of French *grenadiers à cheval* – comprising non-commissioned officers employed in engineering works – took up quarters in Beeskow and Storkow.[25]

The officers and military engineers involved in building fortifications, such as Louis Cayart, who had been a pupil of the famed French fortification engineer, Vauban, were particularly sought after. Cayart was involved in the building of the *Langen Brücke* in Berlin and the French Church in Friedrichstadt. Jean de Bodt came to the country in 1699 and for a time led the fortification building works in Wexel, completed the arsenal (armoury) in Berlin begun by Johann Arnold Nering and also

---

22 Schöning, *Des General-Feldmarschalls Dubislaw Gneomar von Natzmer*, p. 53.

23 In Count Philip Wilhelm's cavalry regiment, formerly Briquemault's, there were in 1698 still 11 Huguenot officers out of 30: Deutsche Staatsbibliothek, Berlin, MS boruss, fols 133, 311. In Wylich and Lottum's infantry regiment (infantry regiment No. 15), which was formed in 1688 out of eight companies from the Varennes regiment, there were in 1690 six German officers, which was one quarter of the officer corps: *Chronik des Ersten Garderegiments zu Fuß und dessen Stammtruppenteilen 1675–1900* (Berlin, 1907), p. 30.

24 Jany, *Geschichte der Königlich Preußischen Armee*, pp. 297 et seq.

25 O. von Schwerin, *Das Regiment gens d'armes und seine Vorgeschichte* (2 vols, Berlin, 1912), vol. 1, p. 53.

completed further building works at the fortifications of Küstin and Kolberg.[26] In 1728 he entered the service of Saxony and there advanced to the rank of Lieutenant-General and Inspector of the engineering *corps*. Under his leadership re-building works at the Dresden fortifications and at the Königstein were executed. He was a key participant in the development of the art of fortification building and in the education and training of the military engineer *corps* in the armies of Prussia and Saxony.[27]

Those army units which were predominantly Huguenot were characterized by a number of idiosyncrasies vis à vis the older Brandenburg units. The regiments 'on a French footing' consisted of 12 to 16 companies, with each company numbering some 50 to 60 soldiers. The Brandenburg companies on the other hand were over 100 soldiers strong and as a rule had eight to ten companies to a regiment. The 'French footing' brought certain military advantages. The number of officers in the regiment as a whole was relatively high, which enabled a stronger control and surveillance of the soldiers and at the same time facilitated the leadership of the companies in training and in combat. Another particularity was that the Huguenot units were imbued with a pervading Calvinist religious ethos, emphasizing obligation and loyalty, which guaranteed a strong adherence to duty and discipline, but had little in common with the cudgel and stick discipline that was established in the eighteenth century under Friedrich Wilhelm I and Friedrich II.[28]

Certainly in the eighteenth century the refugee units and their officers amalgamated relatively quickly with the Brandenburg troops to form a homogeneous army and officer corps, but the influence of the professionalism of individual Huguenot soldiers continued to be discernable in the eighteenth-century Prussian army. The names of the refugees' descendants constantly occur in the Prussian army lists well into the twentieth century.[29]

Officers from Huguenot families also played a noteworthy role in military literature: René L'Homme de Courbière compiled a representation of the history of the Prussian military system and a series of works on Prussian military administration.[30] Gerhard von Pelet-Narbonne wrote a comprehensive history of the Brandenburg-Prussian cavalry along with further publications on this topic; he was descended

---

26   For biographical details of Jean de Bodt, see R. Loeber 'Biographical Dictionary of Engineers in Ireland 1600–1730', *Irish Sword*, 13/50 (1977): 44.

27   For military engineers in Brandenburg, see U. von Bonin, *Geschichte des Ingenieurkorps und der Pioniere in Preußen* (2 vols, Berlin, 1877–8), vol. 1.

28   'Reglement vor die Königlich Preußische Infanterie von 1726', in *Bibliotheca Rerum Militarum*, Quellen und Darstellungen zur Militärwissenschaft und Militärgeschichte 4 (Osnabrück, 1968), p. 538.

29   See C. Jany, *Die alte Armee von 1655 bis 1740: Formation und Stärke* (Berlin, 1905); C. Jany, 'Die Dessauer Stammliste von 1729', in *Urkundliche Beiträge und Forschungen zur Geschichte des Preußischen Heeres*, ed. Great General Staff, Kriegsgeschichtliche Abteilung 2/8 (Berlin, 1905).

30   See R. L'Homme de Courbière, *Geschichte der Brandenburgisch-Preussischen Heeres-Verfassung* (Berlin, 1852).

from Jacques de Pelet de Roucoulle, a colonel of the *grands mousquetaires*.[31] Adolf
Friedrich Johannes von Crousaz compiled a history of the Prussian Cadet *corps* and
the officer *corps*.[32] These and other works were products of their time and were
impregnated with a monarchistic spirit, but, nevertheless, distinguished themselves
by a high level of professional and technical military science and decisively influenced
the face of official military historiography in nineteenth-century Prussia-Germany.

III

To what extent did Huguenots play individual prominent roles? An imposing group
of them formed the backbone of the high command. The best known personality
was undoubtedly Friedrich Herman von Schomberg, whose military development
reflected an archetypal seventeenth-century military service. Schomberg stemmed
from a Protestant noble family from the Palatinate. At the age of 13 he arrived at
the French military academy at Sedan (a school for young nobles who subsequently
wanted to join the army), studied at the University of Leiden in 1632 and in 1633
entered the Dutch army as a volunteer. During the following years he, like many
officers, changed his 'military nationality'. In 1655 he was a French lieutenant-
general, in 1660 a general in the Portuguese army, in 1673 he was in the English
service and ultimately in 1674 he renewed his French service, and became a marshal
of France. After the revocation of the Edict of Nantes he left France and once again
entered the Portuguese service until the Great Elector summoned him to Brandenburg
in 1687. Although he was only engaged in this army for a year, Schomberg was
invested with the highest military authority and official positions by the Elector. He
was Field Marshal and at the same time a privy councillor of State and of War and
was, moreover, a *stadtholder* of Prussia. Without doubt his career made an enormous
impact on the Huguenot refugees who sought service in the Brandenburg army and in
the administration. Schomberg had under his command in Brandenburg an auxiliary
corps with 5,300 infantry soldiers and 600 cavalry troopers, which at the beginning
of the War of the Grand Alliance, or Nine Years' War (1688–97), marched up to
the Lower Rhine against France. Schomberg transferred in 1688 to the service of
William of Orange, who landed with him in England later that year and, thereafter,

---

31   Jacques de Pelet, Seigneur de Rocoulle (d.1698), was Colonel of the *grands
mousquetaires*. His wife was Marthe du Val, widow of Essaie du Maz de Montbail, younger
brother of Louis du Maz de Montmartin, whose widow Marguerite de Roussay arrived in
Brandenburg with her young sons and sister-in-law, Marthe (above). The sons became pages
in the court of the Grand Elector. The eldest boy was wounded at the siege of Stralsund
in 1715 and became a captain of the castle guard of the Prince of Anhalt-Dessau. Another
member of the family, Charles Louis Emile de Pelet, Baron de Montmartin, was lieutenant in
the regiment of Duke Leopold von Brunswick in Frankfurt-am-der-Oder: Erman and Reclam,
Mémoires pour l'histoire des Réfugiés François, vol. 3, pp. 114–16.

32   G. von Pelet-Narbonne, *Geschichte der Brandenburg-Preussen Reiterei von den
Zeiten des Grossen Kurfürsten bis zur Gegenwart* (2 vols, Hamburg, 1905); A. von Crousaz,
Geschichte des königlich Preussischen Kadetten-Corps (Berlin, 1857).

sent the Marshal to Ireland where Schomberg fell on 10 July 1690 at the battle of the Boyne.[33]

Schomberg's sons followed their father. The second, Meinhard, entered Brandenburg service in 1688, and was the envoy of the electorate of Brandenburg in England and later remained in the English service. The younger son, Charles, became Governor of the large fortress at Magdeburg in 1687 and in the first two years of the Nine Years' War he commanded Brandenburg-Prussian troops in the Lower Rhine theatre of war.[34]

Further noteworthy Huguenot military officers include Jacques Laumonier, Marquis de Varennes, Joël de Cornuaud, and Andreas Rouvillas de Veyne.[35] Varennes, who had been a lieutenant-colonel in France, came to Brandenburg in 1686 and became Colonel of the infantry regiment bearing his name in Soest which was made up of predominantly Huguenot officers and men.[36] In 1691 Varennes was promoted to Major-General and in 1703 to Lieutenant-General, and he commanded Brandenburg-Prussian troops in the Nine Years' War and the War of the Spanish Succession.[37]

In 1686 Cornuaud established a battalion of Huguenots in Brandenburg (at Havel), advanced to colonel in 1689 and in 1696 became a major-general. De Veyne commanded a dragoons regiment (post-1705) as a major-general.[38] Jean Quirin de Forcade, Marquis de Biaix (1663–1729) transferred to the Elector's Life Guards at the age of 22 and advanced from captain (of infantry) up to lieutenant-general (in 1729). From 1714 he was Commandant of the Berlin city garrison and one of Friedrich Wilhelm I's confidants.[39]

---

33   See M. R. Glozier, *Marshal Schomberg, 1615–1690: 'The Ablest Soldier of His Age': International Soldiering and the Formation of State Armies in Seventeenth-Century Europe* (Brighton, Portland, 2005).

34   Ibid., pp. 119–20.

35   Jacques Laumonier, Marquis de Varennes (b.1641 – d. 2 December 1717): Haag, *La France Protestante*, vol. 6, pp. 425–6. Joël de Cornuaud (b.1637 at Pujols, Guienne – d.1718), of the house of Cornuaud de Fonbourgarde. His sister married M. Jourgniac de Marcoux, and their daughter was betrothed to Colonel de Saint-Sauveur. Cornuaud's brother fathered four boys who all followed careers in arms: Joseph (d.1715), commanded Varennes's infantry regiment in Prussia; Cornuaud de Barthelot (d.1717) was a lieutenant-colonel in Prussia; Cornuaud de Baugerie, commanded Burke's English infantry regiment; Jean-Jacques was a lieutenant-colonel in Prussia: Haag, *La France Protestante*, vol. 4, pp. 64–6.

36   Lehmann, 'Die brandeneburgische Kriegsmacht', p. 502.

37   Cornuaud's regiment included the following officers in 1686: Jean de Favolles (lieutenant-colonel); André Rouvillas de Veyne (major); d'Artis, Lot de Saint-Martin (captains); Fouquet, de Beaufort, de Bauchardis, de La Salle, Jean du Périer de Fontange, Pierre Portal, Montfort, La Motte, Charles de Wisson de Saint-Maurice, Saint-Blancard, de Brogard, Hercule de Gertout, de Témelac, de Péguilhem, Alexandre de La Faye, de Carmasse (lieutenants): Haag, *La France Protestante*, vol. 4, pp. 64–6.

38   Lehmann, 'Die brandenburgische Kriegsmacht', p. 502 et seq.

39   See D. Harms, 'Das Edikt von Potsdam vom 29.Oktober 1685. Die Integration und der soziale Aufstieg von Ausländern in der preußischen Armee des 17. und 18. Jahrhunderts', in B. R. Kroener (ed.), *Potsdam. Staat, Armee, Residenz in der preußisch-deutschen Militärgeschichte* (Frankfurt-am-Main, Berlin, 1993), pp. 168–70.

A succession of generals and officers of Huguenot origin also served in the army of Friedrich the Great, above all from the families of La Motte-Fouqué and von Forcade, who in the campaigns of the Silesian wars came to rank and honours, titles and office. To these belonged amongst others, Ernst Heinrich August, Baron de La Motte-Fouqué, who fought in the battles of Prague (1757), Leuthen (1757) and Landshut (1760).[40] Friedrich Wilhelm Quirin de Forcade, Marquis de Biaix, a son of the aforementioned Berlin city garrison commander, rose in the royal service to lieutenant-general and participated in the successful siege of Breslau (1757) and in the following year in the court-martial of the Prussian generals who, in November 1757, handed this town over to the Austrians.[41]

IV

The Huguenot soldiers brought a strong impetus for the field of military training. They were at the forefront in the setting up of a cadet institute. The concept of preparing young nobles for war duties in their own schools was not in any way new at that time. At the beginning of the seventeenth century, the Prince of Orange and the Count of Nassau put forward similar suggestions. Johan VII of Nassau set up a military school in Siegen and appointed the well-known military theorist Johann Jacobi von Wallhausen as director.[42] In Cassel, Moritz, Landgrave of Hesse-Cassel, established a *collegium* with similar aims. All these institutions were only allotted a short life. The furies of the Thirty Years' War disrupted the setting up of military educational establishments in the German states. After 1648, new initiatives were set in motion by sovereigns and private individuals; in the electorate of Brandenburg so-called 'knights' academies sprung up, but only operated for a short time.

With the incorporation of Huguenots a clear transformation was effected. Separate companies were established in 1682 for the cadets (in France the term for younger sons of noble families without an inheritance), who found accommodation in the army. The Huguenot refugees brought this institution with them to Brandenburg. After 1688 the Huguenot units had their own cadet companies, likewise the Guards in Berlin, to which came principally young nobles from districts east of the River Elbe. Gradually the Huguenot cadet companies were disbanded since the cadets transferred to regular regiments at the age of 16 to 18 years. At the beginning of the eighteenth century there was a central cadet corps in Berlin. Alongside this there were independent small cadet schools set up in Kolberg and Magdeburg.

---

40 He was descended from Charles de La Motte-Fouqué (1625–1701), Baron de Thonnaiboutonne et de Saint-Saurin, seigneur de La Greve, from Bordeaux: W. Gahrig (ed.), *Hugenotten, Willkommen in der Mark: Die Mark Brandenburg – Zeitschrift für die Mark und das Land Brandenburg*, Heft 48 (Berlin, 2003), pp. 33–4, 34–9; Deutsche Staatsbibilothek zu Berlin, Preussischer Kulturbesitz, MS boruss. 311, fol. 5.

41 Jany, *Geschichte der Königlich Preußischen Armee*, p. 359; Schwerin, *Das Regiment gens d'armes*, vol. 1, p. 54.

42 G. Parker, *The Military Revolution: Military Innovation and the Rise of the West, 1500–1800* (Cambridge, 1988), p. 163.

Under the control of absolutist (and later Prussian-German) militarism this institution developed in a reactionary manner. Originally, however, the concept had been to educate, train and develop young officers, which had its origins in the military reform ideas of the beginning of the seventeenth century. The aim had been to create a military power from native burghers, farmers and nobles for the protection of the country to counter the gathering storm of the Thirty Years' War, whereby young nobles and sons of burghers could be trained to be officers.[43]

Huguenots also successfully introduced the concept of establishing militia troops from the local Brandenburg population. In France the Secretary of State for War, Louvois, had been involved with such plans in 1660. The maintenance of a standing army proved to be expensive, the losses of war were not easy to make good; therefore, it was essential to supplement the employment of expensive foreign mercenaries with the cheaper conscription of native farmers and burgher-townspeople. In this field there was also a Huguenot tradition which reached back to the time of the French religious wars in the sixteenth century. At that time the Huguenot military forces consisted of mercenaries and miscellaneous local units. In Brandenburg-Prussia, Friedrich Wilhelm and his successors likewise made efforts to build up local militias. In 1701 a royal decree in relation to the militia was issued. In practice this had limited success. However, it is unmistakable that certain Huguenot experiences in relation to the founding of local militias played their part.[44]

The incorporation of Huguenot soldiers in the Brandenburg army did not change the socio-political character of this fighting force or its class-structured duties in the service of the Hohenzollern dynasty. But Brandenburg-Prussian military history, and not least the spiritual life in this army, received an impulse which influenced further military development. Certainly the Calvinistic Huguenot military conception of obedience and discipline, without resorting to control by the cudgel, could not be implemented in practice in the eighteenth-century Prussian army. It needed the cataclysm of the French Revolution and defeat on the battlefield to create a breakthrough and bring about a new mode of thinking in the military field.[45]

---

43   See H. Rosenberg, *Bureaucracy, Aristocracy and Autocrat: The Prussian Experience, 1660–1815* (Cambridge, MA, 1958).

44   Lynn, *Giant of the Grand Siècle*, pp. 371–9.

45   Ibid., pp. 298–330.

Appendix 1: Varennes's Infantry Regiment, called the 'French Foot'

Establishment
1 colonel
12 staff officers
15 companies, each containing a captain, lieutenant, ensign, sergeant, lance-corporal,
    corporal, 8 musicians and labourers, and 40 soldiers
1 company of cadets, containing 50 men

Personnel
12 staff officers
256 officers
630 soldiers and cadets

Total strength
898 men

Appendix 2: The 'Brandenburg Foot'

1 colonel
12 staff officers
8 companies, each containing a captain, lieutenant, ensign, sergeant, lance-corporal,
    corporal, 8 musicians and labourers, and 125 soldiers

Personnel
12 staff officers
144 officers
1,000 soldiers

Total strength
1,156 men

Appendix 3: Briquemault's cavalry regiment, attached to the 'French Foot'

Establishment
1 colonel
12 staff officers
10 troops, each containing a captain (*rittmeister*), lieutenant, cornet, sergeant
    (*wachtmeister*), corporal, 7 musicians and labourers, and 40 troopers

Personnel
12 staff officers
140 officers
400 troopers

Total strength
552 men

Appendix 4: Cavalry regiment attached to the 'Brandenburg Foot'

Establishment
1 colonel
12 staff officers
6 troops, each containing a captain, lieutenant, cornet, sergeant, corporal, 7 musicians
      and labourers, and 50 troopers

Personnel
12 staff officers
84 officers
300 troopers

Total strength
396 men

Appendix 5: The *grands mousquetaires*

Establishment
1 colonel
Staff: a pastor, auditor (*Gerichtsoffizier*) and doctor
2 troops, each containing a lieutenant-colonel, major, two captains, 2 lieutenants, 2
      cornets, 2 quartermasters, 6 brigadiers (*entsprechen Korporalen*), 2 labourers,
      4 musicians, 22 volunteers (*Diener*) and gentlemen-of-horse (*Pferdeknechte*),
      65 troopers

Table 1   Monthly cost of the French and Brandenburg Foot regiments, according to the Prussian army establishment of 1 January 1684 (all figures in *Talers*)

Overall soldier costs

Cavalry		Infantry	
Staff *per* regiment	24,575	Staff *per* regiment	20,000
Officers *per* company	19,300	Officers *per* company	13,450
Troopers	450	Soldiers	300

Soldier costs per regiment

1. Brandenburg Foot

Cavalry		Infantry	
Staff	24,575	Staff	20,000
Six officers	115,800	Eight officers	107,700
300 troopers	135,000	1,000 soldiers	300,000
Total	275,375	Total	427,700

2. French Foot

Cavalry		Infantry	
Staff	24,575	Staff	20,000
Ten officers	193,000	16 officers	215,200
400 troopers	450	630 soldiers	189,000
Total	397,575	Total	424,200

Source: F. von Schroetter, 'Die brandenburgisch-Preußische Heeresverfassung unter dem Großen Kurfürsten', *Staats- und socialwissenschaftliche Forschungen*, 11/5 (Leipzig, 1882): 56.

Table 2 **Monthly soldier costs for cavalry regiments attached to the Brandenburg Foot and the** *Grands Mousquetaires*

Grands Mousquetaires

First Company and staff officers	134,850
Second Company	126,900
Total	261,750

Cavalry Regiment

Total	275,375

Source: Schroetter, 'Die brandenburgisch-Preußische Heeresverfassung unter dem Großen Kurfürsten': 56; Schwerin, *Das Regiment gens d'armes*, vol. 1, p. 73.

Chapter 10

Integration and Social Ascent of Huguenot Soldiers in Brandenburg-Prussia
The Impact of the Edict of Potsdam[1]

Detlef Harms

When examining tolerance in Brandenburg-Prussia, 29 October 1685 is a significant date.[2] On this day the Elector Friedrich Wilhelm (1640–88), referred to as the Great Elector, signed an edict in Potsdam Castle 'regarding those rights, privileges and other benefits which His Excellency the Elector of Brandenburg has resolved to graciously allow within his territory, so that those Reformed Protestants of the French nation, will establish themselves in that same place'.[3] This document, which history has recorded as the Edict of Potsdam, bestowed on Huguenots who wished to settle there, comprehensive political, economic and religious rights in conjunction with material concessions such as privileges, subventions and tax advantages within a certain time frame. Moreover, Huguenot immigrants were granted their own separate jurisdiction in accordance with French laws along with independent French Protestant settlements.

The Great Elector had a variety of motives for assisting persecuted French Protestants. In the aftermath of the Thirty Years' War (1618–48), Friedrich Wilhelm

---

1   First published as 'Das Edikt von Potsdam vom 29.Oktober 1685. Die Integration und der soziale Aufstieg von Ausländern in der preußischen Armee des 17. und 18. Jahrhunderts', in B. R. Kroener (ed.), *Potsdam. Staat, Armee, Residenz in der preußisch-deutschen Militärgeschichte* (Frankfurt-am-Main, Berlin, 1993). The article was kindly translated by Mrs Vivien Costello of the Huguenot Society of Great Britain and Ireland.

2   29 October 1685 in Brandenburg according to the Julian Calendar, but 8 November 1685 since 1582 in Catholic countries since the adoption by them of the Gregorian Calendar.

3   *Corpus Constitutionum Marchicarum, Oder Königl. Preußis. und Churfürstl. Brandenburgische in der Chur- und Marck Brandenburg, auch incorporirten Landen publicirte und ergangene Ordnungen, Edicta, Mandata, Rescripta [et]c.: Von Zeiten Friedrich I. Churfürstens zu Brandenburg, [et]c. biß ietzo unter der Regierung Friderich Wilhelms, Königs in Preußen [et]c. ad annum 1736. inclusivè*, ed. C. O. Mylius (2 vols, Berlin, Halle, 1737-55), vol. 2, 2/1, no. 65, p. 183; E. Muret, *Geschichte der französischen Kolonie in Brandenburg-Preußen* (Berlin, 1885), p. 301; M. Kohnke, 'Das Edikt von Potsdam: Zu seiner Entstehung, Verbreitung und Überlieferung', in *Jahrbuch für Geschichte des Feudalismus*, Akademie der Wissenschaften der DDR Berlin 9 (Berlin, 1985), p. 241 (copy of documents, p. 271).

had ambitiously set himself the target of transforming the territories under his rule into a stable, disciplined state structure that would not only be internally capable of achieving economic and military strength but also externally able to pursue an influential foreign policy. The circumstances under which this policy was launched were the worst imaginable, since Potsdam and likewise the Mark of Brandenburg had been extensively laid waste and depopulated during the course of the Thirty Years' War. Thus the Elector from the outset of his reign made every effort to acquire foreign settlers, above all for Brandenburg, who would participate in the re-building of his domain. Artisans, merchants and manufacturers with their specialist skills and knowledge were particularly sought after; but farmers and academics as well as soldiers and their officers were also offered beneficial conditions for a new start. Manifest religious tolerance was a key expedient adopted vis à vis the repopulation initiative, to ensure state security and the integration of the population. Friedrich Wilhelm had comprehended the advantageousness of this policy, aptly described some time later by his grandson, King Friedrich Wilhelm I (1713–40): 'But the land will be cultivated and is in good condition, therefore, when the children grow up, and my son gets involved in war, he will have no shortage of people. That also is a form of wealth; I consider people to be the greatest riches.'[4]

I

French religious refugees had already been emigrating from their native country before 1685. The Huguenots were accorded comprehensive rights in the Edict of Nantes of 13 April 1598 by Henri IV (1589–1610), at the same time as Catholicism in France was elevated to the status of a state religion.[5] However, in 1629 they lost important special privileges, although their freedom of worship had not yet been endangered.[6] Huguenots were pre-eminent in commerce and trade and over-represented in leading administrative and military positions. Because of their influence, but above all for economic reasons, Calvinism was still tolerated. Louis XIV, the so-called 'Sun King' (1643–1715), believed in French religious uniformity and under the slogan 'one King, one faith, one law', re-established punitive rigorous measures against the Huguenots. By 1685 they had lost all their public appointments and the King tried to force them to convert to Catholicism through coercion.

As a Protestant, Friedrich Wilhelm had repeatedly tried to intervene with the French king against the oppression of Protestants. However, Louis XIV had resolved, with the Edict of Fontainebleau of October 1685, effectively to revoke the Edict of

---

4   *Die Briefe Friedrich Wilhelms I an den Fürsten Leopold von Anhalt-Dessau*, ed. O. Krauske (Berlin, 1905), p. 212.

5   E. Mengin, *Das Edikt von Nantes: Das Edikt von Fontainebleau* (Flensburg, 1963).

6   Under the Edict of Nantes French Protestants could never gain new places of worship, but the number they could use was reduced for various reasons – Huguenot nobles converting, but also towns losing the right to have *temples*, usually as a result of legal proceedings. It was a slow process of erosion.

Nantes.[7] This forbade Huguenots to practise their religion. Protestant marriages were declared invalid and emigration was forbidden, under penalty of being sentenced to the galleys. Despite the threat of punishment, an immense flood of refugees was engendered. England, The Netherlands, Switzerland and the Protestant German territories gave refuge to thousands of Huguenots.

Friedrich Wilhelm had already issued a number of edicts since 1661 which accorded immigrants various advantageous conditions, whereby he had attracted Netherlanders, Bohemians, Swiss and Austrian Jews into the country. Given the worsening repression in France, the flow of Huguenot immigrants also escalated. The number of refugee Huguenots who fled to Brandenburg-Prussia after the Edict of Potsdam can be estimated, after evaluating the extant records up to 1720, as being between 13,000 and 16,000. Until 1690 the majority of all *réfugiés* (about 60 per cent) went to Brandenburg, first came Protestant Palatines and Walloons, then followed Huguenots who had initially fled to Switzerland along with Protestants from the principality of Orange.[8] Immigration to Brandenburg-Prussia essentially emanated via Frankfurt-am-Main, Cologne and Amsterdam.[9] At the reception centres the newcomers were registered, provided with money and furnished with recommendations for a place of settlement. The Edict of Potsdam specified locations for the establishment of French colonies. In Brandenburg the places envisaged were Stendal, Werven, Rathenow, Brandenburg and Frankfurt-an-der-Oder. In the duchy of Magdeburg the towns of Halberstadt, Calbe and Magdeburg were designated and in the duchy of Prussia the town of Königsberg was selected. Ultimately though, the choice of place of settlement was left to the Huguenots themselves.

Berlin became an especially favoured place of refuge not only because of its proximity to the Elector's residence but also because a French Protestant community had been established there since 1672. A further reason to which the existence of the French community in Berlin can be attributed is the presence there of the Master of the Horse, Lieutenant-General Louis de Beauveau, Comte d'Espence, who had been in Brandenburg service since 1668. A commission of the office of the Commissioner-General under the command of the Lord Marshal, Joachim Ernst von Grumbkow, undertook the examination of refugees. The proceedings of the administrative authorities, which also involved erstwhile refugees such as the aforementioned Beauveau d'Espence, were considered, in the opinion of relevant Huguenots, to be well organised and benevolent. Thus the number of French who settled in Berlin rose from 500 in the year 1685 to about 5,400 in the year 1700, comprising some 20 per

7   H. Duchhardt, 'Die Konfessionspolitik Ludwigs XIV und die Aufhebung das Edikts von Nantes', in H. Duchhardt (ed.), *Der Exodus der Hugenotten: Die Aufhebung des Edikts von Nantes 1685 als europaisches Ereignis*, Beihefte zum Archiv für Kulturgeschichte 24 (Cologne, Wien, 1985), p. 29.

8   J. Wilke, 'Zur sozialstruktur und demographischen analyse der Hugenotten in Brandenburg-Preußen, insbesondere der in Berlin', in I. Mittenzwei (ed.), *Hugenotten in Brandenburg-Preußen*, Studien zur Geschichte der Akademie der Wissenschaften der DDR, Zentralinstitut für Geschichte 8 (Berlin, 1987), p. 30.

9   See 'Base de Donnees du Refuge Huguenot' database, hosted by the Ecole des Hautes Etudes en Sciences Sociales, Centre National de La Recherche Scientifique (CNRS) and the Centre d'Analyse et de Mathematique Sociales (CAMS): URL http://cams-atid.ivry.cnrs.fr.

cent of the town's inhabitants. Christoph, Count zu Dohna, reported in his memoirs how in 1686 he found

> Berlin full of French people, masses of whom had fled there, attracted by the beneficial welcome prepared for them by the Great Elector ... On a daily basis one saw the arrival of merchants, artists, manufacturers and especially also quantities of officers and noblemen.[10]

There was no immediate large scale Huguenot immigration of textile workers and soldiers into nearby Potsdam after the revocation of the Edict of Nantes. A Huguenot community was not established there until 1723. The extant French church, which remains as an architectural monument, was not built until the years 1751 to 1753 at the instigation of Friedrich II (1740–86). Nevertheless, Potsdam experienced an unprecedented increase in prosperity after 1660 due to the Elector Friedrich Wilhelm's choice of the town as his second residence. With the completion of a 'Grenadier barracks' and town garrison, the Prussian kings Friedrich Wilhelm I and Friedrich II put their imprint on the face of the town. Foreigners were to contribute decisively to this transformation. There was major participation from foreign master-builders such as the Dutchman, Cornelius Rijckwaert, in the new building works and the development of the grounds of Potsdam Castle up until 1688. Well-known master builders, architects and artists entered into the Brandenburg service at this time alongside soldiers such as the Huguenot Pierre de La Cheise who was Quarter-Master General and, after 1666, Director General of the Berlin fortification works and also the Dutch architect and engineer, Michael Matthias Smids.[11] In addition, subsequent Brandenburg rulers used the technical knowledge and reputation of foreigners such as Jean-Baptiste Broebes, Jean de Bodt (who was for a time a Huguenot engineer on the English establishment, including service in Ireland) culminating with Pierre Louis Moreau de Maupertuis and Voltaire – Catholic Frenchmen of the Age of Reason – for the furtherance of their economic enterprises and for the purpose of 'keeping up appearances'.[12]

II

The immigration and integration of the Huguenot officers and soldiers as well as their influence on Brandenburg-Prussian military affairs was substantial. The type of role played by refugee Huguenot military officers (already envisaged by the

---

10   C. von und zu Dohna, *Die Denkwürdigkeiten des Burggrafen und Grafen Christoph zu Dohna* (Göttingen, 1974), p. 60.

11   Pierre de La Cheise (1629–73): E. and E. Haag, *La France Protestante; ou Vie des protestants français qui se sont faut un nom dans l'histoire* (10 vols, Montpellier, 1992), vol. 6, pp. 178–9.

12   F. Mielke, *Potsdamer Baukunst* (Frankfurt, Berlin, Wien, 1981); *Der Große Kurfürst (Sammler, Bauherr, Mäzen, 1620–88)* (exhibition catalogue), ed. under general direction of Staatlichen Schlösser und Gärten Potsdam-Sanssouci (Potsdam, 1988); *Friedrich II und die Kunst* (200th anniversary exhibition catalogue), ed. under general direction of Staatlichen Schlösser und Gärten Potsdam-Sanssouci (Potsdam, 1986).

Elector Friedrich Wilhelm early in his deliberations) was clarified by his letter of 31 December 1685 to Field Marshal Georg von Derfflinger:

> You are also aware how great the sympathy is which we have for those unfortunate banished people from France of the Protestant religion and that we are engaged in the work of forming a new cavalry regiment and a new infantry regiment [from among their number].[13]

The Elector viewed the role of the Huguenots in relation to the development of the Brandenburg-Prussian army to be of just as much importance as their contribution to expanding the population and the economy. The consequences of the Thirty Years' War were very clearly evident in military affairs. In 1648 the Elector's army consisted only of some fortress and garrison troops. Military contractors – men such as Wallenstein – had commanded their own contingents which they themselves financed and maintained. These troops were, therefore, only of limited use to the head of state. In order to protect a reigning sovereign who had wide-ranging foreign policy ambitions it would be essential to have a standing, well-prepared, regulated force under the direct command of the ruler. For that reason Friedrich Wilhelm of Brandenburg resolved in 1660 to establish a standing army. After participating in the First Northern War (1655–60), the Elector omitted to carry out the customary disbandment of the troops. He continued to employ six infantry regiments, each 5,500 men strong, which formed the core of the Brandenburg standing army. In 1666 seven cavalry regiments, with a strength of 1,260 men under arms, were retained. In that same year (1666) the total effective, battle ready, peacetime army under the Elector's command comprised 2,000 cavalry, 6,140 infantry and 5,000 garrison unit men. By the beginning of the 1680s the army's total strength had risen to about 25,000 men.[14] A crucial problem for the continuing existence of the army was finance. In the difficult conflict with the Brandenburg estates (the governing body of the realm), the Elector succeeded for the first time in concluding a treaty with the legislative assembly in 1653, to implement an army tax from which a standing army could be maintained.

Just as there was a labour shortage in the fields of trade, commerce and administration after the Thirty Years' War so there was also an acute scarcity of army personnel, above all of officers. It was, therefore, established practice for absolutist states to engage seasoned foreign officers. In the opinion of (Germanic) rulers, citizens of other German territorial states were also to be classified in this category. Amongst the best know high ranking army officers in the Brandenburg service during the second half of the seventeenth century were the Austrian-born Georg von Derfflinger and Friedrich II, Landgrave of Hesse-Homburg.[15]

---

13   K. W. von Schöning (ed.), *Das General-Feldmarschalls Dubislav Gneomar von Natzmer auf Gannewitz Leben und Kriegsthaten* (Berlin, 1838), p. 52.

14   C. Jany, *Geschichte der Königlich-Preußischen Armee bis zum Jahre 1807* (5 vols, Berlin, 1928–37), vol. 1, p. 274; P. Kiehm, 'Anfänge eines stehengen Heeres in Brandenburg 1640 bis 1655 unter Kurfürst Friedrich Wilhelm', *Militärgeschichte*, 24/6 (1985): 515.

15   Biographical notices of all these generals appear in K. von Priesdorf (ed.), *Soldatisches Führertum. Die Generale der brandenburgisch-preußischen Armee* (10 vols, Hamburg,

The commissioning of Huguenots proved to be of far-reaching significance for the enlargement and development of the Brandenburg army. Former officers of the French crown, most of whom were Calvinists, had already served in the Brandenburg-Prussian army before the promulgation of the 1685 Edict of Potsdam. Amongst these was Pierre de La Cave, who had left France in 1630 and had entered Brandenburg service during the Thirty Years' War.[16] Since his appointment as an ensign of the Elector's Life Guards, La Cave proved himself in various capacities, advancing to major-general in 1669. At this point we must return to Louis, Comte d'Espence. In 1668 he received a commission as colonel of the company of Life Guards. Besides his aforementioned activities in the commissariat for French refugees, he served Brandenburg in various political missions to France in 1679–80 and to England in 1688.[17]

The integration of the enormous inflow of Huguenots into the Brandenburg-Prussian forces was considerably expedited by officers of French origin who had already been commissioned prior to the proclamation of the Edict of Potsdam. For example, Major-General François, Comte du Hamel, a Catholic Frenchman, who in 1674 had taken over a newly raised cavalry regiment, found himself inundated by refugees with requests for commissions.[18] The Huguenot Charles Ancillon reported in 1690 in his work on the *History of the settlement of the refugees in the states of His Highness the Elector of Brandenburg* that the lure of the Brandenburg army was so great, that initially not all former officers could be accommodated: 'Therefore, for a period they obtained an allotted subvention and could settle themselves wherever they wanted, either in an urban or rural area.'[19]

As was the case with all other immigrants, the incorporation of the Huguenot soldiers was processed via the general office of the commissioner (*commissaire*) for war. Soon after the arrival of a substantial number of officers, General Henri de Beauvais-Briquemault, Baron de Saint-Loup, received an order from the Elector 'to accommodate all French officers and do this on the same footing as is laid down in French regiments, according to the organizational framework as described by the assorted French officers who have come here'.[20] Briquemault arrived in Brandenburg in 1680 after some years of military service in the French army at the rank of colonel. On 1 January 1681 he obtained a commission as major-general in Brandenburg and in 1683 he established a cavalry regiment. From November 1685 to March 1686

1936–42), vol. 1 'Die Generale von den Anfängen der brandenburgisch-preußischen Armee bis 1740'.

16   Haag, *La France Protestante*, vol. 6, pp. 171–2.

17   Louis de Beauveau, Seigneur de Grandru (later Comte d'Espence) (d.1727 at Berlin). He was a *maréchal de camp* in France by 1664, but was in Brandenburg service by 1672: ibid., vol. 2, pp. 136–9.

18   H. Schnitter, 'Die Réfugiés in der brandenburgischen Armee', in G. Bregulla (ed.), *Hugenotten in Berlin* (Berlin, 1988), p. 315.

19   C. Ancillon, *Geschichte der Niederlassung der Réfugiés in den Staaten seiner kurfürstlichen Hoheit von Brandenburg* (Berlin, 1690; reprinted Berlin, *Geschichtsblätter des Deutschen Hugenotten-Vereins* 15/8, 1939), p. 45.

20   *Das General-Feldmarschalls Dubislav Gneomar von Natzmer*, p. 53; Haag, *La France Protestante*, vol. 2, pp. 130–36.

he served in the commissariat for French refugees. At the turn of the year 1686 the Briquemault regiment was selected to relocate to Hungary as the Brandenburg contingent for the Emperor's war against the Turks. The arrival of the Huguenot reinforcements was most timely for the Imperial campaign against the Ottoman Empire.

The number of Huguenot officers who had joined the Brandenburg-Prussian army by 1700 is estimated to be 600. An exact figure is not possible since soldiers are not identified in the extant lists of settlers.[21] The numbers of immigrant junior officers and rank-and-file soldiers remain conjectural. In any event, a new infantry regiment was established under the command of Colonel Jacques Laumonier, Marquis de Varennes, in January 1686, alongside the Briquemault cavalry regiment.[22] The garrison for its 630 soldiers was located at Soest in Westphalia. Joël de Cornuaud was another Huguenot who transferred to the Brandenburg service.[23] In May 1686 he was ordered to establish an additional Huguenot infantry regiment.

The immigrant Huguenots were accorded extensive privileges. The Elector's generous incentives were particularly attractive to Huguenot soldiers, accompanied as they were by the guarantee of freedom of worship. Incorporation into the Brandenburg service resulted in their being accorded a rank at least equivalent to that which they had held in France. Ancillon wrote: 'Those who before their flight had led a regiment, immediately again became a regiment commander here. They were even promoted to Major-General.'[24] In the lower ranks likewise advancements in rank ensued. Even regiment commanders who had previously been pensioned in France were given the rank of major-general and provided with an annual stipend of 500 *Talers*. The Brandenburg service provided Huguenot officers and non-commissioned officers who had suffered religious persecution with the opportunity to advance or even accelerate their military careers.

III

As the influx of Huguenot officers became overwhelming during the winter of 1685/6 and it was no longer possible to absorb them into the existing Huguenot regiments, the Elector decided to form regiments composed entirely of gentlemen-officers. Following the prototype of the French king's household troop (*maison du roi*), which consisted of young nobles, a decree was issued on 3 February 1687 to form two companies of *grands mousquetaires*. In addition to a double-strength company structure (*Primaplana*), initially each 65 officers counted as a company of musketeers. The Elector himself and Field Marshal Friedrich Hermann von Schomberg acted as commanders. Schomberg, who had been born in the Palatinate and had been in the service of the Electorate of Brandenburg since March 1687,

---

21   Many lists are reproduced in J. P. Erman and P. C. F. Reclam, *Mémoires pour servir à l'histoire des Réfugiés François dans les États du Roi* (9 vols, Berlin, 1782–99), vol. 2, p. 185.

22   Haag, *La France Protestante*, vol. 6, pp. 425–6.

23   Ibid., vol. 4, pp. 64–6.

24   Ancillon, *Geschichte der Niederlassung der Réfugiés*, p. 45.

became for the Huguenot refugees a shining example of the promotional prospects in the Brandenburg army. Schomberg spearheaded the expansion of the *grands mousquetaires*. At the age of 73 he re-assigned himself to William III, Prince of Orange and it was in his service in Ireland that he ultimately fell at the battle of the Boyne.[25]

The high esteem in which Friedrich Hermann von Schomberg was held by the Huguenot officers, and more importantly by Friedrich Wilhelm, was transferred to his sons. After the example of their father, Charles and Meinhard in turn served in various European armies. Charles von Schomberg came to Brandenburg in 1686. Later he became Governor of Magdeburg and Colonel of the Electress Dorothea's Life Guards. In 1689 an independent regiment with ten companies was transferred to him. Meinhard von Schomberg, during his nine-month term of service with the Elector of Brandenburg was appointed General of the Artillery and took over from his father as Colonel of the *grands mousquetaires*.

The *grands mousquetaires* were billeted in accordance with the Elector's anticipated requirements, at Prenzlau with 100 officers, at Angermunde with 30, Eberswalde 24, Wrietzen 16, Templin 30 and Strausberg 20 officers including the company commanders. The first company was under the command of Christoph, Count zu Dohna, who was born near Geneva and had excelled himself in the campaign against the Turks. The command of the second company was taken over by Lieutenant-Colonel des Vignolles de Saint-Bonnet.[26] The quartering of the officers, as was then customary, was incumbent on the towns, who had to shoulder the problem that 'certain previously specified officers would meet with the same standard of accommodation and quarters in every location'.[27] Each musketeer held the rank of second-lieutenant with a monthly pay of 10 *Talers*. One orderly was shared amongst three men. For French non-commissioned officers there was a comparable military formation, the *grenadiers à cheval*. It consisted of 65 men and had its garrison in Beeskow-Storkow. The commander was Major du Puy.[28]

One consequence of the establishment of the French regiments was a substantial level of expenditure. Additional costs arose from the taking over of the French

25 See M. R. Glozier, *Marshal Schomberg (1615–1690): 'the ablest soldier of his age': International Soldiering and the Formation of State Armies in Seventeenth-Century Europe* (Brighton, Portland, 2005), pp. 117–20.

26 Charles des Vignolles de Saint-Bonnet, Marquis de Cournonteral (b.1663), had been assisted to Berlin via Frankfurt-am-Main in 1686, having arrived there from his native Besançon: Deutsche Staatsbibliothek zu Berlin, Preussischer Kulturbesitz (hereafter SBPK), D PRF FFM 104 238r 04 et 238v. A possible kinsman is Edouard de Vignoles (b.1677), a lieutenant of dragoons in Prussia and a captain in Poland at the time of his death at Dresden. Also, Louis de Vignoles (b.1666) was a cadet in Cornuaud's regiment in Prussia: Haag, *La France Protestante*, vol. 9, p. 501.

27 See O. von Schwerin, *Das Regiment gens d'armes und seine Vorgeschichte* (2 vols, Berlin, 1912), p. 53.

28 Possibly either Major du Puy, from Bass-Guienne, Philippe du Puy de La Bousquetie, from Upper Languedoc, or Captain David du Puy, from Dauphiné, all recorded in the Berlin census, 31 December 1699: SBPK, D WEZ col 1699 Ber liste 177 3997, D PRF FFM 107 327 04, CH AES exul 26 13 153 19.

organisational structure in the newly established regiments. Whilst a cavalry regiment 'on a Brandenburg footing' consisted of six companies with 300 soldiers, a French cavalry regiment had at its disposal ten companies with 400 soldiers. This structure required 44 per cent more in terms of soldiers' pay. The greater number of officers occasioned by the larger number of companies was even more extreme in the infantry. The number of companies in the French regiments was 16, which was double the size of the Brandenburg troop units (equalling 1,000 soldiers). The adoption of the French structure, with the larger number of officer positions, was undertaken not only because of the numerous Huguenot military immigrants but also because of the Elector's concepts for the development of the Brandenburg army. The availability of officers allowed new units to be speedily established according to requirements.

In their refuge, the *officiers* were enabled to assimilate socially and professionally, in that they had no difficulty in finding employment in the Brandenburg service coupled with remuneration and accommodation. Extant biographical details on Huguenot officers provide testimony for the rapid social ascent of a number of them. Under the rule of Friedrich Wilhelm (d.1688) and Friedrich III (King 1701–13), no less than 19 French officers attained the rank of general. In recognition of the available military talent, there were also constant promotions amongst the lower ranks. The extant records allow us to present the career development of the Huguenot Samuel de Saint-Sauveur as a case study. In 1687 he is described as a sergeant in the Third Company of Varennes's infantry regiment; in 1705 he served as a captain in the Life Guards company of the same regiment and, in 1716, he was a major in Dienhoff's regiment.[29] In 1727, equipped with many years' experience, he was transferred to a training role with new officer recruits. He became second-in-command of the central cadet corps in Berlin.[30]

The adoption of the French regimental structure and appropriate army tactics facilitated the incorporation of Huguenot soldiers in Brandenburg. The assumption of a French-style organizational structure demonstrates the Elector's recognition of the direct military benefits deriving from Huguenot immigration. The success of the incorporation convinced the Elector that his army had acquired militarily experienced and loyal subjects.

IV

The mass immigration of foreigners during a period when the vast majority of the population lacked the means to communicate with distant places or to experience other lifestyles and cultures inevitably engendered considerable social problems. The resentment of the native population was fed by its own deficient living conditions as well as the raising of special taxes, the benefits of which Friedrich Wilhelm dispensed to the Huguenots.[31] J. P. Erman and P. C. F. Reclam, the descendants

---

29   SBPK, MS boruss. 311, fols 22, 37, 315.

30   A. von Crousaz, *Geschichte des Königlich Preußischen Kadetten-Corps* (Berlin, 1857), pp. 31, 68.

31   Muret, *Geschichte der französischen Kolonie in Brandenburg-Preußen*, p. 17.

of Huguenot refugees and resident in Prussia at the end of the eighteenth century, presented an idealised picture of the assimilation problems in their history of the Huguenot refugees. Above all they say that, in the early years of residing in the Mark of Brandenburg, 'one was not sufficiently enlightened to be tolerant'.[32] There was a comparable resentment of the Huguenot refugees amongst German military officers. Christoph zu Dohna reported that the incorporation of the Huguenots into the army 'at the very least created envy. Both in political and military circles there was a great deal of it'.[33] Dohna identified General Hans Adam von Schöning as one of their most vehement objectors, who worked extremely hard to oppose Dohna's favourable treatment of the refugees and intrigued against Marshal Schomberg and his son Meinhard.[34] For example, Schöning ordered his nephew, Lüdecke Ernst von Schöning,

> who commanded the Life Guard regiment ... not to give a military salute to the Marshal [Schomberg] when he encountered his regiment. Schomberg, who was irritated by this type of unprincipled behaviour, ordered me [Dohna], to do the same, whenever Schöning, at the head of the Life Guards regiment, would meet the *grands mousquetaires*.[35]

Thereupon, Hans Adam von Schöning reputedly swore 'to shoot a cannon ball in front of his [Schomberg's] face should this happened again'.[36]

Problems occurred constantly in Prenzlau, where a company of the *grands mousquetaires* was stationed. There were reports of

> unruliness ... amongst the high-spirited men ... and in the Prenzlau winter of 1698/9 a rambunctious carnival boiled over and came to a head – with black consequences for the guilty parties – on the other hand there were also incessant, pestering complaints from the local inhabitants about being hunted down in an unwarranted manner and similar [complaints] by the French.[37]

Dohna was well aware of these problems and, therefore, considered it necessary, with the 'many young nobles from the Languedoc, Gascony, Normandy, Picardy, Poitou and so on, most of them spirited people ... to keep a tight rein on them and on the other hand, if possible to win their friendship'.[38] In contrast to the idealised descriptions given by Ancillon, Erman and Reclam and others, dissentions amongst Huguenots themselves were not uncommon and had to be grappled with, in relation to military matters as well as about grants, benefits and promotions. Christoph zu Dohna mentions in his memoirs, without giving any details, that *réfugiés* were

---

32   H. Krum (ed.), *Preußens Adoptivkinder. Die Hugenotten. 300 Jahre Edikt von Potsdam. Unter Verwendung von 'Mémoires pour servir à l'histoire des réfugiés françois dans les états du roi' von J. P. Erman und F. Reclam 1782–1789* (Berlin, 1985), p. 205.

33   Dohna, *Die Denkwürdigkeiten ... Christoph zu Dohna*, p. 61.

34   Ibid., pp. 61, 96; *Das General-Feldmarschalls Dubislav Gneomar von Natzmer*, p. 74.

35   Dohna, *Die Denkwürdigkeiten ... Christoph zu Dohna*, p. 74.

36   Ibid., p. 74.

37   Schwerin, *Das Regiment gens d'armes und seine Vorgeschichte*, p. 67.

38   Dohna, *Die Denkwürdigkeiten ... Christoph zu Dohna*, p. 80.

antagonistic towards him.[39] The background of a duel in 1692 in which Dohna shot the Huguenot Lieutenant-Colonel de Souville points to a universal problem within a standing army, the personal enrichment of officers at the expense of their subordinates. Dohna challenged de Souville to a duel, because the latter 'thought that he could copy the majority of officers in Germany by withholding a certain small "cut" from the pay of his cavaliers and soldiers'.[40]

Latterly, General Dubislav Gneomar von Natzmer, who was appointed as the Elector's adjutant-general in 1687, also entertained reservations about the Huguenots and in July 1688 he spearheaded intensive efforts to establish a German company of *grands mousquetaires* whose purpose would be to achieve a counter-balance against the privileged position of the Huguenot *grands mousquetaires*. Probably the determining factor for this policy was the easily influenced Friedrich III's somewhat ambivalent attitude towards entirely French regiments compared to that of Friedrich Wilhelm, who had died on 29 April 1688. The aforesaid Natzmer received his commission as the real colonel of the German company of *grands mousquetaires* in October 1689.[41]

The integration of Huguenot soldiers was expedited so that sometime after 1700, facilitated by the transformation and re-structuring of regiments, a blending with German officers had taken place. In 1690 there were six German officers in the Wylich und Lottum infantry regiment (Infantry Regiment No. 15) formed in 1688 out of eight companies from Varennes's regiment.[42] On the other hand the officer list of the Varennes regiment in 1705 testifies to the fact that the companies' senior officers were still, without exception, French.[43] In 1698 there were still 12 *réfugiés* amongst 30 officers of the former Briquemault cavalry regiment, the majority of whom had begun their service in Brandenburg between 1685 and 1687.[44]

There were many factors which contributed to the mixing of regiments. Thereby the segregation of the immigrants from the German regiments could be prevented, which in the event of war could have had negative consequences in relation to the co-operation of troops. On the other hand Brandenburg benefited from the increased efficiency arising from the widespread dispersion of Huguenots who infused the army with French concepts vis à vis organizational and tactical principles. Ultimately though, with the constant re-armament of the army and the appointment of numerous new officers, the need for more independent (and exclusively French) companies of officers and non-commissioned officers ceased to exist. The *grenadiers à cheval* unit was disbanded in 1701 and in 1708 it was decided that no further additions were

---

39   Ibid., p. 144.

40   Ibid., p. 131. Jean de Bardonenche de Souville came from Dauphiné and held the rank of major when he appeared in the census of Berlin on 31 December 1699: SBPK, D WEZ col 1699 Ber liste 175 3952.

41   Ibid.

42   *Chronik des I Garderegiments zu Fuß und dessen Stammtruppenteilen 1675–1900* (Berlin, 1907), p. 30.

43   SBPK, MS boruss. 311, fol. 37.

44   Ibid., fol. 135.

needed for the *grands mousquetaires*. In 1712 pensions of a mere 636 *Reichstaler* were introduced for the musketeers by the Military Council.[45]

V

The history of the Huguenots in the Brandenburg-Prussian army did not end with the dissolving of the exclusively French regiments. In the eighteenth century Huguenots still immigrated to Prussia along with other foreigners during the reigns of Friedrich Wilhelm II and Friedrich II. This developed into an increasingly significant winning factor in the context of absolutist Europe. Extant officer lists also testify to further Huguenots who, having been born in France, departed their native country in order to enter the Brandenburg service. On the other hand there were also many nobles with French names whose officer commissions indicate that their birthplace was Berlin or that their fatherland was Prussia. These were mostly descendants of Huguenot immigrants. It is highly probable that in the eighteenth century, some officers of the Varennes infantry regiment established in 1687 were descendants of the original officers. For example, in 1740 the Second Company of this regiment was led by Colonel Friedrich Wilhelm, Marquis de Varennes (age 40, birthplace Berlin) and it included Ensign Georg Wilhelm de Varennes (age 15, birthplace Berlin).[46]

The family de La Motte-Fouqué was also closely connected with the Prussian army. Ernst Heinrich August, Baron de La Motte-Fouqué, whose forefathers left France for religious reasons, served in a number of capacities in the Prussian army from 1715.[47] He was in a high ranking position during the Silesian wars (1740–2; 1744–5). His younger brother, Henri-Charles-Frédéric, Baron de Saint-Saurin, and sons – Heinrich Karl and Heinrich August – also embarked upon military careers.[48] Huguenot family traditions likewise characterised the von Forcade family.[49]

The large number of Huguenots in the Brandenburg army up until the end of the eighteenth century also resulted in an intensive injection of French ideas which encompassed all spheres of the Prussian forces. Thus developments which had been tried and tested in France were perfected in Brandenburg-Prussia. Administrative and tax systems, which form the bedrock of a stable standing army, were refined with the aid of French paradigms. Recognisable French prototypes influenced the systematic army training regime as well as the command structure of units. The

---

45 C. Jany, 'Der Dessauer Stammliste von 1729', in *Urkundliche Beiträge und Forschungen zur Geschichte des Preußischen Heeres*, ed. Great General Staff, Kriegsgeschichtliche Abteilung 2/8 (Berlin, 1905), p. 129.

46 SBPK, MS boruss. 311, fols 33, 35, 36.

47 He was descended from Charles de La Motte-Fouqué (1625–1701), Baron de Thonnaiboutonne et de Saint-Saurin, Seigneur de La Greve, from Bordeaux: W. Gahrig (ed.), *Hugenotten, Willkommen in der Mark: Die Mark Brandenburg – Zeitschrift für die Mark und das Land Brandenburg*, Heft 48 (Berlin, 2003), pp. 33–4.

48 Ibid., pp.34 –9; SBPK, MS boruss. 311, fol. 5.

49 Portraits of General Heinrich August, Baron de La Motte-Fouqué, and General Johann Quirin von Forcade are reproduced in Schnitter, 'Die Réfugiés in der brandenburgischen Armee', p. 323.

influence of Huguenot immigrants was particularly significant in improving the level of officer training, which was decisively upgraded. Through the establishment of cadet companies, a continuous training programme for a new generation of officers was achieved, into which young nobles were accepted in order to prepare themselves for military service. The appointment of Samuel de Saint-Sauveur as second-in-command of the central cadet corps in Berlin gives eloquent expression to the wealth of French influence in this field. An analogous indication of this influence was the adoption of numerous French military concepts and terminology. Thus there was an input in the sphere of fortifications with terms such as *fort* and *casemate* (gun turret) and in the realm of military ranks with grades such as sergeant, lieutenant, captain, major, as well as *garde*, *fusilier* (in the infantry) and cadet, being adopted. This also occurred in relation to military formations with words such as *battalion* coming into use.

The incorporation of foreign soldiers was of major import for the quantitative and qualitative development of the Prussian army during the seventeenth and eighteenth centuries. Notwithstanding that all absolutist armies of that period employed officers, non-commissioned officers and soldiers of various nationalities, the large number of refugee Huguenot soldiers, nevertheless, attained a special elite status in Brandenburg-Prussia. With decisive assistance from Prussian rulers and senior army commanders they succeeded in becoming integrated into the Prussian army, despite the many difficulties placed in their path. Given relevant qualifications and aptitude, all leading military positions were open to them. Accordingly the Huguenots distinguished themselves by demonstrating an ethos of loyalty to the state, religious piety and, usually, an assiduous attitude to duty and discipline. Although definitive research on the integration of French Protestant officers still needs to be undertaken using extant biographical sources, it can already be demonstrated that this topic is important, not only in relation to the military history of Germany (and Prussia especially), but also to Europe as a whole.

Chapter 11

Huguenot Soldiers in Brandenburg-Prussia under Friedrich Wilhelm and Friedrich III (1640–1713)
The State of Research in German Military, Migration and Confessional History[1]

Matthias Asche

University of Tübingen, Germany

The large exodus of French Huguenots[2] after the 1685 revocation of the Edict of Nantes[3] marked one of the most important migration movements of refugees based on faith in early modern Europe.[4] It was also a confessionally inspired movement

---

1 Translated by Matthew Glozier.

2 H. W. Wagner, 'Der Hugenottenring', in H. W. Wagner (ed.), *Hugenotten in Hamburg, Stade, Altona, Tagungsschrift zum Deutschen Hugenottentag Hamburg, 23–26 April 1976*, Geschichtsblätter des Deutschen Hugenotten-Vereins 14 (Obersickte, 1976), pp. 12–13; T. Kiefner, 'Die Zusammensetzung des deutschen Refuge. Neuberechnung des "Hugenottenringes"', *Der Deutsche Hugenott*, 54 (1990): 54–6, 94, 125–6: M. Röhling, 'Zur Zusammensetzung des deutschen Refuge und zum Arbeitsgebiet des Deutschen Hugenotten-Vereins', *Der Deutsche Hugenott*, 55 (1991): 101–4; W. Beuleke, *Studien zum Refuge in Deutschland und zur Ursprungsheimat seiner Mitglieder*, Geschichtsblätter des Deutschen Hugenotten-Vereins 16 XVI. Zehnt, Heft 3 (Brunswick, Obersickte, 1966).

3 G. E. Reaman, *The Trail of the Huguenots in Europe, the United States, South Africa and Canada* (London, 1963); M. Yardeni, *Le refuge protestant* (Paris: Universitaires de France, coll. L'historien, 1985); H. Duchhardt (ed.), *Der Exodus der Hugenotten. Die Aufhebung des Edikts von Nantes 1685 als europäisches Ereignis*, Beihefte zum Archiv für Kulturgeschichte 24 (Cologne, Vienna, 1985); R. von Thadden and M. Magdelaine (eds), *Die Hugenotten, 1685–1985* (second edition, Munich, 1986).

4 T. Klingebiel, 'Vorreiter der Freiheit oder Opfer der Modernisierung? Zur konfessionell bedingten Migration im frühneuzeitlichen Europa', in C. Friederich (ed.), *300 Jahre Hugenottenstadt Erlangen. Vom Nutzen der Toleranz. Ausstellungskatalog* (Nuremberg, 1986), pp. 21–8; A. Pettegree, 'Protestant Migrations during the Early Modern Period', in S. Cavaciocchi (ed.), *Le migrazione in Europa, Secc. XIII–XVIII. Atti della "Venticinquesima Settimana di Studi", Prato 3–8 maggio 1993* (Florence, 1994), pp. 441–58; H. Schilling, 'Confessional Migration as a Distinct Type of Old European Longdistance Migration', in Cavaciocchi (ed.), *Le migrazione in Europa*, pp. 175–89; A. Schunka, 'Glaubensflucht als Migrationsoption. Konfessionell motivierte Migrationen in der Frühen Neuzeit', *Geschichte in Wissenschaft und Unterricht*, 56 (2005); 547–64; M. Asche, 'Migrationen im Europa der

with which contemporaries showed a great deal of sympathy. Although difficult to quantify today, realistic estimates[5] of their number in France between 1670 and 1700 are about 900,000; approximately 150,000 left the country. The largest number of Huguenots went to England (50,000 including those that ventured to Ireland and the English colonies in North America), the Netherlands (35–50,000 including some at the African Cape colony) and to German territories (27,100–34,350). Of this last number between 16,000 and 20,000 went to Brandenburg-Prussia.[6] Smaller contingents distributed themselves among Switzerland (10,000), Denmark (2,000) and Russia (600). The confessional faith of the respective territories was almost exclusively Protestant – usually Calvinist, Reformed or Anglican.

Looking after the refugees following the Revocation was a responsibility divided between the Protestant powers of Europe. The economically and demographically advanced Netherlands, like Switzerland and England, donated funds to facilitate refugee transportation, the establishment of congregations and the building of new settlements. The close connection between Protestant states and the refugees of the later seventeenth century operated on three levels: it was aided by the dynastic connection between Protestant ruling families, by a network of legal and administrative privileges accorded to refugees and by favourable conditions of admission to other countries, and, finally, by the diplomatic projects designed to accommodate Huguenots based on the capacity of individual territories to assist them.

It is important to emphasise that the refugees did not all come cap-in-hand, begging from their new hosts. Although the French exodus included people from almost all levels of society, most possessed highly attractive skills in manufacturing, specialized crafts, sciences, language teaching and military affairs.[7] Their competitive position is evident in the granting of special privileges for manufacturing and working conditions in their new homes.[8] For instance, relief from compulsory army service and the quartering of troops on their households meant that the largest part of the mercantile, technical, military and intellectual

---

Frühen Neuzeit – Versuch einer Typologie', *Geschichte, Politik und ihre Didaktik. Beiträge und Nachrichten für die Unterrichtspraxis. Zeitschrift für historisch-politische Bildung*, 32 (2004): 74–89.

5   B. Dölemeyer, 'Hugenotten im europäischen Refuge. Zu den rechtlichen Rahmenbedingungen ihrer Aufnahme', *Hugenotten*, 63 (1999): 75–85.

6   F. David, 'Les colonies françaises en Brandebourg-Prusse. Une étude statistique de leur population', in M. Böhm, J. Häseler and R. Violet (eds), *Hugenotten zwischen Migration und Integration. Neue Forschungen zum Refuge in Berlin und Brandenburg* (Berlin, 2005), pp. 69–93; F. David, 'Les colonies des réfugiés protestants français en Brandebourg-Prusse (1685–1809). Institutions, géographie et évolution de leur peuplement', *Bulletin de la société de l'histoire du Protestantisme française*, 140 (1994): 111–42.

7   M. Kohnke, 'Das Edikt von Potsdam. Zu seiner Entstehung, Verbreitung und Überlieferung', *Jahrbuch für Geschichte des Feudalismus*, 9 (Berlin, 1985): 241–75.

8   B. Dölemeyer, 'Die Aufnahmeprivilegien für Hugenotten im europäischen Refuge', in B. Dölemeyer (ed.), *Das Privileg im europäischen Vergleich* (Frankfurt-am-Main, 1997), pp. 303–28.

elite of the refugees in the Netherlands, England and Switzerland remained free from such burdens.[9] At the same time, the majority of Huguenot craftsmen and agricultural workers gained a place in civil society in most German territories. German rulers recruited them with very generous privileges for the most offered to leading Huguenots who would encourage their brethren to settle also.[10] In this context of liberal privileges and international refugee politics many German rulers, controlling absolute states, benefited from their ability to override normal laws in favour of the constantly growing needs of absolutist states for highly qualified specialists. The near-permanent state of war in seventeenth-century Europe, with its attendant destruction and depopulating of whole regions of central Europe, further privileged those German rulers who were ready and willing to aid Huguenot settlement. The Thirty Years' War had traced an arc of devastation from the northeast to the southwest, straight across Germany.[11]

The Huguenot exodus was regarded subsequently as the salvation of the electorate of Brandenburg,[12] for no German territory had been so thoroughly affected by the

---

9   H. P. H. Nusteling, 'The Netherlands and the Huguenot Émigrés', in H. Bots, G. Posthumus Meyjes and F. Wieringa (eds), *Vlucht naar de vrijheid. De Hugenoten en de Nederlanden* (Amsterdam, Maarssen, 1986); W. Frijhof, 'Migrations religieuses dans les Provinces-Unies avant le second Refuge', *Revue du Nord*, 80 (1998): 573–98; B. Cottret, *The Huguenots in England: Immigration and Settlement, c.1550–1700* (Cambridge, 1991); H. M. Davis and M. H. Davis, *French Huguenots in English-Speaking Lands* (New York, 2000); R. D. Gwynn, *Huguenot Heritage: The History and Contribution of the Huguenots in Britain* (Brighton, Portland, 2001); L.-E. Roulet (ed.), *Le Refuge Huguenot en Suisse. Die Hugenotten in der Schweiz. Ausstellungskatalog* (Lausanne, 1985); J.-D. Candaux (ed.), *Die Hugenotten in der Schweiz* (Lausanne, 1985).

10   M. Preetz, 'Die Privilegien für die deutschen Hugenotten', *Der Deutsche Hugenott*, 12 (1940): 18–30, 102–12, 150–59; 13 (1941): 29–43; 25 (1961): 76–85, 107–23; 26 (1962): 7–22; M. Preetz, 'Die deutschen Hugenottenkolonien als Experiment des Merkantilismus', PhD thesis (Jena, 1930); D. Mempel (ed.), *Gewissensfreiheit und Wirtschaftspolitik. Hugenotten- und Waldenser-Privilegien 1681–1699* (Trier, 1986); T. Kiefner (ed.), *Die Privilegien der nach Deutschland gekommenen Waldenser* (Stuttgart, Berlin, Cologne, 1990); especially for Brandenburg-Prussia: C. O. Mylius, *Recueil des Edits, Ordonnances, Règlements et Rescripts, contenant les privilèges et les droits attribués aux François Réfugiés, dans les États du Roy de Prusse, et reglant tant pour l'ecclesiastique que pour l'administration de la justice, ce qui concerne les Colonies Françoises établies dans les États de sa Majesté. Auxquels sont joints la Discipline des Églises Réformées de France; et quelques autres édits traduits de leur langue originale pour l'usage de ses Colonies* (Berlin, 1750).

11   G. Franz, *Der Dreißigjährige Krieg und das deutsche Volk* (fourth edition, Stuttgart, New York, 1979).

12   S. Jersch-Wenzel, *Juden und 'Franzosen' in der Wirtschaft des Raumes Berlin/ Brandenburg zur Zeit des Merkantilismus*, Einzelveröffentlichungen der Historischen Kommission zu Berlin 23 (Berlin, 1978); H. Krum, *Preußens Adoptivkinder. Die Hugenotten. 300 Jahre Edikt von Potsdam. Unter Verwendung von 'Mémoires pour servir à l'histoire des réfugiés françois dans les états du roi' von J. P. Erman und F. Reclam 1782–1789* (Berlin, 1985); A. Bonifas and H. Krum, *Les huguenots à Berlin et en Brandebourg de Louis XIV à Hitler* (Paris, 2000); E. Muret, *Geschichte der Französischen Kolonie in Brandenburg-Preußen, unter besonderer Berücksichtigung der Berliner Gemeinde. Aus Veranlassung*

Thirty Years' War.[13] Also, after 1648 it was beset by invasions of Swedish troops. The enormous social breadth of Huguenot settlers, spanning ministers of religion to manufacturers and encompassing craftsmen and farmers,[14] was responsible, in the long run, for the spectacular success of the 1685 Edict of Potsdam issued by Friedrich Wilhelm.[15] The fundamental innovative achievement of this general inducement lay less in the sum of the single privileges accorded to mercantile and specialist activity,[16] but in the grant of the general freedom to establish residence in the whole Hohenzollern territorial complex between Königsberg and Cleves. In effect, large-scale immigrant settlement was only possible in the northeast regions of the Mark of Brandenburg, formerly depopulated by war. In this regard the Potsdam edict far outstripped in generosity the privileges granted to the Huguenots by other German rulers.

Economic reasons were not the sole rationale for Huguenot privileges in Brandenburg. Apart from the personal piety of the Elector, greater affairs in Western Europe affected domestic issues and played a central role in the efficacy of the

---

der zweihundertjährigen Jubelfeier am 29. Oktober 1885 (Berlin, 1885; reprinted Berlin, 1990).

13   M. Asche, *Neusiedler im verheerten Land – Kriegsfolgenbewältigung, Migrationssteuerung und Konfessionspolitik im Zeichen des Landeswiederaufbaus. Die Mark Brandenburg nach den Kriegen des 17. Jahrhunderts* (Münster, 2006).

14   J. Wilke, 'Zur Sozialstruktur und demographischen Analyse der Hugenotten in Brandenburg-Preußen, insbesondere der in Berlin', in I. Mittenzwei (ed.), *Hugenotten in Brandenburg-Preußen*, Studien zur Geschichte der Akademie der Wissenschaften der DDR, Zentralinstitut für Geschichte 8 (Berlin, 1987), pp. 27–99.

15   H. J. Beeskow, 'Zur Vorgeschichte des Edikts von Potsdam 1685. Bemerkungen zur Kirchenpolitik des brandenburgischen Kurfürsten Friedrich Wilhelm', *Jahrbuch für brandenburgische Landesgeschichte*, 35 (1984): 53–62; B. Zilch, 'Das Edikt von Potsdam. Zur 300. Wiederkehr der Aufnahme der Réfugiés in Brandenburg-Preußen', *Zeitschrift für Geschichtswissenschaft*, 33 (1985): 823–37; M. Kohnke, 'Das Edikt von Potsdam'; H. J. Giersberg (ed.), *Das Edikt von Potsdam 1685. Die französische Einwanderung in Brandenburg-Preußen und ihre Auswirkungen auf Kunst, Kultur und Wissenschaft. Ausstellung der Staatlichen Schlösser und Gärten Potsdam-Sanssouci in Zusammenarbeit mit dem Zentralen Staatsarchiv Merseburg und dem Staatsarchiv Potsdam. Potsdam-Sanssouci, Neues Palais 24. August bis 10. November 1985* (Potsdam, 1985).

16   N. von Preradovic, 'Die Hugenotten in der brandenburg-preußischen Wirtschaft 1685–1786', in H. Helbig (ed.), *Führungskräfte der Wirtschaft. Mittelalter und Neuzeit 1350–1850. Büdinger Vorträge* (Limburg, 1973), pp 149–66; S. Jersch-Wenzel, 'Der Einfluß zugewanderter Minoritäten als Wirtschaftsgruppen auf die Berliner Wirtschaft in vor- und frühindustrieller Zeit', in O. Büsch (ed.), *Untersuchung zur Geschichte der Frühindustrialisierung vornehmlich im Wirtschaftsraum Berlin/Brandenburg* (Berlin, 1971), pp. 193–223; S. Jersch-Wenzel, 'Ein importiertes Ersatzbürgertum? Die Bedeutung der Hugenotten für die Wirtschaft Brandenburg-Preußens', in Thadden and Magdelaine (eds), *Die Hugenotten*, pp. 160–71; I. Mittenzwei, 'Die Hugenotten in der gewerblichen Wirtschaft Brandenburg-Preußens', *Zeitschrift für Geschichtswissenschaft*, 34 (1986): 494–507; J. Wilke, 'Der Einfluß der Hugenotten auf Wirtschaft, Wissenschaft und Kultur', in M. Stolpe and F. Winter (eds), *Wege und Grenzen der Toleranz. Edikt von Potsdam 1685–1985* (Berlin, 1987), pp. 36–50; J. Wilke, 'Der Einfluß der Hugenotten auf die gewerbliche Entwicklung', in G. Bregulla (ed.), *Hugenotten in Berlin* (Berlin, 1988), pp. 227–80.

Potsdam edict. In this, the Elector was partly led by the example of his predecessors; Johann Sigismund (1608–19) and Georg Wilhelm (1619–1640) faced significant political and religious problems as Calvinists ruling over subjects who held fast to the Lutheran faith.[17] Calvin's teachings were essentially concentrated among courtiers and a few nobles in Brandenburg. With the massive immigration of Huguenot brothers-in-faith, Friedrich Wilhelm hoped to strengthen Calvinism in his domain[18] while furthering his foreign policy goals.

Brandenburg remained an absolutist state and it was intent on shoring up its position within the structure of the Holy Roman Empire with the creation of a strong standing army. These ambitious goals were cherished by Friedrich Wilhelm. With the accession of his son, Friedrich III, in the year 1688 – from 1701 he was known as Friedrich I, King in Prussia – a large number of the most important court offices were firmly in the hands of Calvinists, both Frenchmen and Brandenburgers.[19]

I

The number of refugee soldiers accommodated in the armies of Friedrich Wilhelm and Friedrich III was not insignificant. However, in the overall study of the history of the Huguenots in Brandenburg-Prussia references to the soldiers among them

---

17   U. Stutz, 'Kurfürst Johann Sigismund von Brandenburg und das Reformationsrecht', in *Sitzungsberichte der preußischen Akademie der Wissenschaften zu Berlin. Philosophisch-Historische Klasse 1922* (Berlin, 1922), pp. 4–38; W. Delius, 'Der Konfessionswechsel des Brandenburgischen Kurfürsten Johann Sigismund', *Jahrbuch für Berlin-Brandenburgische Kirchengeschichte*, 50 (1977): 125–9; H. J. Beeskow, 'Der Konfessionswechsel des brandenburgischen Kurfürsten Johann Sigismund im Jahre 1613', *Herbergen der Christenheit*, 14 (1983/84): 7–18; R. von Thadden, 'Die Fortsetzung des "Reformationswerkes" in Brandenburg-Preußen', in H. Schilling (ed.), *Reformierte Konfessionalisierung. Das Problem der 'Zweiten Reformation'* (Gütersloh, 1986), pp. 233–50; M. Rudersdorf and A. Schindling, 'Kurbrandenburg', in A. Schindling and W. Ziegler (eds), *Die Territorien des Reichs im Zeitalter der Reformation und Konfessionalisierung. Land und Konfession 1500–1648* (second edition, Münster, 1991), vol. 2, pp. 34–66; B. Nischan, *Prince, People and Confession: The Second Reformation in Brandenburg* (Philadelphia, 1994).

18   G. Heinrich, 'Religionstoleranz in Brandenburg-Preußen. Idee und Wirklichkeit', in M. Schlenke (ed.), *Preußen. Beiträge zu einer politischen Kultur* (Reinbek, 1981), pp. 61–88; H. D. Heimann, 'Brandenburger Toleranz zwischen Anspruch, Mythos und Dementi. Historisch-politische Annäherungen an das "Edikt von Potsdam"', *Zeitschrift für Religions- und Geistesgeschichte*, 52 (2000): 115–25; E. Birnstiel, 'Die Aufnahme hugenottischer Glaubensflüchtlinge in Brandenburg-Preußen. Ein Akt der Toleranz?', in A. Flick and A. de Lange (eds), *Von Berlin bis Konstantinopel. Eine Aufsatzsammlung zur Geschichte der Hugenotten und Waldenser*, Geschichtsblätter der Deutschen Hugenotten-Gesellschaft 35 (Bad Karlshafen, 2001), pp. 9–33; J. Luh, 'Zur Konfessionspolitik der Kurfürsten von Brandenburg und Könige in Preußen 1640–1740', in H. Lademacher, R. Loos and S. Groenveld (eds), *Ablehnung – Duldung – Anerkennung. Toleranz in den Niederlanden und in Deutschland. Ein historischer und aktueller Vergleich* (Münster, New York, Munich, Berlin, 2004), pp. 306–24.

19   P. Bahl, *Der Hof des Großen Kurfürsten. Studien zur Amtsträgerschaft Brandenburg-Preußens* (Cologne, Weimar, Vienna, 2001).

are few. It is to the classical works of older, Prussian military historiography,[20] rather than to recent studies, that one must look for the contribution of Huguenot soldiers.[21] The study of them remains today a specialist field of German military historiography, so that the work of Helmut Schnitter[22] and Detlef Harms[23] represents the current level of knowledge. In the larger scheme of things, Huguenot soldiers in Brandenburg-Prussia are mainly ignored – wholly in contrast to the substantially

---

20   G. A. von Mülverstedt, *Die brandenburgische Kriegsmacht unter dem Großen Kurfürsten. Quellenmäßige Darstellung aller einzelnen, in der Zeit von 1640–1688 bestehenden kurbrandenburgischen Regimenter und sonstigen Truppenkörper nebst den Festungen, der Marine etc.* (Magdeburg, 1888; reprinted Wiesbaden, 1981); H. Sommer, *Das brandenburgisch-preußische Heer in seiner Entwickelung seit dem Anfang des 17. Jahrhunderts bis auf die neueste Zeit* (Berlin, 1898); C. Jany, *Die Anfänge der alten Armee* (Berlin, 1901), vol. 1; C. Jany, *Die alte Armee von 1655 bis 1740. Formation und Stärke* (Berlin, 1905); C. Jany, *Geschichte der Königlich Preußischen Armee vom 15. Jahrhundert und des Deutschen Reichsheeres* (5 vols, Berlin, 1928–37), vol. 1 'Von den Anfängen bis 1740' (1928); O. von der Osten-Sacken und von Rhein, *Preußens Heer von seinen Anfängen bis zur Gegenwart* (3 vols, Berlin, 1911–14), vol. 1; G. Lehmann, 'Die brandenburgische Kriegsmacht unter dem Großen Kurfürsten', *Forschungen zur Brandenburgischen und Preußischen Geschichte*, 1 (1888): 451–525; F. von Schrötter, *Die brandenburg-preußische Heeresverfassung unter dem Großen Kurfürsten* (Leipzig, 1882); F. von Schrötter, 'Das preußische Offizierkorps unter dem ersten Könige von Preußen', *Forschungen zur Brandenburgischen und Preußischen Geschichte*, 27 (1914): 97–167; K. von Priesdorff, *Soldatisches Führertum* (10 vols, Hamburg, 1936–42), vol. 1 'Die Generale von den Anfängen der brandenburgisch-Preußischen Armee bis 1740'; A. B. König, *Biographisches Lexikon aller Helden und Militairpersonen, welche sich in preußischen Diensten berühmt gemacht haben* (2 vols, Berlin, 1788–9) [continued under the title: *Militairisches Pantheon oder biographisches Lexikon aller Helden und Militairpersonen, welche sich in preußischen Diensten berühmt gemacht haben* (2 vols, Berlin 1797)]; K. von Bredow and E. von Wedel, *Historische Rang- und Stammlisten des deutschen Heeres* (Berlin, 1905); C. Chambeau, 'Der Anteil der Hugenotten in der preußischen Wehrmacht', *Zeitschrift für Heereskunde*, 107 (1939): 15–22.

21   H. Bleckwenn, *Unter dem Preußen-Adler. Das brandenburgisch-preußische Heer 1640–1807* (Munich, 1978); M. Guddat (ed.), *Handbuch zur preußischen Militärgeschichte 1701–1786* (Hamburg, 2001); H. Müller, *Das Heerwesen in Brandenburg und Preußen von 1640 bis 1806. Die Bewaffnung* (second edition, Berlin, 2001); O. Groehler, *Das Heerwesen in Brandenburg und Preußen von 1640 bis 1806. Das Heerwesen* (second edition, Berlin, 2001).

22   T. Schmidt and H. Schnitter, 'Die Hugenotten in der Brandenburgisch-Preussischen armee', *Militärgeschichte*, 24/3 (1985): 233–9; H. Schnitter, 'Unter dem brandenburgischen Adler – Hugenotten in der brandenburgischen Armee', *Blätter für Heimatgeschichte: Studienmaterial 1986* (Berlin, 1986): 51–5; H. Schnitter, 'Die Réfugiés in der brandenburgischen Armee', in G. Bregulla (ed.), *Hugenotten in Berlin* (Berlin, 1988), pp. 311–26; H. Schnitter, *Unter dem roten Adler. Réfugiés im brandenburgischen Heer Ende des 17./Anfang des 18. Jahrhundert* (Berlin, 1996).

23   D. Harms, 'Das Edikt von Potsdam vom 29 Oktober 1685; Die Intergration und der soziale Auftieg von Ausländern in der Preußischen Armee des 17. und 18. Jahrhunderts', in B. R. Kroener (ed.), *Potsdam: Staat, Armee, Residenz in der Preußisch-deutschen Militärgeschichte* (Frankfurt-am-Main, Berlin, 1993), pp. 159–71.

developed historiography in the area in English, Irish and Netherlands history[24] – not least because the purely French regiments soon disappeared. In this sense it is perhaps not surprising that little more has appeared on them, beyond the works of Schnitter and Harms.

The arrival of the Huguenot officers occurred at a time of army reconstruction and the building up of standing troops in Brandenburg. One year after his 1640 accession, Friedrich Wilhelm was forced to conclude a separate peace with the Swedish queen Christina which gave some relief to his country; though plunder by soldiers and mercenary groups continued for another decade. In the Thirty Years' War the lack of organised logistics in the Brandenburg army was clearly revealed. Friedrich Wilhelm lacked both an appropriate recruiting system and the financial ability to sustain soldiers under his command for long periods of time. Brandenburg troops mostly performed garrison duties and were essentially enlisted for set periods as mercenaries privately contracted by military entrepreneurs. After completing war service, mercenaries were rapidly disbanded.[25]

The origins of the standing army[26] are to be found in the two large wars fought by Friedrich Wilhelm against Sweden and Poland over the sovereignty of the Polish lands bordering Prussia and the acquisition of Swedish Pomerania (the First Northern War, 1655–60 and the Scanian War, 1675–9). After the peace treaties were concluded, in each case it was possible to retain at least some infantry and cavalry regiments on a standing basis. This state of affairs continued into the 1680s, with a gradual ebb and flow of additional garrison units and new regiments and some reduction in army size depending upon political and financial circumstances. Soldiers were still quartered on civilians[27] well into the reign of Friedrich III and stability came slowly to the Brandenburg-Prussian army in the form of an effective recruiting system developed during the reign of King Friedrich Wilhelm I (1713–40).

The increasing complexity of the standing army in Brandenburg was connected with the recruitment of competent and battle-tested officers from foreign countries, particularly since it could fall back on only very limited native forces. Among the regimental commanders serving between the 1670s and 1680s there existed a

---

24   M. R. Glozier, *The Huguenot Soldiers of William of Orange and the Glorious Revolution of 1688: The Lions of Judah* (Brighton, Portland, 2002); P. Rambaut and R. Vigne, *Britain's Huguenot War Leaders* (London, 2003).

25   B. R. Kroener, 'Der Krieg hat ein Loch ... Überlegungen zum Schicksal demobilisierter Söldner nach dem Dreißigjährigen Krieg', in H. Duchhardt (ed.), *Der Westfälische Friede. Diplomatie – politische Zäsur – kulturelles Umfeld – Rezeptionsgeschichte* (Munich, 1998), pp. 599–630.

26   C. Jany, 'Der Anfang des stehenden Heeres in Brandenburg', *Forschungen zur Brandenburgischen und Preußischen Geschichte*, 51 (1939): 178–80; P. Kiehm, 'Anfänge eines stehenden Heeres in Brandenburg 1640 bis 1655 unter Kurfürst Friedrich Wilhelm', *Militärgeschichte*, 24 (1985): 515–20.

27   O. Büsch, *Garnisonen und Garnisonsorte in Brandenburg 1640–1806* (Berlin, 1967).

very high proportion of non-Brandenburgers.[28] They affected the force not only in terms of their cultural outlook, but also by introducing their considerable technical military knowledge. France dominated Europe in the second half of the century as a model absolute and military state. French officers in the service of King Louis XIV included both Protestants and Catholics. They were professional due in part to their practice-oriented training at military academies visited frequently by foreigners.[29] As a result, long before the publication of the Potsdam edict, some officers from France had entered Brandenburg service. Pierre de La Cave (1605–79) is supposed to be the first French officer in the electoral army.[30] He arrived in the reign of Georg Wilhelm, in 1632, and in 1641 created the Prussian infantry bodyguard company (*Preußische Kompanie Leibgarde zu Fuß*), which consisted of pikemen and musketeers. La Cave died in 1679, holding the rank of major-general;[31] he was also Governor of the fortress of Pillau, an important strategic position during the Scanian War (1675–9).

French officers came in greater numbers in the later 1660s and throughout the 1670s to strengthen the Brandenburg army. The best-known of them include Louis de Beauveau, Comte d'Espence (1620–88; colonel of his own cavalry regiment from

---

28   E. Opgenoorth, *'Ausländer' in Brandenburg-Preußen als leitende Beamte und Offiziere 1604–1871* (Würzburg, 1967), p. 21.

29   A. Joubert, 'Les gentilhommes étrangers – Allemands, Anglais, Ecossais, Flamands, Bohémiens, Danois, Polonais – à l'Académie d'Équitation d'Angers au XVIIe siècle d'après un document inédit (1601–1635)', *Revue d'Anjou*, 26 (1893): 5–22; W. Frijhoff, 'Etudiants étrangers à l'Académie d'Equitation d'Angers au XVIIe siècle', *Lias. Sources and Documents to the Early Modern History of Ideas*, 4 (1977): 13–84; M. Ratouis, *Les origines de l'Académie d'équitation civile et de l'équitation militaire de Saumur 1593–1830* (Saumur, 1879); E. Merzeau, *L'Académie protestante de Saumur 1604–1685. Son organisation et ses rapports avec les églises réformées* (Alençon, 1908); D. de Chavigny, *L'église et l'Académie protestante de Saumur* (Saumur, 1924); L.-J. Métayer, *L'Académie protestante de Saumur* (Paris, 1933; reprinted Carrière-sous-Poissy, 2005); M. Durosoy, *Saumur. Historiques de l'École d'application de l'arme blindée et de la cavalerie* (Paris, 1978); P. G. Grandchamp (ed.), *Saumur – l'École de Cavalerie. Histoire architecturale d'une cité de cheval militaire* (Paris, 2005); M. Nicolas, *Histoire de l'ancienne Académie protestante de Montauban (1598–1659) et de Puylaurens* (Montauban, 1885); E. Doumergue, *L'Académie et la Faculté de Montauban 1598 – 1809 – 1906* (Montauban, 1906); C. Peyran, *Histoire de l'ancienne Académie réformée de Sedan* (Strassbourg, 1846); A. Joubert, *Les étudiants allemands de l'Académie protestante de Saumur et leur maître de danse* (Angers, 1889).

30   La Cave probably left France soon after the Edict of Grace was concluded at Nîmes in 1629: von Priesdorff, *Soldatisches Führertum*, no. 36; Bahl, *Der Hof des Großen Kurfürsten*, p. 451.

31   Also his son, Wilhelm (1648–1731) who became a major-general: von Priesdorff, *Soldatisches Führertum*, no. 97.

1668),[32] Henri d'Hallard (called 'Elliot', 1620–81; from 1672 an infantry colonel),[33] François, Marquis du Hamel (1630–1709; from 1674 a cavalry colonel),[34] Bernhard du Huet (or 'von Hutten', 1630–98; from 1678 an infantry colonel)[35] and Henri de Briquemault, Baron de Saint-Loup (1620–92; in Brandenburg service from 1680 and from 1683 a cavalry colonel).[36] Their early arrival in Brandenburg is proof that not all so-called Huguenot officers were refugees. The Comte d'Espence, for example, left his homeland in the 1660s and not for reasons of conscience. By contrast, du Hamel was a Catholic who remained in Brandenburg service well into the 1690s. From 1674 his cavalry regiment possessed a Reformed preacher.

Some of those French officers who come to Brandenburg before the Potsdam edict took on non-military functions as civilian administrators. After the edict some of them put their administrative skills to good use, serving as refugee commissioners due to their organizational and logistical skill and linguistic abilities. The Comte d'Espence, the actual founder of the Huguenot municipality in Berlin in the year 1672,[37] was the first to obtain French Reformed pastors. He also planned and developed social infrastructure for the constantly increasing number of refugees in Berlin since the early 1680s.[38] A similar function was performed by de Briquemault for the northwestern part of the Hohenzollern territorial domains. As Governor of the fortress of Lippstadt (from 1681) and a refugee commissioner (from 1685) he was responsible not only for the reception of the Huguenots, but also for their settlement and the distribution of relief funds. Among other things, the French Reformed refugee communities in Lippstadt, Hamm, Soest, Minden, Cleves, Emmerich and Duisburg owe their emergence to him.[39]

---

32 J. T. Lorenz, 'Louis de Beauveau, comte d'Espence', *Die Kolonie*, 5 (1881): 49–51; von Priesdorff, *Soldatisches Führertum*, no. 33; Bahl, *Der Hof des Großen Kurfürsten*, p. 426. He probably brought from France his nephew, Louis de l'Hôpital (1669–1755) from 1684 a page in the Elector's service before enjoying a military career that saw him attain the rank of lieutenant-general: von Priesdorff, *Soldatisches Führertum*, no. 236.

33 Ibid., no. 48.

34 Ibid., no. 49.

35 Ibid., no. 95.

36 Ibid., no. 53.

37 E. Birnstiel, *Die Hugenotten in Berlin oder Die Schule der Untertanen* (Berlin: Deutscher Kunstverlag, 1986); E. Birnstiel and A. Reinke, 'Hugenotten in Berlin', in S. Jersch-Wenzel and B. John (eds), *Von Zuwanderern zu Einheimischen. Hugenotten, Juden, Böhmen, Polen in Berlin* (Berlin, 1990), pp. 13–152; G. Fischer, *Die Hugenotten in Berlin* (third edition, Berlin, 1988); Bregulla (ed.), *Hugenotten in Berlin*; F. Hartweg, 'Die Hugenotten in Berlin. Eine Geschichte, die vor 300 Jahren begann', in F. Hartweg and S. Jersch-Wenzel (eds), *Die Hugenotten und das Refuge. Deutschland und Europa* (Berlin, 1990), pp. 1–56; J. Wilke, 'Die Französische Kolonie in Berlin', in H. Schultz (ed.), *Berlin 1650–1800. Sozialgeschichte einer Residenz* (second edition, 2 vols, Berlin, 1992), vol. 2, pp. 353–430.

38 U. Fuhrich-Grubert, *Die Französische Kirche zu Berlin. Ihre Einrichtungen 1672–1945*, Tagungsschriften des Deutschen Hugenotten-Vereins 11 (Bad Karlshafen, 1992).

39 J. E. Bischoff, *Lexikon deutscher Hugenotten-Orte mit Literatur- und Quellen-Nachweisen für ihre evangelisch-reformierten Réfugiés-Gemeinden von Flamen, Franzosen,*

Only in 1685 did French officers have the opportunity to command their own Huguenot regiments.[40] This was, of course, prompted by the massive influx of refugees in the first year following the publication of the Potsdam edict and led to the establishment of purely French regiments with Huguenot officers and staff, in which French was the language of command at all levels. In 1686 an infantry and a cavalry regiment, consisting of ten companies and five troops respectively, was commanded by Henri de Briquemault with its main garrison place at Lippstadt (altogether 750 men). In the same year an infantry regiment, consisting of 16 companies, was created under the direction of Jacques de Laumonier, Marquis de Varennes (1642–1717); its main garrison place was at Soest (approximate strength 800 men).[41] Yet another infantry regiment, consisting of four companies, was under the direction of Joël de Cournaud (or Courneaud, 1637–1718) with its garrison place in the city of Brandenburg-an-der-Havel (approximate strength 190 men).[42] In the following year, in 1687, there was created the *grands mousquetaires*, consisting of two companies of French officers, who after the model of the French king's musketeers (in the royal household, or *maison du roi*) were elite household troops personally subordinated to the Elector and commanded by his field marshal: first, Friedrich Hermann von Schomberg (1615–90)[43] then Count Christoph von Dohna-Schlodien (1665–1733),[44] with the main garrison places at Prenzlau and Fürstenwalde-an-der-Spree (approximate strength 120 men).[45] From 1688 a similar regiment existed for French non-commissioned officers, the *grenadiers à cheval* commanded by Colonel Charles du Puy de l'Espinasse (d.1695) with its garrison places at Beeskow and Storkow (strength 65 men).

Although no comparative studies exist of this phenomenon, it must be assumed the French regiments in Brandenburg were unique in Germany. Other German rulers employed French officers primarily as regimental commanders. The creation of purely Huguenot regiments, in particular the elite units of the *grands mousquetaires* and the *grenadiers à cheval*, was an expression of the value placed in accommodating French Huguenots in the army throughout the years 1685–7. No permanent posts in the regular Brandenburg army existed for those French refugees

---

Waldensern und Wallonen, Geschichtsblätter des Deutschen Hugenotten-Vereins 22 (Bad Karlshafen, 1994).

40   The office of quartermaster-general of the Brandenburg army between 1678 and 1729, was occupied exclusively by French military engineers: 1678–88 de Maistre; 1688–95 Charles du Puy de l'Espinasse; 1695–1701 Etienne Marges; 1701–1702 Charles Jacques de Lux, Baron de Brion; 1702–29 Pierre de Montargues (Peter von Montargues): von Priesdorff, *Soldatisches Führertum*, nos 119, 186.

41   Ibid., no. 88.

42   Ibid., no. 105.

43   M. R. Glozier, *Marshal Schomberg, 1615–1690: 'the ablest soldier of his age': International Soldiering and the Formation of State Armies in Seventeenth-Century Europe* (Brighton, Portland, 2005).

44   *Die Denkwürdigkeiten des Burggrafen und Grafen Christoph zu Dohna (1665–1733)*, ed. R. Grieser (Göttingen, 1974).

45   For the *grands mousquetaires*, see Schnitter and Schmidt, 'Die Hugenotten in der brandenburgisch-preußischen Armee': 238.

who arrived in such large numbers. Friedrich Wilhelm strove to supply the officers with positions commensurate with their rank.[46] In the *grands mousquetaires*, the lowest member ranked as a second-lieutenant and to their number was entrusted special military and diplomatic missions where the ability to speak good French was required.

The existence of purely French regiments marked, however, only a short episode in Brandenburg military history. After the late 1680s the strong influx of French refugees subsided and the French units under Friedrich III in the 1690s gradually dissolved. The cavalry regiment of Colonel de Briquemault became the *Kürassier-Regiment Nr. 5*; his infantry regiment became the *Infanterie-Regiment Nr. 9*. The infantry regiment of Colonel de Varennes (divided in 1687) became the *Infanterie-Regimenter Nr. 13* and *15*,[47] while that of Cournaud became the *Infanterieregiment Nr. 20*. The *grands mousquetaires* were not altered until 1708, while the *grenadiers à cheval* were completely dissolved between 1697 and 1701. In the officer lists of the royal Prussian army of 1713 – naming all officers and troop bodies, at the time of the death of Friedrich I and the assumption of rule by Friedrich Wilhelm I – only mixed regiments are to be found. However, four regiments of French origin (two cavalry and two infantry) remained.[48] Characteristically, in those regiments, the portion of officers of French descent was significantly high.[49]

II

The most important writers about the refugees in Brandenburg-Prussia were Jean Pierre Erman and Pierre Chrétien Frédéric Reclam. Their influence was great upon the future research of the Huguenots in Brandenburg-Prussia. Both men wrote in the late eighteenth century and, according to them about 600 French officers and cadets

---

46 Harms, 'Das Edikt von Potsdam': 164; C. Ancillon, *Histoire de l'Etablissement des François Réfugiés dans les Etats de Son Altesse Electorale de Brandebourg*: (Berlin, 1690; republished Berlin, *Geschichtsblätter des Deutschen Hugenotten-Vereins*, 15/8, 1939), p. 45.

47 *Chronik des Ersten Garde-Regiments zu Fuß und dessen Stamm-Truppen, 1675–1900* (Oldenburg, Berlin, 1902).

48 One infantry regiment each belonging to de Varennes and Etienne, Comte du Trossel (d. after 1713) and the cavalry regiment of Benjamin Hieronymus de Cournauld, Chevalier du Portail (1654–1730), later Governor of the fortress of Peitz; André Reveillas de Veyne (1653–1723): von Priesdorff, *Soldatisches Führertum*, nos 160, 147, 134.

49 In the infantry regiments of du Trossel and de Varennes the portion of French officers was 16 (30 per cent); in the two cavalry regiments of de Veyne and du Portail it was about 48 (61 per cent).

came to Brandenburg;[50] an assertion that all later authors have accepted uncritically.[51] Although available studies rightly stress the high number of Huguenot soldiers in the Brandenburg army under Friedrich Wilhelm and Friedrich I,[52] a complete quantified overview of them is still lacking. Existing literature tends to repeat biographical data or the military achievements of the French officers and is consequently limited in scope.

Most French officers entering the military service of the Elector of Brandenburg – a lesser power on the European stage – were of fairly humble origin. Members of the higher nobility may have been attracted by increased pay and relatively fluid promotion possibilities, but the motivation of most French officers coming to Brandenburg will never be known. The little secure biographical data we have for them suggests they were as likely to use Brandenburg as a stepping stone to senior employment elsewhere. The primary example of this, at senior level, is Friedrich Hermann von Schomberg (1615–90). Though no Huguenot, strictly speaking, but rather an Anglo-German native Heidelberger of the Reformed confession, he was naturalised as a Frenchman in 1668. Only now has his military career been thoroughly investigated in the context of expatriate French officers, owing to the recent work of Matthew Glozier[53] – who also includes important comments on Schomberg's sons, Meinhard (1641–1719)[54] and Charles (1645–93).[55] The study highlights the connection between later seventeenth-century armies and those mercenary-filled ones that existed at the start of the century. Before coming to Brandenburg, Schomberg had served the Calvinist *stadhouder* in the Netherlands, the Lutheran king of Sweden, the Catholic king of Portugal, the Anglican king of England and the 'Most Catholic' king of France. His insensitivity to the confession of his employer marks Schomberg as the type of career military entrepreneur still usual in the era of the Thirty Years' War. His break with Louis XIV in 1685 only occurred because Schomberg – from 1674 a French duke, and from 1675 a marshal of France – was not ready to give up his religion. Schomberg went, nevertheless, for a year into the service of the Catholic king of Portugal before he came in the year

---

50   J. P. Erman and P. C. F. Reclam, *Mémoires pour servir à l'histoire des réfugiés françois dans les états du roi* (9 vols, Berlin, 1782–99), vol. 2, p. 185; M. Yardeni, 'Erudition et engagement. L'historiographie huguenote dans la Prusse des Lumières', *Francia*, 9 (1981): 584–601; V. Rosen-Prest, *L'historiographie des Huguenots en Prusse des Lumières. Entre mémoire, histoire et légende. Jean Pierre Erman et Pierre Chrétien Frédéric Reclam, Les Mémoires pour servir à l'histoire des réfugiés François dans les ètats du Roi (1782–1799)*, La Vie des Huguenots (Paris, 2002); V. Prest, 'Les Mémoires pour servir à l'histoire des réfugiés François dans les ètats du Roi, d'Erman et Reclam. Actualité et intérêt', *Bulletin de la société de l'histoire du Protestantisme française*, 144 (1998): 603–16.

51   'One estimates the number of officers at 3,000 who fled France, of whom 500–600 came to Brandenburg': Muret, *Geschichte der Französischen Kolonie*, p. 51.

52   Between 1640 and 1740, 26 of the 257 generals were Huguenots; cited in von Priesdorff's *Soldatisches Führertum*, p. 34.

53   Glozier, *Marshal Schomberg*, ch. 7.

54   Ibid., p. 99–101; von Priesdorff, *Soldatisches Führertum*, no. 64.

55   Glozier, *Marshal Schomberg*, p. 160–5; von Priesdorff, *Soldatisches Führertum*, no. 63.

1687 to Brandenburg. There Schomberg made a short, but steep career rise which terminated abruptly in 1688 with his transfer into the substantially more prestigious service of the Dutch *stadhouder*, William III.[56] Schomberg died in 1690 at the battle at the Boyne as 'general of all his Majesty's forces'; in the meantime he had been heaped with English honours as Duke of Schomberg, Baron Teyes, Earl of Brentford and Marquis of Harwich, and been naturalised.

That the military career followed by Schomberg does not represent an individual case – though certainly a particularly salient one – is shown by two further examples. The Catholic François, Comte du Hamel, left the Brandenburg army after almost 20 years in order to enter Venetian service. He was probably from Lorraine originally and was initially in Palatine service. Jeremias Chauvet (d.1696),[57] who was probably from Lorraine originally and initially in Palatine service, came into the service of Eleonore Desmier d'Olbreuse,[58] companion of Georg Wilhelm, Duke of Brunswick-Lüneburg-Celle. Chauvet went, in 1693, into the service of the Elector Johann Georg IV of Saxony and died in the rank of Field Marshal. These three examples of French officers who regarded the Brandenburg army as one stage in a broader career could surely be increased if further analysis was brought to bear upon the biographical details of other Huguenots. Nevertheless, it must be accepted that there remained a sizeable number of French officers who made their home in Brandenburg-Prussia.

While it is difficult to determine officer numbers, it is far more difficult to do so for the refugee French non-commissioned officers and simple soldiers in the Brandenburg army. Schnitter and Schmidt say: 'alone in the troop units of Briquemault, Varennes and Cournaud, which were recruited after 1685 exclusively from among the refugees, there stood already 1,100 soldiers to which can be added a number of non-commissioned officers.'[59] Curt Jany – formerly one of the best connoisseurs of Brandenburg-Prussian army strength – says French officers represented over 15 per cent of the Brandenburg officer corps. He estimates the portion of Frenchmen among the simple soldiers at approximately 5 per cent.[60] But does this figure include the little-regarded Savoyard Waldensians, 800 of whom entered Brandenburg service between 1688 and 1690?[61] One cannot hope to use the yearly register of the French

---

56   Glozier, *Marshal Schomberg*, p. 150–5.

57   A. Flick, 'General und Feldmarschall Jeremias Chauvet', *Celler Chronik*, 6 (1994): 31–45; A. Flick, 'Jeremias Chauvet. Eine militärische Karriere in der Pfalz und am Hof in Celle', *Pfälzer Heimat*, 47 (1996): 88–94.

58   F. Geyken, '"Mutter der Könige" oder "Das Fräulein aus Poitou"? Widersprüche im Bild der Eleonore Desmiers d'Olbreuse (1639–1722) in *Der Deutsche Hugenott*, 58 (1994): 77–85; R. du Vinage, *Ein vortreffliches Frauenzimmer. Das Schicksal von Eleonore d'Olbreuse (1639–1722), der letzten Herzogin von Braunschweig-Lüneburg-Celle* (Berlin, 2000); A. Stammann and E. Krampen, Eleonore d'Olbreuse. Die letzte Herzogin zu Celle, in *Frauen im Celler Land. Ein Streifzug durch die Jahrhunderte* (Celle, 2004): 37–41.

59   Schmidt and Schnitter, 'Die Hugenotten in der brandenburgisch-preußischen Armee': 234.

60   Jany, *Geschichte der Königlich Preußischen Armee*, p. 274.

61   T. Kiefner, *Die Waldenser auf ihrem Weg aus dem Val Cluson durch die Schweiz nach Deutschland 1532–1755* (4 vols, Göttingen, 1985–97), vol. 2, pp. 44, 242; K. F. W. Dieterici,

colony in Brandenburg-Prussia, listing the residences of the refugees, in an attempt to clear-up the issue since the registers did not begin until 1697.[62] Besides, military staff were not subject to the legal regulations of the Potsdam edict, in particular they were free from the usual colony jurisdiction[63] that affected civilians because they were ruled over by that of the Brandenburg army.[64] Only complex prosopographical studies which examine the documents of the individual Brandenburg-Prussian cities and domains for the residential addresses of refugees, and follow them systematically after recruiting and advertisements, could help here.

The simple French soldiers and the non-commissioned officers, probably veterans of earlier service at higher levels, cannot be included among the citizens of Berlin and they did not stand in a particularly close relationship with the Huguenot elite.[65] For its part the French elite successfully and lastingly created a form of control over the French colony in Brandenburg-Prussia which saw its rapid formation into a socially exclusive group.[66] The special role of the refugees and their descendants within the state was, for a long time, reinforced not by cultural or national separation, but by the closed nature of their French Reformed community and its French language. Due to their comparatively long-standing economic, legal and religious privileges, the French colony followed a different course of development than the rest of

---

Die Waldenser und ihre Verhältnisse zu dem brandenburg-preußischen Staat (Berlin, Posen, Bromberg, 1831); M. Behaim-Schwarzbach, *Hohenzollerische Colonisationen. Ein Beitrag zu der Geschichte des preußischen Staates und der Colonisation des östlichen Deutschlands* (Leipzig, 1874), pp. 91, 102.

62 R. Béringuer, 'Die Colonieliste von 1699. Role Générale des François Refugiez dans les Etats de S.A Sérénité Electorale de Brandebourg, comme ils se sont trouvez 31. Dècembre 1699' (Berlin, 1888, reprinted Berlin, 1990).

63 W. Grieshammer, 'Studien zur Geschichte der Réfugiés in Brandenburg-Preußen bis 1713', PhD thesis (Berlin, 1935), p. 61; J. Wilke, 'Rechtsstellüng und Rechtsprechung der Hugenotten in Brandenburg-Preußen (1685–1809)', in von Thadden and Magdelaine (eds), *Die Hugenotten*, pp. 100–114; K. Brandenburg, 'Die Rechtsprechung in der Kolonie', in Bregulla (ed.), *Hugenotten in Berlin*, pp. 281–97.

64 Schnitter, 'Die Réfugiés in der brandenburgischen Armee': 317.

65 Kiefner, *Die Privilegien*, p. 1326.

66 Rudolf von Thadden, 'Vom Glaubensflüchtling zum preußischen Patrioten', in von Thadden and Magdelaine (eds), *Die Hugenotten*, pp. 186–97; F. Hartweg, 'Hugenotten(tum) und Preußen(tum)', in Mittenzwei (ed.), *Hugenotten in Brandenburg-Preußen*, pp. 313–52; E. Birnstiel, 'Dieu protège nos souverains. Zur Gruppenidentität der Hugenotten in Brandenburg-Preußen', in Hartweg and Jersch-Wenzel (eds), *Die Hugenotten und das Refuge*, pp. 107–28; V. Prest, 'Prediger, Aufklärer, Hugenotten und Preußen. Identitätsfragen am Ende der französischen Kolonie anhand der Mémoires pour servir à servir l'histoire des réfugiés francais dans les états du Roi (1782–1799) von J. P. Erman und P. C. F. Reclam', in T. Höpel and K. Middell (eds), *Réfugiés und Emigrés. Migration zwischen Frankreich und Deutschland im 18. Jahrhundert* (Leipzig, 1997), pp. 76–94; U. Fuhrich-Grubert, '"Refugirte" und "Emigrirte" im Berlin des ausgehenden 18. Jahrhundert. Zur Konstruktion von kultureller Identität einer Migrationsbewegung', in Höpel and Middell (eds), *Réfugiés und Emigrés*, pp. 111–34; U. Fuhrich-Grubert, 'Hugenotten in Preußen 1685–1945. Von den verachteten "Paddenschluckern" zu den besten Deutschen', *Der Deutsche Hugenott*, 66 (2002): 3–27.

Brandenburg-Prussia right up to its dissolution as a separate entity within the state in 1809. The special privileges accorded to the Huguenots of Brandenburg, in contrast to those given in other parts of Europe, proved hard to remove. As a consequence, the generous privileges and the preferential treatment of the refugees did not lead to a rapid integration of these new subjects into the broader Brandenburg-Prussian polity.

The Huguenot officers well understood their advantages in pay and conditions compared to the native Brandenburgers. They, therefore, maintained a high appreciation for the court in deference to their special position in the state. However, for these reasons the French officers remained disinterested in being integrated into the state or the army more generally. In view of the still insufficient level of research on this topic, the findings of Detlef Harms must apply: 'The impact of the immigration and integration of the Huguenot officers and soldiers as well as their influence on Brandenburg-Prussian military affairs was substantial.'[67] After all, Harms is the first researcher to raise this issue for discussion.[68]

There existed among the native population strong reservations about the influence of the Frenchmen, and the German population opposed the quartering upon them of Huguenot soldiers and officers. Conflict surrounded Huguenot accommodation in the garrison places, where soldiers were expected to live among citizens before the age of the separate barracks in the later eighteenth century.[69] In Prenzlau alone – next to Potsdam the largest and most important garrison place for French officers – approximately 100 members of the *grands mousquetaires* were quartered. Although there are studies of the garrison town of Prenzlau, the specific problems of living together experienced by French soldiers and a German civilian population, caused by linguistic conflicts among others, have not been well considered.[70] The autobiography of Count Christoph von Dohna refers to everyday life among the French officers

---

67 Harms, 'Das Edikt von Potsdam': 170.

68 Ibid.: 166.

69 R. Pröve, 'Der Soldat in der "guten Bürgerstube". Das frühneuzeitliche Einquartierungssystem und die sozioökonomischen Folgen', in Kroener and Pröve (eds), *Krieg und Frieden*, pp. 191–217; H. W. Hermann and F. Irsigler (eds), *Beiträge zur Geschichte der frühneuzeitlichen Garnisons- und Festungsstadt. Referat und Ergebnisse der Diskussion eines Kolloquiums in Saarlouis vom 24.–27.6.1980*, Komm. für Saarländische Landesgeschichte und Volksforschung 13 (Saarbrücken, 1983); H. T. Gräf, 'Militarisierung der Stadt oder Urbanisierung des Militärs? Ein Beitrag zur Militärgeschichte der frühen Neuzeit aus stadtgeschichtlicher Perspektive', in R. Pröve (ed.), *Klio in Uniform? Probleme und Perspektiven einer modernen Militärgeschichte in der Frühen Neuzeit* (Cologne, Weimar, Vienna, 1997), pp. 89–108; B. Sicken (ed.), *Stadt und Militär. Wirtschaftliche Impulse, infrastrukturelle Beziehungen, sicherheitspolitische Aspekte* (Paderborn, 1998).

70 K. von Albedyll, 'Prenzlau als Garnison der Garde-Kavallerie', *Heimatkalender Prenzlau*, 10 (1935): 129–31; O. Gründel, 'Bürgerrock und Uniform. Die Garnisonsstadt Prenzlau 1685–1806', in H. Hülsbergen and H. Wilderotter (eds), *Ortstermine. Stationen Brandenburg-Preußens auf dem Weg in die moderne Welt. Teil der gemeinsamen Landesausstellung Berlin und Brandenburg Preußen 2001. Landwirtschaft, Industrie, Militär, Universität* (Berlin, 2001), pp. 6–23; B. Engelen, 'Fremde in der Stadt. Die Garnisonsgesellschaft Prenzlaus im 18. Jahrhunderts', in K. Neitmann and J. Theil (eds), *Die Herkunft der Brandenburger. Sozial- und mentalitätsgeschichtliche Beiträge zur*

– their fixed culture and customs and their arrogance towards non-noble and civilian personnel.[71] It tells us much about the self-confident, elitist Huguenot troops. But it must be taken into consideration that – after Berlin, Magdeburg, Halle and Wesel – Prenzlau was the fifth-biggest urban settlement of refugees in Brandenburg-Prussia, which consisted predominantly of Walloon, Huguenot, Palatine and numerous francophone Swiss settlers.[72] The *grands mousquetaires* at the end of the century were relatively problem-free, despite their strongly French culture. However, they were not at first accommodated in the private houses of other refugees, because the Potsdam edict explicitly assured Huguenots of freedom from quartering for the first six years after their settlement.[73]

The resentment of the native Brandenburg officers towards their Huguenot brothers-in-arms was substantially more serious. Both belonged to the court, but the refugees enjoyed a special proximity to the Elector.[74] The native officers looked upon the Frenchmen openly with envy and disfavour as specialists from abroad who were immediately granted advanced rank in their officer *corps*.[75] Friedrich Wilhelm and Friedrich III reacted to a number of latent, smouldering conflicts: for example, the *grands mousquetaires* regiment was augmented in 1688 by a company of native Brandenburg *gens d'armes* in addition to the two noble Huguenot cadet companies.[76] They were also subordinated to the supreme command of Dubislav Gneomar von Natzmer (1654–1739).[77] The gradual pooling of the French into the German regiments and the refusal of Friedrich III to fill up the purely French regiments again with Huguenots saw them gradually lose their specific French character.

Bevölkerung Brandenburgs vom hohen Mittelalter bis zum 20. Jahrhundert (Potsdam, 2001), pp. 113–26.

71   Grieser, *Die Denkwürdigkeiten*, pp. 80, 111, 131; Harms, 'Das Edikt von Potsdam': 167.

72   Muret, *Geschichte der Französischen Kolonie*, p. 259; K. Manoury, *Die Geschichte der französisch-reformierten Provinzgemeinden* (Berlin, 1961), p. 139; W. Beuleke, *Die Südfranzosen in den uckermärkischen Hugenottenkolonien Prenzlau, Potzlow und Strasburg* (Sickte, 1980); W. Beuleke, 'Die Hugenottengemeinde Prenzlau', *Genealogie*, 14 (1965): 416–21.

73   § 5 Potsdam edict.

74   P. M. Hahn, 'Aristokratisierung und Professionalisierung. Der Aufstieg der Obristen zu einer militärischen und höfischen Elite in Brandenburg-Preußen von 1650–1725', *Forschungen zur Brandenburgischen und Preußischen Geschichte N.F.*, 1 (1991): 161–208.

75   Grieser, *Die Denkwürdigkeiten*, p. 61.

76   O. von Schwerin, *Das Regiment gens d'armes und seine Vorgeschichte* (2 vols, Berlin, 1912).

77   K. W. von Schöning (ed.), *Des General-Feldmarschalls Dubislav Gneomar von Natzmer auf Gannewitz Leben und Kriegsthaten mit den Hauptbegebenheiten des von ihm errichteten und 48 Jahre als Commandeur en Chef geführten bekannten Garde-Reuter-Regiments Gens d'armes. Ein Beitrag zur brandenburgisch-preußischen Armee-Geschichte* (Berlin, 1838); H. G. Bloth, 'Soldat und Vermittler. Generalfeldmarschall Dubislav Gneomar von Natzmer (1654–1739)', *Baltische Studien N.F.*, 70 (1984): 81–111.

The occasional hiring-out of Brandenburg troops to William III under the guidance of Schomberg[78] – including the purely Huguenot regiments – was likewise a measure by which Friedrich Wilhelm could calm the displeasure of his native officer corps. After 1688, French regiments were almost permanently abroad, during the Wars of the Grand Alliance (1688–97) and the Spanish succession war (1701–13) in the theatres of the Rhine and in northern Italy. Research emphasises, again and again, the special loyalty of the French officers to the Brandenburg electors and later Prussian kings due to their specific combat motives – the embittered opposition to Louis XIV, and the highly disciplined Calvinist ethic; exactly the traits highlighted by Max Weber.[79] Indeed, the Huguenots retained concrete hope in a return to their homes in France throughout the Wars of the Grand Alliance and the Spanish succession war.[80] The question remains unanswered, however, whether they fought for personal religious reasons, simple fanaticism (in the same way as Oliver Cromwell's Puritan 'Ironsides' had),[81] or whether these assumptions are the result of historiographical misinterpretation.

The historiography generated by the Huguenot elite among the *bourgeois* citizens of Berlin at the end of the eighteenth century continues to resonate in today's literature. It has been accepted uncritically, as is evidenced by the recent 'Huguenot legends' publication.[82] It has also formed a firm component in the self-understanding

---

78   R. Wiebe, 'Untersuchung über die Hilfeleistung der deutschen Staaten für Wilhelm III. von Oranien im Jahre 1688', PhD thesis (Göttingen, 1939); T. A. Boeree (ed.), 'Les officiers français en service hollandaise après la revocation de l'édit de Nantes pendant la période 1686–1689', *Bulletin de la commission de l'histoire des èglises wallones*, series 4, 1 (1928): 1–65; R. D. Gwynn, 'The Huguenots in Britain, the "Protestant International" and the Defeat of Louis XIV', in R. Vigne and C. Littleton (eds), *From Strangers to Citizens: The Integration of Immigrant Communities in Britain, Ireland and Colonial America 1550–1750* (Brighton, Portland, 2001), pp. 412–46.

79   See Schnitter and Schmidt, 'Die Hugenotten in der brandenburgisch-preußischen Armee': 236.

80   L. H. Boles, *The Huguenots, the Protestant Interest, and the War of the Spanish Succession, 1702–1714* (New York, 1997); B. Dölemeyer, 'Der Friede von Rijswijk und seine Bedeutung für das europäische Refuge', *Der Deutsche Hugenott*, 66 (2002): 51–73; C. Read, 'Les démarches des réfugiés huguenots auprès des négociateurs de la paix de Ryswick pour leur rétablissement en France (1697)', *Bulletin de la société de l'histoire du Protestantisme française*, 40 (1891): 169–88, 384–7; R. Schmertosch, *Denkschriften französischer Réfugiés zu den Friedensverhandlungen von Rijswijk* (Pirna, 1898).

81   C. F. Firth, *Cromwell's Army: A History of the English Soldier during the Civil Wars, the Commonwealth and the Protectorate* (London, 1902; reprinted London, 1967); M. A. Kishlansky, *The Rise of the New Model Army* (Cambridge, 1979); I. Gentles, *The New Model Army in England, Ireland and Scotland 1645–1653* (2 vols, Oxford, Cambridge, MA, 1994); T. Uenlüdag-Puschnerat, 'Wir sind keine bloße Söldnerarmee. Cromwells Revolutionsarmee 1645–49', *Militär und Gesellschaft in der Frühen Neuzeit*, 6 (2002): 108–24.

82   For the 'Huguenot legends' publication, see E. François, 'Die Traditions- und Legendenbildung des deutschen Refuge', in Duchhardt (ed.), *Der Exodus der Hugenotten*, pp. 177–193; E. François, 'Vom preußischen Patrioten zum besten Deutschen', in von Thadden and Magdelaine (eds), *Die Hugenotten*, pp. 198–212; R. von Thadden, 'Hugenotten und

and collective identity of Huguenot officer descendants.[83] A military career in royal Prussian or imperial German service remained, well into the early twentieth century,[84] an adequate vocational field for refugee descendants.[85] Yet the contribution of Huguenots cannot be overestimated; French military engineers helped to reform the army of Brandenburg-Prussia in the eighteenth century along French lines.[86] They contributed to the systematic training of troops in times of peace and raised the general education level of officers through cadet companies consisting of young noblemen.[87] The purely Huguenot regiments were a brief episode in Brandenburg-Prussian military history, and the portion of French officers and soldiers in the electoral army was reduced slowly, but continuously, through the 1690s. The short-

Hugenottengedenken 1685–1985', in Stolpe and Winter (eds), *Wege und Grenzen der Toleranz*, pp. 15–20; U. Fuhring-Grubert, 'Hugenotten in Preußen 1685–1945. Von den verachteten "Paddenschluckern" zu den besten Deutschen', *Der Deutsche Hugenott*, 66 (2002): 3–27; J. Desel, *Hugenotten in der Literatur. Eine Bibliographie. Hugenotten, Waldenser, Wallonen und ihr Umfeld in Erzählung, Biographie, Hagiographie, Drama, Geschichtsschreibung und Gedicht*, Geschichtsblätter des Deutschen Hugenotten-Vereins 25 (Bad Karlshafen, 1996).

83 Appropriate expressions of eighteenth- and nineteenth-century Huguenot descendants show this. For instance, see the letter written by First-Lieutenant de Saint-Julien to Jean Pierre Erman at the end of the 1700s: 'My father was a refugee, this says everything; and if I did not have other reasons to honour his memory then this fact alone would prompt me to. By the way, it has always been my tendency, and we have achieved noble status by it, to be an upright man and to serve faithfully my native country: this, to the refugees, is our reason for being.' The military historian Major-General René de l'Homme de Courbière said: 'It is the highest honour to serve our incomparable King with loyalty and devotion and to be always ready to sacrifice myself in order to contribute to the common Weal; I flatter myself that the descendants of the refugees do me the honour to include me among the number of those who possess the greatest eagerness to serve their new native country': Muret, *Geschichte der Französischen Kolonie*, p. 52.

84 Chambeau, 'Der Anteil der Hugenotten': 22.

85 For example, see genealogical overview of the Forcade family to which belonged Jean Quirin, Marquis de Biaix de Forcade (1663–1729), originating from Pau and from 1714 commander of the city of Berlin. Three generations of the family served in the Brandenburg-Prussian officer *corps*: Harms, 'Das Edikt von Potsdam': 169.

86 Two engineers trained under Vauban include Jean Cayart (1645–1702) and Jean de Bodt (1670–1745): H. J. Kuke, *Jean de Bodt (1670–1745). Architekt und Ingenieur im Zeitalter des Barock* (Worms, 2002); Schnitter and Schmidt, 'Die Hugenotten in der brandenburgisch-preußischen Armee': 237; Harms, 'Das Edikt von Potsdam': 168; U. W. B. von Bonin, *Geschichte des Ingenieurkorps und der Pioniere in Preußen* (2 vols, Berlin, 1877–8; reprinted Wiesbaden, 1981); M. Jähns, *Geschichte der Kriegswissenschaften vornehmlich in Deutschland* (2 vols, Munich, Leipzig, 1890), vol. 2, 'XVII. und XVIII. Jahrhundert bis zum Auftreten Friedrichs des Großen'; H. Delbrück, *Geschichte der Kriegskunst im Rahmen der politischen Geschichte* (4 vols, Berlin, 1900–20), vol. 4 'Neuzeit'.

87 A. F. J. von Crousaz, *Geschichte des Königlich Preußischen Kadetten-Corps, nach seiner Entstehung, seinem Entwicklungsgange und seinen Resultaten, aus den Quellen geschöpft und systematisch bearbeitet* (Berlin, 1857); N. von Benstatt-Wahlberg, *Aus den Voranstalten des Kadetten-Corps und der Haupt-Kadettenanstalt zu Lichterfelde* (2 vols, Hanover, 1891); K. H. Freiherr von Brand, *Geschichte des Königlich Preußischen Kadettenkorps* (Munich, 1981).

term nature of the massive Huguenot exodus into Brandenburg-Prussia led to a durable change in the paradigm of military affairs: one that far removed Prussia from Swedish and Dutch models in favour of the French one.[88] Thus, the Huguenots had a profound influence on Brandenburg-Prussia on the eve of its ascent to become one of Europe's great powers – at least in military terms.

---

88   P. M. Hahn, 'Magnifizenz und dynastische Legitimation durch Übernahme kultureller Muster. Die Beziehungen der Hohenzollern zum Haus Oranien und den Niederlanden im 17. Jahrhundert', in P. M. Hahn and H. Lorenz (eds), *Formen der Visualisierung von Herrschaft. Studien zu Adel, Fürst und Schloßbau vom 16. bis zum 18. Jahrhundert* (Potsdam, 1998), pp. 9–56; J. Häseler, 'Franzosen im Dienste des Aufstiegs Preußens', in G. Lottes (ed.), *Vom Kurfürstentum zum "Königreich der Landstriche". Brandenburg-Preußen im Zeitalter von Absolutismus und Aufklärung* (Berlin, 2004), pp. 175–92.

Chapter 12

'The court at Celle … is completely French'
Huguenot Soldiers in the Duchy of Brunswick-Lüneburg[1]

Andreas Flick

Huguenot Society of Germany

The Dutchman Constantijn Huygens reported in June 1680 in his travel diary that Frenchmen would stand in the highest favour at the court of Georg Wilhelm, Duke of Brunswick-Lüneburg, due to the influence of the Duchess, Eléonore Desmier d'Olbreuse.[2] Celle (north-east of Hanover in Lower Saxony) was the residence of the dukes of Brunswick-Lüneburg. The adventurer and writer, Baron Karl Ludwig von Pöllnitz, stated (a few years after the death of the ducal couple and long after the Revocation in France) that the Frenchmen in Celle had raised the reputation of the court more than its own native-born members. He reports:

> I have been told that the French are so utterly presumptuous, that one of them, on an occasion when he lunched with the Duke, having duly noted that amongst the twelve people at the table there was no one except the Duke who was not French, turned to the aforesaid Duke and commented, 'it is a remarkable fact, your Grace, that there are no foreigners here except you'.[3]

Such clear criticism was already loud in the lifetime of the ducal couple, and is expressed in a biting comment made by Duke Georg Wilhelm's sister-in-law, Sophie, Electress of Hanover: 'The court at Celle, one can say, is completely French …

1 Translated by Matthew Glozier. For an expanded version of the article in German, see 'Der Celler Hof, so sagt man, ist ganz französisch: Hugenotten am Hof und beim Militär Herzog Georg Wilhelms von Braunschweig-Lüneburg', *Celler Chronik*, 12 (Beiträge zum 300. Todestag Herzog Georg Wilhelms von Braunschweig-Lüneburg, Celle, 2005): 65–98.

2 C. Huygens, 'Voyage de Cell, 1680', *Journalen van Constantijn Huygens, den Zoon (Handschrift van de Koninklijke Akademie van Wetenschappen te Amsterdam)*, 3 (Historisch Genootschap, new series 46, Utrecht, 1888): 10. The Calvinist Constantijn Huygens, Jr. (d.1697) was the secretary of William of Orange.

3 Pöllnitz quoted in 'Celle in Reisebeschreibungen und Briefen. 2. Aus Pöllnitz Reisebriefen', *Cellesche Zeitung (Der Sachsenspiegel)*, 8/27 (September 1929): 59.

one hardly sees Germans there any more.'[4] Indeed, the Duke's cosmopolitan tastes
drew critics long before the arrival of most French refugees. Georg Wilhelm said in
1675:

> I am astonished that there are still people who are alarmed about the large number of
> French [people] in my court. I think that I have sufficiently proved that these people have
> never been able to hinder me from attending to the business of the Empire.[5]

The Lower Saxon aristocracy shaped not only the diplomacy but also the internal
administration of the duchy. However, the Duke never succeeded in quelling criticism
of outsiders at his court. It entered German historiography and, for example, recurs
in Ferdinand Neigebaur's 1859 book which described Eléonore d'Olbreuse. For him
it was a 'weakness' of Georg Wilhelm to allow 'only foreigners and Frenchmen' to
enjoy favour in Celle.[6] Completely different, but understandable, on the other hand,
is the judgement of René Martel, Marquis d'Arcis, Envoy of Louis XIV to Celle. He
said the 'large number of foreigners who are in their service ... raises their people a
little above the backwardness which one still meets in many regions of Germany'.[7]

The court lists from that time reveal how many French people were present in
Celle; although not all of them were Huguenots, most of them were.[8] The French
company of actors was, for example, entirely so, but the musicians of the court

---

4   'La cour de Cell à ce qu'on dit est toute Françoise ... on n'y voit casi plus d'Allemand':
E. Bodeman (ed.), 'Briefwechsel der Herzogin Sophie von Hannover mit ihrem Bruder,
dem Kurfürsten Karl Ludwig von der Pfalz, und des Letzteren mit seiner Schwägerin, der
Pfalzgräfin Anna', *Publikationen aus den K. Preußischen Staatsarchiven*, 26 (Leipzig, 1885):
410.

5   H. de Beauclaire, *Une mésalliance dans la maison de Brunswick (1665–1725):
Eléonore Desmier d'Olbreuze, Duchesse de Zell* (Paris, 1884). Published in German as *Die
letzte Herzogin von Celle: Eleonore Desmier d'Olbreuze 1665–1725*, ed. Baron E. Grote
(Hanover, 1886), p. 84.

6   J. F. Neigebaur, *Eleonore d'Olbreuse, die Stammmutter der Königshäuser von
England, Hannover und Preußen. Ermittlungen zur Geschichte ihrer Heirath mit dem
Herzoge von Braunschweig-Celle und der damaligen Zeit, in besonderer Beziehung auf
Ebenbürtigkeitsheirathen* (Brunswick, 1859), p. 52 *et passim*.

7   R. E. Wallbrecht, *Das Theater des Barockzeitalters an den welfischen Höfen Hannover
und Celle*, Quellen und Darstellungen zur Geschichte Niedersachsens 83 (Hildesheim, 1974),
p. 11.

8   Niedersächsisches Hauptstaatsarchiv, Hanover (hereafter NHStAH), Celle 44/74,
'Liste der Beamten von Georg Wilhelm'; Celle 44/935, 'Hauptregister der Ausgaben für den
Celler Hofstaat, 1684–1706'. See also Herzog's Georg Wilhelm zu Celle hohe u. niedere
Minister u. Diener u. deren Besoldung, vom Jahre 1682 (Aus einem offiziellen Besoldungs-
Register), *Neues vaterländisches Archiv oder Beiträge zur allseitigen Kenntnis des Königreichs
Hannover und des Herzogthums Braunschweig* (22 vols, Lüneburg, 1822–32), vol. 1 (1828),
pp. 308–20. For example, the nobleman Jean de Carlin and Estienne Languillett, and the
valet of the Duchess, George Guyon (called 'La Perle'), were all undoubtedly Catholics:
Bistumsarchiv Hildesheim, Bestand Kirchenbücher, Hanover-St Clemens. Kirchenbuch-
Abschrift. Taufbuch 1671–1699. Traubuch 1667–1711. Sterbebuch 1666–1710; C. Meyer-
Rasch, *Alte Häuser erzählen. Von Menschen und Schicksalen der Stadt Celle* (2 vols, Celle,
1962), vol. 2, p. 185.

orchestra were predominantly Catholic.[9] In view of the sparse seventeenth-century Catholic, Reformed Protestant (Calvinist)[10] and Lutheran Protestant[11] church records, it is sometimes difficult to determine the denomination of the French courtiers and military officers specified in the court registers. But also the confessional affiliation of some officials in Celle whose names do not appear in any church registers, remains uncertain.[12] Moreover, the entries in the register of the Lutheran court chapel in Celle leave some questions unanswered concerning the denominational affiliation of the Frenchmen recorded therein.[13] It must also be said that the confessional boundaries between Catholics, Lutherans and Protestants of the Reformed faith were not always strictly observed by some individuals. Wilhelm Beuleke, the Huguenot historian, rightly concludes as a result of his painstaking research into the church registers of Lower Saxony:

> There were Frenchmen living in Celle and Hanover – a considerable number of whom were undoubtedly religiously indifferent – who had lived together more or less peacefully since at least 1665. Through this longstanding coexistence at the court, their confessional differences had lessened and receded, bringing about a *rapprochement*, which was impossible at the court of Louis XIV because of the persecution and exclusion of the Protestants.[14]

The fact that 90 of the 300 *réfugiés* (30 per cent) resident in Celle were in the service of the court,[15] says a great deal about the Celle Huguenot colony, which, therefore, possessed a very different composition to most others in Germany.[16] This says

---

9   See Flick, 'Der Celler Hof, so sagt man, ist ganz französisch': 74–6.

10   Not all of the Reformed Protestants in Celle were Calvinists: Evangelisch-reformierte Gemeinde, Celle, Kirche 1, no. 13, 'Protokollbücher des Französisch-reformierten *consistoire* (Presbyterium)', vol. 1, 1687–1729, 1732–5, 1737–50.

11   Stadtkirche Trauregister I. 4 1659–73, 1684–99, 1700–14, 5 1674–83; III, 2 1630–78, 3 1679–1707; IV. 3 1660–90, 4 1691–1723.

12   For the Roman Catholic Church in Celle see F. W. Woker, *Geschichte der katholischen Kirche in Hannover und Celle. Ein weiterer Beitrag zur Kirchengeschichte Norddeutschlands nach der Reformation* (Paderborn, 1889). The confessional faith of Colonel de Villiers is uncertain; he spent his life in Holland as a native of Alsace, and in Celle as a Dutchman. So too his brother, Captain de Villiers: Huygens, 'Voyage de Cell, 1680': 19. Wilhelm Beuleke includes none of these people on his list of Huguenots in Lower Saxony.

13   Evangelisch-lutherisches Kirchenbuchamt, Celle: Schlosskapelle. Tauf-, Trau- und Sterbebuch 1667–1706 (with gaps).

14   W. Beuleke, *Die Hugenotten in Niedersachsen*, Quellen und Darstellungen zur Geschichte Niedersachsens 58 (Hildesheim, 1960), p. 147. (The names of the courtiers and soldiers in this chapter follow the form set down by Beuleke.)

15   Ibid., p. 174.

16   Literature relating to the Huguenots in Celle includes H. Tollin, 'Geschichte der hugenottischen Gemeinde von Celle', *Geschichtsblätter des Deutschen Hugenotten-Vereins*, 2, 7/8 (Magdeburg, 1893); G. Stolze, *Die Bedeutung der unter Herzog Georg Wilhelm eingewanderten französischen Hugenotten für die Stadt Celle* (Göttingen, 1963); A. Flick, A. Hack and S. Maehnert, *Hugenotten in Celle*, catalogue of exhibition in Celle Palace, 9 April – 8 May 1994 (Celle, 1994); A. Flick and S. Maehnert, *Archivbestände der Französisch-reformierten Gemeinden Lüneburg und Celle. Mit einer geschichtlichen Einleitung und einer*

much about the attitude of the rulers of Celle. The Nestor of nineteenth-century German Huguenot research, Henri Tollin, speaks of 'the noble character of the Celle Huguenot colony'.[17] He states that whilst 15 Huguenot ladies secured positions at the courts of Celle alone, there was by comparison only one at the court of Hanover (duchy of Brunswick-Calenberg) and none at all at that of Wolfenbüttel (duchy of Brunswick-Wolfenbüttel). Whilst it would undoubtedly be too simplistic to think of the Celle Huguenot refuge primarily as a court community, nevertheless even those Huguenots who were not directly involved with the court found their lives entangled with it.[18]

I

The most important Huguenot in Celle was undoubtedly Eléonore Desmier d'Olbreuse (1639–1722),[19] Georg Wilhelm's spouse. She was born on 3 January 1639 at the small château d'Olbreuse in the Poitou. Eléonore was descended from several generations of Reformed Protestant Poitevin nobility. At a time when it was quite usual for young children of the landed aristocracy to seek their fortunes with other aristocratic families, she secured a position as a lady-of-honour to the Duchess de Trémoïlle.[20] Eléonore subsequently became chamber-lady to the Huguenot Princess, Emilie de Tarent. The Prince and Princess de Tarent's Calvinist faith reduced the possibility of their having a career in France and barred them from advancement at the court of Louis XIV. The couple, therefore, departed for the Netherlands, taking Eléonore with them. Here the Prince de Tarent received a senior military position.

Bibliographie, Geschichtsblätter des Deutschen Hugenotten-Vereins 24 (Kleine Schriften zur Celler Stadtgeschichte 1, Bad Karlshafen, Celle, 1997).

17   Tollin, 'Geschichte der hugenottischen Gemeinde von Celle', p. 20.

18   For example the Huguenot baker, Barbière. There are Huguenot craftsmen mentioned in the Celle court lists, including the clock-maker, Mathurin Brachet, and the French master tinsmith, Charles Houel, from Poitou, but they are exceptional cases: NHStAH Fürstlich Cellesche Kammerregister, Des 76cA/230, 1705/6, fol. 457. In 1693 Brachet married as his second wife, Christine Chappuzeau, in Celle. He died in Hanover, 28 March 1715. Houel, from Normandy, married the chamber lady Marie Migault. He died in 1714 at Lübeck: Beuleke, *Die Hugenotten in Niedersachsen*, p. 123.

19   Literature on Eléonore Desmier d'Olbreuse includes Beauclaire, *Une mésalliance dans la maison de Brunswick*; L. Marelle, *Eleonore d'Olbreuse. Herzogin von Braunschweig-Lüneburg-Celle. Die Großmutter Europas* (Hamburg, 1936); Neigebaur, *Eleonore d'Olbreuse*; F. Sander, 'Eleonore d'Olbreuse, Herzogin von Braunschweig-Lüneburg-Celle', *Die Französische Colonie*, 3 (1893): 49–53 and 4: 69–75; F. Geyken, '"Mutter der Könige" oder das "Fräulein aus Poitou"? Widersprüche im Bild der Eleonore Desmier d'Olbreuse (1638–1722)', *Der Deutsche Hugenott*, 58/3 (1994): 77–85 and 58/4: 102–7; R. du Vinage, *Ein vortreffliches Frauenzimmer. Das Schicksal von Eleonore Desmier d'Olbreuse (1639–1722), der letzten Herzogin von Braunschweig-Lüneburg-Celle* (Berlin, 2000). For an expanded list, see Flick and Maehnert, *Archivbestände der Französisch-reformierten Gemeinden Lüneburg und Celle*.

20   See R. Mosen, *Das Leben der Prinzessin Charlotte Amélie de la Trémoïlle, Gräfin von Oldenburg (1652–1732). Erzählt von ihr selbst* (Oldenburg, Leipzig, 1892).

In 1663 Eléonore met Georg Wilhelm von Brunswick-Lüneburg, then Duke of Calenberg-Göttingen, for the first time in Cassel. She was there with the Princess de Tarent, a native-born Countess of Hesse-Cassel. The Duke from the ancient dynasty of Guelphs must have been impressed by her at this first meeting, since he visited her in Holland one year later, in December 1664. He again paid her a visit in March 1665, remaining near her thereafter. But his interest in Eléonore was interrupted by the sudden death of his brother, Christian Ludwig, in Celle. Moreover his third brother, Johann Friedrich, had seized the government of the duchy of Brunswick-Lüneburg through a *coup d'état*. Only after this conflict was resolved did Georg Wilhelm commence his rule of Brunswick-Lüneburg as its duke in 1665.

Eléonore d'Olbreuse had come to Celle on the occasion of Christian Ludwig's funeral. On 15 November 1665, she contracted a morganatic marriage with the Lutheran Georg Wilhelm, since the Duke was now relieved of the contractual promise not to marry which had been imposed on him by his brother, Ernst August in 1658. Therefore, initially, Eléonore remained a bride with neither the name nor the status of an official ducal wife. She received the title 'Lady of Harburg'. On 22 July 1674 Georg Wilhelm obtained the title of Countess von Wilhelmsburg from the Emperor Leopold for his wife Eléonore and their daughter, Sophie Dorothea. On the understanding that, on his death, the principality of Brunswick-Lüneburg would descend to his youngest brother, Ernst August, Georg Wilhelm's official marriage with Eléonore Desmier d'Olbreuse took place on 12 April 1676 in the chapel in the ducal palace of Celle.

Eléonore remained faithful to her Reformed Protestant (Calvinist) religion in the Lutheran duchy of Brunswick-Lüneburg. The crucial characteristic of the Huguenots in exile was their steadfast adherence to the French Reformed denomination, the Confession of Faith (*confession de foi*) of 1559, and to the church discipline, the *discipline ecclésiastique des églises réformées de France*. The Duchess's private *temple*, where French Reformed services were celebrated, lay in the third floor of the ducal palace above the Lutheran court chapel. This was a room that functioned as a religious meeting place for the still small, fledgling Huguenot community in Celle.[21] Gregorio Leti[22] described these services in 1687:

> The dominant religion is that of the Prince, who is Lutheran, but the Catholics do not suffer under him. At the moment one finds here also the Reformed Protestants [...], encouraged by the Duchess, who lets a minister come on short notice to the ducal chapel for both her and the other Reformed Protestants who are at the court or who live in the city.[23]

---

21 A. Flick, '1700–2000: 300 Jahre Evangelisch-reformierte Kirche in Celle', *Celler Chronik*, 9 (Beiträge zur Geschichte und Geographie der Stadt und des Landkreises Celle, Celle, 2000): 61.

22 Gregorio Leti (1630–1701), converted to the Reformed faith and lived temporarily in Geneva, England, at different German courts and in Amsterdam. He left numerous writings, among them the work entitled *Abrégé de l'histoire de la maison Sérénissime et Electorale de Brandenburg* (Amsterdam, 1667), in which he reports on Celle.

23 A. Flick, 'Gregorio Leti und sein Bericht über den Celler Hof aus dem Jahr 1687', *Celler Chronik*, 8 (Celle, 1998): 79.

At the time the incumbant was the Duchess's cousin, Louis Suzannet de La Forest-Puycouvert, successor to Etienne de Maxuel de La Fortière, a former minister of Mauzé-sur-le-Mignon in Poitou. [24] De La Forest was described as being 'a man of good family, [who] leads an exemplary life, is well educated and a scholar'.[25]

Leti counted less than 150 refugees in Celle. Soon afterwards the number had risen to approximately 300 refugees (many of whom became soldiers). They lived in the Lutheran town of Celle and its suburbs, forming a local French Reformed church which required its own place of worship. And this was only achieved after a proposal from the representatives of the local French Reformed church in the west Celle suburb, where most courtly officials and officers lived in freehold houses.[26] The proposal for the establishment of a common church building for both Lutherans and Calvinists was rejected both by the Lutheran church and by the state.[27] The Huguenots finally founded their *temple*, the current Evangelical Reformed church, in the year 1700 with ducal permission. However, Calvinist court services continued to take place in the Duchess's chapel, conducted by her personal chaplains.[28]

Eléonore promoted the Celle Huguenots and the local French Reformed church to a considerable extent.[29] Numerous high-placed courtiers and soldiers were leading members of the church consistory (*consistoire*).[30] The courtly character of their congregation is reflected in the hierarchical seating order in the Celle *temple*, an otherwise uncommon practice among Huguenot worshippers – 'give honour to those who are entitled to honour'. For example, the Marquise de La Roche-Giffard and the Duchess's ladies-in-waiting took the first pew; the next pew in line was allocated to the German Reformed ladies of rank, followed by the English envoy along with his Huguenot wife, and the first of the pews to the left of the pulpit went to old Scottish major-general Andrew Melville.[31]

Eléonore gave assistance to numerous Huguenot refugees who were in a distressed state because of the Revocation, and also gave the Celle Reformed ministers money to be distributed amongst the needy. She donated large sums for the building of the *temple* and for the attached manse. She also contributed to the rental

---

24   Louis Suzannet de La Forest lived in Celle from spring 1686, until his death on 25 July 1703: Beuleke, *Die Hugenotten in Niedersachsen*, p. 111.

25   But at the time, the Duchess showed so much eagerness and devotion for her religion that, in Leti's words, she 'could simply not be more forward': Flick, 'Gregorio Leti': 79.

26   For Huguenots in the west Celle suburb, see Flick, Hack and Maehnert, *Hugenotten in Celle*, pp. 66–90. No taxes were levied on the freehold houses.

27   NHStAH, Celle 48/65, vol. 22, 1699.

28   Ibid., vol. 49, 6 August 1705.

29   For the history of the French Reformed church in Celle, see A. J. Enschédé, 'L'église Française de Celle en Allemagne', *Bulletin historique et littéraire de la société de l'histoire du protestantisme Français*, 41/12 (1892): 247–51; Tollin, 'Geschichte der hugenottischen Gemeinde von Celle'; Flick, Hack and Maehnert, *Hugenotten in Celle*; Flick and Maehnert, *Archivbestände der Französisch-reformierten Gemeinden Lüneburg und Celle*.

30   Evangelisch-reformierte Gemeinde Celle, Best. 2, 13, 'Protokollbücher des Französisch-reformierten *consistoire* (Presbyterium)', vol. 1, 1687–1729, 1732–5, 1737–50.

31   Kanzelabkündigung vom 24. Dezember 1700, in Tollin, 'Geschichte der hugenottischen Gemeinde von Celle', p. 28.

of the *maison française*, and for the salaries of the Huguenot teachers there and not least she guaranteed the ongoing payment of the minister's salary.[32] In addition, she supported Huguenots beyond the borders of the duchy, especially the activities of the theologian and politician, Pierre Jurieu, who was living in exile in Rotterdam.[33]

The fact that the Huguenots found in Eléonore a person of their faith and culture, and in whom they could have confidence at Georg Wilhelm's court, predestined Celle as a place of refuge. In order to make herself feel more at home at the court of her husband, Eléonore (contemptuously called 'the Miss from Poitou' by her sister-in-law) also began to surround herself with her compatriots, all of her Reformed Protestant denomination.[34] Among them were some close relatives, including her older sister and lady-of-honour, Angélique Desmier d'Olbreuse,[35] their eldest brother, Alexandre Desmier, Seigneur d'Antigny-Olbreuse (whose tomb in the Lutheran town-church at Celle is still adorned with his military uniform, sword and periwig),[36] their half-brother, Henri Desmier, Seigneur du Beignon,[37] as well as her half-brother, Jean Desmier, Seigneur du Parc.[38] Amongst the remaining court officials, who often originated from Poitou, were other relatives.

In the 1660s approximately 77–80,000 Protestants lived in Poitou, against whom repressive measures were already being taken long before the Revocation. The fact that Protestants were barred from practicing many occupations in France and that in the year 1681 the *dragonnades* (the obligatory quartering of dragoons on Protestant households) began, coupled with the forcible conversion of almost 39,000 Poitevin Huguenots to Catholicism, led to the (forbidden) emigration of numerous Huguenots from the region. The prohibition on Protestant services in France after 1685 had, besides the destruction of all existing Huguenot churches in Poitou, serious consequences in the Duchess's home-town of Mauzé.[39] With this background it is understandable that numerous Poitevins went, after their escape from France, to Celle, where they found in Eléonore a zealous ducal spokeswoman. Henri Tollin remarks:

---

32   The *maison française* served as a poor-house and hospital as well as a lodging house for transients: ibid.: 14.

33   See F. R. J. Knetsch, *Pierre Jurieu, Theoloog en politikus der refuge* (Kampen, 1967).

34   Cited in Beauclaire, *Une mésalliance dans la maison de Brunswick*, p. 60.

35   Following her divorce from the imperial general, Heinrich V, Count von Reuß-Burck: Beuleke, *Die Hugenotten in Niedersachsen*, p. 105; NHStAH Fürstlich Cellesches Kammerregister, Des 76cA/218–19, 1692–5, fol. 576.

36   See the Celle church register, 21 January 1687, when he was aged 61. He married as his second wife lady-of-honour Sylvie de Sainte-Hermine: Beuleke, *Die Hugenotten in Niedersachsen*, p. 106.

37   Already in Celle in 1666, he died there on 13 April 1675 after the Rhine campaign due to a heavy malarial fever; he was 28 years old: ibid.

38   Killed at the siege of Crete in 1668: ibid.

39   See Y. Krumenacker, *Les Protestants du Poitou au XVIIIe siècle (1681–1789)*, Vie des Huguenots 1 (Paris: Editions Honoré Champion, 1998).

Eleonore's [Celle] palace was like the château d'Olbreuse in Poitou, the ark which saved the condemned. Here they could hold their religious services ... here was their homeland. Here Protestant Poitou assembled itself.[40]

II

On 7 August 1684, Georg Wilhelm issued an edict, which promised Reformed Protestant refugees from France admission and support in the duchy of Brunswick-Lüneburg.[41] Obviously the regent suspected Louis XIV's intent before the Revocation, and hoped that numerous Huguenot craftsmen and manufacturers would animate the duchy economically. The numerous French people in Celle offered the possibility of opening up Georg Wilhelm's court to French culture, which had become the model for the princes of Europe, not least because of the splendour of the court of the 'Sun King', Louis XIV.[42] The Celle court's major-domo, Armand de Lescours, was one of numerous Huguenot courtiers; he rapidly gained recognition and wealth.[43] Sophie of Hanover wrote of him:

---

40   Tollin, 'Geschichte der hugenottischen Gemeinde von Celle', p. 11.

41   See T. Klingebiel, *Die Hugenotten in den welfischen Landen. Eine Privilegiensammlung*, Geschichtsblätter des Deutschen Hugenotten-Vereins 23 (Bad Karlshafen, 1994).

42   Among Georg Wilhelm's high-ranking Huguenot officials was the senior hunt master Olivier de Beaulieu-Marconnay (1 September 1660–11 November 1751). He received 1,241 *Talers* annually, and married the court lady Marie Chrêtien de Barbigant (d. 19 December 1742 aged 73), also from Poitou: Beuleke, *Die Hugenotten in Niedersachsen*, p. 107; M. van Bellen, 'Über die Verbindung der Familien de Beaulieu Marconnay und Suzannet de la Forest mit der hannoverschen Adelsfamilie von Düring. Ein Kapitel aus der Geschichte adeliger Hugenotten in Celle', *Der Deutsche Hugenott*, 55/1 (1994): 3–16. Further Huguenot courtiers under the Duke include the chamberlains Paul de Caumont-Montbeton and Henri de Pouguet de Faillac, the French personal chamber secretary Christophe Chappuzeau, his father, the principal page at court, Samuel Chappuzeau, the grand falconer and keeper of the 'Kaninchengarten' Etienne de Maxuel de la Fortière, the principal page at court Pierre (Jean) Vincent and secret Envoy Jean (de) Robethon: see Beuleke, *Die Hugenotten in Niedersachsen*, pp. 104–37. Robethon was later one of the most hated men on the political scene in England and was described by one of his contemporaries as a 'prying, impertinent, venomous creature, for ever crawling in some slimy intrigue': R. Hatton, *George I: Elector and King* (Cambridge, MA, 1978), p. 164; J. Marlow, *The Life and Time of George I* (London, 1973)' p. 70; A. Flick, 'Huguenots in the Electorate of Hanover and their British links', *Proceedings of the Huguenot Society of Great Britain and Ireland*, 37/3 (2000): 339. Some areas of the palace in Celle were named after the ducal barber and valet Daniel Ceaullier (Collieu, Caulier), probably because he resided there: Stadtarchiv Celle, Sign. N1, A1, 'Extracted from the furniture inventory carried out in the year 1703 by the old paperhanger la Fontaine ... at that time existing in Celle castle'.

43   He supervised the running of the kitchen and cellar, kept an account of all expenditure, prepared for guests, looked after all aspects of the catering and their entertainment as well as being present to receive them on their arrival. He also accompanied the Duchess when travelling: W. Dinger, 'Armand de Lescours Oberhofmarschall der Herzogin Eleonore d'Olbreuse. Einblick in die Geschichte einer Hugenottenfamilie', *Cellesche Zeitung*, 4 (April 1967: Sonderbeilage; 150 Jahre Cellesche Zeitung): 13; NHStAH, Dep 84 KG Hann 9, Domestica 125, 'Lescourscher Stammbaum'.

Mr. Lescour is held in great favour by his master, the Duke of Celle, who was happy to permit him to look after his interests; he wagered his money, like the lotteries in England; the King has a high opinion of him; he has made his fortune in Celle from gaming, since he arrived quite 'bald' [destitute] along with his sisters to whom he gives considerable assistance.[44]

Moreover, there belonged to the ducal household of the Duchess many other Huguenots of rank and influence.[45] Equally as court ladies and ladies-of-honour to the Duchess there were a large number of Huguenots.[46]

Gregorio Leti, to whom we owe the most detailed contemporary description of the Celle court, writes that at Celle one must put on 'the appearance of a soldier, huntsman or musician' to be accepted. However, there were numerous exceptions to

---

44 Bodeman (ed.), *Briefwechsel .... Sophie von Hannover*, p. 156.

45 Jacques Rozemont, Seigneur de Boucoeur, later accredited as envoy from Celle to the French court came from Orléanais: Vinage, *Ein vortreffliches Frauenzimmer*, p. 223; Beuleke, *Die Hugenotten in Niedersachsen*, p. 116. David de Vaux from Poitou: ibid., p. 132. Stablemaster Gabriel de Villars-Malortie (1660–1736) held the office of upper court master in Ahlden: ibid., p. 113. Charles du Verger de Monroy from Poitou (d.1718): ibid., p. 107. Louis August du Verger de Monroy, Seigneur de Bessé et de Paisay (11 April 1671–1743), *ancien* from 1714. In 1743 he lost a leg at the battle of Dettingen as a Hanoverian lieutenant-general: ibid., p. 107; Beauclaire, *Une mésalliance dans la maison de Brunswick*, p. 69; Evangelisch-reformierte Gemeinde Celle, Best. 2,13, 'Protokollbücher des Französisch-reformierten *consistoire* (Presbyterium)', vol. 1, 1687–1729, 1732–5, 1737–50.

46 Marie Chrêtien de Barbigant (1669–1742), from 1686 a court lady to the Duchess, married de Beaulieu-Marconnay: Beuleke, *Die Hugenotten in Niedersachsen*, p. 107. Charlotte de Bourdon, at court since 1677: ibid., p. 114. Dorothée Louise, daughter of Anton de Chareard, Court-Marshal to the Duke of Saxony-Jena. She married de Farcy de Saint-Laurent: ibid., p. 112; W. Schuchardt, 'Amaury de Farcy de Saint Laurent, Hugenotte. Kommandant der Festung Kalkberg und der Stadt Lüneburg. Generalleutnant der hannoverschen Kavallerie. Drost des Amtes Ebstorf', *Fundstück: Zweites Heimatbuch für den Landkreis Lüneburg* (Lüneburg, 1993), pp. 209–23; NHStAH Fürstlich Cellesche Kammerregister, Des 76cA/218–19, 1692–5, fol. 576. Marianne du Faur de Pibrac (1674–1743), at court from 1695: Beauclaire, *Une mésalliance dans la maison de Brunswick*, p. 70; Beuleke, *Die Hugenotten in Niedersachsen*, p. 110. Hélène de Lescours, at court from 1683. In 1698 she married the French envoy to Celle, de Bourgeauville: ibid., p. 118. Anne de Lescours (d.1738 aged over 78), married Ludwig Justus Sinold, called 'von Schütz', envoy of Georg Wilhelm in England: ibid., p. 118. Marie Anna de Melvill(e): Beauclaire, *Une mésalliance dans la maison de Brunswick*, p. 70. Louise Marie de La Motte-Fouqué, a relative of the Duchess from Poitou, married the British envoy in Celle and Hanover, Jaques Cresset: ibid., p. 67; Beuleke, *Die Hugenotten in Niedersachsen*, p. 117. Marie Cathérine de Maxuel de La Fortière: Beauclaire, *Une mésalliance dans la maison de Brunswick*, p. 67. Marquise Louise Artémise de La Roche-Giffart (d.1743), from Poitou, married Henri de La Chapelle, Marquis de La Roche-Giffart; she married secondly the Duchess's cousin, Jacques de Sarragand du Breuil: Beuleke, *Die Hugenotten in Niedersachsen*, p. 108. Judith de Thomas (d.1736), married as her second husband François de Beauregard: ibid., p. 111; NHStAH Fürstlich Cellesche Kammerregister, Des 76cA/218–9, 1692–5, fol. 576. Her sister-in-law Madeleine Sylvie de Sainte-Hermine de La Laigne (d.1739) was related to Madame de Maintenon: Beuleke, *Die Hugenotten in Niedersachsen*, p. 106; Vinage, *Ein vortreffliches Frauenzimmer*, p. 208.

this rule, including the ducal surgeons and physicians.[47] Skilled Huguenot doctors were distributed among the regiments of the army, including surgeon César Teissier,[48] along with the physician, François Tessier,[49] both of whom served in the field with medical officer Isaac Bataillé (Bouteiler)[50] and pharmacist André Couturier-Fondousme.[51]

The link between army and court was strong. Huguenots who were important cultural figures at Celle's court also played a role in training soldiers. One such person, the senior page, Samuel Chappuzeau (called a most versatile *poète vagabond*), attended the outstanding Celle Cadet school.[52] It was the same institution patronised by the later *general-en-chef* of the cavalry Jacques d'Amproux du Pontpiétin and Pierre de Montfort (who went on to serve under William III of Orange); both trained at the Celle cadet school.[53] The cadet training academy, endowed by Georg Wilhelm, was considered to be one of the first and most appropriately equipped military cadet schools of the time.[54] The experienced teacher Samuel Chappuzeau, familiar with numerous courts in Europe, instructed the pupils in etiquette, politeness, gallantry and French. He arrived at the Celle court in 1682, at the age of 57, and from 1676 his son, Christophe, held an enviable position as French chamber secretary to the Duke and Duchess. The tight connection between army and court in Celle is exemplified by Samuel Chappuzeau, who continued with his historical-geographical, lexical and translation work, and produced one of the first German court newspapers with the title *Mercure*. He was permitted to dine with Duke Georg Wilhelm on a monthly basis, reading the latest edition of the *Mercure* aloud after the meal.[55]

---

47   Among the important officials at court was the Champagne-born surgeon Jean de l'Estocq, whose son, Armand, later became the surgeon and trusted friend of Catherine the Great of Russia: A. Kleinschmidt, 'L'Estocq (Johann Hermann, Reichsgraf von)', in J. S. Ersch and J. G. Gruber (eds), *Allgemeine Enzyklopädie der Wissenschaften und Künste* (167 vols, Leipzig, 1818–89; reprinted Grazt, 1969), vol. 43, pt. 2, pp. 234–5; Flick, 'Gregorio Leti': 79.

48   Beuleke, *Die Hugenotten in Niedersachsen*, p. 132.

49   Ibid., p. 133.

50   Ibid., p. 129.

51   Ibid., p. 126; Flick, Hack and Maehnert, *Hugenotten in Celle*, p. 142; NHStAH Fürstlich Cellesche Kammerregister, Des 76cA/230, 1705/6, fol. 457.

52   S. Haake-Kress, *Hessen im 17. Jahrhundert aus der Sicht des hugenottischen Schriftstellers Samuel Chappuzeau (1625–1701)*, Zeitschrift des Vereins für hessische Geschichte und Landeskunde 91 (Hesse, 1986): 51.

53   Personal communication with Anne de Montfort, 7 February 2001 (not cited in Beuleke).

54   'Lebensgeschichte des Churbraunschweigischen commandirenden Generals der Cavalerie, Chef eines Dragonerregiments und Gouverneurs der Festung Stade, Jacques d'Amproux du Pontpietin', *Annalen der Braunschweig-Lüneburgischen Churlande*, 6/4 (Hanover, 1792): 621.

55   Haake-Kress, *Hessen im 17. Jahrhundert*, p. 13.

III

When Georg Wilhelm took up the government of the duchy in 1665, he saw from the outset that one of its most pressing concerns must be the establishment of a battle-ready standing army. He was obliged to entirely rebuild Brunswick-Lüneburg's army, because the majority of the officers had followed his brother Johann Friedrich to Hanover after the death of Christian Ludwig in 1665.[56] Georg Wilhelm intended to create a considerable armed force for his duchy, with one of his various aims being, thereby, to enhance his reputation amongst the princes of Europe. That he succeeded, partly in co-operation with his brothers, is confirmed by the French envoy in The Hague, Godefroy d'Estrades, in 1668.[57]

Since it proved impossible to find sufficient qualified officers among his native nobility, Georg Wilhelm was dependent on the recruitment of foreign military professionals. It was standard practice in seventeenth-century Europe for soldiers frequently to cross national borders and change allegiance and for foreign officers to receive high command: 'The sword was at that time just as stateless as were the arts', confirms Henri Tollin.[58] Thus, for example, the armies of Britain were three times – under Feversham, Galway and Jean-Louis (later Earl) Ligonier – commanded by Huguenot generals between 1688 and 1762, who even led British troops against their French compatriots.[59] And in the Brandenburg army there were reputedly more than 600 officers as well as 1,100 non-commissioned officers who were *réfugiés*.[60]

Numerous French officers (mostly Huguenots) had left their homeland and entered into military service with foreign princes long before the Revocation in France.[61] But the large inflow of Huguenot soldiers into the Protestant German territories took place only after 1685. They emanated from a well-organized, battle-tested army with excellent training and discipline.[62]

On the German side criticism of the recruitment practices of the Duke of Brunswick-Lüneburg was loud. Thus his sister-in-law, Sophie of Hanover, wrote, 'it does not please me that he has so many Frenchmen in his army, who so frequently go around with lowered heads like harbingers of doom'.[63] Also the German officers

56 J. Walter, *Personengeschichtliche Quellen in den Militaria-Beständen des Niedersächsischen Hauptstaatsarchives in Hannover*, Veröffentlichungen der Niedersächsischen Archivverwaltung 38 (Göttingen, 1997), p. 35.

57 Schirmer, 'Das Heer Herzog Georg': V/8; NHStAH Fürstlich Cellesche Kammerregister, Des 76cA/230, 1705/6, fol. 457.

58 Tollin, 'Geschichte der hugenottischen Gemeinde von Celle', p. 14.

59 P. Rambaut and R. Vigne, *Britain's Huguenot War Leaders* (London, 2002).

60 H. Schnitter, 'Unter dem brandenburgischen Adler – Hugenotten in der brandenburgischen Armee', *Blätter für Heimatgeschichte. Studienmaterial 1986* (Berlin, 1986): 51–5.

61 Celle officers present before 1685 include François de Beauregard, Jeremias Chauvet, Henri du Faur de Pibrac and Charles de La Motte-Chevallerie.

62 H. Schnitter, 'Die Réfugiés in der brandenburgischen Armee', in G. Bregulla (ed.), *Hugenotten in Berlin* (Berlin, 1988), p. 316.

63 Bodeman (ed.), *Briefwechsel .... Sophie von Hannover*, p. 200.

viewed the Frenchmen with suspicion, since they saw their own influence and chances of promotion reduced.[64]

Huguenots were not alone among the high-ranking foreign officers in the service of the Duke; for example Calvinist Scots such as John Mollesson and Andrew Melvill rose to senior positions in Celle.[65] However, the Celle duke displayed a much greater tendency to employ French officers than his brothers; and they were to be met with everywhere in Celle.[66] But not all French soldiers were Huguenots, and Major-General de La Croix de Fréchapelle and the Breton nobleman Anton Simon, Marquis de Bois-David[67] – 'eager Catholics and convinced adventurers' – led Celle troops from 1682 to 1705.[68] Bois-David and his family ranked among the first members of the local Catholic church in Celle in the reign of Georg Wilhelm.[69]

Among the Huguenot officers in the duchy of Brunswick-Lüneburg were one lieutenant, 11 captains, six majors, five lieutenant-colonels, 11 colonels, seven major-generals, five lieutenant-generals, two generals as well as a field marshal.[70] They were of a high calibre and it is worth relating here in brief the careers of a few of them. Major-General François de Beauregard, from Château-Thierry near Montpellier, arrived in Celle in 1669 and was later described by Samuel Chappuzeau as being 'beautiful, spirited, eloquent, courageous'.[71] Gregorio Leti said he was 'educated, in body and spirit, on all points, intelligent and careful, in all very kindly. Therefore, he cuts an excellent figure at court, and where learning has always been esteemed and protected.'[72] Another of these desirable refugee recruits was Colonel George de Boisrenaud de Launay, from Louvigny's Osnabrück Dragoons regiment.

---

64   A. Melvill, *Memoirs of Sir Andrew Melvill. Translated from the French*, foreword by Sir Ian Hamilton (London, New York, 1918), p. 216. This is a modern version of André de Melvill, *Memoires de Chevalier de Melvill* (Amsterdam, 1704). A comparable situation is recorded in Brandenburg: see U. Michas, 'Das Salz in der Suppe. Hugenotten als brandenburgische Soldaten', *Die Mark Brandenburg, Heft 48, Die Hugenotten. Willkommen in der Mark* (Berlin, 2003), p. 22.

65   Beuleke, *Die Hugenotten in Niedersachsen*, p. 115. Melvill married Eléonore's friend, Nymphe de La Motte-Chevallerie.

66   B. von Poten, 'Die Generale der Königlich Hannoverschen Armee und ihrer Stammtruppen', *Beiheft zum Militär Wochenblatt*, 6/7 (Berlin, 1903).

67   Bistumsarchiv Hildesheim. Bestand Kirchenbücher. Kirchenbuch Celle. Taufbuch 1706–1852. Traubuch 1706–1852. Sterbebuch 1718–52. Bois-David was supreme commander of the 6,000 men of the Hanover-Celle corps in Hungary, with the Huguenot Jeremias Chauvet (from 1692 to his departure from the military service in 1705), leaders of the Celle troops: E. Kittel, *Memoiren des Generals Graf Ferdinand Christian zur Lippe (1668–1724)* (Lemgo, 1959), p. 22; von Poten, 'Die Generale der Königlich Hannoverschen Armee': 255. It is uncertain to which denomination Lieutenant-Colonel de Luc or the brothers Boccage belonged.

68   G. Schnath, *Geschichte Hannovers im Zeitalter der neunten Kur und der englischen Sukzession 1674–1714* (2 vols, Hildesheim, 1976), vol. 2, 1693–8, p. 52.

69   Woker, *Geschichte der katholischen Kirche in Hannover*, p. 243.

70   Beuleke, *Die Hugenotten in Niedersachsen*, p. 180. Indeed, Beuleke does not mention all of those officers on the Celle and Lüneburg lists.

71   Tollin, 'Geschichte der hugenottischen Gemeinde von Celle', p. 5.

72   Flick, 'Gregorio Leti': 86.

He served from 1680 to his death in 1691 in the Celle Horse Guards.[73] De Launay was typical in that he married one of the Duchess's Huguenot court ladies, Charlotte de Bourdon.[74] Gregorio Leti said of him: 'He is highly educated, a perfect cavalier, and in every way a good soldier; and just as good a man at the court, being full of spirit and well educated.'[75] The De Launay family motto was *In sanguine robur, in candore fides* (In blood strength, in loyalty integrity).[76]

Amaury de Farcy de Saint-Laurent, from Vitré in Brittany, was from 1672 a page of the hunt in Cassel before being transferred (in 1674 on the recommendation of the Prince of Orange) to Celle. He began his military career as a *piquenier* – a humble rank-and-file pikeman – and later fought with honour at Ramillies, Oudenaarde and Malplaquet. In 1700 Georg Wilhelm made major-general de Saint-Laurent Bailiff of Ebsorf. As a sign of his competence and the trust placed in him, in 1717 he was appointed Commandant of the fortress of Kalkberg and of the city of Lüneburg by Great Britain's new king, George I. Like many others, he married a Huguenot lady of the court, Dorothee Louise de Chareard.[77] He also became an *ancien* of the French Reformed church in Celle.

A host of other refugees joined Brunswick-Lüneburg's army; many of them had wives, sisters or near-relations who also served at court.[78] Furthermore, Huguenots

---

73   Kittel, *Memoiren ...Christian zur Lippe*, p. 79.

74   Beuleke, *Die Hugenotten in Niedersachsen*, p. 114; Poten, 'Die Generale der Königlich Hannoverschen Armee': 262.

75   Leti quoted in Flick, 'Gregorio Leti': 86.

76   Meyer-Rasch, *Alte Häuser erzählen*, p. 19.

77   Poten, 'Die Generale der Königlich Hannoverschen Armee': 57; L. von Estorff, *Das Geschlecht der von Estorff in der Geschichte seiner Heimat des Bardengaues und des späteren Herzogtums Lüneburg* (Uelzen, 1925), p. 106.

78   General Jacques d'Amproux du Pontpiétin (d.1738 aged over 70), Lieutenant-Colonel of Reck's infantry regiment (1711), recieved General Lucius's regiment in 1729, was a brigadier by 1735: Beuleke, *Die Hugenotten in Niedersachsen*, p. 114; B. von Poten, 'Pontpietin', *Allgemeine Deutsche Biographie* (56 vols, Berlin, 1875–1912; republished 1970), vol. 26 (1888), pp. 92, 414–16. Major-General Louis d'Amproux du Pontpiétin of whom Beuleke writes: 'Louis is supposed, with the page Jean Louis d'Amproux, to have "received" in 1691 in Celle 300 *Talers* for its [his regiment's] "installation and lining"': Beuleke, *Die Hugenotten in Niedersachsen*, p. 114. Colonel Pierre de Ballanger (1660–1702): ibid., p. 136. Captain Paul Bancelin, at Metz from 1696 to 1698 before travelling to Berlin: ibid., p. 134. Major Pierre Marin des Basques (d.1745), in Lüneburg in 1695 and Celle from 1697: ibid., p. 138. Captain Thomas de Beauregard: brother of François, in Celle between 1669 and 1692, afterwards returning to France where he became a Catholic: ibid., p. 111. Captain Henri Charles Rogier de Belleville (d.1706), from Thouars in Poitou: ibid., p. 136. Colonel Charles de Bimont-Malortie (*c*.1650/4–1720), fought on Crete in 1668: ibid., p. 113. Officer of artillery Isaac du Bois, in Celle between 1702 and 1708: ibid., p. 127. Second-Lieutenant Pierre du Bois (1665–1700): ibid. Captain Isaac de Boitou (1663–1749), from Saint-Malo, Brittany: ibid., p. 136. Colonel Daniel de Bourdon (1663–1745), town commander of Hamelin: ibid., p. 114. Colonel Jeromé de Courgelon, allegedly a cousin of the Duchess, in Celle from 1687, major commanding the Celle mounted guard (1690), lieutenant-colonel (1695), colonel (1702–6), later a general: Kittel, *Memoiren ... Christian zur Lippe*, p. 79; Meyer-Rasch, *Alte Häuser erzählen*, p. 51. Major-General René Henri Crux de Monceaux:

also appear at rank-and-file level too, with one regimental Fourier (an NCO charged with arrangements for accommodation, maintenance and so forth), Johann Giton, in the town of Uelzen. 'Due to the cause of [the persecution of the Protestant] religion in France', Giton could not provide his birth certificate.[79]

These soldiers were primarily stationed in Celle and Lüneburg, the location of the second Huguenot colony in Brunswick-Lüneburg. But the army was variously located within the duchy. Huguenot soldiers were also garrisoned at Harburg or Uelzen. Although Georg Wilhelm's plans for Lüneburg involved it developing as an extensive Huguenot colony with craftsmen and manufacturers, it was the soldiers who predominated in the around 50-strong Huguenot colony.[80] The Calvinist town commanders were quasi-protectors of the small local French Reformed church in the orthodox Lutheran town of Lüneburg. The Scottish colonel John Mollesson, who

---

Beuleke, *Die Hugenotten in Niedersachsen*, p. 116. Lieutenant-Colonel Jacques de Dompierre de Jonquières (d.1729): ibid. Colonel Henri du Faur de Pibrac: (b.1638), in Celle from 1667. Commissioned colonel (3 August 1692), he later fought at Steinkirk aged 54: ibid., p. 110. Captain Henri de La Forçade, from Béarn, served in Lüneburg from 1695 to 1706: ibid., p. 137. Commander of the Harburg fortress Lieutenant-General David de Gauvain from Metz: ibid., p. 120; A. Flick, 'Auf den Spuren der Hugenotten in Uelzen und Umgebung', *Der Deutsche Hugenott*, 61/1 (1997): 12–14. Colonel Louis de Malortie, in Celle from 1682: Beuleke, *Die Hugenotten in Niedersachsen*, p. 113. Major Benjamin de Malortie, possibly Jacques's son, and, therefore, brother of Louis (above): ibid. Lüneburg city commander Colonel S. Louis de Malortie, Seigneur de Faverolles-Glatigny, from Normandy, in Celle from 1682: ibid. Major Jean Basquin de Martin, from Lorraine: ibid., p. 136. Major-General Charles de La Motte-Chevallerie (1648–1717), from Poitou, began his career as a page in Heidelberg. Under Georg Wilhelm he received an infantry regiment (1685), was Governor of Kalkberg and Commandant of Lüneburg: ibid., p. 116; Poten, 'Die Generale der Königlich Hannoverschen Armee': 53. He also held the office of *ancien* in the Celle French Reformed church and was at the same time ducal synod-commissioner: Tollin, 'Geschichte der hugenottischen Gemeinde von Celle', p. 9. Major Charles du Pont de Boisragon, in Celle from 1696 to 1706, originally from Poitou and imprisoned in 1690 'for his religion' in the château of Pierre-Encise near Lyon: Beuleke, *Die Hugenotten in Niedersachsen*, p. 110. Lieutenant-Colonel Abraham de Raquet, Seigneur de Quissy et de Mora (d.1720 aged 63), from Brie, was captain-commandant of Ahlden at the time of the scandal surrounding Sophie Dorothea: ibid, p. 107; Schnath, *Geschichte Hannovers*, p. 185. Lieutenant-General Fréderic Henri Suzannet de La Forrest married Elisabeth de Courcillon, a relative of Philippe, Marquis de Dangeau: Beuleke, *Die Hugenotten in Niedersachsen*, p. 112. Colonel Jacques de Vigny-Launois, in Lüneburg from 1686: ibid., p. 136. Captain de Vigneulles, in Lüneburg 1688–93 and in Celle from 1699: ibid., p. 754. Possibly synonymous with Pierre de Vignoles (b.1677), a lieutenant of dragoons in Brandenburg, and later captain of the *gardes du roi* of the King of Poland: E. and E. Haag, *La France protestante ou vies des protestants français qui se sont fait un nom dans l'histoire* (10 vols, Montpellier, 1992), vol. 9, p. 501. Lüneburg city commandant colonel Guillaume de Waller, *Die Hugenotten in Niedersachsen*, p. 137.

79   Sergeant Juergen Geveron can also be counted even if he is not registered with Beuleke: Flick, 'Auf den Spuren': 11; Stadtarchiv Celle (hereafter StA), Sign. 5CH1, 'Einquartierungsrechnung de Anno 1669': Bl. 408.

80   Flick and Maehnert, *Archivbestände der Französisch-reformierten Gemeinden Lüneburg und Celle*, p. 14; Evangelisch-reformierte Gemeinde Celle, Kirche 1/2, 'Kirchenbuch der Französisch-reformierten Gemeinde in Lüneburg, 1689–1713'.

had come in 1665 to be fortress commandant of Lüneburg-Kalkberg, and the town commander Guillaume de Waller were also Protestants of the Reformed faith, as were, of course, the Huguenots, Louis de Malortie, Seigneur de Faverolles-Glatigny (appointed 1687) and Charles de La Motte-Chevallerie (appointed 1703).[81]

Contemporary reports survive in relation to some of the Huguenot officers who served the Duke of Celle. Amongst them were Amaury de Farcy de Saint-Laurent,[82] Jacques d'Amproux du Pontpiétin[83] and Jeremias Chauvet, who occupied the highest military office in the duchy as field marshal.[84] Chauvet was not of noble origin, but came from humble stock (his father is said to have been a craftsman). He was born around 1620 either in Pfalzburg (Lorraine) or in Bischweiler (Lower Alsace). His military career led him through the Portuguese service (under Friedrich Hermann von Schomberg) and that of the Palatinate until finally, in 1670, he came to Celle. Andrew Melvill reports in his memoires:

> At this time Chauvet, who was then without employment, came to Celle, where His Highness, knowing his merits, wished to retain him in his service. He consented only on condition that he should be made a Major-General, which request was granted, to the prejudice of all the other Colonels, who were greatly annoyed. They did not, however, leave the service, as they had at first threatened, if they were to be superseded by a new-comer. It must be admitted that in truth Chauvet merited the distinction; for it cannot be gainsaid that he possessed all the qualities which tend to make a great Captain.[85]

Chauvet, who proved his military gifts in subsequent campaigns, was promoted by Georg Wilhelm to the principal position of field marshal in 1685. He became president of the council of war and was thus the Duke's right-hand man in all military matters. A description of Chauvet at the Celle court is given by Gregorio Leti, who wrote:

> He is one of the most important men at this court ... In addition to his great experience in the art of war, his cleverness as a councillor of state and in all state matters, he is also very upright, very polite, very kind, especially to foreigners ... But whatever the true profession of this man might be, be it war or weapons, he is never weary of taking pleasure in attending to the organisation and protection of this court and to welcome it in his house.[86]

Chauvet, who left the Celle service after a disagreement for that of Saxony in 1693, returned the following year to his position as field marshal to Georg Wilhelm and president of the council of war. He died on 13 August 1699, aged over 80, and

---

81 Following the death of the Duke, two further Reformed town commanders were appointed: Jean de Casacau de Soubiron (1749) and Georg Ludwig de La Chevallerie (1763).

82 Poten, 'Die Generale der Königlich Hannoverschen Armee': 57.

83 Beuleke, *Die Hugenotten in Niedersachsen*, p. 114.

84 On Chauvet, see Poten, 'Die Generale der Königlich Hannoverschen Armee': 254 and A. Flick, 'General und Feldmarschall Jeremias Chauvet', *Celler Chronik*, 6 (Beiträge zur Geschichte und Geographie der Stadt und des Landkreises Celle, Celle, 1994): 31–45.

85 Ibid.: 33.

86 Flick, 'Gregorio Leti': 80.

was immediately buried under an arch of the Lutheran town church in Celle to the right of the Luther Hall with a triple peal of bells. According to Calvinist custom no funeral oration was delivered.

The Huguenot soldiers in Georg Wilhelm's army had fought in the most diverse European theatres of war, for example some served under Venetian direction against the Turks at the great siege of Candia (Heraklion) on Crete in 1668.[87] Others had experience of the Franco-Dutch war of 1672–8, fighting on the sides of Holland and Brandenburg, against France and Sweden; then in 1683 and 1692–3 again against the Turks, this time in Hungary. They also fought in the Palatinate (1688–97), as well as in the war of the Spanish succession (1701–14), in which Celle troops on the side of the Emperor fought against France.

A number of Huguenot soldiers were killed while serving Brunswick-Lüneburg. Included among them was the youngest half-brother of Eléonore Desmier d'Olbreuse, Jean Desmier, who fought on Crete in 1668, in the defence of Candia and met his death there.[88] Colonel Henri du Faur de Pibrac, who had commanded Celle forces, fell in 1692 at the battle of Steinkirk (in Flanders) and Jean Basquin de Marin, from Pfalzburg in Lorraine, died in combat in Celle service at the Speyerbach, on 15 November 1703. The same is true of both the brothers Louis and Benjamin de Malortie.

IV

'The court at Celle is very magnificent, and, it is said, very merry and conducted not at all in a forced manner', wrote Samuel Chappuzeau in praise of Celle in the year 1674.[89] Less flattering was the judgement of Constantijn Huygens, who described Celle court life – despite the presence of the Huguenots, whose puritanical mores were well known – as an unrestrained place where enthusiasm for pleasure seeking was widespread.[90] The quote which begins this chapter shows the straightforward criticism levelled at the pro-Huguenot court by those close to it; an attitude understandable from the German perspective in relation to the dominance of French court officials and military officers. Naturally the numerous immigrants, of which there were representatives of other countries, contributed in large measure to the

---

87   See F. von der Decken, *Feldzüge Herzog Georg Wilhelms von Celle* (Hanover, 1838).

88   Beuleke, *Die Hugenotten in Niedersachsen*, p. 106; Beauclaire, *Une mésalliance dans la maison de Brunswick*, p. 42; L. H. F. von Sichart, *Geschichte der Königlich-Hannoverschen Armee* (5 vols, Hanover, 1866–71), vol. 1, pp. 339–576.

89   S. Chappuzeau, 'Jetztlebenden Europae Dritter Theil: Begreiffend Die Beschreibung einer Raise in Teutschland in den Monaten April, May, Junio, Julio und Augusto des Jahres 1669 ... Frankfurt am Mayn 1685', published in S. Chappuzeau, *L'Europe viuante, ou Relation nouuelle, historique et politique de tous ses estats, selon la face qu'ils ont sur la fin de l'année M.DC.LXVI, etc.* (Geneva, 1666/7), p. 296.

90   Tollin, 'Geschichte der hugenottischen Gemeinde von Celle', p. 10.

cultural diversity of the Celle court during the baroque period.[91] Undoubtedly the French facilitated the transformation of the Celle court from a German to a French-style court ethos, modelled on Versailles in every respect. So the court assisted Georg Wilhelm in becoming an important mediator of French culture in north-west Germany, just as the army gave him a strong military presence there. In the Lutheran duchy of Brunswick-Lüneburg he was also the instigator of a degree of religious tolerance, so that in Celle Reformed and Catholic Christians and Jews were tolerated and could celebrate their religious services.

But the baroque splendour of Georg Wilhelm's court died with him in 1705, when Celle's role as a court residence had to be relinquished to Hanover. When the Celle troops were combined with those of Hanover, only one French officer remained, Major-General Louis de Saint-Pôl des Estangs.[92] At this time, Celle still possessed seven senior Huguenot officers, beside the two commanders of the ducal body guard and the dragoons.[93] After the Duke's death, Eléonore d'Olbreuse withdrew to the palace at Lüneburg, where she remained as a dowager until 1717, when she returned to Celle. This she did in order to be nearer her daughter, Sophie Dorothea, following the Königsmarck affair which saw her banished to Ahlden castle.[94] Eléonore died on 5 February 1722 in Celle; she was 83 years old.[95] In accordance with her last will she was buried without a funeral oration, in accordance with Huguenot practice. During the mourning ceremonies that followed, the Reformed officers were recognisable by the fact that they had bound black mourning crape about their bodies.[96] In the years that followed, the noble, courtly character of the Celle Huguenot colony remained strong, well into the eighteenth century, during which time (ever smaller) numbers of the French Reformed church community retained their independence up to the year 1805. After that year it, together with the local German Reformed church, joined the Evangelical Reformed church of Celle.

---

91 In addition, the ducal chamber servant Giorgio Casarotti; the horticulture master Gaspario Ferri; the Italian chamber secretary Giuseppe Pignata; Giovanni Francesco bailiff Stechinelli; Colonel von Bucco; the Italian master bricklayer Jovanni Sale; and the painter Giovanni Bastista Tornielli; all these count alongside the family Guizetti and the Italian comedy players already mentioned: NHStAH, Celle 44/935: Hauptregister der Ausgaben für den Celler Hofstaat, 1685–1705.

92 Beuleke, *Die Hugenotten in Niedersachsen*, p. 138.

93 NHStAH, Cal. 22/71, 'Liste der vornehmsten Offiziere, 1705'. Although some Huguenot descendants do appear on the Hanoverian army lists in the eighteenth and nineteenth century: see 'Woher erhielt unser vaterländisches Militär am Ende des 17ten und zu Anfang des 18ten Jahrhunderts die vielen Officiere von französischer Abkunft? und wo sind wohl deren Nachkommen geblieben?', *Hannoversches Magazin*, 38 (13 May 1818): 594–600.

94 See Schnath, *Geschichte Hannovers*.

95 See Flick, Hack and Maehnert, *Hugenotten in Celle*.

96 NHStAH Dep. 84B/600, fol. 123.

Chapter 13

Huguenots in the Army of Savoy-Piedmont
Protestant Soldiers and Civilians in the Savoyard State in the Seventeenth and Eighteenth Century[1]

Paola Bianchi
University of Aosta, Italy

From the seventeenth to the eighteenth century Catholic and Protestant states shared a common course of action by deciding to enrol professional soldiers and officers who were recruited from a wide international market. After the Thirty Years' War, bodies of itinerant mercenaries survived but became increasingly specialised. In part this reflects and emphasises the consolidation of migration routes used by soldiers across Europe.[2] Among those who played an important role in this typical form of military service in the early modern period, as illustrated by the studies referred to in this chapter, were Huguenots affected by the revocation of the Edict of Nantes. This chapter explores the movements of some of them as they travelled to one of France's neighbours, Savoy-Piedmont, which, from the late seventeenth century onwards, had become increasingly independent of the earlier political influence exerted by its powerful neighbour.[3] The study also explains how the presence of Huguenot soldiers, and Protestants in general, fits into a Savoyard social fabric that also welcomed other categories of Protestant groups employed in lay professions.

I

In order to understand this phenomenon, it is important to go back to the sixteenth century when the territories of Savoy-Piedmont became a target for migratory waves

---

1   Translated by Lucinda Byatt.

2   It is difficult to provide a concise bibliography on this subject which has produced a number of studies. For a synthesis that is historiographically up to date, see J. Black, *European Warfare, 1660–1815* (London, 1994) and *European Warfare, 1494–1660* (London, 2002).

3   G. Symcox, *Victor Amadeus II: Absolutism in the Savoyard state (1675–1730)* (London: Thames and Hudson, 1983); C. Storrs, *War, Diplomacy and the Rise of Savoy, 1690–1720* (Cambridge, 1999).

of Protestants from France and Geneva. This led to the birth of the Waldensian enclave, which has survived to the present day, in a mountainous area that follows the curve of the Alps and comprises the Chisone, Pellice and Germanasca valleys.[4]

The Waldensians, namely the remnants of the medieval sect who had survived continuing condemnation and persecution, had already settled in Piedmontese territory by the time of the French occupation of Piedmont (1536–59). Therefore, when Emanuele Filiberto regained possession of Savoy-Piedmont in 1559, the Waldensian presence already represented a political problem. There are no specific studies on this aspect, but traces exist of the degree to which Lutheran and Calvinist doctrines had penetrated the Savoy aristocracy and even the court of Turin itself through the influence of its Duchess, the French Princess, Marguerite de Valois.[5] As for south-western Piedmont, in the areas around Cuneo and Pinerolo, various branches of the Reformed movement had joined the Cathar-Waldensian settlements. Cuneo, a city close to France and the marquisate of Saluzzo (which had been affected by the spread of Protestant ideas before it was annexed to the Savoy-Piedmontese territories), offered fertile grounds for contact with Protestants.[6] Trade with Provence and Switzerland, and the frequent transit of armies comprising considerable numbers of Lutheran and Calvinist French soldiers had fostered these exchanges, perhaps more so than in other areas of Piedmont. Maximilien-Henri, Marquis de Saint-Simon, was not inventing anything when, in his *Histoire de la guerre des Alpes* (History of the War of the Alps: a late eighteenth-century work that described the military campaigns of the War of the Austrian Succession, and focused in particular on the siege of Cuneo in 1744), he used the city's sixteenth-century history to underline the tenacity of a small, but hardened group of Huguenot settlers. According to Saint-Simon, when Emanuele Filiberto made his first ducal entrance into Cuneo in 1561 all the subjects came to pay homage to him, except for those from the Angrogna and Luserna valleys, whose disobedience was incited by Huguenots who had arrived from France. Between 1575 and 1576 the Duke was again welcomed to the city with his son, Carlo Emanuele, and again – as Saint-Simon observed – the Huguenots who had settled in the surrounding valleys caused trouble.[7]

---

4   On the history of the Waldensian community in Piedmont, see essays published in A. de Lange (ed.), *Dall'Europa alle valli valdesi. Atti del convegno 'Il Glorioso Rimpatrio 1689–1989'* (Turin, 1990); G. P. Romagnani (ed.), *La Bibbia, la coccarda e il tricolore. I valdesi fra due Emancipazioni 1798–1848* (Turin, 2001).

5   P. Merlin, *Emanuele Filiberto. Un principe tra il Piemonte e l'Europa* (Turin: SEI, 1995), pp. 238–67.

6   Having been occupied since 1588, the marquisate of Saluzzo was annexed to Piedmont in 1601: see M. Fratini (ed.), *L'annessione sabauda del Marchesato di Saluzzo. Tra dissidenza religiosa e ortodossia cattolica. Secoli XVI–XVIII* (Turin, 2004).

7   H. de Saint-Simon, *Histoire de la guerre des Alpes* (Amsterdam, 1770), pp. 214–15. The author was *aide-de-camp* to Louis-François de Bourbon, Prince de Conti (1717–76), the French commander who, together with the Spaniard Jayme Miguel de Gusman, Marquis de La Mina (1689–1767), led the French and Spanish army against the Savoy troops in the campaign of 1744. On the spread of the Reformation in Cuneo, see P. Bianchi and A. Merlotti, *Cuneo in età moderna. Città e Stato nel Piemonte di antico regime* (Milan, 2002), pp. 79–103.

In response to strong pressure exerted by the allies, first Spanish and then French, and in order to avoid upsetting the equilibrium created by the climate of the Counter-Reformation in the various Italian states, Emanuele Filiberto (1553–80) and his successor, Carlo Emanuele I (1580–1630), finally undertook proper military campaigns to repress the heterodox minorities residing inside the duchy and along the border with France.[8] By the late sixteenth and early seventeenth centuries, these campaigns had alternated with phases of temporary compromise during which the Waldensians were granted the right to worship, to build schools and to convene synods on the condition that they abstained from proselytising to the Catholic population.

The real political turning point, at both a domestic and international level, was not reached before the reign of Vittorio Amedeo II as duke (1684–1713) and subsequently king (1713–30). France's growing interference in the affairs of Savoy-Piedmont had become a form of protection that was overly oppressive and, after the revocation of the Edict of Nantes, Vittorio Amedeo felt that he could not simply obey. In 1685 Louis XIV had ordered the Piedmontese ruler to crush the Waldensian community, but although at first he was unable to oppose this request, Vittorio Amedeo II soon turned the presence of the Waldensian minority to his advantage by entering an alliance with the United Provinces and Britain.[9]

Between the summer and autumn of 1685, a considerable number of Huguenots chose to travel from France to Geneva, passing through Piedmont and staying in houses in those Piedmontese valleys that had for years welcomed the Waldensians. A community of Huguenots, whose livelihood depended not on arms but on trade, settled around Nice where, in spite of the ban of 1685, they succeeded in surviving underground, thanks above all to contacts with England. The then Governor of Nice, Don Antonio di Savoia (1620–88), one of Duke Carlo Emanuele I's illegitimate sons, was given the task of ordering a house-to-house search but was eventually forced to give his tacit consent to the undisturbed continuation of the valuable economic activities in the area around the port. In October 1685 Don Antonio wrote to Vittorio Amedeo that every day fugitives arrived from France who were heading for Piedmont, many of whom were determined to reach Germany (*alamagna*).[10]

---

8   P. Bianchi, 'La riorganizzazione militare del Ducato di Savoia e i rapporti del Piemonte con la Francia e la Spagna. Da Emanuele Filiberto a Carlo Emanuele II', in Enrique García Hernán and Davide Maffi (eds), *Guerra y Sociedad en la Monarquía Hispánica. Política, Estrategia y Cultura en la Europa Moderna (1500–1700). Congreso internacional de historia militar, Madrid 9–12.III.2005* (Madrid, 2006), pp. 189–216.

9   On these aspects, see the studies published in de Lange (ed.), *Dall'Europa alle valli valdesi*, in particular G. Symcox, 'The Waldensians in the Absolutist State of Victor Amadeus II' (pp. 237–50) and R. Oresko, 'The Diplomatic Background to the Glorioso Rimpatrio: The Rupture Between Victor Amadeus II and Louis XIV (1688–1690)' (pp. 251–78).

10   On Don Antonio and on the situation in Nice, see P. Bianchi, 'Principi, militari, cortigiani: gli illegittimi dei Savoia fra esercito, diplomazia e cariche curiali', in P. Bianchi and L. C. Gentile (eds), *L'affermarsi della corte sabauda. Dinastie, poteri, élites in Piemonte e Savoia fra tardo medioevo e prima età moderna* (Turin, 2006), pp. 305–60.

In January 1686, pandering to Louis XIV's continued demands, Vittorio Amedeo revoked the previous measures of tolerance granted to the Waldensians; but, from 1687 onwards, his policy started to assume tones that were more and more clearly anti-French.[11] At the end of August 1689, a band of nearly 1,000 Huguenots and Waldensians, who had left Piedmont under the guidance of the pastor Henri Arnaud, set out from Geneva in a march that became known in Protestant tradition as the *glorieuse rentrée*. The return of this group of Protestants to Piedmont was in fact encouraged by the Duke of Savoy himself, who used the event to rupture the alliance with France. The sovereign had not only started secret negotiations with the Waldensians but had already entered into a military alliance with the Swiss cantons, well aware that William III was closely watching the affairs of the Piedmontese community. All this helped to prompt the Duke of Savoy in 1690 to intervene in the Nine Years' War (1688–1697), with the aim of freeing Piedmont from French hegemony, but also with a view to gaining favour with the Protestant powers. Therefore, in 1694 he granted limited freedom of worship to the Waldensians, marking a return to the situation prior to 1686. By doing so, he opened the way to a partial absorption of Waldensian soldiers in the Savoy-Piedmont army fighting against the French, and also for the settlement in Turin of a new group of Protestants.[12]

The operations against the French army under Marshal Catinat exploited the widespread popular dislike of the invaders. Alongside a regiment of volunteers recruited in Mondovì (a city that, until 1690, had opposed ducal rule and had witnessed open anti-Savoy uprisings), the Waldensians were initially organised into an irregular battalion and later enrolled into two standing regiments together with other Protestants and predominantly French refugees from Switzerland.[13]

The role of the *religionari* (an expression used to describe Protestants in general, but which often referred to French Calvinists alone), most of whom were paid directly by the States General of the United Provinces or by the English crown, was again exploited by Vittorio Amedeo II during the war of the Spanish Succession (1702–13). At the end of the war, Savoy policy again oscillated between the temptation to react and the adoption of greater caution, but any sign of renewed repression of the Protestant minorities was met with complaints and pressure from Britain. In this context, the actions of the English representative in Turin, John Molesworth, finally led to a decree being passed in 1730 in which it was established that Piedmontese Waldensians could worship freely (including giving sermons and holding meetings

11   I. Soffietti, 'La legislazione sabauda sui valdesi dal 1685 al 1730', in de Lange (ed.), *Dall'Europa alle valli valdesi*, pp. 279–92.

12   P. Bianchi, 'Militari, banchieri, studenti. Presenze protestanti nella Torino del Settecento', in P. Cozzo, F. De Pieri and A. Merlotti (eds), *Valdesi e protestanti a Torino. XVIII–XX secolo* (Turin, 2005), pp. 39–63.

13   On the various aspects of the late seventeenth-century revolts in Savoy territories and on the development of the political conditions that led to the anti-French choice made by Vittorio Amedeo II during the Nine Years' War, see the useful studies in G. Lombardi (ed.), *La guerra del sale (1680–1699). Rivolte e frontiere del Piemonte barocco* (3 vols, Milan, 1986). Among the various studies, it is worth mentioning that by G. Symcox, 'Two Forms of Popular Resistance in the Savoyard State of the 1680s: The Rebels of Mondovì and the Vaudois' (vol. 1, pp. 275–90).

of pastors) solely in the Pellice and Chisone valleys; diplomatic pressure was also applied in the 1690s during the Nine Years' War by English and Dutch ambassadors. They were entitled to trade and attend fairs outside these boundaries provided that they did not move there and did not use the occasion to spread the Reformed faith; could work on Catholic feast days, but only in their own homes; were obliged to negotiate with foreigners through the sovereign; and were able to set up schools and publish books on religious subjects in their respective residential centres provided they avoided mixing with or involving Catholics.

Map 1 The Savoyard State in 1713, after the Peace of Utrecht

The outbreak of the war of the Polish Succession (1733–8) a few years later again saw the involvement of various groups of Waldensians from Piedmont, on this occasion not fighting to defend their own lands but rather as allies of the French troops occupying the Imperial possessions of Lombardy and Emilia. The Waldensians were also engaged, both as irregular companies and standing troops, in the last war that Piedmont fought during the first half of the century, the war of the Austrian Succession (1740–8), again as part of the alliance against the French.[14]

The decision to make 'heretics' and Catholics fight side-by-side caused a variety of confessional reactions. The Waldensians for their part continued to boast of their invincible tradition as militiamen; this was countered by the growing loyalty of the Piedmontese *La Regina* (Queen's) infantry regiment established in 1734 and described as a compact regiment made up of Waldensians alone. In fact, the troops of the regiment did not include Waldensian soldiers solely, but also Catholic militia. The percentage of *religionari*, in this as in other regiments serving Savoy, changed considerably from year to year. In other words, these were military units whose religious physiognomy was far from homogeneous, being instead conditioned by contingent factors such as intermittent recruiting. The Rietman, Guibert, Ghidt, du Pasquier, Roquin, Thonatz, Rehbinder, Schulenburg and de Portes infantry regiments, named after the men who commanded them, welcomed both Lutherans and Huguenots.[15] De Portes, in particular, raised and commanded a regiment officered and manned by French refugees in Savoy service.

---

14   On the difference between the commissioned army (made up of career soldiers), ancient bodies of militia (introduced into the Savoy troops in the late sixteenth century) and provincial regiments (units that were recruited only occasionally, and were introduced from 1713–14), see P. Bianchi, *Onore e mestiere. Le riforme militari nel Piemonte del Settecento* (Turin, 2002).

15   Johan Rietman commanded the Swiss Kalbermatten infantry regiment from 21 December 1731 to 1744. The Swiss Guibert Regiment of Infantry ('the fighting regiment'), was commanded by Alexander Guibert de Saissac from 10 November 1733 to 1746. Franz Frederick Ghidt commanded a Swiss infantry regiment from 24 November 1733 till it was disbanded in 1737. Jacques du Pasquier commanded a Swiss infantry regiment from 24 November 1733 to 1737, when it was disbanded. Albert Louis Roquin de Suerdon commanded a Swiss infantry regiment from 14 November 1733 to 1737; thereafter, its command passed to Jean Rodolfe von Diesbach (from 17 May 1737) thence to Augustine Roquin (from 10 April 1744). Conrad Thonatz commanded this Swiss infantry regiment from 15 March 1734 to 1737. Karl Frederick, Baron von Bourgsdorff commanded a German infantry regiment from 20 December 1723; thereafter, its command passed to Frederick Wilhelm, Baron von Leutrum (from 10 January 1749), then Karl Heinrich von Wangenheim (from 12 July 1755), and Ludwig Anton, Baron von Brempt (from 10 December 1763). Commanders of the German Schulenburg (Schoulembourg) or *royal allemand* infantry regiment, 1695–1798 include Christopher Daniel Birkoltz, Baron von der Schulenburg (from 3 June 1729), Heinrich Hasswich Falchemberg, Baron von der Schulenburg (from 23 March 1754), Hernst Frederick von Leuthen (from 7 July 1757) and Daniel Gotfried Zietten (from 17 December 1763). Existing from 1703, the de Portes regiment of foreign infantry was commanded by Louis de Portes from 4 November 1703 to 1739. Thereafter, its command passed to Pierre Audibert (from 10 March 1739), then Jean du Monfort de Varache (from 6 April 1746) and Eugene Alexandre de Sury (from 16 November 1769).

Some of the oldest Savoyard regiments were associated with Huguenots. The Savoy Regiment was first raised in 1624 as the *régiment de Fleury* with a strength of 1,500 men in 15 companies, all French with some Protestants among them. In 1640 it became the *régiment français de S.A.R.* (French regiment of His Royal Highness) only changing its name in 1664 to become the *régiment de Savoye de S.A.R.* It ranked second in order of seniority and by century's end the officer *corps* was resolutely Savoyard and Piedmontese with its commanders drawn from the high aristocracy.[16] The Savoyard *régiment de la marine* was commanded by a possible Huguenot from 1728 to 1734 – Colonel Jacob d'Alerthon (commissioned 25 April 1728). Other units commanded by men with French-sounding names were actually loyal, and ultra-Catholic, Savoyards: for example, between 1739 and 1742, Paul Seyssel, Baron de La Serre (commissioned 14 April 1739), commanded the *régiment d'Aoste*. Some other colonels may well have had refugee origins, including Jean Augustin Gouett, who commanded the *régiment de Nice* from 16 April 1739. Similarly, Jean Jacques du Pacquier (or Paquier), was colonel of a Savoy regiment bearing his name in 1733, having previously served Spain. He and three brothers reached the rank of lieutenant-general, major and captain in Savoyard service, but his regiment was dissolved by Carlo Emanuele III in 1739 and it remains unclear whether the family's origins lay in the French Protestant diaspora.[17]

Three commanders of Savoyard regiments were undoubtedly of Huguenot origin. The most prominent of them was Louis de Portes, who became a general of Infantry and Governor of Alessandria. His family, originally from Dauphiné, migrated to Lausanne, Switzerland, due to their Protestant faith and Louis de Portes entered Savoyard service as a cadet in the corps of *gentilshommes*, then commanded a regiment in 1690. In 1699 he became a naturalised Swiss citizen in the canton of Bern, and in 1703 raised a regiment composed of French *rifugiati* or refugees in the service of Savoy. He was successively a major-general (1709), lieutenant-general (1717), and general (1720), before being raised to the title of Count of Verriè in Savoy. He did not convert to Catholicism and retired to Geneva where he later died.[18] Two Huguenots of slightly lesser standing include Jean Pierre Audibert, a lieutenant-general in Savoy and *bourgeois de Vevai* in France by origin. After the revocation of the Edict of Nantes he was naturalised in the canton of Béarn, having come from Languedoc and been a refugee by cause of his religion.[19] Alexandre Guibert de Seissac was born in Guienne where he was eventually proscribed due to his religion at the time of the revocation. He abandoned his homeland in favour of Switzerland. Afterwards he joined the Savoyard army and commanded the ostensibly

---

16   The names of Seyssel, Chabod de Saint-Maurice, Clermont, Della Chiesa and du Verger all belong to Savoyard or Piedmontese families, from the high aristocracy. They were not French, but faithful subjects of the Savoyard dynasty.

17   F. Girard, *Histoire abrégée des officiers suisses qui se sont distingués aux services étrangers dans des grades superieurs* (3 vols, Fribourg, 1781–2), vol. 2, pp. 189, 289.

18   Ibid., vol. 2, pp. 227–9.

19   Ibid., vol. 1, pp. 47–8.

Swiss infantry regiment, called 'the fighting regiment', that bore his name from 10 November 1733 to 1746.[20]

II

During the seventeenth and eighteenth centuries the recruitment of foreign officers was used by the rulers of Savoy-Piedmont not only as a means of guaranteeing professional leadership for the troops but also to reduce the claims made by the old local military aristocracy. The role played by a number of figures from German-speaking areas – who were generically known as *alemanni* or Germans – was particularly important in this sense. The preferential treatment received by Swiss troops over the past two hundred years or so had been gradually eroded by soldiers recruited from German and northern European states. Some names have become linked not only to the military history of the Savoy-Piedmont domains but also to that of other European countries. Their international, scope and itinerant professionalism marks them as representative figures akin to Huguenot soldiers who were often of lesser standing in Savoy.

A case in point, for example, is that of the Schulenburg family, descendants of one of the many branches of a dynasty originating in Brandenburg who, from the late fifteenth century onwards, sent officers to the German, Italian and English courts.[21] The Schulenburg distinguished themselves in Piedmont during the first half of the eighteenth century. Johann Matthias was a brigadier in the Savoy army from 1698 to 1711; during the same period he was also appointed lieutenant-general (in 1702) of Augustus II of Poland's troops, and then moved to the Republic of Venice in 1715. His brother, Daniel Bodo, and nephew, Ludwig Ferdinand, then followed him to Italy: the former joined the Venetian troops and was eventually recruited into the Polish army; the latter was engaged by the Emperor to fight in Lombardy in 1735 and in the 1747 expedition against Genoa.[22] In 1723 another Schulenburg, Karl, moved to Piedmont. These were third and fourth cousins of Levin Friedrich, who died in Turin in 1729 at the age of 58, having been appointed marshal, general of artillery and Governor of Alba, as well as being sent on delicate missions to Hanover and Genoa on behalf of Vittorio Amedeo II. His brother, Friedrich August, nephew, Christoph Daniel, and the latter's son, Heinrich Hartung, also joined the Savoy army.

Bernhard Otto, Baron von Rehbinder, had a much more influential role, and he succeeded in maintaining his position until the start of Carlo Emanuele III's reign.[23] Born in 1662 in Revel, now the city of Tallinn, which was under Swedish rule at the time, Rehbinder came from a Lutheran family of noble stock, originally from the

---

20   Ibid., pp. 320–22.

21   On the genealogy of the Schulenburg family, see J. H. Zedler, *Grosses Vollständiges universal Lexikon aller Wissenschaften und Künste* (64 vols, Leipzig, Halle, 1732–54; reprinted Graz, 1961–4), vol. 35, col. 1501–35. On their presence in Piedmont, see Bianchi, *Onore e mestiere*, p. 102.

22   F. Venturi, *Settecento riformatore. 1 Da Muratori a Beccaria. 1730–1764* (Turin, 1969), pp. 246–7.

23   Bianchi, *Onore e mestiere, passim.*

Grand Duchy of Livonia. His father, Otto, was a privy councillor: an excellent visiting card for the young officer who, having enrolled in the *royal allemand* regiment in the pay of the Elector Palatine, then came to Piedmont with the allied troops of the Emperor, the Prussians and a number of German principalities. In 1707 Rehbinder was already on the payroll of the Duke of Savoy as Governor of Biella, in charge of recruiting a regiment of German infantry. Between 1713 and 1730 the Baltic officer rose rapidly through the military ranks, from infantry commander to brigadier, and from Governor of Pinerolo to field marshal. Having abjured his Lutheran faith and converted to Roman Catholicism, probably under pressure from his wife, Maria O'More, a noblewoman of Irish origin whose ancestors included several generations of turbulent Catholic rebels, in 1713 Rehbinder was made a member of the *ordine dell'Annunziata* (Supreme Order of the Most Holy Annunciation), a Savoy order of knighthood, and in 1718 became a naturalised subject of Savoy.

Once the Rehbinder family had come to court and had forged links with a number of families belonging to the Piedmontese landed nobility, they lived in a palace in the heart of Turin. It had been used in 1695 by Karl Philipp von Hohenzollern, brother of Friedrich III, Elector of Brandenburg, the commander of the *alemanni* battalions who fought alongside the Piedmontese during the Nine Years' War. By 1739 Rehbinder had been widowed and, although getting on in years, he married the noblewoman, Cristina Margherita Piossasco, who was then 16 years old. However, suspicion and jealousy of the foreign officer increased during the reign of Carlo Emanuele III (1730–73). At the outbreak of the War of the Polish Succession, Rehbinder was again placed at the head of the Piedmontese infantry, but the French allies, through Cardinal Fleury in Paris, turned down the suggestion that he should be appointed in charge of the joint French and Piedmontese armies. Rehbinder's isolation grew during the last years of his life and his presence was restricted mainly to court ceremonies. The general died in Turin in November 1742 and was buried in the church of Santo Spirito. He was outlived by the regiment that was named after him, the Rehbinder regiment, made up of soldiers of Roman Catholic and Lutheran faith, which initially passed to the command of his stepson, Karl Friedrich Burgsdorf, and then to another Protestant officer well known to Piedmontese military historians, Friedrich Wilhelm von Leutrum.[24]

Born in Karlhausen, Baden, in 1692, son of Baron Friedrich, a member of the Württemberg court, Friedrich Wilhelm von Leutrum only partly followed in Rehbinder's wake. He came to Piedmont as a boy, in 1706, in the retinue of Prince Eugène, together with his elder brother, Karl Magnus, who soon left to serve the rulers of Sweden and Austria. Of Karl Magnus' sons, it is known with certainty that Karl Alexander also fought in Piedmont, where he was killed at the battle of Madonna dell'Olmo (1744), as did his brother Karl August Emanuel. Having fought for Austria against the Prussians in the Seven Years' War (1756–63), Karl August Emanuel enrolled in the service of the King of Sardinia in 1764; he was made a count by Vittorio Amedeo III in 1781 and married a German noblewoman in Württemberg, who later gave birth to a son, Karl Emanuel, in Alessandria.

---

24   See P. Bianchi, *'Baron Litron' e gli altri. Militari stranieri nel Piemonte del Settecento*, preface by P. Del Negro (Turin, 1998).

Unlike the Rehbinders, the Leutrums preserved strong links with their native land and did not intermarry with the Piedmontese nobility. In this their experience of Savoy service echoes that of the Huguenots a generation before. The contribution made by Friedrich Wilhelm, who spent his entire career in the service of Savoy, working his way up to the rank of infantry commander and Governor of Cuneo, has entered the collective imagination, together with the memory of his professionalism, his sense of duty and, also, his discretion. His role in freeing the city of Cuneo from the Franco-Spanish siege of 1744 inspired a series of novels and even well-known popular songs. As a Lutheran who refused to convert to Roman Catholicism, Friedrich Wilhelm von Leutrum asked to be buried in a small Protestant church in Val Luserna (one of the Waldensian valleys); he also renounced the possibility of being invested with the Order of the Annunciation, as Rehbinder had been. He died in 1755, leaving his nephew, Karl August Emanuel, in Piedmont; the latter became the last great career army officer given to the court of Turin by this family, and he re-established contacts with Württemberg whence derived his roots.

The cases of the Schulenburg, Rehbinder and Leutrum families, although not identical, stemmed from a common background of international exchanges and military service to highlight a few noteworthy examples, which, however, must be seen against the dense network of military relationships spread throughout Savoy-Piedmont. In order to illustrate more clearly the phenomenon of this mix of foreign and native soldiers, troops and civil population, Protestant and Catholic, it is useful to turn briefly to a more limited geographical area, but one that was at the heart of the Piedmontese strategic system: the urban area of Turin.

III

By signing a separate peace in 1696 with Louis XIV, Vittorio Amedeo II undertook to expel the Huguenots in order to prevent the spread of the Reformation. The pastors and most of the Protestants who had settled in Turin subsequently left Piedmont and moved to Switzerland or to German principalities that had embraced the Reformation. But, as was explained earlier, a Protestant minority remained. The risk of friction between the Duke and Rome was constantly looming.[25] In 1692, for example, a brief from Pope Innocent XII had expressed the Church's disapproval of Vittorio Amedeo II's decision to allow 40 Huguenot families to settle in Turin.[26] In 1721 a similar document, signed by Pope Clement XI, denounced the fact that Protestant soldiers based in Turin and Alessandria enjoyed the right to worship according to their own faith; the Pope exhorted the Duke's mother, Giovanna Battista di Savoia-Nemours, to intercede by convincing her son to ban such 'heretical' practices that were pernicious for Catholics. But Vittorio Amedeo II defended his position by stating that troops in the de Portes regiment (one of the two bodies of foreign Protestants, together with

---

25   G. P. Romagnani, 'Presenze protestanti a Torino tra Sei e Settecento', in G. Ricuperati (ed.), *Dalla città razionale alla crisi dello Stato d'Antico Regime (1730–1798)*, *Storia di Torino* 5 (Turin, 2002), pp. 423–51.

26   Archivio di Stato di Torino (hereafter AST), Corte, Materie ecclesiastiche, Eretici, m. 1 non inv, 11 November 1692.

the Schulenburg regiment, then employed by the Savoy rulers) had always been carefully monitored and ordered to celebrate Reformed religious rites 'in secret'.[27] Tension on this subject continued, to a varying degree, throughout the century, but was regulated by an endless series of compromise situations.

The Protestant presence in Turin can only be quantified with reasonable certainty after 1724, the year when the sovereign decided to impose an annual census on the urban population who were divided into groups according to religious persuasion. Later censuses have only survived up to the middle of the eighteenth century, given that after 1752 a description was no longer included of the separate confessional groups. Therefore, it is impossible today to assess whether the community increased or shrank over the course of the entire century.[28] In 1725 a royal decree attempted to curb the number of *religionari* residing in the capital, many of whom had lived there for several years. The sovereign ordered the *vicario di polizia* to take steps to reduce the phenomenon of permanent residence. Protestants were given the chance to stay in inns and to exercise business activities with other traders, provided that they did not manage them in person. However, once again, these provisions were widely disregarded both by the authorities and by the Protestants themselves, who did not hesitate to rent business premises and turn them into houses if the occasion arose.[29]

Interesting data can be extracted from the surveys, bearing in mind, however, that some categories, such as military officers and diplomats, were not included. In 1726, for example, out of a total population of 63,819 inhabitants, there were 144 Protestants and 1,056 Jews in Turin. At the time of the severe economic crisis of the 1730s, the number of Protestants fell, ranging between a minimum of 45 and a maximum of 86 persons up until 1751. The population started to rise again during the 1750s and this was accompanied, proportionally, by an increased number of Protestants, climbing to between 150 and 200 in all. The peak was reached in 1769–71, when a total of 216 of them were recorded. Numbers fell again during the closing decades of the century, when the number of Protestants shrank to 70 or 80 individuals every year. Although fragmentary and broken, these figures offer information regarding the composition and location of the groups covered by the census. Between the 1720s and 1730s, the Protestants came from Geneva, Lyons, Nîmes and Languedoc. In 1752, among the Protestants the *vicario* counted 17 households from Geneva, 3 from Switzerland, 2 from Nîmes and 4 from Lucerna, giving a total of 135 individuals. Most were merchants, shopkeepers and bankers, but there were also professional figures, including lawyers, as well as domestic servants, labourers, grooms, tailors, wigmakers and watchmakers. The considerable number of so-called *ginevrini* (namely those from Geneva) dealers may have concealed the

27 Ibid., 16 January 1721.

28 Documents in AST, Corte, Provincia di Torino, Città di Torino, m. 5, n. 1, m. 2 addendum, n. 6, m. 5 d'add., n. 5, and m. 22, n. 6; Corte, Materie ecclesiastiche, Eretici, m. 1, n. 11, and m. 1 d'add. For census of 1725, 1726, 1728, 1729, 1731, 1733, 1735, 1740, 1744, 1752: Romagnani, 'Presenze protestanti a Torino', p. 428.

29 D. Balani, *Il vicario tra città e Stato. L'ordine pubblico e l'annona nella Torino del Settecento* (Turin, 1987); P. Bianchi, '"Politica e polizia" in una realtà d'antico regime: le sfide contro vecchi e nuovi disordini nello Stato sabaudo fra Sei e Settecento', *Bollettino storico bibliografico subalpino*, 103 (2005): 473–504.

presence of various French Huguenot exiles, originally from the Languedoc and Cévennes regions.

Among the families registered in Turin were the brothers Pierre and Paul Tallian (or Talhan), who arrived there in 1695; the brothers Pierre and Paul Torras, who were involved in major financial operations during the mid-century wars of succession; and the brothers, Mathieu and Jacques Nadal, who later became associated with Jean-Abraham Haldimann and Pierre Long d'Yverdon as promoters of the firm 'Haldimann, Long & Nadal', which was active in Turin until the 1770s. Other likely Huguenots include the brothers Perraud, the banker Giovanni André, the silk merchant and banker Giovanni Long, in association with the refugee Pietro Barde, the bankers Jean Giraudet and David Gadagnon, who operated in partnership, Giovanni Lobié, a banker and dealer of cloth and silk, the merchants Luigi and Giovanni Chiametton, and the gentlemen Sancton and Leukeus. Twenty years later the situation had not changed much. The earlier occupations had survived, but new individuals had also arrived: for example, the Leclercs, the Bouers, Jacques-Louis and Guillaume Aubert, members of a family with numerous branches originally from the Dauphiné and recorded as 'bourgeois citizens' from Geneva who were very active in Turin up until the 1780s.[30]

It is difficult to assess how old the Protestant presence in Turin was, even if it seems plausible to imagine that the city would have accepted groups of Protestants among the garrison troops in the capital or in diplomatic legations from the earliest settlements. Diplomatic relations between Savoy-Piedmont and the Protestant countries (Bern, Basel, Britain) dated back to the early sixteenth century. Relations were subsequently established during the course of the seventeenth century with Holland, Saxony and Prussia, and were strengthened during the eighteenth century. The question of contacts with Geneva and with the Swiss was more complex because ancient rivalries with the dukes prevented the signing of international agreements and the establishment of diplomatic representatives in Turin.[31] The study of the role played by chapels for private worship within the foreign embassies in the Piedmontese

---

30　Romagnani, 'Presenze protestanti a Torino', pp. 437–40.

31　See D. Carutti, *Storia della diplomazia della corte di Savoia (1494–1773)* (4 vols, Turin, 1875–80); A. Bazzoni, 'Relazioni diplomatiche tra la Casa di Savoia e la Prussia nel secolo XVIII', *Archivio storico italiano*, 15 (1872): 3–21, 193–209, 377–90; L. Bulferetti, *Le relazioni diplomatiche tra lo Stato sabaudo e la Prussia durante il regno di Vittorio Amedeo III* (Milan, 1941). For Anglo-Piedmontese relations, see F. Sclopis, 'Delle relazioni politiche tra la dinastia di Savoia e il governo britannico (1240–1815); Ricerche storiche', *Memorie della Regia Accademia delle Scienze di Torino* (1854): 261–2; C. Contessa, 'Aspirazioni commerciali intrecciate ad alleanze politiche della Casa di Savoia coll'Inghilterra nei secoli XVII e XVIII', *Memorie della Regia Accademia delle Scienze di Torino*, 64 (1913–14): 1–50; F. Venturi, 'Il Piemonte dei primi decenni del Settecento nelle relazioni dei diplomatici inglesi', *Bollettino storico bibliografico subalpino*, 54 (1956): 227–71; J. Black, 'The Development of Anglo-Sardinian Relations in the First Half of Eighteenth Century', *Studi piemontesi*, 12 (1983): 48–60; G. Pagano De Divitiis, 'Il Mediterraneo nel XVII secolo. L'espansione commerciale inglese e l'Italia', *Studi storici*, 27 (1986): 109–48. On the growth of diplomatic missions in the seventeenth and eighteenth century, see Storrs, *War, Diplomacy and the Rise of Savoy*, pp. 122–70.

capital might offer interesting information, but no overall reconstruction of the development of foreign delegations in Turin has yet been made. It is only known that throughout the eighteenth century the various ambassadors chose their own residences individually, given that they could not yet rely on institutional premises used by the embassies.

Turning to the military presence, the first foreigners to settle in Turin were about 70 Swiss (but Catholic) soldiers who were recruited to form the body known as the *guardia*, which survived until the early 1830s.[32] Duke Carlo Emanuele I (1580–1630) had used some Swiss troops on the battlefield, but also Germans, Frenchmen and soldiers from Lorraine, including a number of Huguenots.[33] Clear rifts between these early foreign units became evident during the years of civil war (1638–42) when the supporters of Duchess Christine (who had become regent after the death of Vittorio Amedeo I) fought against those who backed the Princes Tomaso and Maurizio (the brothers of the deceased Duke). During this period the Swiss who had settled in Piedmont, and formed a regiment of companies originating also from the Protestant cantons of Bern, Basel and Fribourg, were divided and some supported the Princes and others the regent: the soldiers from Bern and Basel supported Prince Tomaso's troops, while the company from Fribourg remained loyal to Christine of France.[34]

After this period of seventeenth-century crisis and civil war had passed, in traditional relations between Piedmont and its resident foreigners, embassy staff and soldiers continued to receive preferential treatment compared to the normal state policy. For example, the application of the law of *ubena* was suspended in their favour. This law gave rulers the prerogative of allocating to the treasury of the host country the property of a foreigner who died, excluding the possibility that any inheritance belonging to persons who had become naturalised Piedmontese subjects should leave the country, destined for spouses or fellow countrymen.[35] The essential role of these groups of foreigners prompted the introduction of a policy of tacit tolerance, at the risk of having to cope with the ever-present danger of cultural and religious contamination.

At a more formal level, the regulations drew a distinction between regiments that were wholly Protestant and mixed regiments: the former were exempt from

---

32   On their establishment beside the ducal palace, see W. Barberis, *Le armi del principe. La tradizione militare sabauda* (Turin, 1988), pp. 124–9.

33   Unfortunately their names and number remain a mystery. The primary sources, which are not easy to search in this period, have not yet been studied seriously by anyone. Other information comes from secondary sources: see N. Brancaccio, *L'esercito del vecchio Piemonte. Gli ordinamenti. Parte I: Dal 1560 al 1814* (Rome, 1923) and Girard, *Histoire abrégée des officiers suisses, passim*.

34   In the absence of more recent studies, see Brancaccio, *L'esercito del vecchio Piemonte*, pp. 42, 91–3, 147–50.

35   The law of *ubena* was suspended during the French occupation and while Piedmont was annexed to Napoleonic France, re-introduced after the Restoration and then lapsed at the end of the nineteenth century: see M. C. Scopi, 'Ricerche storico-giuridiche sul diritto d'ubena negli Stati sabaudi con particolare riguardo alla legislazione militare', graduation thesis (University of Turin, Faculty of Jurisprudence, 1997/8).

confessional obligations, such as kneeling when a procession went past or in front of a sacred image, whereas the mixed regiments had to show respect for the Roman Catholic religion while continuing to include minority groups from other faiths.[36] Faced with the inevitable mixing of different religions, complaints were not slow to emerge. In the early eighteenth century, for example, a Lutheran soldier from the Schulenburg regiment was condemned to death in Turin, and was assisted by a Protestant pastor; the case immediately provoked an angry reaction from the Archbishop who demanded that, in other similar cases, religious comfort should be denied in public because it might provide an occasion for preaching.[37] A number of Protestant officers continued to settle in Turin, sometimes accompanied by their families and households. In response to this widely accepted practice, the clergy tried to convince landlords not to accept Protestants or to report their conduct to the Inquisition.[38]

However, one episode shows how such excessive zeal on the part of the Catholic clergy against the Protestants was counterproductive for the political authorities. In the spring of 1758 the Jesuit priest Carlo Melano di Portula, having spent many years abroad, including a long period in Prussia, returned to Savoy-Piedmont where he became rector of the College in Chambéry, in Savoy. Between 1757 and 1758 the Jesuit had – without the sovereign's permission – printed 1,000 copies of a work of Roman Catholic precepts entitled *Heures et instruction chretiennes à l'usage des troupes de S.M. le Roy de Sardaigne* (Hours and Christian instruction for the use of the troops of His Royal Highness the King of Sardinia). The books were soon made available in Piedmont, where they were falsely attributed to a Turin-based publisher (*'chez les frères Reycend, Guibert et Silvestre, avec aprobation et permission'*: 'by the brothers Reycend, Guibert and Silvestre, with aprobation and permission'). When the first copies began to circulate, state officials were quick to intervene and ordered their sequestration. The Jesuit's teachings could have fomented malcontent among the numerous Protestant soldiers, leading to defections or forms of insubordination that could not be risked among professional troops, even in peace time.[39]

IV

Savoyard diplomacy … offers an excellent example of the constant interaction between war and diplomacy – between campaigning and negotiating what John Lynn identifies as a key component in the type of 'war process' which characterised contemporary warfare.[40]

These are the words of Christopher Storrs, writing with reference to the period 1690–1720. The same argument can in fact be applied to later decades when Savoy-

---

36   AST, Corte, Materie militari, Levata di truppe straniere, m. 1 non inventariato.

37   Ibid., m. 1, n. 7, undated report on this case.

38   Romagnani, 'Presenze protestanti a Torino', p. 445.

39   The episode is described in A. Merlotti, *Il silenzio e il servizio. Le Epoche principali delle vita di Vincenzo Sebastiano Beraudo di Pralormo* (Turin, 2003), pp. 62–3.

40   Storrs, *War, Diplomacy and the Rise of Savoy*, p. 124.

Piedmont was involved in two wars (the war of the Polish Succession and that of the Austrian Succession), before experiencing a relatively long period of peace prior to the clash with revolutionary France (1748–92). During this period foreign soldiers were subject to a policy of demobilisation that resulted in their numbers virtually being halved, falling to about 6,000 men throughout Savoy-Piedmont; the overall number of so-called national troops shrank from 40–50,000 to about 30,000 soldiers.[41]

However, demobilisation did not mean demilitarisation, nor a breakdown in contacts with foreign troops. During the second-half of the eighteenth century the army was employed to maintain public order and to defend the frontiers in a state whose military image was now firmly in place. In the meantime, Piedmont's reputation grew as an example of a state that had successfully expanded its own domains through its skilful choice of international alliances. The recruitment of so many Protestant soldiers was another consequence of this relaxed attitude to dealings with foreign powers.

It was no coincidence, therefore, that in 1749, Philip Stanhope, fourth Earl of Chesterfield, should write from London to his 18-year-old son who was then on a grand tour, advising him to visit Turin and to spend a few months in the city in order to study and learn the arts of court ceremony and diplomacy. Lord Chesterfield's *Letters to his Son*, which was published posthumously in London in 1774 and soon circulated in translation, became a model for other handbooks of conduct and served to spread the reputation of the educational establishment attended by the English aristocrat's son in Turin: the *Accademia Reale*.

This was a cavalry school founded between 1677 and 1678 and housed in a building adjacent to the royal palace in Turin. The *Accademia Reale di Torino* (controlled directly by the court and not by a religious order, as was the case with numerous other *seminaria nobilium* in Piedmont and many other European countries) attracted a student population that was mainly Catholic but also included a number of young Protestants. The papacy had, as usual, attempted to curb this initiative, but with little success. The privileges enjoyed by the students and the jurisdictional policy of Savoy had helped to keep the Turin-based institution going. This is not the place to describe the various transformations which the *Accademia Reale* underwent during the eighteenth century. It is sufficient to say that throughout this period it attracted members of the top European aristocracy (Italians, but also Englishmen, Germans, Poles and Russians), intended for senior ecclesiastic, military and diplomatic careers. Through the *Accademia Reale* (where, among other things, the number of courses on military subjects was increased during the eighteenth century), the students came into contact with the main venues of Turinese social and cultural life: the court, salons, theatres, literary and scientific circles, and the noble *casini* (houses, or families). From this point of view, Turin was increasingly seen as a laboratory of modern political education.[42] As has been seen, foreign soldiers

---

41   See P. Bianchi, 'Guerra e pace nel Settecento: alcune riflessioni sul caso sabaudo', *Studi settecenteschi*, 22 (2002): 89–102.

42   See P. Bianchi, '"Quel fortunato e libero paese". L'Accademia Reale e i primi contatti del giovane Alfieri con il mondo inglese', in M. Cerruti, M. Corsi and B. Danna (eds), *Alfieri*

(among them Huguenots) played a very important role in this laboratory, alongside a wide variety of other social arenas.

This short study ends with a document that sums up, clearly, the highly pragmatic grounds on which the presence of *religionari* was for a long time tolerated in Savoy-Piedmont. In 1725, to mark the convocation of a council of state, which was also attended by the crown prince (the future Carlo Emanuele III), Vittorio Amedeo II set out a few clear rules of conduct for Protestants living in Turin. These rules were intended to guide the civil and military authorities responsible for keeping public order. The aim was to combat the 'abuses' committed by heretics in the city, but, at the same time, to 'provide a remedy'. They were allowed partial, but controlled, autonomy of movement, which would not turn what was primarily a political choice ('a rule for good governance') into a question of faith (*un fatto di religione*, as the document states).[43] A series of rules of this type was introduced throughout the history of the Savoy domains, and not only in relation to the capital.

The co-existence, in mixed armies, of different religious faiths is, as is well known, characteristic of many European nations. The international aristocracy of officers accustomed to serve more than one sovereign continued to dominate the scene until the fall of the *ancien régime*. Similarly, some minor central European states (both Catholic and Protestant) specialised in offering collective mercenary troops (both officers and simple rank-and-file soldiers) to countries that could afford to pay temporarily for their use. Between the seventeenth and eighteenth centuries, Savoy-Piedmont was a perfect example of this practice and it employed high-quality mercenaries without interrupting, on the other hand, the tradition of military service provided abroad by numerous members of aristocratic families who were subjects of Savoy.

Throughout the *ancien régime*, the military history of the Savoyard domains must essentially be studied in a wider context, stretching across most of Europe. Taking the contacts between different cultures and faiths inside the same country as a starting point helps us to see beyond the old national stereotypes that for years have influenced, both positively and negatively, the history of the territories ruled by Savoy's dukes, the future kings of Italy.

---

e il suo tempo (Florence, 2003), pp. 89–112; P. Bianchi, 'La fortuna dell'Accademia Reale di Torino nei percorsi europei del viaggio di formazione', in R. Maggio Serra, F. Mazzocca, C. Sisi and C. Spantigati (eds), *Vittorio Alfieri. Aristocratico ribelle (1749–1803)* (Milan, 2003), pp. 150–53; P. Bianchi, 'In cerca del moderno. Studenti e viaggiatori inglesi a Torino nel Settecento', *Rivista storica italiana*, 115/3 (2003): 1021–51. On this subject, see also A. Merlotti, 'Note sulla sociabilità aristocratica nell'Italia del Settecento: i "casini de' nobili"', in G. Barbarisi, C. Capra, F. Degrada and F. Mazzocca (eds), *L'amabil rito. Società e cultura nella Milano di Parini* (Milan, 2000), pp. 45–69; A. Merlotti, '"Compagni de' giovenili errori". Gli amici di Alfieri fra Accademia Reale e Société des Sansguignon (1772–1778)', in Maggio Serra *et al.* (eds), *Vittorio Alfieri. Aristocratico ribelle*, pp. 154–6; A. Merlotti, 'Gentildonne e sociabilità aristocratica nella Torino del secondo Settecento', in M. L. Betri and E. Brambilla (eds), *Salotti e ruolo femminile in Italia tra fine Seicento e primo Novecento* (Venice, 2004), pp. 125–52.

43   AST, Corte, Materie giuridiche, Materie giuridiche per categorie, Ministri e segreterie, m. 1, n. 26, 30 January 1725.

Chapter 14

Huguenot Soldiers in Russia

A Study in Military Competence

Matthew Glozier
University of Sydney, Australia

Russia was by no means as popular a destination for Huguenot refugees as some other countries. However, Russia was an Orthodox land (arguably attractive to the Huguenots for that reason) and Peter the Great went out of his way to encourage the settlement of communities of foreign experts. As a result, some Huguenot soldiers and civilians made their way to Russia and, throughout the early years of the eighteenth century, many of them arrived from established communities in Germany and just one source cites 45 families of Huguenot descent that settled in Russia in the early 1700s.[1] As in other countries, such as Great Britain and the Netherlands, many Huguenot families adopted variant spellings of their surname and this fact causes some problems for researching the Huguenots in Russia.[2]

I

Many Huguenots were attracted to the duchy of Muscovy from service in the armies of Brandenburg-Prussia, whither many of the French refugees had been encouraged in 1685, when Elector Friedrich Wilhelm promulgated his Edict of Potsdam.[3] Friedrich Wilhelm also did a great deal to encourage their reception in Russia, where many Huguenots fled after finding the refuge of Sweden somewhat less than welcoming. Nevertheless, they found sympathy from one Swede, himself descended from a Huguenot refugee of sorts:

> Count Gustav de La Gardie[4] has received letters from Moscow, informing him that there have there established themselves a prodigious number of French of the Reformed religion, that the Tsars have received them perfectly well, have granted them the free

---

1   E. Amburger, 'Hugenottenfamilien in Rußland', *Der Herold*, 5 (1963/5): 125–35.

2   J. Kämmerer, *Rußland und die Hugenotten im 18. Jahrhundert (1689–1789)* (Wiesbaden, 1978), p. 15.

3   R. Stupperich, 'Brandenburgisch-russische Verhandlungen über Aufnahme der Hugenotten in Rußland', *Zeitschrift für osteuropäische Geschichte*, 8 (1934): 72.

4   Count Gustav Adolf de La Gardie, Baron of Ekholmen (1647–95), Swedish statesman, was descended from Jacques d'Escouperie de Bussol de La Gardie (1520–88), from Caunes in Languedoc, founder of the family in Sweden.

exercise of their religion, and many privileges and franchises. A strange metamorphosis, Monseigneur, that France, formerly so polite, and so full of humanity, should have become barbarous to such a degree that the most faithful subjects of its King are compelled to seek asylum in Muscovy, and that they there find the repose and safety denied to them in their own country.[5]

The old Elector's son, Friedrich III, also strongly encouraged the refugees to come to Berlin. Over 20,000 refugees made their way to Brandenburg. The early links between Huguenots in Berlin and Russia is evident in the fact that Friedrich sent word of his father's death in 1688 to Russia, via the Huguenot Jean Reyer-Chapliez, who was charged with requesting free entry into all parts of Russia for his fellow refugees.[6]

Peter the Great, supported by his brother, Ivan, granted an Imperial *ukase* (encouragement), which gave the Huguenots permission to settle in Russia, and guaranteed military employment with pay proportionate to their rank to any who desired it. Significantly, the Huguenots were also promised their freedom from service in the Tsar's armies, if ever they should be able to return to their homes in France.[7] How much this concession came from the prompting of William III in the Dutch Republic is impossible to say; the meeting which took place between the Prince and Peter in 1697 was private, attended only by the Swiss general, and close personal friend of the Tsar, Guillaume Lefort.[8] That Geneva-born, Dutch-trained general, at least, was pleased to see French refugees arrive in Muscovy.[9] In his home city of Geneva he had seen too many skilled Huguenot craftsmen volunteer to be soldiers in William's 1688 invasion force. He thought they would be happier pursuing their civilian occupations in a land that offered them both freedom of conscience and stable employment:

> Those whom are in Geneva among the refugees, both craftsmen and soldiers (so one may say to them), they must come find liberty here; they need only come to Königsberg to see M. Reyer Chapliez, my intimate friend, to get passports, according to which they will find here [in Russia] very good terms of admission.[10]

---

5   Lefort quoted in M. C. Weiss, *History of the French Protestant Refugees from the Revocation of the Edict of Nantes to Our Own Days*, ed. H. W. Herbert (2 vols, New York, 1854), vol. 1, p. 581.

6   Ibid., pp. 581–2; Kämmerer, *Rußland und die Hugenotten*, pp. 20–24.

7   Weiss, *Histoire de France Protestante*, vol. 1, p. 582.

8   G.u, *The Anglo-Russian Entente Cordiale of 1697–1698: Peter I and William at Utrecht*, East European Monographs (Boulder, New York, 1986), pp. 1, 13; J. F. M. A. de Voltaire, *Histoire de l'Empire de Russie sous Pierre le Grand. Par l'auteur de l'histoire de Charles XII* (2 vols, Geneva, 1759–63), vol. 2, pp. 143–4; M. C. F. F. Posselt, *Der General und Admiral Franz Lefort. Sein Leben und seine Zeit. Ein Beitrag zur Geschichte Peters des Großen* (2 vols, Frankfort-am-Main, 1866), vol. 2, p. 420.

9   Barary, *The Anglo-Russian Entente Cordiale of 1697–1698*, p. 13.

10   Lefort quoted in Posselt, *Der General und Admiral Franz Lefort*, vol. 2, p. 105; Kämmerer, *Rußland und die Hugenotten*, p. 48; For Lefort's career and actions, see N. J. Hugou de Bassville (ed.), *Précis historique sur la vie et les exploits de François Le Fort*.

Indeed, Peter took from the Dutch Republic and Britain 60 specialists (many of them Scottish Catholics). In Britain this occurred by special arrangement, tempering William III's proclamation 'prohibiting his Majesty's subjects to enter into the service of foreign princes and states without licence'.[11] A third of Lefort's Russian regiment would eventually consist of Huguenot soldiers.[12] However, unlike their experience in Britain and the Netherlands, the refugees do not seem to have joined the elite Guards regiments of Peter the Great, which he reserved for training up his own Russian nobility in the latest military techniques.[13]

Not every French refugee was a soldier, of course, but some of the most significant military figures in both Brandenburg and Russia were French Protestants.[14] There was little enough employment in Western Europe in the few years of peace following the 1697 Peace of Ryswick, and this prompted a number of Huguenot officers, predominantly engineers, to seek employment further away in Eastern Europe.[15] The Brandenburg-based Colonel Reyer-Chapliez (called in Russia Reyer-Czaplicz) took many of them into Poland, where Prince Karol I Stanislas Radziwill employed a number of Huguenots.[16] Meanwhile, in Russia, Peter the Great sought eagerly to increase the potential of his army by employing foreign military specialists.[17]

Citoyen de Genéve. Général et Grand-Admiral de Russie (Geneva, 1784; reprinted 2 vols, Lausanne, 1786).

11   N. Luttrell, *A Brief Historical Relation of State Affairs from September 1678 to April 1714* (6 vols, Oxford, 1857), vol. 4, p. 339; N. G. Ustrialov, *Istoriya tsarstvovaniya Petra Velikago* (6 vols, St Petersburg, 1858–63), vol. 3, p. 101; I. Grey, 'Peter the Great in England', *History Today*, 6 (1956): 234; Barary, *The Anglo-Russian Entente Cordiale of 1697–1698*, p. 50. For their use by Peter, see M. J. Okenfuss, 'Technical Training in Russia under Peter the Great', *History of Education Quarterly*, 13 (1973): 327 *passim*.

12   F. M. A. de Voltaire, *The History of Charles the XIIth, King of Sweden*, trans. W. S. Kenrick [incl. *The Life of Peter the Great*, trans. J. Johnson] (London, 1780), ch. 6.

13   I. de Madariaga, *Catherine the Great: A Short History* (Yale, 1990), p. 11.

14   W. Beuleke, *Studien zum Refuge in Deutschland und zur Ursprungsheimat seiner Mitglieder*, Geschichtsblätter der Deutschen Hugenotten-Vereins 12/3 (Obersickte, Brunswick, 1966), p. 4; Stupperich, 'Brandenburgisch-russische Verhandlungen': 60–61.

15   C. Read, 'Les démarches des réfugiées huguenots auprès des négocieteurs de la paix de Ryswick pour leur rétablissement en France 1697', *Bulletin de la société de l'histoire du Protestantisme française*, 40 (1891): 169–88, 384–7.

16   See letter from Prince Karol I Stanislas Radziwill (1669–1719), Great Chancellor of Lithuania, April 1699: New York State University at Boulder, Arts and Sciences Libraries, Polish Royal Documents, 'Prince Charles Stanislaus Radziwill – letter dated 1699'; Kämmerer, *Rußland und die Hugenotten*, p. 66; J. Krusche, 'Die Entstehung und Entwicklung derständigen diplomatischen Vertretung Brandeburg-Preußens am Carenhofe bis zum Eintritt Rußlands in die Reihe der europäischen Großmächte', *Jahrbücher für Kultur und Geschichte der Slaven*, 8 (1932): 212, 215; K. Forstreuter, *Preußen und Rußland im Mittelalter. Die Entwicklung ihrer Beziehungen vom 13. bis 17. Jarhhundert* (Königsberg, Berlin, 1938), pp. 173–5.

17   Kämmerer, *Rußland und die Hugenotten*, p. 19; Stupperich, 'Brandenburgisch-russische Verhandlungen': 70.

How many Huguenots sought employment in Russia is impossible to determine. One figure, of 626 refugees arriving from the United Provinces, suggests the Huguenot presence was small.[18] Many came straight from the Netherlands, but their origins lay in France, unlike the majority of early eighteenth-century arrivals who came via a generation spent in Germany. The most important Huguenot families in Russia possessed a variety of skills and founded military dynasties such as those of Clapier de Colongue, from Provence, de Marin, from Metz, Vechery de Coulon, Gervais, Scalon and Gendre.[19] Their integration into the foreign officer corps in Russia was aided by the fact that many Huguenots came from respectable families, actually enjoying, or on the verge of, noble status. The social acceptability of a large number of them meant that barriers to employment in the army could be crossed with relative ease. Thus families, such as the Lestocqs, transformed themselves from *haute bourgeois* doctors of medicine, into army officers enjoying noble status: one of the earliest Lestocqs was the physician of Georg Wilhelm, Duke of Brunswick-Lüneburg-Celle.[20] The physician's son left his father at Celle, and ventured to Russia where he, too, was a doctor to many of the foreign officers in Peter the Great's 'foreign quarter' at St Petersburg. Other members of the family joined the army of Brandenburg-Prussia, and one of their descendants was a colonel at the siege of Paris in 1870.[21] Another example of this process of social elevation through service in foreign armies can be seen in the descendants of Isaac-Pierre Souchay de Duboissière (1748–88), a Huguenot jeweller from Hanau, who had learnt his trade in Geneva, Paris and London, before travelling to Russia.[22] His son, Jean-Pierre Souchay de Duboissière (1763–1830), became an officer and surveyor in the Russian army *c*.1760.[23]

Strong links also existed between Huguenot serving officers and their civilian kinsfolk. For example, in 1710, Cornelius Possiet de Roussier, a major-general in the Russian army, was instrumental in encouraging his relation, Pierre Vincent Roussier, a vintner, to depart The Hague for Russia.[24] Some early advertising of Russia as a place fit for refugee settlement found its way into international Huguenot circles through the writings of Samuel Chappuzeau, who travelled there from Celle in the 1690s. However, it should be said that his description of the country exposes his

18   H. Dalton, *Zur Geschichte der evangelischen Kirche in Rußland* (2 vols, Gotha, 1887–9; republished in one vol. Leipzig, 1893 and Amsterdam, 1968), p. 54; E. and E. Haag, *La France protestante ou vies des protestants français qui se sont fait un nom dans l'histoire* (10 vols, Montpellier, 1992), vol. 6, pp. 329–30.

19   Amburger, 'Hugenottenfamilien in Rußland': 127–9, 133.

20   Georg Wilhelm, Duke of Brunswick-Lüneburg-Celle (1624–1705), married the Huguenot Eleanor, daughter of Alexandre Desmier d'Olbreuse.

21   Major-General J. F. Maurice (ed. and trans.), *The Franco-German War, 1870–71* (London, 1900).

22   O. Döhner, *Das Hugenottengeschlecht Souchay de la Duboissière und seine Nachkommen*, Deutsches Famililensarchiev. Ein genealogisches Sammelwerk 19 (Neustadt-an-der-Aisch, 1961).

23   Amburger, 'Hugenottenfamilien in Rußland': 133.

24   The Possiet de Roussier family originated in Annonay in the Vivarais: Kämmerer, *Rußland und die Hugenotten*, p. 66; Muralt, *Chronik*, p. 33.

profoundly French sensibilities: 'Muscovy must be considered little for the freedom of its inhabitants [who cannot] leave their country and foreigners cannot cross it without trouble; all and sundry being badly treated.'[25]

II

One trait, present in Huguenots as a result of their Calvinist upbringing and lived experience, was that which Britain's James II chose to call 'republicanism'. In truth, this was the Protestant Resistance Theory which had been born during the Dutch Revolt (1568–1648) and which held that it was just to oppose any monarch who interfered with his or her subjects' consciences; an idea that had its origins among the French thinkers during the Wars of Religion, as advocated by men such as Duplessis-Mornay. Arguably, the Huguenots saw William III in this light in 1688, and the idea proved of assistance to the Russian Empress Elizabeth, who included Huguenots among those who participated in her *coup*, which removed her cousin, Ivan VI, from his Imperial throne in 1741.[26] Jean-Armand Lestocq, a keen student of revolutionary literature, was deeply involved in the *coup*.[27] Lestocq may well have been influenced by any one of a number of Huguenot pastors attached to the Protestant courts of northern Europe. Paul-Emile de Mauclerc, from the court of Stettin, and Jacques Pérard, from that of Anhalt-Zerbst, represent the popularity and influence of Calvinist theology in royal Protestant German circles throughout northern Europe.[28] Significantly, every member of the Prussian royal family had a Huguenot tutor, following the Revocation in France. However, it is true that many contemporaries saw Lestocq as nothing more than a self-interested opportunist: after all, Russia in 1741 was not Britain in 1688.[29] Equally, it was the great Huguenot, Henri de Navarre's ability to compromise, rather than his inherent dynamism, which

---

25   Samuel Chappuzeau (1625–1701): S. Chappuzeau, *Suite de l'Europe viuante, contenant la relation d'vn voyage fait en Allemagne aux mois d'Auril, May, Iuin, Iuillet & Aoust de l'année M.DC.LXIX. Où l'on void quelle est la face presente de plusieurs Estats d'Électeurs et de Princes de l'Empire, l'origine de leurs maisons, leur accroissement & leurs alliances, auec les portraits des Princes & des Princesses, suiuis des eloges des personnes les plus illustres de ce temps, etc.* (2 vols, Geneva, 1671), vol. 2, p. 261; H. Eggers, *Das altfranzösische Geschlecht Chappuzeau. Eine genealogische Skizze nebst Anhang. Fortgeführt von C. Chappuzeau* (Hanover, 1968).

26   Ivan VI Antonovic: Madariaga, *Catherine the Great*, pp. 1, 5, 6, 58.

27   Jean-Armand, Count von Lestocq (1692–1767): Kämmerer, *Rußland und die Hugenotten*, pp. 40 n. 226, 111–19; Muralt, *Chronik*, p. 15; Dalton, *Zur Geschichte der evangelischen Kirche*, p. 46.

28   Paul-Émile de Mauclerc (1698–1742) and Jacques Pérard (1713–66): Kämmerer, *Rußland und die Hugenotten*, p. 121.

29   S. M. Solov'ev, *Istorija Rossii s drevnejšich vremen* [History of Russia from most ancient times] (14 vols, Moscow: Izdatel'stvo social'noekonomiceskoj literatury, 1896; reprinted 29 vols, Moscow 1959–66), vol. 11, pp. 173, 181–2, 321.

appealed to Catherine the Great, when she reflected on French history, 20 years after the *coup*.[30]

One of the first refugees to find his way to Russia was Etienne Vechery de Coulon, an experienced engineer, who had found refuge in the Netherlands after 1685 and accompanied William of Orange to England in 1688.[31] He was followed quickly by the Lefort brothers. Though identified as Swiss by some historians, General François Lefort and his brother, Admiral Ami Lefort, were of French Huguenot ancestry and had been affected by the same forces as other Huguenot refugees such as Vechery de Coulon. François Lefort had also served William of Orange in the Netherlands before travelling to Russia.[32] Others arrived, fitfully, throughout the 1690s: among them was Abraham Roussier, originally from Verneuil, in Angoumois, and a friend of Lefort, who first appeared in Russia in 1698. Once they had established themselves in the forces of the Tsar of Muscovy, a small number of Huguenot soldiers attracted their kinsmen and compatriots to the same service. For example, Adelbert Vechery de Coulon arrived in Russia in 1726, on the recommendation of his kinsman, Etienne.[33]

The Huguenot diaspora ensured that a number of new arrivals, though they possessed French surnames, were quite Germanised by the time they reached Russia. Their view of the relationship between armies and the states they served was, arguably, affected by the experience of these German kingdoms in a period of flux. A good exponent of this process is Baron Ludwig Nickolas von Hallard, from Kursachsen in Brandenburg. More precisely he was Louis-Nicholas, Baron de Hallard, son of Henri de Hallard, a long-time Huguenot officer in the service of the Elector of Brandenburg.[34] He used the German version of his name and was thoroughly Germanised by the time of his arrival in Russia; Hallard became an engineer officer in the Russian army *c.*1700 and was a general officer *c.*1720.[35]

Though most early Huguenot arrivals came straight from the Netherlands, or from Brandenburg-Prussia, not all were soldiers. Jean Dupré and *Maître* du Buisson were both pastors from Dieppe; Jean and Pierre Marteille were pastors from Bergerac;

---

30   Madariaga, *Catherine the Great*, p. 4; V. Rjeoutski, 'La communauté francophone de Moscou sous le règne de Catherine II', *Revue des Etudes Slaves*, 68/4 (Paris, 1996): 445–61.

31   Haag, *La France protestante*, vol. 4, p. 83.

32   A. Babkine (ed.), 'Les Premiers Lettres de Russie du Général Lefort', *Canadian Slavonic Papers*, 16 (1974): 380–402; Haag, *La France protestante*, vol. 9, pp. 57–8.

33   K. H. Heyking, *Aus Polens und Kurlands letzten Tagen. Memoiren des Baron Karl Heinrich Heyking (1752–1796)*, ed. A. Heyking (Berlin, 1897), p. 244.

34   Henri de Hallard (d.1681): E. Winter, *Frühaufklärung. Der Kampf gegen den Konfessionalismus in Mittel- und Osteuropa und die deutsch-slawische Begegnung. Zum 250. Todestag von G. W. Liebniz*, Beiträge zur Geschichte des religiösen und Wissenschaftlichen Denkens 6 (Berlin, 1966); Tastevin, *Histoire*, p. 12; Kämmerer, *Rußland und die Hugenotten*, p. 16.

35   Louis-Nicholas, Baron de Hallard (1659–1727): Kämmerer, *Rußland und die Hugenotten*, p. 67; A. S. Pushkin, *Istorija Pugačeva (Polnoe sobranie socinenij)* [History of the Pugachev Rebellion] (2 vols, Leningrad, 1938–40), vol. 1, pp. 303–4.

Philippe Marantier de La Ramée and Pierre de La Ramée were humanist scholars.[36] Many civilian Huguenots were assisted into Russia by existing connections between Brandenburg and major Russian towns, such as Smolensk.[37] Huguenot merchants continued to foster trade links: for example, Barthélémy Pelletier, of Leipzig, and Charles-Jean Salomé, of Magdeburg, pursued a prosperous trade with their agent in St Petersburg, Pierre Pesché, throughout the early years of the eighteenth century.[38]

In Russia, the refugees were greeted by their new masters with a mixture of tolerance and self-interest, familiar to the story of the Huguenots as a group.[39] This was, perhaps, not surprising as the refugees brought with them a wide range of specialist knowledge in areas as diverse as fireworks, medicine, theology, chemistry, optics, pedagogy, trade, engineering and, of course, their own language.[40] Under Peter the Great, instruction in the French language was increasingly sought after and, later, for her own amusement, Catherine the Great translated French works.[41] Peter, similarly, encouraged the adoption of French fashions in clothing at his royal court.[42] Throughout the eighteenth century, French tutors were sought-after by leading Russian nobles for the education of their sons, who could not hope to rise in Imperial service, by entering the cadet corps, Moscow University or private boarding schools, without instruction.[43] Despite the growth of state academies throughout the century, the value of private education remained strong: leading military figures, such as Prince Ferdinand of Brunswick, proved that private instruction could equip a great nobleman with the skills needed in public life:

> Ferdinand's education was entirely confined to his personal house … This is not normally the environment best suited for forming a Prince, but such an education can be most successful providing it is supervised by intelligent and vigilant parents who set a good example in all things. So it proved in this case.[44]

---

36 Dalton, *Zur Geschichte der evangelischen Kirche*, pp. 54–6; Haag, *La France protestante*, vol. 6, pp. 329–30; vol. 7, pp. 286–7; Amburger, 'Hugenottenfamilien in Rußland': 126; E. von Muralt, *Chronik der vereiningten französischen und teutschen reformierten Gemeinde in St. Petersburg, nebst Beiträgen zur Geschichte der Stiftung protestantischer und besonders reformierter Kirchen, zum Kirkenrechte und zur Geschichte der Ausländer im russischen Reiche* (Dorpat, 1842), p. 28.

37 Kämmerer, *Rußland und die Hugenotten* , p. 24.

38 Amburger, 'Hugenottenfamilien in Rußland': 132; Haag, *La France protestante*, vol. 8, pp. 180–83; Muralt, *Chronik*, p. 63; G. Pozé, 'Zapiski pridvornago bril'jantščika Pozé o preby vanii ego v Rossi (1729–64) (Perevod s francuzsko, neizdannoj rukopisi)', *Bulletin de la société de l'histoire du Protestantisme française*, 1 (1870): 92–3.

39 Kämmerer, *Rußland und die Hugenotten* , p. 27.

40 A. W. Fechner, *Chronik der Evangelischen-Gemeinden in Moskau. Zum dreihundertjährigen jubiläum der Evangelisch-Lutherischen St. Michaelis-Gemeinde zusammengestellt* (2 vols, Moscow, 1876), vol. 1, pp. 167, 197, 202, 203, 293.

41 In 1767 Catherine translated Marmontel's *Bélisaire*: Madariaga, *Catherine the Great*, p. 95; C. Duffy, *European Warfare in the Age of Reason* (London, 1987), p. 51.

42 Madariaga, *Catherine the Great*, p. 13.

43 Ibid., p. 148.

44 J. Mauvillon, *Geschichte Ferdinands Herzogs von Braunschweig-Lüneburg* (2 vols, Leipzig, 1794), vol. 1, p. 18.

The tsars were not ignorant of the enormous value of skilled craftsmen, such as Philippe Behagle, who learnt his trade in France at the Gobellin tapestry factory.[45] However, under the increasingly absolutist Russian crown, service of any sort had militaristic overtones. The tsars relied upon both Huguenot refugees and Baltic German nobles to fill administrative positions throughout Russia as the skills, education and character of local nobles often left much to be desired.[46] Thus many Huguenot civil, military and household officers shared broadly similar experiences in the service of the tsars. This fact links a number of Huguenots who, in other countries, might have been inclined to construct social or occupational barriers between themselves and others. Internationalism and diversity of service were both strong characteristics of the Huguenot experience in Russia. For example, two members of the Russian judiciary, Johann Joachim Balleux, son of a household teacher to the Counts of Orlov, and Peter Lobry, son of a wig maker, both studied jurisprudence at Königsburg *c*.1740.[47] Another judge, Gottlieb Wilhelm Battrai, from Magdeburg, was the son of a master-founder. From the same social *milieu* came Alexandre Daniel Feray, the son of a French-language teacher, who was the father of Major-General Frederick Feray, who led Russian armies against the Turks in the Seven Years' War and served in Finland and Orenburg before meeting his end in the Caucuses in 1794.[48] Each of these men was descended from a Huguenot refugee.

III

In a relatively short time, a small number of Huguenot officers became very important in Russia. This may have owed something to the fact that Russia's nobility was itself small, comprising no more than 50,000 males in 1752.[49] While it is true that foreign nobles were not generally integrated into local elites, they were instrumental in training them. Even as late as 1762, 74 (17 per cent) of the 435 young Russian nobles who presented themselves at the Herald Master's College for employment in the army or civil administration were illiterate.[50] In this atmosphere, the skills of Huguenot military engineers, such as Alexandre Clapier de Coulon and Jean de Marin, were highly valued: both men were promoted by the president of the War College, Baron Karl von Münnich.[51]

---

45   Philippe Behagle (d.1734): Kämmerer, *Rußland und die Hugenotten*, p. 83.

46   Madariaga, *Catherine the Great*, p. 73.

47   Johann Joachim Balleux (b.1727), of Neustrelitz: Amburger, *Beiträge*, pp. 204–5.

48   Major-General Frederick Feray (d.1794): Kämmerer, *Rußland und die Hugenotten*, p. 69; Amburger, 'Hugenottenfamilien': 134.

49   Madariaga, *Catherine the Great*, p. 19.

50   Thirty-two of the illiterates were over 20 years old, while seven were over 50. More than half owned land, but no serfs, suggesting they were among the poorest applicants: ibid., p. 72.

51   N. E. Brandenburg, *Materialy dlja istorii artillerijskago upravlenija v Rossi 'Prikaz artillerii' (1701–1720)* (St Petersburg, 1876), p. 215; Amburger, *Anwerbung*, p. 113; Amburger, 'Hugenottenfamilien in Rußland': 128.

Clapier de Coulon became the dominant force in Russian military engineering in the first half of the eighteenth century.[52] His co-religionist and compatriot Louis-Nicholas de Hallard was described as 'one of the most masterful generals of the Tsars ... one of the best engineers of his time'.[53] Other Huguenot officers supervised purely aristocratic army corps. Until his death in 1732, the Comte d'Auvremont was Inspector of the Noble Cadets' corps. Under his guidance the corps came to resemble similar units of young, noble volunteers in France, the Netherlands and Germany.[54] Many of the Huguenots who came to Russia from Berlin were influenced by Abel Burja, head of Berlin's *Collège Français*, who said: 'I have the happiness to be esteemed by the chief [persons], and loved by the Cadets' in Russia.[55]

Peter the Great's desire to expand his navy also attracted Huguenot involvement, though of much smaller significance. Guillaume Barré, a Huguenot soldier who arrived in Russian from Germany, was one of the few French Protestant officers in the Tsar's navy *c.*1720.[56] Not all was plain sailing, so to speak, and the appointment in 1717 of the Huguenot Baron de Saint-Hilaire as Director of the Russian Sea Academy sparked a long-running disagreement with Count A. Matveev.[57] Their dispute grew so violent that, at one point, Saint-Hilaire was 'ejected through a window' by the imperious Matveev.[58] The Huguenot association with martial and naval academies is significant. Their connection with pedagogy, whether of the French language as private tutors or of the gentlemanly arts of riding and fencing, is a common feature of their story. For example, Hugh Trevor-Roper described the financial necessity for many refugees of tutoring the often dull-witted scions of noble families, and says that it was a 'dispiriting' experience for Huguenot gentlemen of the calibre of Paul Rapin de Thoyras.[59]

Military academies were introduced all over Europe at the beginning of the Age of Reason, as a response to the increasingly ponderous size of armies across the continent. Such large forces required increasingly professional and well-trained personnel to guide them, while countries such as Brandenburg-Prussia and Russia expected large numbers of the nobility to serve for at least some time in the army. The result was that the schooling of young gentlemen came to be directed through state-run academies, which taught mathematics, geometry, siege-craft and military history as

---

52   Kämmerer, *Rußland und die Hugenotten*, p. 61.

53   Puskin, *Polnoe sobranie socinenij*, vol. 10, pp. 303–4.

54   Amburger, 'Hugenottenfamilien in Rußland': 128; P. Lusanov, *Suchoputnyj šljachetskij korpus pri grafe Miniche, 1732–1741* (St Petersburg, 1907).

55   Abel Burja [n.b. Bourgeois] (1752–1816): Kämmerer, *Rußland und die Hugenotten*, p. 65; A. Burja, *Observations d'un voyageur sur la Russie, la Finlande, la Livonie, la Curlande et la Prusse* (Maastricht, 1787), pp. 52–6.

56   Haag, *La France protestant*, vol. 1, p. 22.

57   On Matveev's career, see A. Matveev, *Russkij diplomat vo Francii (zapisksi Andreja Matveeva)*, ed. I. S. Sarkova (Leningrad, 1972).

58   Dalton, *Zur Geschichte der evangelischen Kirche*, p. 55; L. Pingaud, *Les Français en Russie et les Russes en France* (Paris, 1886), p. 14.

59   H. Trevor-Roper, 'A Huguenot Historian: Paul Rapin', in I. Scouloudi (ed.), *Huguenots in Britain and their French Background, 1550–1800* (London, 1987), p. 6.

a means of introducing young men to the rudiments of warfare.[60] The Prussian Cadet corps academy opened in 1717 and was soon followed by the Russian land Cadet corps artillery and engineering academy (1732), the Dutch artillery academy (1735), the Woolwich engineering and artillery academy in England (1741), the Mezières engineering academy in France (1749), the *École Militaire* in Paris (1751) and the Wiener-Neustadt academy in Austria (1752). Alongside these state institutions there existed private academies, which also operated in Russia: those at Angers, Brienne and Caen in France acquired an international reputation in the eighteenth century.[61]

In many ways, Huguenots were natural teachers for such institutions: first and foremost, they spoke French which was considered an accomplishment for any officer. Secondly, more often than not, they displayed traits which came from a close association with Calvinist instruction. These were necessary for any teacher: they were didactic and pedagogical (though admittedly sometimes pedantic and unoriginal) without being overly dogmatic and many possessed a strong moral sense of right and wrong. As the century progressed, Russia's elite increasingly opened up to the influence of the French *philosophes* and discussions focused as much on the moral and philosophical implications of warfare as on the strict mechanics of it. The high moral code of many Huguenot teachers also assisted academies in dealing with one of the great evils inherent in such closed communities of young men – bullying and hazing – of which Huguenot teachers were far less tolerant than Russian or Prussian natives.

Russia did not enjoy a good reputation in regard to the treatment of its foreign experts. Despite Peter the Great's original promise that they could depart Russia at will, later Huguenot soldiers found themselves subjected to tyrannical and, at times, capricious masters. They often enjoyed little freedom of movement and were expected to endure long periods of regimental or garrison life, separated from friends and family.[62] While these duties were expected of soldiers throughout Europe, Russian service contained the added discomfort of campaigns in Siberia and against the Turks. Neither was it an attractive prospect for civilised Frenchmen: between 1771 and 1777, Jean Clapier de Coulange, the son of the Huguenot General Alexandre de Coulange, faced just such service, when he was appointed Troop Commander in Siberia.[63] Like most soldiers serving under these conditions, Huguenots were prey to the evils of garrison life. Gambling was one of the greatest of these temptations and, when combined with the normal expectations of officers to maintain servants, dress expensively and entertain their peers, this often meant Huguenot officers in Russia

---

60 Duffy, *European Warfare in the Age of Reason*, p. 15.

61 C. Duffy, *The Military Experience in the Age of Reason* (New York, 1987), p. 48. Significantly, the academy at Caen was founded by the Huguenot Jacques Moisant de Brieux. His grandson, François Moisant de Brieux, captain in the service of Holland, died at The Hague, his will dated 1 December 1727: Records of the Prerogative Court of Canterbury Farrant Quire Numbers: 251 – 313 PROB 11/618.

62 Kämmerer, *Rußland und die Hugenotten*, p. 27; Stupperich, 'Brandenburgisch-russische Verhandlungen': 67; W. L. Blackwell, 'The Old Believers and the Rise of Private Industrial Enterprise in early Nineteenth-Century Moskow', *Slavonic Review*, 24 (1965): 407–24.

63 Amburger, 'Hugenottenfamilien in Rußland': 127.

suffered chronic debt. The ease with which prominent military leaders could obtain credit only added to their financial problems: Lieutenant-General Vechery de Coulon accrued debts of 3,000 *rubles* and most of his peers were in a similar position.[64]

Huguenots did not suffer these discomforts in silence. However, when they complained, it was as members of an international foreign officer corps in Russia, rather than as a distinct group of French Protestant exiles. Jean Rousset de Missy gave the clearest expression to their concerns: 'It is, for the most part, to the memories concerning Russia that I come ... foreigners inform their enemies of what I speak, solidly esteeming the manners of their homeland, and in consequence adopt an unjust distaste for those of other nations.'[65] He added that, under Peter the Great, Russia was 'an almost barbarous nation'.[66]

This situation was not aided by the generally non-military and unprofessional character of the Russian court nobility and one Catholic French observer perceived a 'total lack of zeal and courage in the Russian magnates, and especially that mob of volunteers – courtiers, Muscovites and Guardsmen – who came out to the active army to deprive deserving officers of their rewards'.[67] In such an environment it was both the poorer Russian nobility and professional foreign officers who suffered the consequences. True, the Russian army was particularly open to non-aristocratic, professional officers. As has been seen, Huguenot officers were the sons of skilled artisans and merchants who had acquired technical skills that were prized in Russia.[68] A similar situation existed in Germany, where the innovation and original thinking of their class marked them out as being worthy of praise:

> Taken as a whole, the bourgeois officers were far better educated than the nobles, even in the higher reaches of knowledge, and they showed far greater decorum in their conduct. In fact there were many nobles who were total ignoramuses. These men from the middle class had an excellent effect on the spirit of the regiment. They nearly all hailed from respectable and decent families. Most of them were volunteers, who wished to advance themselves through military service, and they accordingly cultivate a certain dignity of manner in their off-duty hours. Their example has an astonishing effect. The ordinary hussars strove to catch up with them, so as to be judged equally worthy of promotion.[69]

---

64   J. C. Grot, *Bemerkungen über die Religionsfreiheit der Ausländer im Russischen Reiche in Rücksicht auf ihre verschiedenen Geimeinen, ihre kirchliche Einrichtungen, ihre Gebräuche und ihre Rechte* (3 vols, St Petersburg, Leipzig, 1797–8), vol. 3, pp. 295–6; Muralt, *Chronik*, pp. 11–12; Kämmerer, *Rußland und die Hugenotten*, p. 39.

65   J. Rousset de Missy [pseudonym: Baron Iwan Nestesuranoi], *Memoires du regne de Pierre le Grand, Empereur de Russie, Père de la Patrie, etc.* (4 vols, The Hague, Amsterdam, 1725–6), pp. 55–6; J. Rousset de Missy, *Cérémonial des cours de l'Europe* (Amsterdam, 1739).

66   Rousset de Missy, *Memoires du regne de Pierre le Grand*, pp. 55–6.

67   L. A. Langeron, 'Russkaya Armiya v God Smerti Ekateriny II', *Russkaya Starima*, 83 (1895): 169; Duffy, *The Military Experience in the Age of Reason*, p. 38.

68   Ibid., p. 43.

69   J. G. Lojewsky, *Selbstbiographie des Husaren-Obersten* (2 vols, Leipzig, 1843), vol. 2, pp. 294–5; Duffy, *The Military Experience in the Age of Reason*, pp. 44–5.

Huguenots also benefited from the fact that Russia was more cosmopolitan than most places of refuge in Central or Eastern Europe. Unlike their employment in largely Protestant armies, such as those of Brandenburg-Prussia and Britain, the refugees found themselves serving alongside both Roman Catholic and Orthodox officers. They were but one of a number of expatriate groups in Russia. There were even Roman Catholic Jacobites in the Russian army – the very people who had been the enemy in Ireland in the 1690s. By far the most important of them was Patrick Gordon of Auchleuchries, a Scottish soldier of fortune who had served the tsars of Muscovy for decades: in 1687 he was appointed Envoy Extraordinary to Russia by James II. It was Auchleuchries who induced Peter the Great to ignore the Williamite settlement in Britain, making Russia the only non-Catholic country in Europe which refused to acknowledge the outcome of the Glorious Revolution of 1688.[70]

Not all Scots in Russia were Jacobites or Roman Catholic, though Gordon met success in fostering a 'Catholic' party among anti-William expatriate Britons.[71] A letter, addressed by Protestant pastors and elders in Russia to the city of Geneva in 1720, confirms the international character of the 'foreign quarter' at St Petersburg: 'Our assembly is composed of English, Dutch, French refugees, Swiss and Geneves, many of whom are of rank and have held honourable employments at the court.'[72] The acceptability of Calvinist Scots to the Huguenots is evident in the 1693 marriage of Etienne Vechery de Coulon to a daughter of Major-General Crawford, a Scottish veteran of Russian service.[73] In turn, the social acceptability of the Huguenot officers to the nobles of their adoptive country is evidenced by the marriage of Henriette du Plessis to Prince P. Dolgorukov. Henriette was the sister of Franz Adolf Bandré du Plessis, the son of a Huguenot refugee, who arrived in Russia from Saxony in the 1720s. He was an engineer officer in the Russian army *c*.1730 and was later promoted to the rank of lieutenant-general.[74] The professionalism, competence and general honesty of senior Huguenot officers in Russia recommended them to leading Russian magnates. In 1748, an officer of the name de La Rivière became adjutant to Lieutenant-General P. S. Sumarokov because he possessed just these qualities.[75]

---

70   P. Gordon of Auchleuchries, *Tagebuch des Generals Patrick Gordon während seiner Kriegsdienste unter den Schweden und Polen vom Jahre 1653 bis 1661 und seines Aufenthaltes in Rußland vom Jahre 1661 bis 1699*, ed. M. Posselt and M. A. Obolenski (St Petersburg, 1849–53); see also A. F. Steuart, *Scottish Influences in Russian History: From the 16th Century to the Beginning of the 19th Century* (Glasgow, 1913).

71   Barary, *The Anglo-Russian Entente Cordiale of 1697–1698*, p. 23.

72   Dated St Petersburg, 25 April 1720: Weiss, *Histoire de France Protestante*, p. 583.

73   Gordon of Auchleuchries, *Tagebuch des Generals Patrick Gordon*, vol. 2, p. 503.

74   Amburger, 'Hugenottenfamilien in Rußland': 132.

75   Muralt, *Chronik*, p. 30; F. Tastevin, 'Les calvinistes française en Russie', *Feuilles d'Histoire du XVIIe au XXe siècle*, 2/4 (1910): 299.

IV

As with their employment elsewhere in Europe, Huguenots were taken on in Russia because the country was in a state of war and in great need of experienced and competent army personnel. Peter the Great's war with Sweden ensured that confessional divisions among his officers were overwhelmed by the demands of hard campaigning. An unexpected result of the cessation of hostilities with Sweden was the addition of a small number of Huguenots to the Russian army from that of Sweden. Some of these soldiers had served under the de La Gardies, a French family long associated with the Swedish crown.[76] Others were brought into Russian service by leading military figures, like Brigadier Moreau de Brasey, who formed a regiment including some of them under Peter the Great in 1711.[77]

As occurred elsewhere in Europe, tensions within the Huguenot community in Russia were strongly monitored and controlled. Jean Calvin had suggested that 'each of us should watch himself closely ... lest we be carried away by violent feelings'.[78] Calvin hoped that the magistracy, or government, of Reformed communities by lay elders would inspire each disciple's government of their own behaviour, which would aid the purity of their relationship with God via the Scriptures. This principle continued to be observed in Huguenot communities throughout Europe and it contributed greatly to the prevention of homicides within those communities. Where there is a report of a Frenchman being killed in a duel in Russia in 1689, there is a strong suspicion that he was Catholic and not a Huguenot.[79] Strong ministries existed in St Petersburg and Moscow, which both housed Lutheran churches comprehending the Calvinist worship of the Huguenots.[80] Russia was never a 'refuge' for the Huguenots in the way that the Netherlands or Great Britain became, and the spiritual demands of the refugees were looked after by a number of Huguenot pastors, who came, predominantly, from Switzerland. Some of them were second-generation Swiss by the time they arrived in Russia and, like the Genevan Leforts, their roots lay in France: Jean Curchod (*fl.*1774–7) was one of these able pastors, who brought with him pastors from farther parts.[81]

---

76   Fechner, *Chronik der Evangelischen-Gemeinden in Moskau*, vol. 1, pp. 152, 176–7; Tastevin, 'Les calvinistes française en Russie': 201; *Recueil des documents russes tirés des archives de famille des comtes de la Gardie*, ed. G. de Sahler (Ioriev-Dorpat, 1896), vol. 6, pp. 177–80.

77   R. Béringuier, *Die Stammbäume der Mitglieder der Französischen Kolonie in Berlin* (Berlin, 1887), p. 58.

78   J. Calvin, *Institutions of the Christian Religion*, ed. J. T. McNeill and F. L. Battles (2 vols, Philadelphia, 1960), vol. 1, p. 611; M. P. Holt, *The French Wars of Religion, 1562–1629* (Cambridge, 1995; reprinted 1997), p. 24.

79   F. H. du Rouillé (k.1689), from Brabant: Fechner, *Chronik der Evangelischen-Gemeinden in Moskau*, vol. 1, p. 388; P. Avril, *Voyage en divers états d'Europe et d'Asie, entrepris pour decouvrir un nouveau chemin à la Chine* (Paris, 1692), p. 251.

80   L. Gaultier, 'L'Eglise évangélique réformée de Moscou, 1629 à 1901', *Bulletin de la société de l'histoire du Protestantisme française*, 56 (1907): 5–16; Dalton, *Zur Geschichte der evangelischen Kirche*, cf. 'Hugenotten in Rußland'.

81   Muralt, *Chronik*, p. 18; Dalton, *Zur Geschichte der evangelischen Kirche*, p. 66.

So close were links with Swiss Calvinism, that Geneva was approached, in 1725, by a number of prominent refugees, including Dupré, Coulon, Lefort and Pelloutier, who requested that the French colony be considered as a daughter church of the Genevan Republic.[82] This may well have represented a separatist desire on the part of Russia's Huguenots, but there is little evidence that they resented or looked down upon other foreigners in Russia. Only in Russia's backward depths, where a colony of refugees formed on the banks of the Volga, did that community freeze itself in time.[83] One traveller in the early 1800s claimed that the inhabitants of the Volga Huguenot community, refusing to have any cultural traffic with their neighbours, still wore the large-skirted frock coat and high perruke wigs of the court of Louis XIV.[84]

As in other refuges, most Huguenots in Russia maintained a strict watch over their morality and general behaviour. The theologian Abel Burja commented on the good behaviour of the wives and daughters of the Huguenot immigrants, of whom he said their 'education was the same as that of the Cadet *corps*, as much as the difference of the sexes can permit'.[85] He insisted that one lady, Sophie de Lefort, was a 'respectable dame ... applying the same [quality] assiduously to her employment'.[86] Burja ascribed their excellent morals and conduct to the strictures of their Calvinist upbringing and faith.[87] The men of the refuge received just as much praise from him: 'The [French] *seigneurs* adopted approximately the manner of living of the other Europeans [in Russia]; the middle-class men, being usually freed slaves [n.b. apprentices], almost all preserve the manners of their first home [in France], and are [here] in rather small numbers'.[88] Some historians have gone further by claiming that the dispersal of the Huguenots aided the spread of Enlightenment philosophy along with the desacrilisation that was implicit to their Calvinist theology.[89]

Another similarity between Russian military Huguenot families and those elsewhere in Europe was the persistence of the army as a choice of career among their descendants. Just as in Britain and Brandenburg-Prussia, the descendants of Huguenots in Russia continued to serve in the Tsar's army until the end of the Old Regime. In Russia's case, this occurred during the Revolution of 1917. Before that date families such as the Gendres provided generations of soldiers. They were

---

82   Weiss, *Histoire de France Protestante*, p. 583.

83   V. Rjeoutski, 'Les français de la Volga: la politique migratoire russe des années 1760 et la formation des communautées francophones à Saint-Petersbourg et à Moscou', *Cahiers du monde russe*, 39/3 (July–September, 1998): 283–96.

84   Comte A. M. B. C. Pelletier de Lagarde, *Voyage de Moscou à Vienne, par Kow, Odessa, Constantinople, Bucharest et Hermanstadt* (Paris, 1812); published in English as *Journey in some Parts of Russia* (London, 1825), p. 347.

85   Burja, *Observations*, p. 93.

86   Sophie de Lefort (1764–97). Her sister, Angélique, married Baron K. H. Heyking: Burja, *Observations*, p. 93; Kämmerer, *Rußland und die Hugenotten*, p. 107 n. 769.

87   Amburger, *Geschichte*, p. 497; Tastevin, 'Calvinistes': 301.

88   Burja, *Observations*, p. 22.

89   Kämmerer, *Rußland und die Hugenotten*, p. 134; H. R. Trevor-Roper, *The Crisis of the Seventeenth Century: Religion, The Reformation, and Social Change* (1967; reprinted Indianapolis, 2001), p. 184.

descended from Joseph Gendre, a Huguenot refugee who arrived in Russia via Brandenburg. He became a lieutenant-colonel in the Russian army *c*.1720, was an official of the Russian War College by 1725, and ended his career as a major-general *c*.1740.[90] He had two sons, Andreus and Semen Osipovic, who both became officers in the 1760s.[91] A grandson, Wilhelm Gendre, extended the family's military tradition into the nineteenth century.[92]

V

The Huguenots who served Peter the Great and his successors were at the forefront of his wars against Sweden and the Ottoman Empire. They were also prominent throughout the Seven Years' War. Their contribution to the 'westernising' of Russia's army and navy was considerable. Their expertise in engineering, siege-craft and artillery, gained in part during the wars of the Grand Alliance (1688–97), was invaluable to Russia. The story of Huguenot soldiers in Russia contains many parallels to that in Britain and Brandenburg-Prussia. In each of these countries they provided skilled, competent and honest service to their new masters. In each they founded dynasties which continued to serve their adoptive country for generations. If Russia's Huguenot soldiers displayed one marked difference from those elsewhere in Europe, it was that the Huguenots of Moscow and St Petersburg tended to marry among the predominantly German foreign officer corps, rather than into the families of Russian Orthodox nobles. Even in this case, they were merely augmenting and cementing their membership of a separate, professional military class, which clearly had more in common with officers in Germany and Britain, than with the people of Russia.

Those French Protestants who came to Russia were rarely direct escapees of the effects of the Revocation of the Edict of Nantes. Some few came in the 1680s, more followed in the 1690s; but mostly they arrived after 1700, in a wave of second-generation migration from Germany, Britain and the Netherlands. They were adopted eagerly enough and formed one among a number of expatriate groups serving the Tsars. Their relations with other such groups demonstrates the complex character of the Russian 'refuge': they interacted with Jacobites, but mostly married among themselves or with Germans. What they brought with them, and what they fostered more than any of these expatriate communities, was an infrastructure of military training. Through their academies and pedagogic instruction they inculcated professional soldierly ethics into still-wild native nobles. As a group they were rightly respected for their competent approach to soldiering; as individuals, those most senior among them were esteemed for their honest and loyal character. What Russia gained from them was yet another foreign bulwark to the Tsarist regime, though in Russia they retained less of an individual identity than in other services.

---

90   Amburger, 'Hugenottenfamilien in Rußland': 128.

91   Andreus Gendre (1741–96) and Semen Osipovic Gendre (1738–95): Kämmerer, *Rußland und die Hugenotten*, p. 109; Muralt, *Chronik*, p. 27; Tastevin, 'Calvinistes': 299.

92   Wilhelm Gendre (1764–1801): Kämmerer, *Rußland und die Hugenotten*, p. 109.

What the Huguenots got from Russia was yet another place to settle, and one in which their particular skills were valued and put to good use by grateful masters.

Bibliography

Manuscript Sources

Beinecke Rare Book and Manuscript Library, Yale University
William Blathwayt Papers. The James Marshall and Marie-Louise Osborn
  Collection.

British Library
Townshend Papers. Letter Books of Moreau – Polish Ambassador at The Hague
  1687–88: Add. MS 38,494, vol. 3.

Huguenot Library, London University
Costello, V. and R. Flatman, 'British and Irish Sources for Huguenot Officers', paper
  for conference *Huguenot Soldiering* (London, 2001).
Glozier, M., *Huguenot Soldiers in Great Britain, The Netherlands, Brandenburg-
  Prussia, and Russia, c.1672*–1740, index (Sydney, 2001).
Gwynn, R. D., 'Huguenot Army Officers in the Service of the Crown in the Late
  Seventeenth and Early Eighteenth Centuries', index to G. H. Jones Cards.
Jones, G. H., 'Index of Huguenot officers in the service of the British Crown', Index
  (Jones Cards).
Vignoles–Duroure papers, correspondence 26A.
Wagner, H., 'Pedigrees', genealogical charts (Wagner Pedigrees).

Quai d'Orsay, Paris
Archives du Ministère des Affaires Etrangères, *Cahiers Politiques Hollande*.

Royal Irish Academy, Dublin
Dumont de Bostaquet, Isaac, 'Memoirs': MS 12N17.

Printed primary sources

*A Letter from an English Officer in His Majesty's Army in Ireland Giving a True
  Account of the Progress of Affairs in that Kingdom: Together with what Past at
  the Surrender of Waterford and Duncannon: And of His Majesty's March Towards
  Limerick. Dated July 29th, 1690* (London, 1690).
Addison, J., *The Works of the Late Right Honourable Joseph Addison, Esq.: Including
  the Whole Contents of Bishop Hurd's Edition, with Letters and Other Pieces not
  found in any Previous Collection; and Macaulay's Essay on His Life and Works*,
  ed. G. W. Greene (third edition, ed. T. Tickell) (6 vols, New York, 1856).
Ailesbury, T. Bruce, Earl of, *Memoirs of Thomas, Earl of Ailesbury: Written by
  Himself*, ed. W. E. Buckley (2 vols, Westminster: Roxburgh Club, 1890).

Aldrich, R., *The Register of the Most Noble Order of the Garter, from Its Cover in Black Velvet, Usually Called the Black Book: With Notes Placed at the Bottom of the Pages*, ed. J. Anstis (2 vols, London: John Barber, 1724).

Ancillon, C., *Histoire de l'Etablissement des François Réfugiés dans les Etats de Son Altesse Electorale de Brandebourg: Diejenigen, die vor ihrer Flucht ein Regiment geführt hatten, sind sofort wieder Regimentskommandeur geworden. Man hat sie sogar zum Generalmajor befördert* (Berlin: Robert Roger, 1690).

——, *Geschichte der Niederlassung der Réfugiés in den Staaten seiner kurfürstlichen Hoheit von Brandenburg*, Geschichtsblätter des Deutschen Hugenotten-Vereins 15/8 (Berlin, 1939).

Aubigné, A. d', *L'Histoire universelle* (3 vols, Maillé: Moussat [Saint-Jean d'Angely], 1616–20).

Aurignac, N___ d', 'Livre de guerre' (1663), in P. Azan (ed), *Un tacticien du XIIe siècle: Le maréchal de bataille d'Aurignac* (Paris: Chapelot, 1904).

Avaux, J.-A. de Mesmes, Comte d', *Négociations de Monsieur le comte d'Avaux en Hollande, depuis 1679, jusqu'en 1684* (Paris: Durand, 1752–3, 1754).

——, *Négociations du comte d'Avaux en Irlande, 1689–90*, ed. J. Hogan (Dublin: Stationery Office, 1934: reprinted Dublin: Stationery Office for the Irish Manuscripts Commission, 1958).

——, *Négociations de monsieur le comte d'Avaux, ambassadeur extraordinaire à la cour de Suède, pendant les années 1693, 1697, 1698*, ed. J. A. Wijnne, Historisch genootschap, gevestigd te. Nieuwe reeks 33–6 (Utrecht: Kemink and Sons, 1882/3).

——, *The negotiations of Count d'Avaux, ambassador etc.* (4 vols, London, 1755).

Avril, P., *Voyage en divers états d'Europe et d'Asie, entrepris pour decouvrir un nouveau chemin à la Chine* (Paris: Jean Boudot, 1692).

Bellingham, Sir T., *Diary of Thomas Bellingham: An Officer under William III*, ed. A. Hewitson (Preston: Toulmin, 1908).

Béringuer, R. (ed.), *Die Colonieliste von 1699. Role Générale des François Refugiez dans les Etats de S.A. Sérénité Electorale de Brandebourg, comme ils se sont trouvez 31. Dècembre 1699* (Berlin, 1888).

Bodeman, E. (ed.), *Briefwechsel der Herzogin Sophie von Hannover mit ihrem Bruder, dem Kurfürsten Karl Ludwig von der Pfalz, und des Letzteren mit seiner Schwägerin, der Pfalzgräfin Anna*, K. Preußischen Staatsarchiven 26 (Leipzig, 1885).

Boyer, A., *The History of the Reign of Queen Anne, Digested into Annals* (11 vols, London: A. Roper, 1703–13).

Burja, A., *Observations d'un voyageur sur la Russie, la Finlande, la Livonie, la Curlande et la Prusse* (Berlin, 1785; reprinted Maastricht, 1787).

Burnet, G., *A Supplement to Burnet's History of My own Time: Derived from his Original Memoirs, his Autobiography, his Letters to Admiral Herbert, and his Private Meditations: All Hitherto Unpublished*, ed. H. C. Foxcroft (Oxford: Clarendon Press, 1902).

——, *History of My Own Times*, ed. M. J. Routh (6 vols, Oxford: Clarendon Press, 1723–24; reprinted 1833, and vols 1 and 2, ed. O. Airy, Oxford: Clarendon Press, 1897).

Calendar of State Papers, Domestic Series, in the reign of William and Mary, ed. W. J. Hardy and E. Bateson (11 vols, Nendeln, 1913–69).

Calvin, J., *Institutions of the Christian Religion*, ed. J. T. McNeill and F. L. Battles (2 vols, Philadelphia: Westminster, 1960).

Carew, G., *Letters from George Carew to Sir Thomas Roe: Ambassador to the Court of the Great Mogul, 1615–1617*, ed. J. MacLean (London: Camden Society, 1840).

Carletonn, Dudley, *Dudley Carleton to John Chamberlain, 1603–1624: Jacobean Letters*, ed. M. Lee, Jr. (New Brunswick, NJ: Rutgers University Press, 1972).

Chappuzeau, S., *L'Europe viuante, ou Relation nouuelle, historique et politique de tous ses estats, selon la face qu'ils ont sur la fin de l'année M.DC.LXVI, etc.* (Geneva, 1666–7).

——, *Suite de l'Europe viuante, contenant la relation d'vn voyage fait en Allemagne aux mois d'Auril, May, Iuin, Iuillet & Aoust de l'année M.DC.LXIX. Où l'on void quelle est la face presente de plusieurs Estats d'Électeurs et de Princes de l'Empire, l'origine de leurs maisons, leur accroissement & leurs alliances, auec les portraits des Princes & des Princesses, suiuis des eloges des personnes les plus illustres de ce temps, etc.* (Geneva: I. H. Widerhold, 1671).

Churchill, John, Duke of Marlborough, *The Marlborough–Godolphin Correspondence*, ed. H. L. Snyder (3 vols, Oxford: Clarendon Press, 1975).

Clarendon, E. Hyde, Earl of Clarendon, *The Correspondence of Henry Hyde, Earl of Clarendon, and His Brother Laurence Hyde, Earl of Rochester: With the Diary of Lord Clarendon from 1687 to 1690, Containing Minute Particulars of the Events Attending the Revolution and the Diary of Lord Rochester During his Embassy to Poland in 1676*, ed. S. W. Singer (2 vols, London: H. Colburn, 1828).

Clarke, Rev. J. S. (ed.), *The Life of King James the Second, King of England, etc., Collected Out of the Memoirs Writ of His Own Hand* (2 vols, London: Longman and Co., 1816).

Cocks, R., *The Parliamentary Diary of Sir Richard Cocks, 1698–1702* ed. D. W. Hayton (Oxford: Clarendon Press, 1996).

Cokayne, G. E., *The Complete Peerage* (8 vols, London: St Catherine Press, 1887–98; reprinted 12 vols, London: St Catherine Press, 1910–59).

Commynes, P. de, *Mémoires*, ed. J. Calmette and G. Durville (3 vols, Paris: Champion, 1924).

Condé, Louis I de Boubon, Prince de, 'Mémoires du Prince de Condé', in J.-F. Michaud and J.-J.-F. Poujoulat (eds), *Nouvelle collection des mémoires pour servir à l'histoire de France, depuis le XIIIe siècle jusqu'à la fin du XVIIIe*, series 1 (32 vols, Paris, 1836–44), vol. 6 (1839).

Coolhaas, W. P. (ed.), *Generale Missiven van Gouverneurs-Generaal en Raden aan heren XVII der Verenigde Oostindische Compagnie*, Rijksgeschiedkundige Publicatiën 104 (The Hague, 1968).

Dangeau, P. de Courcillon, Marquis de, *Journal du marquis de Dangeau*, ed. Soulié, Dussieux, de Chennevières, Mantz, de Montaiglon, with additions by the Duc de Saint-Simon (19 vols, Paris: Firmin Didot frères, 1854–60).

Defoe, D., *The Memoirs of Capt. George Carleton, an English Officer who Served in the Two Last Wars against France and Spain ... Containing an Account of the*

Conduct of the Earl of Peterborough, etc. (London: E. Symon, 1728; reprinted 1854).

——, *The Earlier Life and the Chief Earlier Works of Daniel Defoe*, ed. H. Morley (London: Routledge, 1889).

——, *The True-Born Englishman and Other Writings*, ed. P. N. Furbank and W. R. Owens (London, New York: Penguin, 1997).

Digges de La Touche, J. J. (ed.), *Registers of the French Reformed Churches of St. Patrick and St. Mary, Dublin*, Huguenot Society Quarto Series 7 (Dublin, 1893).

Douen, O. (ed.), *La Révocation de l'Edit de Nantes à Paris* (3 vols, Paris: Fischbacher, 1894).

Dumont de Bostaquet, I., *Mémoires inédites de Dumont de Bostaquet, Gentilhomme Normand, sur les temps qui ont précédé et suivi la Révocation de l'Edit de Nantes sur le refuge et les expéditions de Guillaume III en Angleterre et en Irlande*, ed. C. Read and F. Waddington (Paris: Michel Lévy frères, 1864).

——, *Mémoires inedites de Isaac Dumont de Bostaquet, gentilhomme Normande*, ed. M. Richard (Paris: Mercure de France, 1968).

——, *Memoirs of Isaac Dumont de Bostaquet: A Gentleman of Normandy*, ed. D. W. Ressinger, Huguenot Society New Series 4 (London, 2005).

Evelyn, J., *Diary*, ed. A. Dobson (3 vols, London: Globe, 1908).

Franco-Irish Correspondence December 1688 – February 1692, ed. S. Mulloy (3 vols, Dublin: Stationery Office for the Irish Manuscripts Commission, 1983–4).

Frederick William, Elector of Brandenburg, *Die Briefe Friedrich Wilhelms I an den Fürsten Leopold von Anhalt-Dessau*, ed. O. Krauske (Berlin, 1905).

Gilbert, J. T. (ed.), *A Jacobite Narrative of the War in Ireland 1688–1691* (Dublin: J. Dollard, 1892; reprinted Shannon: Shannon University Press, 1971).

Gordon of Auchleuchries, P., *Tagebuch des Generals Patrick Gordon während seiner Kriegsdienste unter den Schweden und Polen vom Jahre 1653 bis 1661 und seines Aufenthaltes in Rußland vom Jahre 1661 bis 1699*, ed. M. Posselt and M. A. Obolenski (St Petersburg, 1849–53).

Grimeston, E., *A General Inuentorie of the History of France from the Beginning of that Monarchie ... Written by Ihon de Serres. And Continued [and] Translated out of French into English, by Edward Grimeston* (London: George Eld, 1607).

Hare, F., Bishop of St. Asaph and of Chichester, *The Conduct of the Duke of Marlborough During the Present War* (London: J. Morphew, 1712).

Heinsius, A., *Het Archief van den Raadpensionaris Antonie Heinsius, 1683–97*, ed. H. J. van der Heim (3 vols, The Hague, 1867–80).

Hertford: *Hertford County Records: Notes and Extracts from the Sessions Rolls, 1581–1698*, ed. W. J. Hardy (3 vols, Hertford: Simon and Co. Ltd, 1905).

Heyking, K. H., *Aus Polens und Kurlands letzten Tagen. Memoiren des Baron Karl Heinrich Heyking (1752–1796)*, ed. A. Heyking (Berlin: Ort, 1897).

Hugou de Bassville, N. J. (ed.), *Précis historique sur la vie et les exploits de François Le Fort. Citoyen de Genéve. Général et Grand-Admiral de Russie* (Paris: Laurent, Geneva: Paul Barde, 1784; reprinted 2 vols, Lausanne, 1786).

Huygens, C., *Journalen van Constantijn Huygens, den Zoon (Handschrift van de Koninklijke Akademie van Wetenschappen te Amsterdam)*, pt. 3, Werken von hat Historisch Genootschap, niewe serie 46 (Utrecht, 1888).

James II, *The Memoirs of James II: His campaigns as Duke of York, 1652–1660*, ed. Arthur Lytton Sells (London: Chatto and Windus, 1962).

Journals of the House of Commons: *The Journals and Sessional Papers and Votes of the House of Commons, and Blue Books in General*, ed. R. Flexman *et al.* (81 vols, London: Stationery Office, 1826).

Kervyn de Lettenhove, Baron J. (ed.), *Relations politiques des Pays-Bas et de l'Angleterre, sous le règne de Philippe II* (11 vols, Brussels: F. Hayez, 1882–1900).

Kervyn de Volkaersbeke, P. (ed.), *Correspondance de François de La Noue, surnommé Bras-de-Fer, accompagnée de notes historiques et précédée de la vie de ce grand capitaine* (8 vols, Gand: Duquesne, Paris: De la Haye, 1854).

Knötel, R. and C. Röchling (eds), *Chronik des Ersten Garderegiments zu Fuß und dessen Stamm-truppenteilen 1675–1900* (Oldenburg, Berlin, 1902).

Koser, R., O. Hintze and A. Naudé (eds), *Forschungen zur Brandenburgischen und Preußischen Geschichte*, Verein für Geschichte der Mark Brandenburg (54 vols, Leipzig, 1888–1943).

Krämer, F. J. L. (ed.), *Bijdragen en Mededelingen betreffende de Geschiedenis der Nederlanden* (vol. 19, The Hague, 1898).

Lagarde, Comte A. M. B. C. Pelletier de, *Voyage de Moscou à Vienne, par Kow, Odessa, Constantinople, Bucharest et Hermanstadt* (Paris, 1812).

La Noüe, F. de, *Discours politiques de militaires* (Basle: François Forest, 1587).

Le Fanu, T. P. (ed.), *Registers of the French Church of Portarlington, Ireland*, Huguenot Society Quarto Series 19 (Dublin, 1908).

——, (ed.), *Registers of the French Non-Conformist Churches of Lucy Lane and Peter Street, Dublin*, Huguenot Society Quarto Series 14 (Dublin, 1901).

Le Fanu, T. P. and W. H. Manchée (eds), *Dublin and Portarlington Veterans: King William III's Huguenot Army*, Huguenot Society Quarto Series 41 (London, 1946).

Leti, G., *Abrégé de l'histoire de la maison Sérénissime et Electorale de Brandenburg* (Amsterdam, 1667).

Leven and Melville Papers. Letters and State Papers chiefly Addressed to George Earl of Melville, Secretary of State for Scotland, 1689–1691, ed. W. L. Melville (Edinburgh: Bannatyne Club, 1843).

Lexington, R. Sutton, Lord, *The Lexington Papers*, ed. H. M. Sutton (London, 1851).

Luttrell, N., *A Brief Historical Relation of State Affairs from September 1678 to April 1714* (6 vols, Oxford: Clarendon Press, 1857).

——, *The Parliamentary Diary of Narcissus Luttrell, 1691–1639*, ed. H. Horwitz (Oxford: Clarendon Press, 1972).

Macky, J., *Memoirs of the Secret Services of J. Macky ... including, also, the True Secret History of the ... English and Scots Nobility, ... and other Persons of Distinction, from the Revolution*, ed. A. R. with marginal notes by Dean Swift, transcribed by T. Birch (London, The Hague, 1733).

Matveev, A., *Russkij diplomat vo Francii (zapisksi Andreja Matveeva)*, ed. I. S. Sarkova (Leningrad, 1972).

Maurier, L. Aubery du, *The Lives of all the Princes of Orange, from William the Great, Founder of the Common-wealth of the United Provinces* (1682), trans. T. Brown (London: T. Bennet, 1693).

Melvill, A. de, *Memoires de Chevalier de Melvill* (Amsterdam: Jacques Desbordes, 1704).

——, *Memoirs of Sir Andrew Melvill. Translated from the French*, foreword by Sir Ian Hamilton (London, New York: John Lane, 1918).

Michaud, J.-F., and J.-J.-F. Poujoulat (eds), *Nouvelle collection des mémoires pour servir à l'histoire de France, depuis le XIIIe siècle jusqu'à la fin du XVIIIe*, series 1 (32 vols, Paris, 1836–44).

Misson de Valberg, H., *Memoirs and Observations in his Travels over England*, trans. J. Ozells (London: D. Browne, 1721; French edition, The Hague, 1698).

Molesworth, R., Viscount, *An Account of Denmark as it was in the year 1692*, ed. Rosenkilde and Bagger (London: Timothy Goodwin, 1694; Copenhagen: Strauss and Kramer, 1976).

Montagu, M. W., *The Complete Letters of Lady Mary Wortley Montagu*, ed. R. Halsband (Oxford: Clarendon Press, 1966).

Mulloy, S. (ed.), *Franco-Irish Correspondence December 1688 – February 1692* (3 vols, Dublin: Stationery Office for the Irish Manuscripts Commission, 1983/4).

Mylius, C. O. (ed.), *Corpus Constitutionum Marchicarum, Oder Königl. Preußis. und Churfürstl. Brandenburgische in der Chur- und Marck Brandenburg, auch incorporirten Landen publicirte und ergangene Ordnungen, Edicta, Mandata, Rescripta [et]c. : Von Zeiten Friedrichs I. Churfürstens zu Brandenburg, [et]c. biß ietzo unter der Regierung Friedrich Wilhelms, Königs in Preußen [et]c. ad annum 1736. inclusivè*, ed. C. O. Mylius (2 vols, Berlin, Halle: Waysenhauses, 1737–55).

——, *Recueil des Edits, Ordonnances, Règlements et Rescripts, contenant les privilèges et les droits attribués aux François Réfugiés, dans les États du Roy de Prusse, et reglant tant pour l'ecclesiastique que pour l'administration de la justice, ce qui concerne les Colonies Françoises établies dans les États de sa Majesté. Auxquels sont joints la Discipline des Églises Réformées de France; et quelques autres édits traduits de leur langue originale pour l'usage de ses Colonies* (Berlin, 1750).

Netherlands, States General of the United Provinces of, *Resolutiën der Staten-Generaal van 1576 tot 1609*, ed. H. Rijperman (14 vols, The Hague: RGP, 1950).

O'Kelly, C., *Macariae Excidium, or the Destruction of Cyprus*, ed. G. N. Plunkett and E. Hogan (Dublin: Irish Archeological Society, 1896).

Orlers, J., *Den Nassauschen Lauren-crans: Beschrijvinge ende af-beeldinge van alle de Victorien, so te Water als te Lande, die Godt Almachtich de (...) Staten der Vereenichde Neder-landen verleent hefte (...)* (Leyden, 1610).

Parker, R., *Memoirs of the Military Transactions ... from 1683 to 1718* (London: Austin, 1747).

Parri, E. (ed.), *Vittorio Amedeo II ed Eugenio di Savoia nelle guerre della successione spagnuola; studio storico con documenti inediti* (Milan: Hoepli, 1888).

Pepys, S., *The Diary of Samuel Pepys*, ed. R. Latham and W. Matthews (10 vols, London: Bell and Hyman, 1970–83).

Playstowe, P., *The History of the Wars in Ireland, betwixt Their Majesties Army and the Forces of the late King James, by an Officer in the Royal Army* (London: B. Johnson, 1691).

Pluncket, T., *The Character of a Good Commander: Together with a Short Commendation of the Famous Artillery (more properly Military) Company of London: Also a Brief Encomium on the Duke and Worthy Prince Elector of Brandenburg: Lastly, Plain Dealing with Treacherous Dealers: whereunto is Annexed the General Exercise of the Prince of Orange's Army* (London: William Marshall, 1689).

Priesdorf, K. von (ed.), *Soldatisches Führertum. Die Generale der brandenburgisch-preußischen Armee* (10 vols, Hamburg, 1936–42), vol. 1 'Die Generale von den Anfängen der brandenburgisch-Preußischen Armee bis 1740'.

Rapin de Thoyras, P., *The History of England by M. Rapin de Thoyras*, ed. N. Tyndal (4 vols, London, 1743–7).

Recueil général des anciennes lois Françaises (Paris, 1672–86).

Reglement vor die Königlich Preußische Infanterie von 1726, Bibliotheca Rerum Militarum, Quellen und Darstellungen zur Militärwissenschaft und Militärgeschichte (Osnabrück, 1968).

Reresby, J., *Memoirs of Sir John Reresby. The Complete Text and a Selection from His Letters*, ed. W. H. Speck, (London: Royal Historical Society, 1991).

——, *The Memoirs of ... Sir John Reresby ... Containing Several Private and Remarkable Transactions, from the Restoration to the Revolution inclusively*, ed. J. J. Cartwright (London: Longman, Green and Co., 1875).

Rou, J., *Mémoires inédits et opuscules de Jean Rou, avocat du parlement de Paris; Secrétaire-interprete des Etats Généraux de Hollande*, ed. F. Waddington (2 vols, Paris, The Hague: Société de l'histoire du protestantisme français, 1857).

Rousset de Missy, J., *Cérémonial des cours de l'Europe* (Amsterdam, 1739).

——, [pseudonym: Baron Iwan Nestesuranoi], *Memoires du regne de Pierre le Grand, Empereur de Russie, Père de la Patrie, etc.* (4 vols, The Hague, Amsterdam, 1725–6).

Russell, R., *Letters of Rachel, Lady Russell*, ed. Lord J. (later Earl) Russell (2 vols, London, 1853).

Savile, G., *The Life and Letters of Sir George Savile, Bart., First Marquis of Halifax*, ed. H. C. Foxcroft (2 vols, London: Longmans, Green and Co., 1898).

Sahler, G. de (ed.), *Recueil des documents russes tirés des archives de famille des comtes de la Gardie* (Ioriev, Dorpat, 1896).

Saint-Evremond, C. de Marguetel de, *Véritables Œuvres de M. de Saint-Evremond, publiées sur les Manuscrits de l'Auteur* (5 vols, London: Jacob Tonson, 1706).

——, *Oeuvres de Saint-Evremond*, ed. René de Planhol (3 vols, Paris: A la cité des livres, 1927).

——, *Véritables oevres de Saint-Evremond* (London, 1706; second edition).

Saint-Simon, H., Marquis de, *Histoire de la guerre des Alpes* (Amsterdam: Marc Michel Rey, 1770).

Savage, J., *Memoires of the Transactions in Savoy During this War: Wherein the Duke of Savoy's Foul Play with the Allies, and His Secret Correspondence with the French King, are Fully Detected and Demonstrated, by Authentick Proofs, and Undeniable Matter of Fact: With Remarks upon the Separate Treaty of Savoy with France, and the Present Posture of Affairs with Relation to a General Peace* (London: M. Gylliflower *et al.*, 1697).

Schmertosch, R., *Denkschriften französischer Réfugiés zu den Friedensverhandlungen von Rijswijk* (Pirna, 1898).

Shaw, W. A. (ed.), *Letters of Denization and Acts of Naturaliation for Aliens in England and Ireland, 1603–1700*, Huguenot Society Quarto Series 8 (Lymington, 1911).

Somers, J., Lord, *A Collection of Scarce and Valuable Tracts*, ed. Sir W. Scott (13 vols, London: T. Cadell and W. Davies, 1809–14).

——, 'A list of seven Thousand Men, appointed by his Majesty, in his late Proclamation to be the standing Forces of this Kingdom 1699', in *A Second Collection of Scarce and Valuable Tracts etc.* (4 vols, London, 1750).

——, (ed.), 'A True and Exact Relation of the Prince of Orange's Publick Entrance into Exeter', in *A Second Collection of Scarce and Valuable Tracts etc.* (4 vols, London, 1750).

Story Rev. G., *A Continuation of the Impartial History of the Wars of Ireland* (London: R. Chiswell, 1693).

——, *A True and Impartial History of the Most Material Occurrences in the Kingdom of Ireland During the Last Two Years* (London; R. Chiswell, 1691).

Swift, J., *The Poems of Jonathan Swift*, ed. H. Williams (Oxford: Clarendon Press, 1958).

——, *Miscellaneous and Autobiographical Pieces and Marginalia*, ed. H. Davis (Oxford: Basil Blackwell, 1962).

Talbot, C., *Private and Original Correspondence of Charles Talbot, Duke of Shrewsbury*, ed. W. Coxe (London: Longman, Hurst, Rees, Orme and Brown, 1821).

Ten Raa, F. J. G., F. de Bas and J. W. Wijn (eds), *Het Staatsche Leger, 1568–1795* (8 vols, Breda, The Hague, 1911–64).

Tutchin, J., *The Foreigners: A Poem* (London: A. Baldwin, 1700).

Verburgt, J. W. (ed.), 'Liste des pensions des Officiers Français refugies, d'apres la resolution des Etats Generaux. 1683–1689. 1697. 1698. 1700. 1717', in *Inventaire des Archives Wallonnes* (Bibliothèque Wallonne, 1950).

Vere, Sir Francis, *The Commentaries of Sir Francis Vere*, ed. W. Dillingham (1657), published in E. Arber and T. Seccombe (eds), *Stuart Tracts 1603–1693*, intro. C. H. Firth (New York: Cooper Square Publishers, 1964).

Voltaire, J. F. M. Arouet de, *Histoire de l'Empire de Russie sous Pierre le Grand. Par l'auteur de l'histoire de Charles XII* (2 vols, Geneva, 1759–63).

——, 'Siècle de Louis XIV', in *Oeuvres completes de Voltaire* (69 vols, Paris [Kehl]: Imprimerie de la Société Littéraire-Typographique, 1784–9).

——, *The History of Charles the XIIth, King of Sweden*, trans. W. S. Kenrick [incl. *The Life of Peter the Great*, trans. J. Johnson] (London: Fielding and Walker, 1780).

Walpole, H., *Miscellaneous Correspondence*, ed. W. S. Lewis (New Haven: Yale University Press, Oxford: Oxford University Press, 1980).

Westminster Abbey Registers, ed. J. L. Chester, Harleian Society 10 (London, 1875; reprinted London, 1976).

Whittle, J., *An Exact Diary of the Late Expedition of his Illustrious Highness the Prince of Orange into England etc.* (London, 1689).

Wicquefort, A. de (ed.), *Histoire des Provinces Unis des Pais-Bas* (4 vols, Amsterdam: M. L. E. Lenting and C. A. Chais van Buren, 1861, 1864, 1866, 1874).

Wilkins, W. Walker (ed.), 'A Litany Recommended to the Ecclesiastical Commissioners', in *Political Ballads of the Seventeenth and Eighteenth Centuries* (2 vols, London, 1860).

William III, *Correspondentie van Willem III en van Hans Willem Bentinck, eersten graaf van Portland*, ed. N. Japikse (5 vols, The Hague: Rijks Geschiedkundige Publicatiën, 1927–33).

——, *Letters of William III and Louis XIV and Their Ministers: Illustrative of the Domestic and Foreign Politics of England, from the Peace of Ryswick to the Accession of Philip V of Spain, 1697 to 1700*, ed. P. Grimblot (2 vols, London: Longman, Brown, Green, and Longmans, 1848).

Williams, Sir R., *The Works of Sir Roger Williams*, ed. J. X. Evans (Oxford: Clarendon Press, 1972).

Withers, J., *Secret History of the Late Ministry* (London: J. Barker, 1715).

Secondary Sources

Agnew, D. C. A., *Henri de Ruvigny, Earl of Galway: A Filial Memoir with a Prefatory Life of His Father the Marquis de Ruvigny* (Edinburgh: William Patterson, 1864).

——, *Protestant Exiles from France in the Reign of Louis XIV* (2 vols, London, Edinburgh: D. C. A. Agnew, eighth edition 1886).

Alphen, G. van, *De stemming van de Engelschen tegen de Hollanders in Engeland tijdens de regeering van den koning-stadhouder Willem III 1688–1702* (Assen: Van Gorcum and Co., 1938).

Amburger, E., *Die Anwerbung ausländischer Fachkräfte für die Wirtschaft Rußlands vom 15. bis ins 19. Jahrhundert* (Wiesbaden: Otto Harrassowitz, 1968).

Andrews, S., *Eighteenth Century Europe: The 1680s to 1815* (London: Longman, 1965).

Arthur, Sir G., *The Story of the Household Cavalry* (2 vols, London, 1909–26).

Asche, M., *Neusiedler im verheerten Land – Kriegsfolgenbewältigung, Migrationssteuerung und Konfessionspolitik im Zeichen des Landeswiederaufbaus. Die Mark Brandenburg nach den Kriegen des 17. Jahrhunderts* (Münster, 2006).

Atkinson, C. T., *History of the Royal Dragoons, 1661–1914* (Glasgow: Glasgow University Press, 1934).

Bahl, P., *Der Hof des Großen Kurfürsten: Sudien zur Amsträgerschaft Brandeburg-Preußens* (Cologne, Weimar, Wien: Böhlau, 2001).

Baker, G., *History of the Antiquities of the County of Northampton* (2 vols, London: J. B. Nichols and Son, 1822–41).

Balani, D., *Il vicario tra città e Stato. L'ordine pubblico e l'annona nella Torino del Settecento* (Turin: Deputazione subalpina, 1987).

Barany G., *The Anglo-Russian Entente Cordiale of 1697–1698: Peter I and William at Utrecht*, East European Monographs (Boulder, New York: Columbia University Press, 1986).

Barbarisi, G., C. Capra, F. Degrada and F. Mazzocca (eds), *L'amabil rito. Società e cultura nella Milano di Parini* (Milan: Cisalpino, 2000).

Barberis, W., *Le armi del principe. La tradizione militare sabauda* (Turin: Einaudi, 1988).

Baxter, D., *Servants of the Sword, French Intendants of the Army, 1630–70* (Urbana: University of Illinois Press, 1976).

Baxter, S. B., *William III and the Defense of European Liberty 1650–1702* (New York: Harcourt, Brace and World Inc., 1966).

Beauclaire, H. de, *Une mésalliance dans la maison de Brunswick (1665–1725): Eléonore Desmier d'Olbreuze, Duchesse de Zell* (Paris: Libraire H. Oudin, 1884).

——, *Die letzte Herzogin von Celle: Eleonore Desmier d'Olbreuze 1665–1725*, ed. Freiherr E. Grote (Hanover, 1886).

Beckett, J. C., *Protestant Dissent in Ireland* (London: Faber and Faber, 1948).

Beddard, R., *A Kingdom Without a King: The Journal of the Provisional Government in the Revolution of 1688* (London: Phaidon, 1988).

Benedict, P., 'The Dynamics of Protestant Militancy: France, 1555–1563', in P. Benedict *et al.* (eds), *Reformation, Revolt and Civil War in France and the Netherlands 1555–1585* (Koninklijke Nederlandse Akademie van Wetenschappen, Verhandelingen: Afd. Letterkunde, new series 176, Amsterdam, 1999).

Benstatt-Wahlberg, N. von, *Aus den Voranstalten des Kadetten-Corps und der Haupt-Kadettenanstalt zu Lichterfelde* (2 vols, Hanover, 1891).

Berg, W. E. J., *De réfugiés in de Nederlanden na de herroeping van het Edict van Nantes. Eene proeve van onderzoek naar den invloed, welken hunne overkomst gehad heeft op handel en nijverheid, letteren, beschaving en zeden* (8 vols, Amsterdam: Johannes Müller, 1845).

Béringuier, R. (ed.), *Die Colonieliste von 1699. Role Générale des François Refugiez dans les Etats de S.A. Sérénité Electorale de Brandebourg, comme ils se sont trouvez 31. Dècembre 1699* (Berlin: Mittler, 1888; republished Berlin: Scherer, 1990).

——, *Die Stammbäume der Mitglieder der Französischen Kolonie in Berlin* (Berlin: Mittler, 1887).

Beuleke, W., *Die Hugenotten in Niedersachsen*, Quellen und Darstellungen zur Geschichte Niedersachsens 58 (Hildesheim: Lax, 1960).

——, *Die Südfranzosen in den uckermärkischen Hugenottenkolonien Prenzlau, Potzlow und Strasburg*, Geschichtsblatt Band 18/7 (Sickte, 1980).

——, *Studien zum Refuge in Deutschland und zur Ursprungsheimat seiner Mitglieder*, Geschichtsblätter der Deutschen Hugenotten-Vereins 16 XVI. Zehnt, Heft 3 (Brunswick, 1966).

Bianchi, P., *'Baron Litron' e gli altri. Militari stranieri nel Piemonte del Settecento*, preface by P. Del Negro (Turin: Gribaudo, 1998).

——, with A. Merlotti, *Cuneo in età moderna. Città e Stato del Piemonte d'antico regime* (Milan: Franco Angeli, 2002).

——, 'La fortuna dell'Accademia Reale di Torino nei percorsi europei del viaggio di formazione', in R. Maggio Serra, F. Mazzocca, C. Sisi and C. Spantigati (eds), *Vittorio Alfieri. Aristocratico ribelle (1749–1803)* (Milan: Electa, 2003).

——, 'La riorganizzazione militare del Ducato di Savoia e i rapporti del Piemonte con la Francia e la Spagna. Da Emanuele Filiberto a Carlo Emanuele II', in *Guerra y Sociedad en la Monarquía Hispánica. Política, Estrategia y Cultura en la Europa Moderna (1500–1700). Congreso internacional de historia militar, Madrid 9–12 March 2005* (Madrid, 2006).

——, 'Militari, banchieri, studenti. Presenze protestanti nella Torino del Settecento', in P. Cozzo, F. De Pieri and A. Merlotti (eds), *Valdesi e protestanti a Torino. XVIII–XX secolo* (Turin, 2005).

——, *Onore e mestiere. Le riforme militari nel Piemonte del Settecento* (Turin: Silvio Zamorani Editore, 2002).

——, '"Quel fortunato e libero paese". L'Accademia Reale e i primi contatti del giovane Alfieri con il mondo inglese', in M. Cerruti, M. Corsi and B. Danna (eds), *Alfieri e il suo tempo* (Turin, Asti: *Archivum Romanicum*, 2001).

Bianchi, P. and L. C. Gentile (eds), *L'affermarsi della corte sabauda. Dinastie, poteri, élites in Piemonte e Savoia fra tardo Medioevo e prima età moderna* (Turin, 2006).

Birnstiel, E., *Die Hugenotten in Berlin oder Die Schule der Untertanen* (Berlin: Deutscher Kunstverlag, 1986).

Bischoff, J. E., *Lexikon deutscher Hugenotten-Orte mit Literatur- und Quellen-Nachweisen für ihre evangelisch-reformierten Réfugiés-Gemeinden von Flamen, Franzosen, Waldensern und Wallonen*, Geschichtsblätter des Deutschen Hugenotten-Vereins 22 (Bad Karlshafen: Orth, 1994).

Black, J., *European Warfare, 1494–1660* (London: Routledge, 2002).

——, *European Warfare, 1660–1815* (London: UCL Press, 1994).

Blanc, R., *Histoire du Pays Duraquois (Histoire du château, de la ville, des seigneurs de Duras et de son pays)* (Duras, Eymet: Gombeaud, 1979).

Blanchard, A., *Les ingénieurs du roy de Louis XIV à Louis XVI: étude du corps des fortifications* (Montpellier: Université Paul Valéry, 1979).

Böhm, M., J. Häseler and R. Violet (eds), *Hugenotten zwischen Migration und Integration. Neue Forschungen zum Refuge in Berlin und Brandenburg* (Berlin: Metropol, 2005).

Boles, L. H., *The Huguenots, the Protestant Interest and the War of the Spanish Succession, 1702–1714*, American University Studies 9, History 188 (New York: Peter Lang, 1997).

Bonifa, A., and H. Krum, *Les huguenots à Berlin et en Brandebourg de Louis XIV à Hitler* (Paris: Éditions de Paris/Max Chaleil, 2000).

Bonin, U. W. B. von, *Geschichte des Ingenieurkorps und der Pioniere in Preußen* (2 vols, Berlin, 1877–8; reprinted Wiesbaden, 1981).

Brancaccio, N., *L'esercito del vecchio Piemonte. Gli ordinamenti. Parte I: Dal 1560 al 1814* (Rome: Libreria dello Stato, 1923).

Brandenburg, N. E., *Materialy dlja istorii artillerijskago upravlenija v Rossi 'Prikaz artillerii' (1701–1720)* (St Petersburg, 1876).

Braudel, F., *The Mediterranean World in the Age of Philip II*, trans. S. Reynolds (London: Collins, 1973).

Bregulla, H., *et al.* (eds), *Hugenotten in Berlin* (Berlin: Union Verlag, 1988).

Brereton, J. M., *A History of the Fourth/Seventh Royal Dragoon Guards and Their Predecessors, 1685–1980* (Catterick: The Regiment, 1982).

Brown, P. D., *William Pitt, Earl of Chatham: The Great Commoner* (London: Allen and Unwin, 1978).

Bulferetti, L., *Le relazioni diplomatiche tra lo Stato sabaudo e la Prussia durante il regno di Vittorio Amedeo III* (Milan, 1941).

Caldicott, C. E. J., H. Gough and J. P. Pittion (eds), *The Huguenots and Ireland* (Dublin: Glendale Press, 1987).

Callow, J., *The Making of King James II: The Formative Years of a Fallen King* (Stroud: Sutton, 2000).

Candaux, J.-D. (ed.), *Die Hugenotten in der Schweiz* (Lausanne: Musée historique de l'ancien-Evêché, 1985).

Carroll, S., *Noble Power During the French Wars of Religion: The Guise Affinity and the Catholic Cause in Normandy* (Cambridge: Cambridge University Press, 1998).

Carutti, D., *Storia della diplomazia della corte di Savoia (1494–1773)* (4 vols, Turin: Fratelli Bocca, 1875–80).

Cerny, G., *Theology, Politics and Letters at the Crossroads of European Civilization: Jacques Basnage and the Baylean Huguenot Refugees in the Dutch Republic* (Dordrecht, Boston, Lancaster: Kluwer Academic Publishers, 1987).

Chaline, O., 'La bataille de la Montagne Blanche 8 novembre 1620', in L. Bély and I. Richefort (eds), *L'Europe des traités de Westphalie: Esprit de la diplomatie et diplomatie de l'esprit* (Paris: M. Arnold, 2000).

Chambrier, M., Baroness A. de, *Henri de Mirmand et les réfugiés de Révocation de l'Édict de Nantes, 1650–1721* (Neuchâtel: Attinger frères, 1910).

Chandler, D., *Sedgemoor* (London: Anthony Mott Ltd, 1985).

Childs, J., *The Army, James II and the Glorious Revolution* (Manchester: Manchester University Press, 1980).

——, *The Army of Charles II* (London, Toronto: Routledge and Kegan Paul, 1976).

——, *The British Army of William III 1689–1702* (Manchester: Manchester University Press, 1987).

——, 'Military Élites in Seventeenth-Century England', in F. Bosbach, K. Robbins and K. Urbach (eds), *Geburt oder Leistung? Elitenbildung im deutsch-britischen Vergleich* (Munich: K. G. Saur, 2003).

——, with A. Corvisier and M. Mensah (eds), *La Guerre au XVIIe siècle* (Paris: Autremont, 2004).

Churchill, W. S., *Marlborough: His Life and Times* (4 vols, London: George Harrap, 1933–8).

Clair-Louis, J., *Pourquoi Louis de Durfort-Duras quitta la France* (Paris, 1964).

Claydon, T., *William III and the Godly Revolution* (Cambridge: Cambridge University Press, 1996).

Cobbett: *Cobbett's Parliamentary History of England. From the Norman Conquest, in 1066, to the Year 1803 etc.* (12 vols, London, from 1809).

Cohen, G., *Le Séjour de Saint-Évremond en Hollande et l'entrée de Spinoza dans le champ de la pensée française* (Paris, 1926).

Constant, J.-M., 'The Protestant Nobility in France during the Wars of Religion: A Leaven of Innovation in a Traditional World', in P. Benedict *et al.* (eds), *Reformation, Revolt and Civil War in France and the Netherlands 1555–1585* (Amsterdam: Koninklijke Nederlandse Akademie van Wetenschappen, 1999).

Contamine, P. (ed.), *Histoire militaire de France* (4 vols, Paris: Presses universitaires de France, 1992–4).

Contessa, C., *et al* (eds), *La Campagne di Guerra in Piemonte (1703–1708) el'assedio di Torino (1706)* (9 vols, Turin: Fratelli Bocca, 1908–33).

Corbett, J. S., *England in the Seven Years' War: A Study in Combined Strategy* (London: Longmans, 1907).

Corvisier, A., 'Les Guerres de Religion, 1559–1598', in P. Contamine (ed.), *Histoire militaire de France* (4 vols, Paris: Presses universitaires de France, 1992–4), vol. 1.

Cottret, B., *The Huguenots in England: Immigration and Settlement, c.1550–1700* (Cambridge: Cambridge University Press, 1985).

Courcelles, C. de, *Dictionnaire historique et biographique des généraux français. Depuis le onzième siècle jusqu'en 1823* (9 vols, Paris: Arthus Bertrand, 1820–3).

Crousaz, A. F. J. von, *Geschichte des Königlich Preußischen Kadetten-Corps, nach seiner Entstehung, seinem Entwicklungsgange und seinen Resultaten, aus den Quellen geschöpft und systematisch bearbeitet* (Berlin, 1857).

Cunningham, W., *Alien Immigrants to England* (London: Frank Cass and Co. Ltd, 1897).

Danaher, K. and J. G. Simms (eds), *The Danish Force in Ireland 1690–1691* (Dublin: Irish Manuscript Commission, 1962).

Dalton, C., *English Army Lists and Commission Registers, 1661–1714* (6 vols, London: Eyre and Spottiswoode, 1892–1904).

——, *Life and Times of General Sir Edward Cecil, Viscount Wimbledon* (2 vols, London: S. Low, Marston, Searle and Rivington, 1885).

Dalton, H., *Zur Geschichte der evangelischen Kirche in Rußland* (2 vols, Gotha, 1887–9; republished in one vol. Leipzig, 1893, and Amsterdam, 1968).

Decken, Friedrich von der, *Feldzüge Herzog Georg Wilhelms von Celle* (Hanover, 1838).

Delbrück, H., *Geschichte der Kriegskunst im Rahmen der politischen Geschichte* (4 vols, Berlin: Walter de Gruyter, 1900–20).

Desel, J., *Hugenotten in der Literatur. Eine Bibliographie. Hugenotten, Waldenser, Wallonen und ihr Umfeld in Erzählung, Biographie, Hagiographie, Drama, Geschichtsschreibung und Gedicht*, Geschichtsblätter des Deutschen Hugenotten-Vereins 25 (Bad Karlshafen, 1996).

Deyon, S., *Du loyalisme au refus: les protestants français et leur deputé général entre la Fronde et la Revocation* (Villeneuve-d'Ascq: Universite de Lille III, 1976).

Der Große Kurfürst (Sammler, Bauherr, Mäzen, 1620–88) (exhibition catalogue), ed. under general direction of Staatlichen Schlösser und Gärten Potsdam-Sanssouci (Potsdam, 1988).

Dohna, C. zu, *Die Denkwürdigkeiten des Burggrafen und Grafen Christoph zu Dohna*, ed. R. Grieser (Göttingen: Vandenhoeck and Ruprecht, 1974).

Döhner, O., *Das Hugenottengeschlecht Souchay de la Duboissière und seine Nachkommen*, Deutsches Famililensarchiev. Ein genealogisches Sammelwerk 19 (Neustadt-an-der-Aisch, 1961).

Douen, O., *Les Premiers Pasteurs du Désert (1685–1700)* (2 vols, Paris: Grassart, 1879).

Droste, C., *Overblyfsels van geheugenissen* (2 vols, The Hague, 1728).

Dubost, J.-F., *La France italienne* (Paris: Aubier-Histoire, 1997).

Duchhardt, H. (ed.), *Der Exodus der Hugenotten. Die Aufhebung des Edikts von Nantes 1685 als europäisches Ereignis*, Beihefte zum Archiv für Kulturgeschichte 24 (Cologne, Wien, 1985).

——, 'Die Konfessionspolitik Ludwigs XIV und die Aufhebung das Edikts von Nantes', in H. Duchhardt (ed.), *Der Exodus der Hugenotten: Die Aufhebung des Edikts von Nantes 1685 als europaisches Ereignis* (Cologne, Wien, 1985).

Duffy, C., *European Warfare in the Age of Reason* (London: Routledge and Kegan Paul, 1987).

——, *The Military Experience in the Age of Reason* (New York: Atheneum, 1987).

Dumouriez, C. F. Duperrier-, *Campagnes du Maréchal de Schomberg en Portugal, 1662–1668* (London: Cox, Fils and Baylis, 1807).

Durand, Y., *La Maison de Durfort à l'Époque Moderne: Fontenay-le-Comte* (France: Lussaud, 1975).

Earle, P., *The Life and Times of James II* (London: Weidenfeld and Nicolson, 1972).

Eccles, W. J., *The Canadian Frontier* (New York, London, Toronto: Holt, Rinehart and Winston, 1969).

Eggers, H., *Das altfranzösische Geschlecht Chappuzeau: Eine genealogische Skizze nebst Anhang. Fortgeführt von C. Chappuzeau* (Hanover, 1968).

Engelen, B., 'Fremde in der Stadt: Die Garnisonsgesellschaft Prenzlaus im 18. Jahrhunderts', in K. Neitmann and J. Theil (eds), *Die Herkunft der Brandenburger: Sozial- und mentalitätsgeschichtliche Beiträge zur Bevölkerung Brandenburgs vom hohen Mittelalter bis vum 20. Jahrhundert* (Potsdam: Berlin-Brandenburg, 2001), pp. 113–26.

Erman, J. P., *Memoire historique sur la fondation des colonies francois dans les etats du roi* (Berlin, 1785).

——, with P. C. F. Reclam, *Mémoires pour servir à l'histoire des Réfugiés François dans les États du Roi* (9 vols, Berlin, 1782–99).

Estorff, L. von, *Das Geschlecht der von Estorff in der Geschichte seiner Heimat des Bardengaues und des späteren Herzogtums Lüneburg* (Uelzen: Becker, 1925).

Favre, J., *Précis historiques sur la famille du Durfort de Duras* (Paris, 1858).

Fechner, A. W., *Chronik der Evangelischen-Gemeinden in Moskau. Zum dreihundertjährigen jubiläum der Evangelisch-Lutherischen St. Michaelis-Gemeinde zusammengestellt* (2 vols, Moscow: Deubner, 1876).

Feuchtwanger, E. J., *Prussia: Myth and Reality, the Role of Prussia in German History* (Chicago: Henry Regnery, 1970).

Fischer, G., *Die Hugenotten in Berlin* (Berlin: Union, 1988).

Fisher, H. A. L., *A History of Europe* (London: Edward Arnold and Co., 1936).

Flick, A., *Die Geschichte der Deutsch-reformierten Gemeinde in Celle 1709–1805. Von ihren Anfängen bis zum Zusammenschluß mit der Französisch-reformierten Gemeinde*, Tagungsschriften des Deutschen Hugenotten-Vereins 12 (Bad Karlshafen, 1994).

—— and A. de Lange (eds), *Von Berlin bis Konstantinopel. Eine Aufsatzsammlung zur Geschichte der Hugenotten und Waldenser*, Geschichtsblätter der Deutschen Hugenotten-Gesellschaft 35 (Bad Karlshafen, 2001).

—— with A. Hack and S. Maehnert, *Hugenotten in Celle*, catalogue of exhibition in Celle castle, 9 April – 8 May 1994 (Celle, 1994).

——, and S. Maehnert, *Archivbestände der Französisch-reformierten Gemeinden Lüneburg und Celle. Mit einer geschichtlichen Einleitung und einer Bibliographie*, Geschichtsblätter des Deutschen Hugenotten-Vereins 24 (Bad Karlshafen, Celle: Kleine Schriften zur Celler Stadtgeschichte 1, 1997).

Forstreuter, K., *Preußen und Rußland im Mittelalter. Die Entwicklung ihrer Beziehungen vom 13. bis 17. Jarhhundert* (Königsberg, Berlin: Ost-Europa, 1938).

Francis, A. D., *The Methuens and Portugal, 1691–1708* (Cambridge: Cambridge University Press, 1966).

Fratini, M. (ed.), *L'annessione sabauda del Marchesato di Saluzzo. Tra dissidenza religiosa e ortodossia cattolica. Secoli XVI–XVIII* (Turin: Claudiana, 2004).

Friederich, C. (ed.), *300 Jahre Hugenottenstadt Erlangen. Vom Nutzen der Toleranz. Ausstellungskatalog* (Nuremberg: Tümmels, 1986).

Friedrich II und die Kunst, 200th anniversary exhibition (catalogue), ed. under general direction of Staatlichen Schlösser und Gärten Potsdam-Sanssouci (Potsdam, 1986).

Froude, J. A., *The English in Ireland in the Eighteenth Century* (3 vols, London: Longmans Green, 1872–74).

Fuhrich-Grubert, U., *Die Französische Kirche zu Berlin. Ihre Einrichtungen 1672–1945,* Tagungsschriften des Deutschen Hugenotten-Vereins 11 (Bad Karlshafen, 1992).

Gahrig, W. (ed.), *Hugenotten, Willkommen in der Mark: Die Mark Brandenburg – Zeitschrift für die Mark und das Land Brandenburg*, Heft 48 (Berlin, 2003).

Gibbs, G. G., 'Huguenot Contribution to England's Intellectual Life, and England's Intellectual Commerce with Europe, *c.*1680–1720', in I. Scouloudi (ed.), *Huguenots in Britain and their French Background, 1550–1800* (London: Macmillan, 1987).

Giersberg, H. J. (ed.), *Das Edikt von Potsdam 1685. Die französische Einwanderung in Brandenburg-Preußen und ihre Auswirkungen auf Kunst, Kultur und Wissenschaft. Ausstellung der Staatlichen Schlösser und Gärten Potsdam-Sanssouci in Zusammenarbeit mit dem Zentralen Staatsarchiv Merseburg und dem Staatsarchiv Potsdam. Potsdam-Sanssouci, Neues Palais 24. August bis 10. November 1985* (Potsdam, 1985).

Gimlette, T., *The Huguenot Settlers in Ireland* (Waterford: T. Gimlette, 1888).

Girard, F., _Histoire abrégée des officiers suisses qui se sont distingués aux services étrangers dans des grades superieurs_ (3 vols, Fribourg: Louis Piller, 1781–2).

Glozier, M. R., _Marshal Schomberg, 1615–1690: 'the ablest soldier of his age': International Soldiering and the Formation of State Armies in Seventeenth-Century Europe_ (Brighton, Portland: Sussex Academic Press, 2005).

——, _Scottish Soldiers in France in the Reign of the Sun King: Nursery for Men of Honour_, History of Warfare Series 24 (Leiden, Boston: E. J. Brill, 2004).

——, _The Huguenot Soldiers of William of Orange and the Glorious Revolution of 1688: The Lions of Judah_ (Brighton, Portland: Sussex Academic Press, 2002).

Goldie, M., 'The Huguenot experience and the problem of Toleration in Restoration England', in C. E. J. Caldicott _et al._ (eds), _The Huguenots and Ireland: Anatomy of an Emigration_ (Dublin: Glendale Press, 1987).

Greaves, R. L., _Secrets of the Kingdom: British Radicals from the Popish Plot to the Revolution of 1688–1689_ (Stanford, CA: Stanford University Press, 1992).

Grot, J. C., _Bemerkungen über die Religionsfreiheit der Ausländer im Russischen Reiche in Rücksicht auf ihre verschiedenen Geimeinen, ihre kirchliche Einrichtungen, ihre Gebräuche und ihre Rechte_ (3 vols, St Petersburg, Leipzig, 1797–8).

Gwynn, R. D., _Huguenot Heritage. The History and Contribution of the Huguenots in Britain_ (London: Routledge and Kegan Paul, 1985; reprinted Brighton, Portland: Sussex Academic Press, 2001).

——, 'The Huguenots in Britain, the "Protestant International" and the Defeat of Louis XIV', in R. Vigne and C. Littleton (eds), _From Strangers to Citizens: The Integration of Immigrant Communities in Britain, Ireland and Colonial America, 1550–1750_ (Brighton, Portland: Sussex Academic Press, 2001).

Haag, E. and E., _La France protestante ou vies des protestants français qui se sont fait un nom dans l'histoire_ (9 vols, Paris: Cherbuliez, 1846–59; reprinted 10 vols, Montpellier: Dubief and Poujol, 1992).

Haley, K. H. D., _Shaftesbury_ (Oxford: Clarendon Press, 1968).

Harding, R. R., _Anatomy of a Power Elite: The Provincial Governors of Early Modern France_ (New Haven, CT: Yale University Press, 1978).

Harms, D., 'Das Edikt von Potsdam vom 29 Oktober 1685; Die Integration und der soziale Aufstieg von Ausländern in der Preußischen Armee des 17. und 18. Jahrhunderts', in B. R. Kroener (ed.), _Potsdam: Staat, Armee, Residenz in der Preußisch-deutschen Militärgeschichte_ (Frankfurt-am-Main, Berlin: Propyläen, 1993).

——, _Vom Lehns- und Ritterheer zum Söldnerheer. Zur Entwicklung des Militärwesens im deutschen Feudalreich vom Beginn des 14. bis zum Beginn des 16. Jahrhunderts_ (Potsdam, 1990).

Hartweg, F. and S. Jersch-Wenzel (eds), _Die Hugenotten und das Refuge. Deutschland und Europa_ (Berlin: Colloquium, 1990).

Haswell, J., _James II: Soldier and Sailor_ (London: History Book Club, 1972).

Hatton, R., _George I: Elector and King_ (Cambridge, MA: Harvard University Press, 1978).

Hayes-McCoy, G. A., _Irish Battles: A Military History of Ireland_ (London, 1969; reprinted Belfast: The Appletree Press Ltd, 1990).

—— (ed.), *The Irish at War* (Cork: Mercier Press, 1964).

Hayton, D. W. and G. O'Brien (eds), *War and Politics in Ireland, 1647–1730* (London: Hambledon, 1986).

Höpel, T. and K. Middell (eds), *Réfugiés und Emigrés. Migration zwischen Frankreich und Deutschland im 18. Jahrhundert* (Leipzig: Universitätsverlag, 1997).

Holt, M. P., *The French Wars of Religion, 1562–1629* (Cambridge: Cambridge University Press, 1995).

Horn, D. B., *The British Diplomatic Service, 1689–1789* (Oxford: Clarendon Press, 1961).

Horwitz, H., *Parliament, Policy and Politics in the Reign of William III* (Manchester: Manchester University Press, 1977).

Hughes, T., *Die Conföderation der reformierten Kirchen in Niedersachsen. Geschichte und Urkunden* (Celle, 1873).

Hylton, R., 'The Huguenot Settlement at Portarlington, 1682–1775', in C. E. J. Caldicott *et al.* (eds), *The Huguenots and Ireland* (Dublin: Glendale Press, 1987).

Israel, J. I. (ed.), *The Anglo-Dutch Moment: Essays on the Glorious Revolution and its World Impact* (Cambridge: Cambridge University Press, 1991).

——, 'The Dutch role in the Glorious Revolution', in Israel (ed.), *The Anglo-Dutch Moment* (Cambridge: Cambridge University Press, 1991).

Jahn, J. H. F., *Det danske auxiliaircorps i engelsk tjeneste fra 1689 til 1697: Et krigshistorisk udkast* (2 vols, Copenhagen: Berlingske Bogtrykkeri, 1840–41).

Jähns, M. (ed.), *Geschichte der kriegswissenschaften vornehmlich in Deutschland*, Geschichte der Wissenschaften in Deutschland, new series 21 (vol. 1, Oldenburg, Münich: durch die Historische Kommission bei der Kgl. Akademie der Wissenschaften, 1889; vol. 2, Münich, Leipzig, 1890).

——, *Heeresverfassung und Völkerleben* (Berlin: Allgemeiner Verein für Deutsche Literatur, 1885).

Jany, C., *Die alte Armee von 1655 bis 1740: Formation und Stärke* (Berlin, 1905).

——, 'Der Dessauer Stammliste von 1729', in *Urkundliche Beiträge und Forschungen zur Geschichte des Preußischen Heeres*, ed. Great General Staff, Kriegsgeschichtliche Abteilung 2/8 (Berlin: E. S. Mittler und Sohn, 1905).

——, *Geschichte der Königlich Preußischen Armee vom 15. Jahrhundert und des Deutschen Reichsheeres* (5 vols, Berlin: Karl Siegismund, 1928–37), vol. 1 'Von den Anfängen bis 1740' (1928).

Jersch–Wenzel, S., *Juden und 'Franzosen' in der Wirtschaft des Raumes Berlin/ Brandenburg zur Zeit des Merkantilismus*, Einzelveröffentlichungen der Historischen Kommission zu Berlin 23 (Berlin, 1978).

—— and B. John (eds), *Von Zuwanderern zu Einheimischen. Hugenotten, Juden, Böhmen, Polen in Berlin* (Berlin: Nicolai, 1990).

Jones, J. R., *The Revolution of 1688 in England* (London: Weidenfeld and Nicolson, 1972).

Jorgensen, D., *Danmark-Norge mellom stormaktene, 1688–1697* (Oslo: Universitetsforlaget, 1976).

Jullien, A. (ed.), *Soldats suisses au service étranger* (12 vols, Geneva: A. Jullien, 1908–95).

Kämmerer, J., *Rußland und die Hugenotten im 18. Jahrhundert (1689–1789)* (Wiesbaden: Kommission bei Harrassowitz, 1978).

Kathe, H., *Der 'sonnenkönig'. Ludwig XIV., König von Frankreich, und seine Zeit 1638–1715* (Berlin: Akademie Verlag, 1981).

Kazner, J , *Leben Friedrich von Schomberg, oder Schoenburg* (2 vols, Mannheim, 1789).

Kelly, P., 'Lord Galway and the Penal Laws', in C. E. J. Caldicott *et al.* (eds), *The Huguenots and Ireland* (Dublin: Glendale Press, 1987).

Kiefner, T., *Die Waldenser auf ihrem Weg aus dem Val Cluson durch die Schweiz nach Deutschland 1532–1755* (4 vols, Göttingen: Vandenhoeck and Ruprecht, 1985–97).

King, H. L., *Brandenburg and the English Revolution of 1688* (Oberlin, London, 1914).

Kinross, J., *The Boyne and Aughrim: The War of the Two Kings* (Gloucestershire: Windrush Press, 1997).

Kirby, D., *Northern Europe in the Early Modern Period: The Baltic World, 1492–1772* (London: Longman, 1990).

Kittel, E., *Memoiren des Generals Graf Ferdinand Christian zur Lippe (1668–1724)* (Lemgo: F. L. Wagner, 1959).

Kleinschmidt, A., 'L'Estocq (Johann Hermann, Reichsgraf von)', in J. S. Ersch and J. G. Gruber (eds), *Allgemeine Enzyklopädie der Wissenschaften und Künste* (167 vols, Leipzig: Brockhaus, 1818–89; reprinted Graz: Akademische Druck- u. Veragsanstalt, 1969), vol. 43, pt. 2, pp. 234–5.

Klingebeil, T., *Die Hugenotten in den welfischen Landen. Eine Privilegiensammlung*, Geschichtsblätter des Deutschen Hugenotten-Vereins 23 (Bad Karlshafen, 1994).

Knetsch, F. R. J., *Pierre Jurieu, theoloog en politikus der refuge* (Kampen: I. H. Kok, 1967).

Kohnke, M., 'Das Edikt von Potsdam: Zu seiner Entstehung, Verbreitung und Überlieferung', in *Jahrbuch für Geschichte des Feudalismus,* Akademie der Wissenschaften der DDR 9 (Berlin, 1985).

Köller, H. and B. Töpfer, *Frankreich. Ein historischer Abriß. Teil 1: Von den Anfängen bis zum Tode Heinrichs IV* (Berlin: Deutscher Verlag der Wissenschaft, 1977).

Krauske, O., 'Fürst Leopold von Anhalt-Dessau', in P. Seidel (ed.), *Hohenzollern-Jahrbuch*, 2 (Berlin, Leipzig, 1898).

Krum, H. (ed.), *Preußens Adoptivkinder. Die Hugenotten. 300 Jahre Edikt von Potsdam. Unter Verwendung von 'Mémoires pour servir à l'histoire des réfugiés françois dans les états du roi' von J. P. Erman und F. Reclam 1782–1789* (Berlin: Arani, 1985).

Labillière, F. P. de, *History of a Cevenol Family: A Paper Read Before the Huguenot Society of London, January 11, 1888* (London: Spottiswoode, 1888).

Landwehr, H., *Die Kirchenpolitik Friedrich Wilhelms des Großen Kurfürsten* (Berlin: Ernst Hoffman and Co., 1894).

Lange, A. de (ed.), *Dall'Europa alle valli valdesi. Atti del convegno 'Il Glorioso Rimpatrio 1689–1989'* (Turin: Società di studi valdesi, 1990).

Le Poer, R., second Earl of Clancarty, *Memoir of the Le Poer Trench Family* (Dublin, 1874).

Lee, G. L., *The Huguenot Settlements in Ireland* (London: Longmans, Green and Co., 1936)

Lehmann, G., 'Die brandburgische Kriegsmacht unter dem Großen Kurfürsten', in R. Koser (ed.), *Forschungen zur Brandenburgischen und Preußischen Geschichte* 1 (Leipzig, 1888).

Lenihan, P., *1690: Battle of the Boyne* (Stroud: Sutton, 2003).

Lewis, S., *Topographical Dictionary of Ireland: Comprising the Several Counties, Cities, Burroughs, Corporate, Market and Post Towns, Parishes and Villages* (2 vols, London: S. Lewis, 1837).

Lojewsky, J. G., *Selbstbiographie des Husaren-Obersten von ... ky* (2 vols, Leipzig, 1843).

Lombardi, G. (ed.), *La guerra del sale (1680–1699). Rivolte e frontiere del Piemonte barocco* (3 vols, Milan: Angeli, 1986).

Lowther, J., Viscount Lonsdale, *Memoir of the Reign of James II* (York: T. Wilson and R. Spence, 1808.; reprinted London, Bohn's Standard Library, 1846).

Lot, F., *Recherches sur les effectifs des armées françaises des Guerres d'Italie aux Guerres de Religion 1494–1562* (Paris: Editions de l'École des hautes études en sciences sociales, 1962).

Lynn, J. A., *Giant of the Grand Siècle: The French Army 1610–1715* (Cambridge: Cambridge University Press, 1997).

——, *The Wars of Louis XIV 1667–1714* (London, New York: Longman, 1999).

Lusanov, P., *Suchoputnyj šljachetskij korpus pri grafe Miniche, 1732–1741* (St Petersburg, 1907).

Macaulay, T. B., *The History of England from the Accession of James II* (4 vols, London: Longmans, Green and Co., 1848–61).

Madariaga, I. de, *Catherine the Great: A Short History* (New Haven, CT: Yale University Press, 1990).

Maggio Serra, R., F. Mazzocca, C. Sisi and C. Spantigati (eds), *Vittorio Alfieri. Aristocratico ribelle (1749–1803)* (Milan: Electa, 2003).

Magny, E. Drigon, Comte de, *Nobiliaire de Normandie* (2 vols, Paris: Aubry, 1863–4).

Maguire, W. A. (ed.), *Kings in Conflict: The Revolutionary War in Ireland and its Aftermath 1689–1750* (Belfas: Blackstaff, 1990).

Manoury, K., *Die Geschichte der französisch-reformierten Provinzgemeinden* (Berlin, 1961).

Marelle, L., *Eleonore d'Olbreuse. Herzogin von Braunschweig-Lüneburg-Celle. Die Großmutter Europas* (Hamburg: Hoffmann and Campe, 1936).

Marlow, J., *The Life and Times of George I* (London: Weidenfeld and Nicolson, 1973).

Masson, G., *The Huguenots: A Sketch of their History from the Beginning of the Reformation to the Death of Louis XIV* (London, New York: Cassell, Petter, Galpin, 1882).

Mattingly, G., *The Defeat of the Spanish Armada* (London: Jonathan Cape, 1959).

Maurice, J. F. (ed.), *The Franco-German War, 1870–71, by Generals and Other Officers Who Took Part in the Campaign* (London: Sonnenschein, 1900).

Mauvillon, J., *Geschichte Ferdinands Herzogs von Braunschweig-Lüneburg* (2 vols, Leipzig: Dyk, 1794).

Mehring, F., *Gesammelte Schriften*, ed. T. Höhle, H. Kock and J. Schleifstein (15 vols, Berlin: Dietz, 1964–73).

Meinel, F., *Samuel Chappuzeau 1625–1701* (Borna, Leipzig: Robert Noske, 1908).

Mempel, D. (ed.), *Gewissensfreiheit und Wirtschaftspolitik. Hugenotten- und Waldenser-Privilegien 1681–1699* (Trier: Auenthal, 1986).

Mengin, E., *Das Edikt von Nantes: Das Edikt von Fontainebleau* (Flensburg: Kurt Gross, 1963).

Merlin, P., *Emanuele Filiberto. Un principe tra il Piemonte e l'Europa* (Turin: SEI, 1995).

Merlotti, A., *Il silenzio e il servizio. Le Epoche principali delle vita di me di Vincenzo Sebastiano Beraudo di Pralormo* (Turin: Silvio Zamorani editore, 2003).

——, 'Gentildonne e sociabilità aristocratica nella Torino del secondo Settecento', in M. L. Betri and E. Brambilla (eds), *Salotti e ruolo femminile in Italia tra fine Seicento e primo Novecento* (Venice: Marsilio, 2004).

Merzeau, E., *L'Académie protestante de Saumur 1604–1685. Son organisation et ses rapports avec les églises réformées* (Alençon: Bourchenin, 1908).

Meyer-Rasch, C., *Alte Häuser erzählen. Von Menschen und Schicksalen der Stadt Celle* (2 vols, Celle: Schweiger and Pick, 1962).

Michas, U., 'Das Salz in der Suppe. Hugenotten als brandenburgische Soldaten', in *Die Mark Brandenburg*, booklet 48: 'Die Hugenotten. Willkommen in der Mark' (Berlin, 2003).

Middlekauff, R., *The Glorious Cause: The American Revolution, 1763–89* (New York: Oxford University Press, 1982).

Middleton, R., *Colonial America: A History, 1607–1760* (Cambridge, MA: Beacon Press, 1992).

Mielke, F., *Potsdamer Baukunst: das klassische Potsdam* (Frankfurt, Berlin, Wien: Propyläen, 1981).

Mittenzwei, I. (ed.), *Hugenotten in Brandenburg-Preußen*, Studien zur Geschichte der Akademie der Wissenschaften der DDR, Zentralinstitut für Geschichte 8 (Berlin, 1987).

Moerner, T. von, *Kurbrandenburgs Staatsverträge von 1601 bis 1700* (Berlin: de Gruyter, 1867).

Mosen, R., *Das Leben der Prinzessin Charlotte Amélie de la Trémoïlle, Gräfin von Oldenburg (1652–1732). Erzählt von ihr selbst* (Oldenburg, Leipzig: O.StA., 1892).

Muralt, E. von, *Chronik der vereinigten französischen und teutschen reformierten Gemeinde in St. Petersburg, nebst Beiträgen zur Geschichte der Stiftung protestantischer und besonders reformierter Kirchen, zum Kirkenrechte und zur Geschichte der Ausländer im russischen Reiche* (Dorpat, 1842).

Murdoch, T. (ed.), *The Quiet Conquest: The Huguenots 1685 to 1985* (London: Museum of London, 1985).

Muret, E., *Geschichte der französischen Kolonie in Brandenburg-Preußen, unter besonderer Berücksichtigung der Berliner Gemeinde: Aus Veranlassung der zweihundertjährigen Jubelfeier am 29 Oktober 1885* (Berlin: Büxenstein, 1885).

Murtagh, R. H., *Revolutionary Ireland and its Settlement* (London: Macmillan and Co., 1911).

Nègre, L., *Vie et ministère de Claude Brousson, 1647–1698* (Paris: Sandoz and Fischbacher, 1878).

Neigebaur, J. F., *Eleonore d'Olbreuse, die Stammmutter der Königshäuser von England, Hannover und Preußen. Ermittlungen zur Geschichte ihrer Heirath mit dem Herzoge von Braunschweig-Celle und der damaligen Zeit, in besonderer Beziehung auf Ebenbürtigkeitsheirathen* (Brunswick: Leibrock, 1859).

Neuschel, K. B., *Word of Honour: Interpreting Noble Culture in Sixteenth-Century France* (Ithaca, NY, London: Cornell University Press, 1989).

Nusteling, H. P. H., 'The Netherlands and the Huguenot émigrés', in J. A. H. Bots and G. H. M. Posthumus Meyjes (eds), *La révocation de l'édit de Nantes et les Provinces-Unies* (Amsterdam, Maarssen: APA-Holland University Press, 1986).

O'Callaghan, J. C., *History of the Irish Brigades in the Service of France* (Glasgow: Cameron and Ferguson, New York: P. N. Haverty, 1870; reprinted Shannon: Irish University Press, 1969).

Ogg, D., *England in the Reigns of James II and William III* (Oxford: Clarendon Press, 1957).

Opgenoorth, E., *'Ausländer' in Brandenburg-Preußen als leitende Beamte und Offiziere 1604–1871* (Würzburg: Holzner, 1967).

Pagès, G., *Le Grand Electeur et Louis XIV, 1660–1688* (Paris: Société Nouvelle de Librairie et d'Edition, 1905).

Parker, G., *The Dutch Revolt* (London: Penguin, 1977).

——, *The Military Revolution: Military Innovation and the Rise of the West, 1500–1800* (Cambridge: Cambridge University Press, 1988).

Parrott, D., 'Richelieu, the *Grands*, and French Army', in J. Bergin and L. Brockliss (eds), *Richelieu and His Age* (Oxford: Clarendon Press, 1992).

——, *Richelieu's Army: War, Government and Society in France, 1624–1642* (Cambridge: Cambridge University Press, 2001).

Pelet-Narbonne, G. von, *Geschichte der Brandenburg-Preussen Reiterei von den Zeiten des Grossen Kurfürsten bis zur Gegenwart* (2 vols, Hamburg: Ernst Siegfried Mittler, 1905).

Philippson, M., *Der Große Kurfürst Friedrich Wilhelm von Brandenburg* (3 vols, Berlin: Cronbach, 1897–1903).

Pick, M., *Die französischen Kolonien in der Uckermark* (Prenzlau, 1935).

Pingaud, L., *Les Français en Russie et les Russes en France* (Paris: Perrin, 1886).

Posselt, M. C. F. F., *Der General und Admiral Franz Lefort. Sein Leben und seine Zeit. Ein Beitrag zur Geschichte Peters des Großen* (2 vols, Frankfort-am-Main: Baer, 1866).

Potter, D., *War and Government in the French Provinces: Picardy 1470–1560* (Cambridge: Cambridge University Press, 1993).

Powell, J. S., *Portarlington* (York: Frenchchurch Press, 1994).

Pushkin, A. S., *Istorija Pugačeva (Polnoe sobranie socinenij)* [History of the Pugachev Rebellion] (2 vols, St Petersburg, 1834; republished 2 vols, Leningrad, 1938–40).

Rambaut, P. and R. Vigne, *Britain's Huguenot War Leaders* (London: Instructa, 2002).

——, *Louis de Durfort-Duras, second Earl of Feversham* (Hammersmith: P. Rambaut, 1988).

Reaman, G. E., *The Trail of the Huguenots in Europe, the United States, South Africa and Canada* (London: Genealogical Publishing, 1963).

Reid, J. S., *History of the Presbyterian Church of Ireland* (3 vols, Belfast: W. Mullan, 1867).

Reilly, R., *Wolfe of Quebec* (London, New York: White Lion Publishers, 1973).

Ressinger, D. W., 'Good Faith: the military and the Ministry in Exile, or the Memoirs of Isaac Dumont de Bostaquet en Jacques Fontaine', in R. Vigne and C. Littleton (eds), *From Strangers to Citizens* (Brighton, Portland: Sussex Academic Press, 2001).

Ricuperati, G. (ed.), *Dalla città razionale alla crisi dello Stato d'Antico Regime (1730–1798)*, Storia di Torino 5 (Turin, 2002).

Rietbergen, P. J. A. N., 'William III of Orange (1650–1702) between European Politics and European Protestants: The case of the Huguenots', in H. Bots and G. H. M. Posthumus Meyjes (eds), *La Révocation de l'Edit de Nantes et les Provinces-Unies, 1685* (Amsterdam, Maarssen: APA-Holland University Press, 1986), pp. 35–51.

Ringoir, H., *Hoofdofficieren infanterie van 1568 tot 1813*, Bijdragen van de Sectie Militaire. Geschiedenis 9 (The Hague, 1981).

Roider, K., 'Origins of Wars in the Balkans, 1660–1792', in J. Black (ed.), *The Origins of Wars in Early Modern Europe* (Edinburgh: John Donald, 1987).

Romagnani, G. P. (ed.), *La Bibbia, la coccarda e il tricolore. I valdesi fra due Emancipazioni 1798–1848* (Turin: Claudiana, 2001).

——, 'Presenze protestanti a Torino tra Sei e Settecento', in G. Ricuperati (ed.), *Dalla città razionale alla crisi dello Stato d'Antico Regime (1730–1798)*, Storia di Torino 5 (Turin, 2002).

Rose, C., *England in the 1690s: Revolution, Religion and War* (Oxford: Oxford University Press, 1999).

Rosen-Prest, V., *L'Historiographie des Huguenots en Prusse au temps des lumières entre mémoire, histoire et légende: Jean Pierre Erman et Pierre Chrétien Frédéric Reclam. Mémoires pour servir à l'histoire des réfugiés françois dans les États du Roi (1782–1799)*, La Vie des Huguenots (Paris: Champion, 2002).

Rosenberg, H., *Bureaucracy, Aristocracy and Autocrat: The Prussian Experience, 1660–1815* (Cambridge, MA: Beacon Press, 1958).

Roulet, L.-E. (ed.), *Le refuge huguenot en suisse. Die Hugenotten in der Schweiz. Ausstellungskatalog* (Lausanne, 1985).

Rousset, C., *Histoire de Louvois et de son administration militaire* (4 vols, Paris: Librairie académique Didier, 1864–5; sixth edition 1879).

Rowlands, G., *The Dynastic State and the Army under Louis XIV: Royal Service and Private Interest, 1661 to 1701* (Cambridge: Cambridge University Press, 2002).

——, 'The Monopolisation of Military Power in France, 1515–1715', in R. G. Asch, W. E. Voss and M. Wrede (eds), *Frieden und Krieg in der Frühen Neuzeit* (Munich, 2001).

Russell, F. S., *The Earl of Peterborough and Monmouth: A Memoir* (2 vols, London: Chapman and Hall, 1887).

Rüstow, W., *Geschichte der Infanterie* (2 vols, Nordhausen: Hugo Scheube, 1864).

Saunders, A., *Fortress Builder: Bernard De Gomme, Charles II's Military Engineer* (Exeter: University of Exeter Press, 2004).

Savory, G., *His Britannic Majesty's Army in Germany During the Seven Years' War* (Oxford: Oxford University Press, 1966).

Schnath, G., *Geschichte Hannovers im Zeitalter der neunten Kur und der englischen Sukzession 1674–1714* (2 vols, Hildesheim: Lax, 1976).

Schnitter, H., 'Die Réfugiés in der brandenburgischen Armee', in G. Bregulla (ed.), *Hugenotten in Berlin* (Berlin: Union Verlag, 1988).

——, *Unter dem roten Adler: Réfugiés im brandeburgischen Heer Ende des 17. Anfang des 18. Jahrhundert* (Berlin, 1996).

——, 'Unter dem brandenburgichen Adler – Hugenotten in der brandenburgischen Armee', *Blätter für Heimatgeschichte: Studienmaterial 1986* (Berlin, 1986): 51–5.

Schöning, J. W. von (ed.), *Des General-Feldmarschalls Dubislav Gneomar von Natzmer auf Gannewitz Leben und Kriegsthaten mit den Hauptbegebenheiten des von ihm errichteten und 48 Jahre als Commandeur en Chef geführten bekannten Garde-Reuter-Regiments Gens d'armes. Ein Beitrag zur brandenburgisch-preußischen Armee-Geschichte* (Berlin, 1838).

Schuchardt, W., 'Amaury de Farcy de Saint-Laurent, Huguenotte Kommandant der Festung Kalkberg und der Stadt Lüneburg, Generalleutnant der hannoverschen Kavallerie. Drost des Amtes Ebstorf', in *Fundstücke. Zweites Heimatbuch für den Landkreis Lüneburg* (Lüneburg: Lüneburg District Government, 1993).

Schwerin, O. von*, Das Regiment gens d'armes und seine Vorgeschichte* (2 vols, Berlin, 1912).

Schwoerer, L. G., *'No Standing Armies!': The Antiarmy Ideology in Seventeenth-Century England* (Baltimore: Johns Hopkins University Press, 1974).

Scouloudi, I. (ed.), *Huguenots in Britain and their French Background, 1550–1800* (London: Macmillan, 1987).

Sichart, L. H. F. von, *Geschichte der Königlich-Hannoverschen Armee* (5 vols, Hanover: Hahn, 1866–71).

Simms, J. G., *Jacobite Ireland 1685–91* (Norfolk: University of Toronto Press, 1969).

——, *The Williamite Confiscation in Ireland, 1690–1703* (London: Faber and Faber, 1956).

Smiles, S., *The Huguenots: Their Settlements, Churches, and Industries in England and Ireland* (London: John Murray, 1867).

Solov'ev, S. M., *Istorija Rossii s drevnejšich vremen* [History of Russia from most ancient times] (14 vols, Moscow: Izdatel'stvo social'noekonomiceskoj literatury, 1896; reprinted 29 vols, Moscow, 1959–66).

Speck, W. A., *Reluctant Revolutionaries: Englishmen and the Revolution of 1688* (Oxford: Oxford University Press, 1988).

Stanley, A. P., *Historical Memorials of Westminster Abbey* (London: John Murray, 1868).

Starkey, A., *War in the Age of Enlightenment, 1700–1789* (Westport, CT: Praeger, 2003).

Steuart, A. F., *Scottish Influences in Russian History: From the 16th Century to the Beginning of the 19th Century* (Glasgow: James Maclehose and Sons, 1913).

Stolpe, M. and F. Winter (eds), *Wege und Grenzen der Toleranz. Edikt von Potsdam 1685–1985* (Berlin: Evangelische, 1987).

Stolze, G., *Die Bedeutung der unter Herzog Georg Wilhelm eingewanderten französischen Hugenotten für die Stadt Celle* (Göttingen, 1963).

Storrs, C., *War, Diplomacy and the Rise of Savoy, 1690–1720* (Cambridge: Cambridge University Press, 1999).

Stoyle, M., *Soldiers and Strangers: An Ethnic History of the English Civil War* (New Haven, CT: Yale University Press, 2005).

Strickland, A., *Lives of the Queens of England: From the Norman Conquest* (16 vols, London: Bell, 1840–8).

Symcox, G., *Victor Amadeus II: Absolutism in the Savoyard State, 1675–1730* (London: Thames and Hudson, 1983).

Teensma, B. N. (ed.), *Brazil and the Dutch 1630–1654* (Rio de Janeiro: Sextante Artes, 1999).

Thackeray, F., *History of the Rt. Hon. William Pitt, Earl of Chatham* (London, 1827).

Thadden, R. von and M. Magdelaine (eds), *Die Hugenotten 1685–1985* (Munich: Beck, 1986).

Thierry, A., 'L'Homme de guerre dans l'œuvre d'Agrippa d'Aubigné', in G.-A. Pérouse, A. Thierry and A. Tournon (eds), *L'Homme de guerre au XVIe siècle* (Saint-Etienne: Université de Saint-Etienne, 1992).

Trevor-Roper, H., Lord Dacre of Glanton, 'A Huguenot Historian: Paul Rapin', in I. Scouloudi (ed.), *Huguenots in Britain and their French Background, 1550–1800* (London: Macmillan, 1987).

——, *The Crisis of the Seventeenth Century: Religion, The Reformation, and Social Change* (1967; reprinted Indianapolis: Liberty Fund, 2001).

Trim, D. J. B., 'Edict of Nantes: Product of Military Success or Failure?', in K. Cameron, M. Greengrass and P. Roberts (eds), *The Adventure of Religious Pluralism in Early Modern France* (Oxford, Bern, New York: Peter Lang, 2000).

——, 'Immigrants, the Indigenous Community and International Calvinism', in N. Goose and L. Luu (eds), *Immigrants in Tudor and Early Stuart England* (Brighton, Portland: Sussex Academic Press, 2005).

Troost, W., 'William III, Brandenburg and the Construction of the Anti-French Coalition, 1672–88', in J. I. Israel (ed.), *The Anglo-Dutch Moment: Essays on the Glorious Revolution and its World Impact* (Cambridge: Cambridge University Press, 1991), pp. 299–335.

Vigne, R., *Guillaume Chenu de Chalezac: The 'French Boy'* (Cape Town: Van Riebeeck Society, 1993).

——, and C. Littleton (eds), *From Strangers to Citizens. The Integration of Immigrant Communities in Britain, Ireland and Colonial America, 1550–1750* (Brighton, Portland: Sussex Academic Press, 2001).

——, 'Huguenots at the Court of William and Mary', in C. Wilson and D. Proctor (eds), *1688: The Seaborne Alliance and Diplomatic Revolution: Proceedings of an International Symposium Held at the National Maritime Museum, Greenwich, 5–6 October* (London: Trustees of the National Maritime Museum, 1988).

Vinage, R. du, *Ein vortreffliches Frauenzimmer. Das Schicksal von Eleonore Desmier d'Olbreuse (1639–1722), der letzten Herzogin von Braunschweig-Lüneburg-Celle* (Berlin: Otto Meissners, 2000).

Voltaire, J. F. M. Arouet de, *Anecdotes sur le czar Pierre le Grand; Histoire de l'empire de Russie sous Pierre le Grand*, ed. M. and C. Mervaud, A. Brown and U. Kolving (2 vols, Oxford: Oxford University Press, 1999).

Waddington, F., *Le Protestantisme en Normandie depuis la Révocation de l'Edit de Nantes jusqu'a la fin du dix-huitieme siecle: 1685–1797* (Paris: J.-B. Dumoulin, 1862).

Wagner, H. W. (ed.), *Hugenotten in Hamburg, Stade, Altona, Tagungsschrift zum Deutschen Hugenottentag Hamburg, 23–26 April 1976*, Geschichtsblätter des Deutschen Hugenotten-Vereins 14 (Obersickte, 1976).

Wallbrecht, R. E., *Das Theater des Barockzeitalters an den welfischen Höfen Hannover und Celle*, Quellen und Darstellungen zur Geschichte Niedersachsens 83 (Hildesheim, 1974).

Watson, J. N. P., *Captain-General and Rebel Chief: The Life of James, Duke of Monmouth* (London: George Allen and Unwin, 1979).

Webb, S. S., *Lord Churchill's Coup: The Anglo-American Empire and the Glorious Revolution Reconsidered* (Syracuse, NY: Syracuse University Press, 1995).

Weiss, C., *Histoire des réfugiés Protestants de France depuis la revocation de l'édit de Nantes jusqu'à nos jours* (2 vols, Paris: Charpentier, 1853).

——, *History of the French Protestant Refugees from the Revocation of the Edict of Nantes to Our Own Days*, ed. H. W. Herbert (2 vols, New York: Stringer and Townsend, 1854).

Whitworth, R., *Field Marshal Lord Ligonier: A Story of the British Army, 1702–70* (Oxford: Clarendon Press, 1958).

Wilke, J., 'Zur sozialstruktur und demographischen analyse der Hugenotten in Brandenburg-Preußen, insbesondere der in Berlin', in I. Mittenzwei (ed.), *Hugenotten in Brandeburg-Preußen*, Studien zur Geschichte der Akademie der Wissenschaften der DDR, Zentralinstitut für Geschichte 8 (Berlin, 1987).

Wilson, P., *German Armies: War and German Politics, 1648–1806*, Warfare and History (London: UCL Press, 1998).

Woker, F. W., *Geschichte der katholischen Kirche in Hannover und Celle. Ein weiterer Beitrag zur Kirchengeschichte Norddeutschlands nach der Reformation* (Paderborn, 1889).

Wood, J. B., *The King's Army: Warfare, Soldiers, and Society During the Wars of Religion in France, 1562–1576* (Cambridge: Cambridge University Press, 1996).

Yardeni, M., *Le refuge protestant* (Paris: Universitaires de France, coll. L'historien, 1985).

——, 'The Birth of Political Consciousness among the Huguenot Refugees and their Descendants in England (c. 1685–1750)', in R. Vigne and C. Littleton (eds), *From Strangers to Citizens* (Brighton, Portland: Sussex Academic Press, 2001).

Zedler, J. H., *Grosses Vollständiges universal Lexikon aller Wissenschaften und Künste* (64 vols, Leipzig, Halle: Zedler, 1732–54; reprinted Graz: Adakemische Druck, 1961–4).

Zwitzer, H. L., *De militie van den staat: Het leger van de Republiek der Verenigde Nederlanden* (Amsterdam: Van Soeren and Co., 1991).

Articles in Journals

Amburger. E., 'Hugenottenfamilien in Rußland', *Der Herold*, 5 (1963/5): 125–35.

Anderson, J., 'Combined Operations and the Protestant Wind: Some Maritime Aspects of the Glorious Revolution of 1688', *The Great Circle*, 9 (1987): 96–107.

Asche, M., 'Migrationen im Europa der Frühen Neuzeit – Versuch einer Typologie', *Geschichte, Politik und ihre Didaktik. Beiträge und Nachrichten für die Unterrichtspraxis. Zeitschrift für historisch-politische Bildung*, 32 (2004): 74–89.

Babkine, A. (ed.), 'Les Premiers Lettres de Russie du Général Lefort', *Canadian Slavonic Papers*, 16 (1974): 380–402.

Bazzoni, A., 'Relazioni diplomatiche tra la Casa di Savoia e la Prussia nel secolo XVIII', *Archivio storico italiano*, 15 (1872): 3–21, 193–209, 377–90.

Bellen, M. van, 'Über die Verbindung der Familien de Beaulieu Marconnay und Suzannet de la Forest mit der hannoverschen Adelsfamilie von Düring. Ein Kapitel aus der Geschichte adeliger Hugenotten in Celle', *Der Deutsche Hugenott*, 55/1 (1994).

Beuleke, W., 'Die Hugenottengemeinde Prenzlau', *Genealogie*, 14 (1965): 416–21.

Bianchi, P., 'Guerra e pace nel Settecento: alcune riflessioni sul caso sabaudo', *Studi settecenteschi*, 22 (2002): 89–102.

——, 'In cerca del moderno. Studenti e viaggiatori inglesi a Torino nel Settecento', *Rivista storica italiana*, 115/3 (2003): 1021–51.

——, '"Politica e polizia" in una realtà d'antico regime: le sfide contro vecchi e nuovi disordini nello Stato sabaudo fra Sei e Settecento', *Bollettino storico bibliografico subalpino*, 103 (2005): 473–504.

Black, J., 'The Development of Anglo-Sardinian Relations in the First Half of Eighteenth Century', *Studi piemontesi*, 12 (1983): 48–60.

Blackwell, W. L., 'The Old Believers and the Rise of Private Industrial Enterprise in early Nineteenth-Century Moskow', *Slavonic Review*, 24 (1965): 407–24.

Boeree, T. A. (ed.), 'Les officiers français en service hollandais apres la Révocation pendant la période 1686–1689', *Bulletin de la commission de l'histoire des èglises wallones*, fourth series, 1 (1928): 1–65.

Brooks, W. and P. J. Yarrow, 'Armand de Bourbon, Marquis de Miremont, and his Relations in France and England', *Seventeenth Century French Studies*, 23 (2001): 187–200.

—— ——, 'Three Huguenots at the English Court: Louis de Durfort and his Nieces, Mlle. de Malauze, a Correspondent of Élisabeth Charlotte, Duchesse d'Orléans, and Mlle. de Roye, Governess to the Royal Children', *Seventeenth Century French Studies*, 22 (2000): 181–93.

Celle: 'Celle in Reisebeschreibungen und Briefen. 2. Aus Pöllnitz Reisebriefen', *Cellesche Zeitung (Der Sachsenspiegel)*, 8/27 (September 1929).

Chambeau, C., 'Der Anteil der Hugenotten in der preußischen wehrmacht', *Zeitschrift für Heereskunde*, 107 (1939): 15–22.

Chambrier, A. de, 'Projet de colonisation en Irelande par les refugiés français, 1692–9', *Proceedings of the Huguenot Society of London*, 11/3 (1901): 370–432.

Chappell, C. Lougee, '"The Pains I Took to Save My/His Family": Escape Accounts by a Huguenot Mother and Daughter after the Revocation of the Edict of Nantes', *French Historical Studies*, 22 (1999): 1–64.

Childs, J., 'A Patriot for Whom? "For God and for honour": Marshal Schomberg', *History Today*, 38 (July 1988): 46–51.

——, 'The English Brigade in Portugal, 1662–1668', *Journal of the Society for Army Historical Research*, 53/215 (Autumn 1975): 135–47.

Contessa, C., 'Aspirazioni commerciali intrecciate ad alleanze politiche della Casa di Savoia coll'Inghilterra nei secoli XVII e XVIII', *Memorie della Regia Accademia delle Scienze di Torino*, 64 (1913–14): 1–50.

Costello, V., 'Researching Huguenot Officers in the British Army, 1688–1713', *The Genealogists' Magazine: Journal of the Society of Genealogists*, 28/8 (December 2005): 335–54.

Demere, P. M., 'The Huguenot Redcoats: Captains Raymond and Paul Demeré', *Transactions of the Huguenot Society of South Carolina*, 102 (Charleston, SC, 1997).

Dinger, W., 'Armand de Lescours Oberhofmarschall der Herzogin Eleonore d'Olbreuse. Einblick in die Geschichte einer Hugenottenfamilie', *Cellesche Zeitung*, 4 (April 1967: Sonderbeilage; 150 Jahre Cellesche Zeitung).

Dölemeyer, B., 'Der Friede von Rijswijk und seine Bedeutung für das europäische Refuge', *Der Deutsche Hugenott*, 66 (2002): 51–73.

Ede-Borrett, S., 'A Huguenot Regiment?', *Journal of the Society for Army Historical Research*, 70/283 (autumn 1992).

Eglises Réformées: 'Liste des pasteurs des Eglises Réformées de France réfugiés en Hollande', *Bulletin de la société de l'histoire du Protestantisme française,* 7 (1858): 426–34.

Erstorff, E. O. A. von, 'Biographie des Königl. Großbritt. und Churfürstl. Braunsch. Lüneburgischen General-Lieutnants der Cavallerie, Inhaber eines Regiments zu Pferde, Commendanten der Festung Kalkberg und der Stadt Lüneburg, auch Drosten des Amts Ebstorf: Amaury de Farcy de Saint-Laurent', *Annalen der Braunschweig-Lüneburgischen Churlande*, 5/3 (Hanover, 1791): 586–97.

Ferguson, K. P., 'The Organisation of King William's Army in Ireland, 1689–92', *Irish Sword*, 18 (1990–91).

Finkel, C. F., 'French Mercenaries in the Habsburg-Ottoman War of 1593–1606: The Desertion of the Papa Garrison to the Ottomans in 1600', *Bulletin of the School of Oriental and African Studies, University of London*, 55 (1992).

Flick, A., 'Amaury de Farcy de Saint Laurent. Der Drost von Ebstorf war Presbyter der Celler Hugenottengemeinde', *Cellesche Zeitung*, 22 (November 1997) (Sachsenspiegel 47): 62.

——, 'Auf den Spuren der Hugenotten in Uelzen und Umgebung', *Der Deutsche Hugenott*, 61/1 (1997).

——, 'Der Ancien Dr. med. Robert Scott wurde zuweilen wegen seiner besonderen Frömmigkeit … hinterrucks verspottet und verhöhnet', _Der Deutsche Hugenott_, 56/4 (1992).

——, 'General und Feldmarschall Jeremias Chauvet', _Celler Chronik_, 6 (Beiträge zur Geschichte und Geographie der Stadt und des Landkreises Celle, 1994): 31–45.

——, 'Gregorio Leti und sein Bericht über den Celler Hof aus dem Jahr 1667', _Celler Chronik_, 8 (Beiträge zur Geschichte und Geographie der Stadt und des Landkreises Celle, 1998).

——, 'Huguenots in the Electorate of Hanover and their British links', _Proceedings of the Huguenot Society of Great Britain and Ireland_, 27/3 (2000): 335–50.

——, 'Jeremias Chauvet. Eine militärische Karriere in der Pfalz und am Hof in Celle', _Pfälzer Heimat_, 3 (1996): 88–94.

——, 'Jacques d'Amproux du Pontpietin, ein hugenottischer Offizier in welfischen Diensten', _Hugenotten_, 62/4 (1998): 144–9.

——, A. Hack and S. Maehnert, 'Hugenotten in Celle'. Catalogue to the exhibition _Ausstellung im Celler Schloß_, 9 April – 8 May 1994 (Celle, 1994).

——, '1700–2000: 300 Jahre Evangelisch-reformierte Kirche in Celle', _Celler Chronik_, 9 (Beiträge zur Geschichte und Geographie der Stadt und des Landkreises Celle, 2000).

G. S. (ed.), 'Two unpublished Diaries connected with the Battle of the Boyne', _Ulster Journal of Archaeology_, 4 (1856): 77–95.

Gaultier, L., 'L'Eglise évangélique réformée de Moscou, 1629 à 1901', _Bulletin de la société de l'histoire du Protestantisme française_, 56 (1907): 5–16.

Geyken, F., '"Mutter der Könige" oder das "Fräulein aus Poitou"? Widersprüche im Bild der Eleonore Desmier d'Olbreuse (1638–1722)', _Der Deutsche Hugenott_, 58/3 (1994).

Gotfredson, E., 'Et dansk hjaelekorps i engelsk tjeneste 1689', _Krigshistorisk Tidsskrift_ (Copenhagen, 1990): 12–31.

Guasco, F., 'Vittorio Amedeo II nelle campagne dal 1691 al 1696', _Studi su Vittorio Amedeo II_ (Turin, 1933).

Gwynn, R. D., 'James II in the Light of his Treatment of the Huguenot Refugees in England, 1685–6', _English Historical Review_, 92 (1977): 820–33.

Haake-Kress, S., _Hessen im 17. Jahrhundert aus der Sicht des hugenottischen Schriftstellers Samuel Chappuzeau (1625–1701)_, Zeitschrift des Vereins für hessische Geschichte und Landeskunde 91 (Hesse, 1986).

Hanlon, G. P., 'The Decline of a Provincial Military Aristocracy', _Past and Present_, 155 (May 1997).

Hebbert, F. J., 'Charles Goulon, Master Military Engineer', _Proceedings of the Huguenot Society of Great Britain and Ireland_, 28/2 (2004): 212–19.

——, 'The Memoirs of Monsieur Goulon', _Journal of the Society for Army Historical Research_, 69/279 (Autumn 1991).

Holm, E., 'Om danske og norske indfodte soldater som hjaelpetropper i fremmed krigstjeneste under Kristian V of Frederik IV', _Historik Tidsskrift_, 5/5 (Copenhagen, 1885): 256–78.

Hylton, R. P., 'Dublin's Huguenot Community, 1662–1701', _Proceedings of the Huguenot Society of Great Britain and Ireland_, 24 (1985).

Janssens, U., 'Jean Deschamps (1709–1767) and the French Colony in Brandenburg', *Proceedings of the Huguenot Society of London*, 23/4 (1980): 227–39.

Joubert, A., 'Les gentilhommes étrangers – Allemands, Anglais, Ecossais, Flamands, Bohémiens, Danois, Polonais – à l'Académie d'Équitation d'Angers au XVIIe siècle d'après un document inédit (1601–1635)', *Revue d'Anjou*, 26 (1893): 5–22.

Kettering, S. P., 'Patronage and Kinship in Early Modern France', *French Historical Studies*, 16 (1989).

Kiehm, P., 'Anfänge eines stehengen Heeres in Brandenburg 1640 bis 1655 unter Kurfürst Friedrich Wilhelm', *Militärgeschichte*, 24/6 (1985).

Kohnke, M., 'Das Edikt von Potsdam zu seiner entetehung verbreitung und uberlieferung', *Jahrbuch für Geschichte des Feudalismus*, 9 (1985).

Krusche, J., 'Die Entstehung und Entwicklung derständigen diplomatischen Vertretung Brandeburg-Preußens am Carenhofe bis zum Eintritt Rußlands in die Reihe der europäischen Großmächte', *Jahrbücher für Kultur und Geschichte der Slaven*, 8 (1932).

La Forest, C. de, 'Zur Familien-Geschichte derer von Monroy', *Die Französische Colonie. Zeitschrift für Vergangenheit und Gegenwart der französisch-reformierten Gemeinden Deutschlands*, 17 (1903).

Langeron, L. A., 'Russkaya Armiya v God Smerti Ekateriny II', *Russkaya Starima*, 83 (1895).

Lart, C. E., 'The Huguenot Regiments', *Proceedings of the Huguenot Society of London*, 9 (1911): 482–98.

Layard, H., 'The Duc de Rohan's Relations with the Republic of Venice, 1630–1637', *Proceedings of the Huguenot Society of London*, 4 (1891–3).

Le Fanu, T. P., 'Archbishop Marsh and the Discipline of the French Church of St. Patrick's, Dublin, 1691', *Proceedings of the Huguenot Society of London*, 12/4 (1920): 20–21.

——, 'Dumont de Bostaquet at Portarlington', *Proceedings of the Huguenot Society of London*, 14 (1929–33): 211–27.

——, 'French Veterans at Portarlington', *Journal of the Kildare Archeological Society*, 11/4 (July 1933): 177–98.

Loeber, R., 'Biographical Dictionary of Engineers in Ireland, 1600–1730', *Irish Sword*, 13 (1977–9).

Lorenz, J. T., 'Louis de Beauveau, comte d'Espence', *Die Kolonie*, 5 (1881): 49–51.

Love, R. S., '"All the King's Horsemen": The Equestrian Army of Henri IV, 1585–1598', *Sixteenth Century Journal*, 22 (1991): 511–33.

Magdeleine, M., 'Le réfuge: Le role de Francfort-sur-le-main', *Bulletin de la société de l'histoire du Protestantisme française*, 131/4 (1985): 485–94.

Manchée, W. H., 'Huguenot Regiments in Holland', *Proceedings of the Huguenot London*, 14 (1930–33): 96–100.

——, 'The Huguenot Regiments (supplemental note)', *Proceedings of the Huguenot Society of London*,13 (1927): 395–7.

——, 'Huguenot Soldiers and their Conditions of Service in the English Army', *Proceedings of the Huguenot Society of London*, 16 (1938–41): 233–65.

'Mélanges [review of the Read and Waddington edition of the memoirs of Isaac Dumont de Bostaquet]', *Bulletin de la société de l'histoire du Protestantisme française*, 13 (1865).

Minet, P., 'Huguenots in the Marlborough Wars', *Proceedings of the Huguenot Society of Great Britain and Ireland*, 27/4 (2001): 485–96.

Mitgau, H., 'Georg Wilhelm Lafontaines Chappuzeau-Bildnis in Celle (1699)', *Niedersächsisches Jahrbuch für Landesgeschichte*, 41/2 (Hildesheim, 1970).

Mueller, H., 'Lexikon Celler Musiker, Komponisten, Sänger, Instrumentalmusiker', *Musikpädagogen, Musikwissenschaftler, Instrumentenbauer, Glockengießer, Musikverleger, Musikalienhändler und Musiktherapeuten* (Celler Beiträge zur Landes- und Kulturgeschichte. Schriftenreihe des Stadtarchivs und des Bomann-Museums 31, Celle, 2003).

Muisson: 'La famille Muisson', *Bulletin de la société de l'histoire du Protestantisme française*, 12 (1864): 306–9.

Nischan, B., 'The Second Reformation in Brandenburg: Aims and Goals', *Sixteenth Century Journal*, 14 (1983).

Pablo, J. de, 'Contribution à l'étude de l'histoire des institutions militaires huguenotes, ii. L'armée huguenote entre 1562 et 1573', *Archiv für Reformationsgeschichte*, 48 (1957): 192–216.

Pagano De Divitiis, G., 'Il Mediterraneo nel XVII secolo. L'espansione commerciale inglese e l'Italia', *Studi storici*, 27 (1986): 109–48.

Peschels, S. de, 'History of the de Pechels Family', *Sussex Archaelogical Society Collections*, 25 (1875).

Poten, B. von, 'Die Generale der Königlich Hannoverschen Armee und ihrer Stammtruppen', *Beiheft zum Militär Wochenblatt*, 6/7 (Berlin, 1903).

Potter, D., 'The French Protestant Nobility in 1562: The "Associacion de Monseigneur le Prince de Condé"', *French History*, 15 (2001).

Powell, J. S., 'De Ruvigny's Irish Refuge', *History Today* (August 1990): 16–21.

Pozé, G., 'Zapiski pridvornago bril'jantščika Pozé o preby vanii ego v Rossi (1729–64) (Perevod s francuzsko, neizdannoj rukopisi)', *Bulletin de la société de l'histoire du Protestantisme française*, 1 (1870): 41–127.

Read, C., 'Les démarches des réfugiées huguenots auprès des négocieteurs de la paix de Ryswick pour leur rétablissement en France 1697', *Bulletin de la société de l'histoire du Protestantisme française*, 40 (1891).

Rjeoutski, V., 'La communauté francophone de Moscou sous le règne de Catherine II', *Revue des Etudes Slaves*, 68/4 (Paris, 1996): 445–61.

——, 'Les français de la Volga: la politique migratoire russe des années 1760 et la formation des communautées francophones à Saint-Petersbourg et à Moscou', *Cahiers du Monde russe*, 39/3 (July–September, 1998): 283–96.

Rowlands, G., 'An Army in Exile: Louis XIV and the Irish Forces of James II in France, 1691–1698', *Royal Stuart Paper*, 60 (2001).

——, 'Louis XIV, Vittorio Amedeo II and French Military Failure in Italy, 1689–1696', *English Historical Review*, 115 (2000).

Ruiz, A., 'Une famille Huguenote du Brandenburg au XVIIIe siècle: Les Theremin', *Revue d'Allemagne*, 14/2 (1982): 217–28.

Sander, F., 'Eleonore d'Olbreuse, Herzogin von Braunschweig-Lüneburg-Celle', *Die Französische Colonie*, 3 (1893).

Schmidt, T. and H. Schnitter, 'Die Hugenotten in der Brandenburgisch-Preussischen Armee', *Militärgeschichte*, 24/3 (1985).

Schrötter, F. von., 'Das preußische Offizierkorps unter dem ersten Könige von Preußen', *Forschungen zur Brandenburgischen und Preußischen Geschichte*, 27 (1914): 97–167.

Sclopis, F., 'Delle relazioni politiche tra la dinastia di Savoia e il governo britannico (1240–1815). Ricerche storiche', *Memorie della Regia Accademia delle Scienze di Torino* (1854).

Shaw, W. A., 'The Irish Pensioners of William III's Huguenot Regiments, 1702', *Proceedings of the Huguenot Society of London*, 6 (1901): 295–326.

Shears, P. J., 'Armand de Bourbon, Marquis de Miremont', *Proceedings of the Huguenot Society of London*, 20 (1962): 405–15.

Simms, J. G., 'Eye-witnesses of the Boyne', *Irish Sword*, 6 (1963–4).

——, 'Marlborough's Siege of Cork, 1690', *Irish Sword*, 9 (1969–70).

——, 'Schomberg at Dundalk, 1689', *Irish Sword*, 10 (1971–2): 14–25.

Simoni, A. E. C., 'Walter Morgan Wolff: An Elizabethan Soldier and His Maps', *Quaerendo*, 26 (1996): 66–8.

Speck, W. A., 'The Orangist Conspiracy against James II', *Historical Journal*, 30 (1987): 453–62.

Strayer, B., 'Un "Faux frère": le Sieur de Tillières et les réfugiés huguenots aux Provinces Unies, 1685–1688', *Bulletin de la société de l'histoire du Protestantisme française*, 150 (2004): 507–16.

Stupperich, R., 'Brandenburgisch-russische Verhandlungen über Aufnahme der Hugenotten in Rußland', *Zeitschrift für osteuropäische Geschichte*, 8 (1934).

Sutherland, N. M., 'Calvinism and the Conspiracy of Amboise', *History*, 47 (1962): 111–38.

Tastevin, F., 'Les calvinistes française en Russie', *Feuilles d'Histoire du XVIIe au XXe siècle*, 2/4 (1910).

Thomson S. W., 'The Seventh (Princess Royal's) Dragoon Guards: The Story of the Regiment (1913)', *The Cavalry Journal* (July 1938).

Tollin, H., 'Geschichte der hugenottischen Gemeinde von Celle', *Geschichtsblätter des Deutschen Hugenotten-Vereins*, 2, 7/8 (Magdeburg, 1893).

Tuxen, A., 'Royal Danois: Ludvig XIV's dansk-norske regiment, 1690–98', *Militaert Tidsskrift* (Copenhagen, 1888).

Venturi, F., 'Il Piemonte dei primi decenni del Settecento nelle relazioni dei diplomatici inglesi', *Bollettino storico bibliografico subalpino*, 54 (1956): 227–71.

Vigne, R., '"Le Projet d'Irlande": Huguenot migration in the 1690s', *History Ireland*, 2/2 (Summer, 1994).

——, 'In the Purlieus of St Alfege's: Huguenot Families in Seventeenth- and Eighteenth-century Greenwich', *Proceedings of the Huguenot Society of Great Britain and Ireland*, 27/2 (1999): 257–73.

Vignoles, E. B., 'The MS Memoirs of Pierre de Cosne', *Proceedings of the Huguenot Society of London*, 9/3 (1911).

Wagner, H., 'A List of Pensions to Huguenot Officers in 1692', *Proceedings of the Huguenot Society of London*, 93 (1911): 581–8.

Walter, J., *Personengeschichtliche Quellen in den Militaria-Beständen des Niedersächsischen Hauptstaatsarchives in Hannover*, Veröffentlichungen der Niedersächsischen Archivverwaltung 38 (Göttingen, 1997).

Whitworth, R. H., '1685 – James II, the Army and the Huguenots', *Journal of the Society for Army Historical Research*, 63 (1985).

Theses

Dietz, B., 'Privateering in North-West European Waters, 1568 to 1572', PhD thesis (University of London, 1959).

Ferguson, K., 'The Army in Ireland from the Restoration to the Act of Union', PhD thesis (University of Dublin, 1980).

Herd, G. P., 'General Patrick Gordon of Auchleuchries – A Scot in Seventeenth-Century Russian Service', PhD thesis (University of Aberdeen, 1993).

Hylton, Raymond Pierre, *The Huguenot Settlement at Portarlington, 1692–1771*. MA thesis (University College, Dublin, 1982).

Scopi, M. C., 'Ricerche storico-giuridiche sul diritto d'ubena negli Stati sabaudi con particolare riguardo alla legislazione militare', PhD thesis (University of Turin, Faculty of Jurisprudence, 1997/8).

Stapleton, J., 'Forging a Coalition Army: William III, the Grand Alliance, and the Confederate Army in the Spanish Netherlands, 1688–1697', PhD thesis (The Ohio State University, 2003).

Teulon, F., 'François Vivent, prédicant cévenol', PhD thesis (University of Paris, 1946).

Trim, D. J. B., 'Fighting "Jacob's Wars". The Employment of English and Welsh Mercenaries in the European Wars of Religion: France and the Netherlands, 1562–1610', PhD thesis (University of London, 2002).

Wiebe, R., 'Untersuchung über die Hilfeleistung der deutschen Staaten für Wilhelm III. von Oranien im Jahre 1688', PhD thesis (Georg-August University, Göttingen, 1939).

Index